Communications in Computer and Information Science 1152

Commenced Publication in 2007
Founding and Former Series Editors:
Phoebe Chen, Alfredo Cuzzocrea, Xiaoyong Du, Orhun Kara, Ting Liu,
Krishna M. Sivalingam, Dominik Ślęzak, Takashi Washio, Xiaokang Yang,
and Junsong Yuan

More information about this series at http://www.springer.com/series/7899

Sergio Nesmachnow · Luis Hernández Callejo (Eds.)

Smart Cities

Second Ibero-American Congress, ICSC-CITIES 2019
Soria, Spain, October 7–9, 2019
Revised Selected Papers

 Springer

Editors
Sergio Nesmachnow (iD)
Universidad de la República
Montevideo, Uruguay

Luis Hernández Callejo (iD)
Universidad de Valladolid
Soria, Soria, Spain

ISSN 1865-0929   ISSN 1865-0937 (electronic)
Communications in Computer and Information Science
ISBN 978-3-030-38888-1   ISBN 978-3-030-38889-8 (eBook)
https://doi.org/10.1007/978-3-030-38889-8

This Springer imprint is published by the registered company Springer Nature Switzerland AG
The registered company address is: Gewerbestrasse 11, 6330 Cham, Switzerland

Preface

This CCIS volume presents selected articles from the II Ibero-American Congress of Smart Cities (ICSC-CITIES 2019), held in Soria, Spain, during October 7–9, 2019.

Smart Cities are the result of the increasingly urgent need to orient our lives towards sustainability. Therefore, these cities use infrastructure, innovation, and technology to reduce energy consumption and CO_2 emissions, in order to improve the quality of life of their citizens.

Being a strategic issue that brings new challenges, ICSC-CITIES 2019 was a forum for discussion with the main goal of creating synergies among different research groups to favor the development of Smart Cities and contribute to their knowledge and integration in different scenarios, their possible development, and the strategies to address them.

Subject areas defined by the Steering Committee of ICCS-CITIES 2019 included Energy Efficiency and Sustainability; Infrastructures, Energy, and the Environment; Mobility and Internet of Things; and Governance and Citizenship.

ICSC-CITIES 2019 was organized by the CITIES network, and financed as part of the Ibero-American Program for Science and Technology Development (CYTED).

The conference received 98 submissions for peer review. The reviewing process followed a single-blind procedure using a panel of experts and external reviewers (outside the Program Committee). Each submission had an average of three independent reviews and each reviewer was assigned an average of two submissions. The best 21 articles were selected to be part of this CCIS volume.

Sergio Nesmachnow
Luis Hernández Callejo

Organization

Conference Chairs

Luis Hernández Callejo   University of Valladolid, Spain
Sergio Nesmachnow   Universidad de la República, Uruguay

Program Committee

Rafael Asorey Cacheda	University Center for Defense/Marine Military School, Spain
Jesús Vegas Hernández	University of Valladolid, Spain
Diego Alberto Godoy	University Gastón Dachary, Argentina
Luisenia Fernández	University of Zulia, Venezuela
Roberto Villafafila	Polytechnic University of Cataluña, Spain
Luis García Santander	University of Concepción, Chile
Ronney Mancebo Boloy	Federal Center of Technological Education Celso Suckow Da Fonseca, Brazil
Javier Prieto	University of Salamanca, Spain
Vanessa Guimaraes	Federal Center of Technological Education Celso Suckow Da Fonseca, Brazil
Lilian J. Obregón	University of Valladolid, Spain
Hortensia Amaris	University Carlos III of Madrid, Spain
Mónica Aguado	National Center for Renewable Energies, Spain
Claudia Liliana Zuñiga	University Santiago de Cali, Colombia
Carlos Méndez	National Unversity of Litoral, Argentina
Ponciano Escamilla	National Polytechnic Institute, Mexico
Jorge Gómez	Complutense University of Madrid, Spain
Jorge Mírez	National University of Engineering, Peru
Fabian Castillo	University Libre, Colombia
Juan Leonardo Espinoza	University of Cuenca, Ecuador
Jose Antonio Ferrer	Research Centre for Energy, Environment and Technology, Spain
Mª Del Rosario Heras	Research Centre for Energy, Environment and Technology, Spain
Andrei Tchernykh	Centro de Investigación Científica y de Educación Superior de Ensenada, Mexico
Jamal Toutouh	Massachusetts Institute of Technology, USA
Irene Lebrusán	Harvard University, USA
Belén Carro Martínez	University of Valladolid, Spain
Víctor Alonso Gómez	University of Valladolid, Spain

Financial Sponsors

Technical Sponsor

 Springer

Non-Technical Sponsors

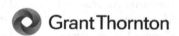

Contents

Segmentation of Thermography Image of Solar Cells and Panels 1
  Estefanía Alfaro-Mejía, Humberto Loaiza-Correa,
  Edinson Franco-Mejía, and Luis Hernández-Callejo

Assessing the Environmental Impact of Car Restrictions Policies:
Madrid Central Case 9
  Irene Lebrusán and Jamal Toutouh

Over-Voltage Protection for Pico-Hydro Generation
Using PV Microinverters 25
  Isabella Cristina Scotta, Gabriela Moreira Ribeiro,
  Wellington Maidana, and Vicente Leite

Detecting Hot Spots in Photovoltaic Panels Using Low-Cost
Thermal Cameras 38
  Miguel Dávila-Sacoto, Luis Hernández-Callejo, Víctor Alonso-Gómez,
  Sara Gallardo-Saavedra, and Luis G. González

Household Energy Disaggregation Based on Pattern
Consumption Similarities 54
  Juan Chavat, Jorge Graneri, and Sergio Nesmachnow

A Hybrid Energy Storage System for Renewable-Based Power Plants 70
  Francisco Díaz-González, Francesc Girbau-Llistuella,
  Mònica Aragüés-Peñalba, Cristian Chillón-Antón,
  and Marc Llonch-Masachs

LoRa-Based IoT Data Monitoring and Collecting Platform 80
  Andres Felipe Fuentes and Eugenio Tamura

Sustainable Mobility in the Public Transportation of Montevideo, Uruguay 93
  Silvina Hipogrosso and Sergio Nesmachnow

IPN Sustainability Program: Solar Photovoltaic Electricity Generation
and Consumption Reduction 109
  P. J. Escamilla-Ambrosio, M. A. Ramírez-Salinas, O. Espinosa-Sosa,
  G. Gallegos-García, M. Morales-Olea, and Luis Hernández-Callejo

Implementation of a Smart Microgrid in a Small Museum: The Silk House 121
  Luís Guilherme Aguiar Figueiredo, Wellington Maidana,
  and Vicente Leite

General Purpose I-V Tester Developed to Measure a Wide Range
of Photovoltaic Systems.   135
  Bhishma Hernández-Martínez, Sara Gallardo-Saavedra,
  Luís Hernández-Callejo, Víctor Alonso-Gómez,
  and José Ignacio Morales-Aragonés

Short Term Load Forecasting of Industrial Electricity Using
Machine Learning.   146
  Rodrigo Porteiro, Sergio Nesmachnow, and Luis Hernández-Callejo

Potential for Thermal Water Desalination Using Microgrid and Solar
Thermal Field Energy Surpluses in an Isolated Community   162
  Jesús Armando Aguilar-Jiménez, Nicolás Velázquez,
  Ricardo Beltrán, Luis Hernández-Callejo, Ricardo López-Zavala,
  and Edgar González-San Pedro

Electric Microgrid in Smart Cities: CEDER-CIEMAT a Case Study   176
  Luis Hernández-Callejo, Oscar Izquierdo Monge, and Lilian J. Obregón

Monthly Characterization of the Generation of Photovoltaic Arrays.
Microgrid Case CEDER, Soria, Spain   185
  Raúl A. López-Meraz, Luis Hernández-Callejo, Luis Omar Jamed-Boza,
  and Víctor Alonso-Gómez

Urban Data Analysis for the Public Transportation System
of Montevideo, Uruguay   199
  Renzo Massobrio and Sergio Nesmachnow

Bus Stops as a Tool for Increasing Social Inclusiveness in Smart Cities.   215
  Víctor Manuel Padrón Nápoles, Diego Gachet Páez,
  José Luis Esteban Penelas, Germán García García,
  and María José García Santacruz

Designing a Backbone Trunk for the Public Transportation Network
in Montevideo, Uruguay   228
  Claudio Risso and Sergio Nesmachnow

Energy Storage Systems for Power Supply of Ultrahigh Speed
Hyperloop Trains   244
  Marcos Lafoz, Gustavo Navarro, Marcos Blanco,
  and Jorge Torres

Noise and Ozone Continuous Monitoring in an Industrial Urban Area
of Northeastern Portugal   256
  Leonardo Campestrini Furst, Manuel Feliciano, Artur Gonçalves,
  and Felipe Romero

Multiobjective Household Energy Planning Using Evolutionary Algorithms ...   269
   Giovanni Colacurcio, Sergio Nesmachnow, Jamal Toutouh,
   Francisco Luna, and Diego Rossit

Control of a Bidirectional Single-Phase Grid Interface for Electric Vehicles....   285
   Matheus Montanini Breve and Vicente Leite

Author Index   301

Segmentation of Thermography Image
of Solar Cells and Panels

Estefanía Alfaro-Mejía[1]([✉]) [iD], Humberto Loaiza-Correa[1]([✉]) [iD],
Edinson Franco-Mejía[1]([✉]) [iD], and Luis Hernández-Callejo[2]([✉]) [iD]

[1] Universidad del Valle, Calle 13 100-00, Cali, Colombia
{estefania.alfaro,humberto.loaiza,edinson.franco}@correounivalle.edu.co
[2] Universidad de Valladolid,
Campus Universitario Duques de Soria, 42004 Soria, Spain
luis.hernandez.callejo@uva.es

Abstract. In this work, two segmentation techniques for photovoltaic
(PV) solar panels are explored: filtering by area and the second to the
method of active contours level-set method (ACM LS). Tuning these
techniques enables the contours of the solar panels to be obtained. Once
these contours are established, morphological operations are used to
refine the obtained edges and the Hough transform technique is used
to find the main lines in the image. The vertices are then found from the
possible intersections between the lines. Finally, the vertices are brought
to the desired position at scale according to the reference of the PV panels projection transformations. The extraction of the region of interest
is evaluated from the Dice similarity coefficient (DSC), Intersection over
Union (IoU), and recall segmentation metrics.

Keywords: Photovoltaic · Thermography imaging · Unmanned aerial
vehicles UAV · Image segmentation · Degradation

1 Introduction

Photovoltaic (PV) solar installations increasingly as part of a transition to renewable energy to help mitigate climate change. As production of panels and inverters increases, PV panels become ever more economically viable [1,2]. In 2017,
there was an increase from 98 GW to 402 GW in overall worldwide clean generation capacity. However, initial investments are substantial and the risk of
production losses are significant if there are system failures. The high levels of
irradiance, necessary for the photovoltaic effect to occur, generate temperature
increases in the cells which reduce the efficiency of the solar panels. Anomalies
or defects may occur during the manufacture, installation, and operation of the
solar panels [3]. Most manufacturers guarantee a lifespan of approximately 25
years for photovoltaic panels but damage to any cell in the chain or from a panel
in the chain can sharply decrease energy production. For this reason, testing

Funded by the Universidad del Valle-Colombia.

S. Nesmachnow and L. Hernández Callejo (Eds.): ICSC-CITIES 2019, CCIS 1152, pp. 1–8, 2020.
https://doi.org/10.1007/978-3-030-38889-8_1

techniques to detect anomalies in a timely manner and take corrective action is of utmost importance. There are different techniques for inspecting PV panels, including techniques such as the I-V curve and image analysis generated by electroluminescence (EL), photoluminescence (PL), and infrared thermography (IRT) [4].

Most faults in solar panels are invisible to the naked eye making manual inspection ineffective. Inspection is not a simple task as solar panels are often in high, difficult to access areas and with little space between them. Inspection carries the further risk of exposure to hazards from circuits with electrical currents of several amps. Deployment of Unmanned Aerial Vehicles (UAV) is an alternative solution for the inspection of photovoltaic modules [2,5–7]. Diagnosis of solar panel failures from aerial infrared thermography techniques using UAVs can be a complex procedure. One challenge is in the acquisition of thermal images: the selection of instruments such as UAVs and cameras is essential to ensure an adequate diagnosis in photovoltaic systems. Often UAVs must be guided both remotely and manually to capture the required images, taking into account multiple considerations such as the height of the UAV, the angles of the camera and the weather conditions which can affect image acquisition and procedures. Another problem is the acquisition of the images considering environmental conditions that may affect the performance of the panels and, indirectly, the usefulness of the data to be processed. Once IRT is acquired, it is necessary to employ processing methods such as Infrared Reflectography (IRR) and pattern recognition techniques which enable the classification of the condition of the solar panels.

In order to draw conclusions regarding best practice solutions for the detection of faults in PV cells and panels, this paper presents research results on segmentation techniques employed to extract information about cells and panels from big photovoltaic generators. The paper is organized as follows: the Benchmark section gives an overview of the equipment employed followed by the methods used and the presentation of results. Error analysis of data is presented with the segmentation metrics. Finally, some conclusions and references are reported.

2   Benchmark

The equipment used for the acquisition of solar panel thermal imaging is described in Table 1. Image acquisition through controlled flights of the UAV was carried out with the DJI Matrice 100 drone which has an A2 flight controller, and a Software Development Kit (SDK) enabling customized development. Thermal imaging was carried out with a Zenumuse XT resolution 336×256 camera, [8]. The PV panels studied were configured in a string of four PV panels of monocrystalline silicon (mono-Si), connected to an electronic load that emulates the energy consumption generated by a resistive load. The image data collected is recorded in [9] (Table 1).

Table 1. Equipment for IR photovoltaic inspection.

UAV Matrice 100		Camera IR Zenmuse XT		ERDM-85 PPV	
Flight endurance (min)	18	Resolution (pixels)	336 × 256	Open circuit voltage (V)	21.78
Full payload (g)	1000	Weight (g)	270	Optimal operating voltage (V)	17.95
Flight speed (m/s)	10	Spectral band (μm)	7–13.5	Maximum power	85

3   Method

The proposed method for segmenting aerial thermal imaging is illustrated in Fig. 1. This method consists of three phases with each containing more detailed stages. The phases are: image acquisition; preprocessing and segmentation; transformations and normalization. Image acquisition includes the definition of initial conditions which may determine some restrictions for correct capture procedure. In the case of Cali, Colombia, for example, the time range for image acquisition is from 10:00 to 15:00 due to registration of irradiance peaks of more than 600 W/m^2, with the hour between 12:00 and 13:00 excluded to avoid the shadow projections generated by the UAV over the analyzed PV panels. The images are only taken if there is no apparent rain or cloudiness. In order to have the panel working near to the Maximum Power Point (MPPT), the condition stage of operation for the solar panels was adjusted to ensure delivery of 80% Voltage open circuit (Voc). The environmental variables, such as external temperature, wind speed, and irradiance are measured to verify that they are within operating ranges used in similar experiments and that the acquired images can be analyzed. The irradiance must be greater than 500 W/m^2 [10], and wind speed 3 m/s < F.S ≤ 5 m/s [5]. The procurement procedure is completed by estimating the acquisition height and the capture angle of the camera so that the emission and reflection remain constant. Once the aerial thermal imaging has been taken, the preprocessing phase begins. Here the thermal imaging enters a steplow filtering process (medium filter) to decrease image noise. The window selection is 25 × 25 and is done heuristically with a sequence of test images. The binarization process of the filtered image is then carrried out, using the Otsu method. This process is

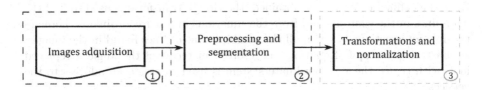

Fig. 1. Acquisition and segmentation method IR images.

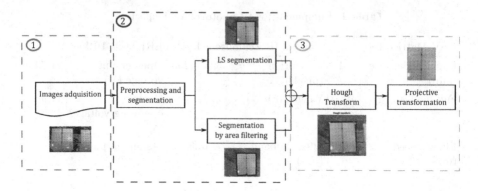

Fig. 2. Acquisition and segmentation method detailed for the IEEE scenario.

complete, one of the two segmentation methods - either the active contour level-set method (ACM LS) or segmentation by area filtering, is chosen, as shown in Fig. 2. Segmentation methods return the contours, after which an edge detector is used. A morphological operation establishes the main lines on the image which are analyzed using the Hough transform technique. Finally, a projective transformation operation is used to generate a normalization of segmented PV panels.

4   Results

Solar panels images were segmented from two proposed techniques; the active contour level sets method (MCA) and the area filtering (AF) approach. For the MCA an initial surface area of 336×256 is defined. To tune the convergence parameters of the implicit surface, ranges are defined for the variables as follows: $-1.5 < \sigma \leq 1.5$, $-7 < \alpha \leq 7$ and $-3 < \epsilon \leq 3$ and compared with an established *ground truth*, according to the initial tests defined as adjustment parameters in the method of active contours: $\sigma = 1.5$, $\alpha = 1.7$ and $\epsilon = 1.5$. Finally, the surface converges to the contour of the solar panels and subsequently an edge detector using a square structural element is deployed. The AF segmentation method consists of the definition of a minimum search area of 0.1 and maximum of 0.9, related to the size of the images, then the possible objects that meet the search criteria are labelled. A dilation operation with a square structural element of 7×7 is used on the contours obtained from both segmentation methods. Once the defined contours are obtained, the Hough transform is used to find the main lines in the contours and from the equations in polar coordinates there are possible intersections between all the combinations of lines found in the images, as illustrated in Eq. 1. Equation 1 is resolved in terms of the angle θ replaced in 1, with (r, θ), the x-y coordinate system is used to assign an address to the vertices.

$$\frac{A_1}{A_2} = \frac{\cos(\theta - \phi_1)}{\cos(\theta - \phi_2)} R = \frac{A_1}{\cos(\theta_R - \phi_1)} \tag{1}$$

With the information on the vertices obtained, a projection transformation is used to ensure that the images have the same composition 3. The vertices are taken to the desired position values obtained from the scale ratio of the PV panel datasheet, as illustrated in Fig. 3.

$$\begin{bmatrix} xt_1 \\ yt_1 \\ 1 \end{bmatrix} = H \begin{bmatrix} xr_1 \\ yr_1 \\ 1 \end{bmatrix} \tag{2}$$

$$xt = H_{(1,1)} \cdot xr_1 + H_{(1,2)} \cdot yr_1 + H_{(1,3)} \cdot 1 \tag{3}$$
$$yt = H_{(2,1)} \cdot xr_1 + H_{(2,2)} \cdot yr_1 + H_{(2,3)} \cdot 1$$
$$1 = H_{(3,1)} \cdot xr_1 + H_{(3,2)} \cdot yr_1 + H_{(3,3)} \cdot 1$$

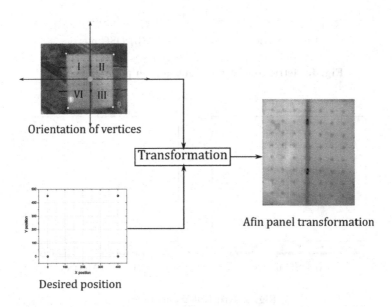

Fig. 3. Affine transformation.

The segmentation methods implemented were tested based on the Dice coefficient and IoU metrics (Table 2).

DSC or IoU measurements are generated with a representative sample of 60 images to compare both the AF and ACM segmentation methods (Fig. 4).

Table 2. Segmentation metrics.

Segmentation method	IoU	DSC	RECALL
AF	0.97	0.94	0.70
ACM LS	0.92	0.96	0.69

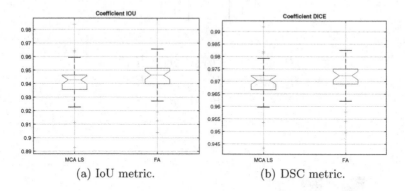

(a) IoU metric.   (b) DSC metric.

Fig. 4. Metric to measure segmentation performance.

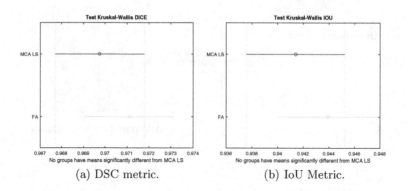

(a) DSC metric.   (b) IoU Metric.

Fig. 5. Kruskall-Wallis test.

5   Conclusions

The image acquisition phase enable the establishment of the relevant variables in the selection of the equipment used for the inspection of PV with thermographic imaging. For the UAV: a flight autonomy of >18 min and an operating temperature $\leq 40\,°C$. For the thermal camera, the spectral range of between 7.5 to 13 µm, resolution 336×256 or higher and compatibility with the UAV communication protocols.

The definition of capture conditions establishes the minimum ranges suitable for the correct processing of the images, among which are: environmental conditions (such as the absence of rain), the acquisition schedule in the time slot of between 11:00 and 12:00 h and 13:00 to 15:00 h (for the specific case of the city Santiago de Cali, Colombia), irradiance levels <600 W/m^2, and wind speed >5 m/s.

In the pre-processing phase, medium filters, Otsu thresholding and, morphological operations were explored to refine the contours obtained from the proposed methods. With a representative sample of 40 images selected by acquisition folders, the medium filter windows were varied from 3×3 to 35×35. The search offers an optimal performance with the 25×25 window.

AF and ACM LS techniques were used for image segmentation, evaluated using the *Sorensen Dice* metrics of 0.92 and IoU of 0.96 for ACM LS and, for the area filtering technique, 0.97 with Dice and 0.94 with IoU. It was found that the AF segmentation method found specific statistical differences using the Kruskal-Wallis test (see Fig. 5) in comparison with the ACM LS method of $P < 0.51$. Finally, we found that AF is better for segmenting panels than ACM LS but without a significant difference.

The morphological operation that improved the edges obtained was the expansion with a square structural element of dimensions 5×5.

Hough transform tuning is used to detect the main lines on the image and all its possible intersections to find the vertices. The vertices found are brought to a desired position from a related transformation or normalization.

There exists a small difference between the two techniques used for the segmentation of photovoltaic panels and cells, in which AF is the better technique according to the metrics Dice and IoU. However, comparing AF against ACM LS methods, the minimum values from FA (which are within the range of a good segmentation process) are above the minimum values from ACM LS.

The segmentation method implemented will enable the state of the photovoltaic system to be analyzed by cell.

References

1. Sundaram, S., Benson, D., Mallick, T.K.: Overview of the PV Industry and Different Technologies, pp. 7–22. Elsevier, Amsterdam (2016). https://doi.org/10.1016/b978-0-12-802953-4.00002-0
2. Pursiheimo, E., Holttinen, H., Koljonen, T.: Inter-sectoral effects of high renewable energy share in global energy system. Renew. Energy **136**, 1119–1129 (2019). https://doi.org/10.1016/j.renene.2018.09.082
3. Mellit, A., Tina, G., Kalogirou, S.: Fault detection and diagnosis methods for photovoltaic systems: a review. Renew. Sustain. Energy Rev. **91**(1–17), 1–17 (2018). https://doi.org/10.1016/j.rser.2018.03.062
4. Abdelhamid, M., Singh, R., Omar, M.: Review of microcrack detection techniques for silicon solar cells. IEEE J. Photovolt. **4**(1), 514–524 (2014). https://doi.org/10.1109/jphotov.2013.2285622

5. Zhang, P., Zhang, L., Wu, T., Zhang, H., Sun, X.: Detection and location of fouling on photovoltaic panels using a drone-mounted infrared thermography system. J. Appl. Remote Sens. **11**(1), 99–110 (2017). https://doi.org/10.1117/1.jrs.11.016026

6. Addabbo, P., et al.: A UAV infrared measurement approach for defect detection in photovoltaic plants, vol. 2, no. 5, pp. 99–110 (2017). https://doi.org/10.1109/metroaerospace.2017.7999594

7. Li, X., Yang, Q., Chen, Z., Luo, X., Yan, W.: Visible defects detection based on UAV-based inspection in large-scale photovoltaic systems. IET Renew. Power Gener. **11**(10), 1234–1244 (2017). https://doi.org/10.1049/iet-rpg.2017.0001

8. Gallardo-Saavedra, S., Hernandez-Callejo, L., Duque-Perez, O.: Image resolution influence in aerial thermographic inspections of photovoltaic plants. IEEE Trans. Ind. Inform. **14**(12), 5678–5686 (2018). https://doi.org/10.1109/tii.2018.2865403

9. Alfaro-Mejía, E., Loaiza-Correa, H., Franco-Mejía, E., Restrepo-Giron, A., Nope-Rodrıguez, S.: Dataset for recognition of snail trails and hot spot failures in monocrystalline Si solar panels. Data Brief **26**, 104441 (2019). https://doi.org/10.1016/j.dib.2019.104441

10. Dotenco, S., et al.: Automatic detection and analysis of photovoltaic modules in aerial infrared imagery. In: 2016 IEEE Winter Conference on Applications of Computer Vision (WACV), pp. 1–9. IEEE (2016). https://doi.org/10.1109/wacv.2016.7477658

Assessing the Environmental Impact of Car Restrictions Policies: Madrid Central Case

Irene Lebrusán[1]([✉])[ID] and Jamal Toutouh[2][ID]

[1] IGLP, Harvard University, Cambridge, MA, USA
ilebrusan@law.harvard.edu
[2] CSAIL, Massachusetts Institute of Technology, Cambridge, MA, USA
toutouh@mit.edu

Abstract. With the increase of population living in urban areas, many transportation-related problems have grown very rapidly. Pollution causes many inhabitants health problems. A major concern for the International Community is pollution, which causes many inhabitants health problems. Accordingly, and under the risk of fines, countries are required to reduce noise and air pollutants. As a way to do so, road restrictions policies are applied in urban areas. Evaluating objectively the benefits of this type of measures is important to asses their real impact. In this work, we analyze the application of Madrid Central (MC), which is a set of road traffic limitation measures applied in the downtown of Madrid (Spain), by using smart city tools. According to our results, MC significantly reduces the nitrogen dioxide (NO_2) concentration in the air and the levels of noise in Madrid, while not arising any border effect.

1 Introduction

According to the United Nations Populations Division, today, 55% of the world's population lives in urban areas. This proportion is expected to increase to 68% by 2050 [23]. This urban agglomerations are giving shape to new challenges from a social, economical, and environmental point of view, being mobility one of them. The fact is that mobility inside the city and inter-cities is a key aspect that determines the development of the urban areas.

The design of most of our cities prioritizes the use of motorized vehicles. This relegates the rest of uses and users with different negative impact over safety and health, as well as over well-being and development, especially for children and the elderly. For example, it has been demonstrated the causal link between the growth of car use and the reduction of children's access to public space in urban contexts, which critically affects their social and physical development [12]. Other authors demonstrate that elderly improve their independence and well-being in environments with safety walking access [13].

Another major concern derived of the rapid development of car oriented cities is the high generation of emissions (air pollutants and noise) and their impact on

© Springer Nature Switzerland AG 2020
S. Nesmachnow and L. Hernández Callejo (Eds.): ICSC-CITIES 2019, CCIS 1152, pp. 9–24, 2020.
https://doi.org/10.1007/978-3-030-38889-8_2

the inhabitants health [19]. Air pollution is the top health hazard in the European Union (EU) [8,26] as it reduces life expectancy, loss of years of healthy life, and diminishes the quality of health. In the EU, it causes more than 400,000 premature deaths, being primarily associated with heart disease and strokes, followed by lung diseases and lung cancer. Noise pollution is also a major environmental health question; the European Environment Agency (EEA) estimates that environmental noise causes at least 16,600 cases of premature death in Europe each year [7]. Exposure to prolonged noise pollution can cause a range of health problems including annoyance, sleep disturbance, increasing hypertension, and cardiovascular diseases [2]. It can also have effects on children's cognition including communication difficulties, impaired attention, increased arousal, frustration, noise annoyance, and consequences of sleep disturbance on performance [10,11].

As road traffic generates the referred problems (e.g., about 80% of the noise pollution is caused by cars [20]), reducing it seems to be an efficient strategy to improve urban livability and their inhabitants health. Accordingly, pedestrianization is a commonly implemented approach to this challenge. Pedestrianization can be defined as to convert a street into a car free space by excluding motor vehicles. It should be coupled with creation of effective public and non-motorized transportation facilities. Absolute pedestrianization is difficult to be implemented. Instead, authorities define road transportation limitation policies. For example,distribution and commercial vehicles may be allowed to enter in a pedestrianized area [16].

Many cities around the world started to shift toward non-car friendly access by implementing different plans and measures [16,19]. However, changes on the spatial configuration of the city requires of a big investment that not all the council can afford. There are several studies that evaluate the impact of pedestrianization implementations [18,19,21,24]. The findings of these studies highlight that this kind of measures have not only environmental health impacts. They positively affect tourism development, job creation, improving safety, enhancing the appearance of urban areas, etc. Figure 1 shows the main benefits of pedestrianization in urban areas. Their conclusions are principally based on the use of surveys and urban simulation.

In this study, we analyze Madrid Central (MC) which has been implemented in Madrid (Spain), as a case study [1]. This low emissions zone (LEZ) gives continuity to dissuasive measures such as fine-tuning the circulation of certain license plates on alternate days or limitations of access to vehicles considered to be the most polluting, among others. But, does this measure have a positive impact over the reduction of pollution? How can we use smart city tools to take the best decision to evaluate benefits of this measure? The interest of this analysis is even bigger as there exists a controversial political use of this measure. Thanks to the virtues of smart city tools, we can analyze objectively the results of this kind of plans. Specifically, we take advantage of smart governance and transparency services to get data shared through open data platforms.

The main contributions of this work are: *(i)* pointing out the potential of open data sources to evaluate the effect of car restrictions implemented in the cities;

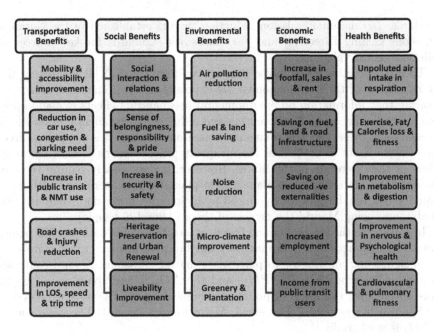

Transportation Benefits	Social Benefits	Environmental Benefits	Economic Benefits	Health Benefits
Mobility & accessibility improvement	Social interaction & relations	Air pollution reduction	Increase in footfall, sales & rent	Unpolluted air intake in respiration
Reduction in car use, congestion & parking need	Sense of belongingness, responsibility & pride	Fuel & land saving	Saving on fuel, land & road infrastructure	Exercise, Fat/ Calories loss & fitness
Increase in public transit & NMT use	Increase in security & safety	Noise reduction	Saving on reduced -ve externalities	Improvement in metabolism & digestion
Road crashes & Injury reduction	Heritage Preservation and Urban Renewal	Micro-climate improvement	Increased employment	Improvement in nervous & Psychological health
Improvement in LOS, speed & trip time	Liveability improvement	Greenery & Plantation	Income from public transit users	Cardiovascular & pulmonary fitness

Fig. 1. Summary of pedestrianization benefits. Image created by Soni and Soni [19].

(ii) analysing the environmental impact of the measures applied in MC; and *(iii)* applying a multidisciplinary approach to assess mobility policies embedded in an international framework of regulations and guidelines. Finally, nothing prevent us to apply the same approach to analyze other initiatives to deal with air quality, noise, and other challenges derived from urban growth.

The rest of the paper is organized as follows: first, we describe the goals, strategies and contextualization of MC, paying especial attention to the directives in which is embedded. Section 3 introduces the materials and methods used in this analysis. The evaluation of the air quality and noise based on the shared open data is shown in Sect. 4. Finally, Sect. 5 presents the conclusions and the main lines of future work.

2   Madrid Central: Purpose, Description and Controversia

The concern over the air quality and noise across the EU leads to the adoption of different environmental and health directives. Those policies have the object to safeguard EU citizens from environment-related pressures and risks to health and wellbeing. Accordingly, emissions are monitored in every member state.

The European Commission adopted in 2013 a Clean Air Policy Package based on `Directive 2008/50/EC` [6] and `2004/107/EC` [5]. It points to the full compliance with the established air quality standards and set different objectives for 2020 and 2030. This EU air quality policy rests on three pillars: *(i)* air quality standards; *(ii)* national emission reduction targets established in the National Emissions Ceiling Directive; and *(iii)* emissions standards for key sources of pollution, as the vehicles.

The EU directive about noise (`Directive 2002/49/EC`) [4] focuses on the determination of three main points: *(i)* exposure to environmental noise; *(ii)* ensuring that information on environmental noise and its effects is made available to the public; and *(iii)* preventing and reducing environmental noise where necessary and preserving environmental noise quality where it is good. The directive of noise is not as exigent as the air quality one, leaving the limit or target values at the discretion of the States. However, it does clearly require the creation of noise maps and noise management plans for agglomerations with more than 100,000 inhabitants. In Spain, 63 municipalities have more than 100,000 inhabitants, being Madrid the biggest of them (3,266,126 people).

Regarding to the air quality and based on latest available data, the EU points that the transport sector is the largest contributor to nitrogen oxide emissions, and a significant contributor to particulate matter emissions. Several countries have exceeded repeatedly the PM_{10} and the NO_2, being Spain one of them. More specifically, the levels of pollution admitted by the EU were exceeded in the Spanish biggest cities (Barcelona, Madrid and Valencia). The main source of NO_2 is road traffic [14].

The EU demanded to Spain the reduction of these pollutants in the air, under the threat of taking the case before the European Court and the risk of important economic sanctions. This process is paralyzed in May of 2018 thanks to the adoption of certain measures to reduce pollutants, such as MC.

MC is a LEZ in Madrid, consisting in car access restrictions in a delimited area of the downtown (see Fig. 2). Those restrictions exclude residents of MC and authorized cars[1]. Otherwise, the access to this area requires vehicles to have

Fig. 2. MC area and the location of the sensor installed in Plaza del Carmen.

---

[1] People with reduced mobility; public transport; security and emergency services; car-sharing or moto-sharing; specific workers; distribution and commercial vehicles.

an environmental sticker[2]. In other words, the measure seeks to eliminate transit traffic, which crosses but has no origin or destination in *Madrid Central.*

MC aims at improving air quality, but also responds to the idea of changing the uses of spaces in the city center, prioritizing the pedestrian one and reducing noise pollution. But as we said, its conformation mainly responds to ensure the objectives demanded by the EU. It should be pointed out that, thanks to this measure, Spain avoided to be brought to the European Court of Justice.

MC convers an area of 4,720,000 m^2, almost the entire *Centro* district, which is formed by the neighborhoods of *Palacio, Embajadores, Cortes, Justicia, Universidad,* and *Sol. Centro* district has 134,881 inhabitants, of which 12,377 are less than 17 years of age and 21,645 people are 65 years old or more. Those groups are more affected by noise and pollutants. Among other benefits referred to citizenship education, to establish the perimeter of MC facilitates the understanding of zonal delimitation and aspires to introduce a behavioral change regarding the use of the car. MC is created by the *Ordenanza de Movilidad Sostenible* (October 5th, 2018) and the traffic restriction started on November 30, 2018. However, the fines for noncompliance did not started until March 16, 2019.

However, and despite of the fact that the European Union have told Spain to reduce their emissions under risk of fine, this restriction to the car use is suspended. After the elections (held on May, 26th 2019) the new government decided to apply a moratorium on fines from July 1st to September 30th 2019, approved under art. 247 of the *Ordenanza de Movilidad Sostenible.* This suspension leaded to the emergence of social movements claiming the paralization of this reversal based on the negative effects over health and environment, and a warning from the EU. After a contentious-administrative appeal filed by environmental groups, a judge has provisionally paralyzed this reversal of MC.

3   Materials and Methods

In order to know more about the objective effects of MC, we analyze different indicators applicable to the dimensions of environmental pollution and noise. The source of data used in this study is provided by the Open Data Portal (ODP) offered by the Madrid City Council[3]. The data gathered by the sensor located in MC (*Plaza del Carmen*) is analyzed to evaluate the impact of the measures carried out (see Fig. 2). The temporal range of this study starts in December of 2016 and finishes in May of 2019, i.e., 30 months grouped in two periods: the 24 months previous to MC (named *Pre-MC*) and six months with the car restrictions (named *Post-MC*).

Following, we introduce the air pollutants evaluated, the outdoor noise metrics studied, and the methodology applied in the evaluation.

---

[2] There are no restrictions for vehicles labeled as 0 and ECO, but parking in the street for ECO vehicles is limited. B and C vehicles can only use car parks.

[3] Madrid Open Data Portal url: https://datos.madrid.es/.

3.1 Air Quality Evaluation

The ODP provides the daily mean concentration of different air pollutants. The sensor located in MC evaluates six air pollutants: carbon monoxide (CO), SO_2, nitrogen monoxide (NO), NO_2, oxides of nitrogen (NOx), and O_3.

The pollutants with the strongest evidence for a public health concern, include particulate matter, SO_2, NO_2, and O_3 [26]. In fact, NO_2 itself caused 241,000 premature deaths among European citizens in 2015 and 2,515,000 of years of life lost [9]. Those pollutants $(SO_2$, NO_2, and $O_3)$, are the ones we analyze, since those are the ones referred to in the guidelines published by the WHO [26] and in the regulations promoted by EU [8] (see Table 1). We have not data regarding particulate matter.

Table 1. WHO and EU maximum concentration of pollutants in the air.

Pollutant	Period	WHO guidelines	EU regulations
SO_2	24 h	$20\,\mu g/m^3$	$125\,\mu g/m^3$
	1 h	–	$350\,\mu g/m^3$
	10 min	$500\,\mu g/m^3$	–
NO_2	1 year	$40\,\mu g/m^3$	$40\,\mu g/m^3$
	1 h	$200\,\mu g/m^3$	$200\,\mu g/m^3$
O_3	8 h	$100\,\mu g/m^3$	$120\,\mu g/m^3$

3.2 Outdoor Noise Evaluation

As there is not a clear international regulation about the outdoor noise, we decided to evaluate this concern taking into account three variants of noise measurements: the equivalent sound pressure, the percentile noise, and the noise pollution (NPL) [17] levels.

The equivalent sound pressure levels (L_{eq}) can be described as the average sound level over a selected period. We study the L_{eq24}, that corresponds to the L_{eq} measured during the whole day (24 h). The L_{eq} measurements are also required for intermediate periods (normally three within a 24 h period) to determine how noise varies with time and hence community activities. Here, we evaluate the L_{eqD}, L_{eqE}, and L_{eqN}, which represent the L_{eq} during the day (from 7:00 h to 19:00 h), the evening (from 19:00 h to 23:00 h), and the night (from 23:00 h to 7:00 h), respectively. According to the Community of Madrid regulations [3], L_{eqD} and L_{eqE} should be lower than 65 dB and L_{eqN} lower than 55 dB.

The percentile noise levels (L_x) are the levels exceeded for x percent of the time, where x is between 0.1% and 99.9%. We evaluate the L_{10}, L_{50}, and L_{90}. The L_{10} takes account of any annoying peaks of noise. The L_{90} is extensively used for rating the outdoor background noise.

The NPL estimates the dissatisfaction caused by road traffic noise comprising the continuous noise level (L_{eq}) and the annoyance caused by fluctuations in that level. It serves as an indicator of the physiological and psychological disturbance of the human system due to the noise pollution in the environment [17]. NPL is equal to L_{eq} plus 2.56 times the standard deviation of the noise distribution. However, it is approximated by $NPL \approx L_{eq} + (L_{10} - L_{90})$.

From the OPD, we get monthly mean values of each metric. This data reports the A-weighted sound level readings to replicate the response of the human ear to the annoyance caused by road traffic noise. Thus, all sound levels referred here are in terms of A-weighted decibel (dBA).

3.3   Methodology

In order to evaluate the impact of MC, we compare the data sensed during Pre-MC and during Post-MC. As MC measures started in December of 2018, this would be consider the first month of every row (number 1). Consequently, November becomes the last one of every year considered (number 12).

The impact on the studied indicators is calculated according to the *gap* for the months M that MC has been active (Eq. 1). The set M is defined as $M = \{December, January, February, March, April, May\}$. The $x_m^{Post\text{-}MC}$ and $\overline{x_m^{Pre\text{-}MC}}$ represent the average value of the indicator x sensed during month $m \in M$. The gap returns the average percentage of decrease or increase for the indicator x.

$$gap = \frac{1}{|M|} \sum_{m \in M} \frac{x_m^{Post\text{-}MC} - \overline{x_m^{Pre\text{-}MC}}}{x_m^{Post\text{-}MC}} \% \tag{1}$$

We use pairwise statistical tests to compare between both periods with a statistical significance of 99% (i.e., p-value < 0.01). When the samples data sets are normally distributed, we use the *Student's t-test*, otherwise, we apply the *Mann-Whitney* non-parametric one.

Giving this data in a specific temporal ordering, it is possible to raise questions about how the indicators are likely to behave in the future [25]. Polynomial regression, which have been successfully used in road traffic prediction [22], is applied here to predict the general future trend in pollution (air and noise) after the implementation of the road traffic restrictions in MC.

These last type of analyses, i.e., statistical tests and regressions, use the highest granularity of the data provided by the ODP: daily concentration of air pollutants and monthly levels of noise.

Finally, there are cases (data sensed) in which the concentration of the air pollutants exceed the maximum/threshold defined by WHO and/or EU (see Table 1). and the mean excess quantity. In this cases, we evaluate both dimensions in which this value is exceeded: the period of time and the mean excess quantity.

4 Results and Discussion

This section evaluates the results of the actions taken in MC in terms of air quality and noise based on the data sensed.

4.1 Air Quality

Table 2 reports the minimum (min), the maximum (max), the mean, the normalized standard deviation, and the gap for the concentration of the pollutants sensed in MC. As these measures are normally distributed, we apply the Student's t-test to asses the statistical significance of the difference between Pre-MC and Post-MC air quality. Figure 3 shows the mean and the standard deviation of the concentration of the pollutants by months. Notice that for the Pre-MC months (in red), the results cover a wider amount of time, corresponding to two different years. Figure 3 also shows the bloxplot of the concentration of the air pollutants for the months that coincide Pre-MC and Post-MC (i.e., from December to May).

Table 2. Summary of the air pollutants sensed. The star($\star$) in the last column indicates there is statistical difference between periods analized (p-value < 0.01).

Metric	Pre-MC			Post-MC			Gap
	min	mean $\pm$ stdev	max	min	mean $\pm$ stdev	max	
SO_2	1.00	$7.82 \pm 50.37\%$	22.00	10.00	$13.97 \pm 21.28\%$	24.00	$\star 56.14\%$
NO_2	15.00	$46.92 \pm 31.27\%$	96.00	8.00	$39.60 \pm 50.42\%$	96.00	$\star -35.65\%$
O_3	1.00	$39.31 \pm 52.32\%$	89.00	5.00	$41.20 \pm 48.94\%$	84.00	22.67%

The concentration of SO_2 increases during Post-MC months in comparison to Pre-MC (gap $= 56.14\%$). Figure 3(a1) shows the concentration of SO_2 for the time previous to MC (from June to November) is close to the Post-MC one. This may be explained by the influence of the meteorological conditions (i.e., wind direction and speed, atmospheric pressure, temperature, and relative humidity) possibly affecting the result in unexpected directions.

For both periods, the mean concentration does not exceed the threshold defined by WHO and EU ($20 \mu g/m^3$), however the maxima values do (see Table 2). In Pre-MC the threshold is exceeded during 0.43% of the time by $0.01 \mu g/m^3$ and in Post-MC during 3.91% of time by 0.09. Thus, this excess is exceptional and negligible, so the EU has not found it problematic in Spain.

Focusing on NO_2, which is the pollutant that almost lead Spain to the European Court, its concentration is significantly reduced in more than one third (gap $= -35.65\%$ and Student's t-test p-value < 0.01). The mean NO_2 concentration for Post-MC is $39.60 \mu g/m^3$, below the threshold established by WHO and EU ($40 \mu g/m^3$). As it can be seen in Fig. 3(b1), the concentration of NO_2 exceeds

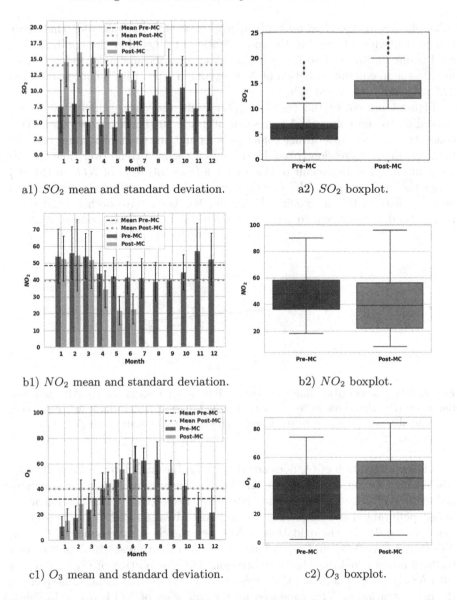

al) SO_2 mean and standard deviation.

a2) SO_2 boxplot.

b1) NO_2 mean and standard deviation.

b2) NO_2 boxplot.

c1) O_3 mean and standard deviation.

c2) O_3 boxplot.

Fig. 3. Mean and standard deviation of the concentration of the air pollutants grouped by months (left side). The red dashed and greed doted lines show the mean value for the months from one to six for Pre-MC and Post-MC, respectively. Boxplot of the concentration of the pollutants (right side). (Color figure online)

during several months the maximum one allowed by WHO and EU for both periods (Pre-MC and Post-MC) but with important differences. During Pre-MC the threshold is exceeded during 64.01% of the time by $9.72\,\mu g/m^3$. During Post-MC the threshold is exceeded, but it does during less time and with a smaller value: 45.81% of the time by $8.26\,\mu g/m^3$. However, it is noticeable that there is a clear downward trend in the concentration of NO_2 after the application of road traffic limitation (see Fig. 3(b1)). Taking into account independently each month, the maximum reduction of NO_2 occurs in April with a concentration of $22.54\,\mu g/m^3$ (gap $= -93.93\%$).

Figure 4 illustrates the trend of NO_2 using the data grouped by weeks. According to the polynomial regression of grade 10 (black dashed line), NO_2 concentration increases during colder seasons and decreases in warmer ones. In turn, the linear regression (black line) shows a declined trend over time for this air pollutant. The behaviour of this variable (concentration of NO_2 in the air) under the application of MC measures point that the traffic restriction has a positive effect in the air quality. Therefore, MC is effective both for this environmental dimension and to avoid fines from the international community.

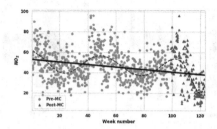

Fig. 4. NO_2 concentration linear regression. Red dots represent the Pre-MC data and the green triangles show Post-MC data grouped in weeks. The black line represents the general trend according to the linear regression. (Color figure online)

The concentration of O_3 does not show a significant difference for both periods of time (see Fig. 3(c1 and c2)). All the O_3 measures are bellow the maximun defined by WHO and EU (100 and $120\,\mu g/m^3$, respectively). The concentration of this pollutant shows an increase during Post-MC (gap $= 22.67\%$). This increment can be due by the oxidation of NO, i.e., the chemical reaction of O_3 and NO that forms NO_2 and O_2, which occurs in urban areas [15]. As the road traffic limitation reduces the concentration NO, the portion of O_3 that reacts with NO is lower. Therefore, the levels of O_3 do not decrease, and subsequently, the concentration of NO_2 produced by the oxidation of NO is lower. In short, this upturn can be a chemical consequence of the reduction in the air of other components concentration.

Finally, the evaluation of the SO_2, NO_2, and O_3 indicates that the final environmental balance may not always coincide with what was intuitively expected.

4.2   Noise Polution

Table 3 reports the min, max, the mean, the normalized standard deviation, and the gap for the levels of noise in MC. As the levels of noise are not normally

Table 3. Summary of the sensed levels of noise. The star($\star$) in the last column indicates that there is statistical difference (p-value < 0.01).

Metric	Pre-MC			Post-MC			Gap
	min	mean $\pm$ stdev	max	min	mean $\pm$ stdev	max	
L_{eqD}	61.30	63.68 $\pm$ 3.56%	68.70	62.10	63.63 $\pm$ 2.01%	65.70	-0.72%
L_{eqE}	60.40	61.96 $\pm$ 1.24%	63.80	60.60	61.18 $\pm$ 0.65%	61.80	$\star-1.51\%$
L_{eqN}	59.00	60.57 $\pm$ 1.32%	62.80	59.70	60.30 $\pm$ 0.80%	61.00	-0.47%
L_{eq24}	60.50	62.70 $\pm$ 2.66%	66.50	61.40	62.40 $\pm$ 1.27%	63.60	-0.96%
L_{10}	63.10	64.53 $\pm$ 1.60%	68.60	63.40	63.88 $\pm$ 0.66%	64.50	$\star-1.51\%$
L_{50}	57.60	58.66 $\pm$ 0.77%	59.60	57.20	57.78 $\pm$ 0.78%	58.60	$\star-1.47\%$
L_{90}	52.40	53.46 $\pm$ 1.46%	55.00	51.30	51.82 $\pm$ 0.97%	52.70	$\star-2.92\%$
NPL	70.70	73.77 $\pm$ 3.40%	80.90	72.60	74.47 $\pm$ 1.69%	76.50	-0.07%

distributed and the size of the samples is low (>30), we apply the Mann-Whitney test to asses the statistical significance of the difference between Pre-MC and Post-MC noise pollution. Figure 5 illustrates the mean of a representative set of different levels (L_{eq24}, L_{10}, L_{90}, and NPL) grouped by months. Figure 6 shows the boxplots of the L_{eq24}, L_{10}, and L_{90} levels of noise.

Regarding the equivalent sound pressure levels (L_{eqD}, L_{eqE}, L_{eqN}, and L_{eq24}), the highest difference between Pre-MC and Post-MC is given by the evening noise (L_{eqE}). This noise is reduced by 1.51% and it is statistically lower than evaluated one during Pre-MC (see Table 3). Among them, the L_{eqN} levels show the lowest decrease. This is mainly explained by the different car affluence during night time, as the nights experience the lightest road traffic flows.

As it can be seen in Fig. 6(a), even if there is not a statistical difference regarding to the L_{eq24} level of noise between both periods, during Post-MC this level of noise is generally lower than during Pre-MC. This metric *averages* the whole noise evaluated during the 24 h of the day. Therefore, in general the noise is lower during MC.

During Post-MC, the reduction of the day noise pollution allows the L_{eqD} be lower than 65 dB, which is the threshold proposed by Community of Madrid regulations (see Sect. 3.2). This value is exceeded just during some periods of March (month number 4 in Fig. 5(b)).

Focusing on the percentile noise levels (L_{10}, L_{50}, and L_{90}), Pre-MC and Post-MC differences are statistically significant. The highest improvement is shown by L_{90} (see Fig. 6(c)), which represents the residual background levels of noise of the urban area analyzed (gap $= -2.92\%$). As the continuous road traffic flow is one of the main sources of the background noise, its reduction provoques a decrease on this type of noise. According to the Mann-Whitney test results, the significance reduction of L_{10} is lower than for the other two percentile levels (p-value < 0.05). The L_{10} considers annoying peaks of noise. This type of maxima levels of noise are reduced by 1.51% with a mean value during Post-MC of 63.88 dBA.

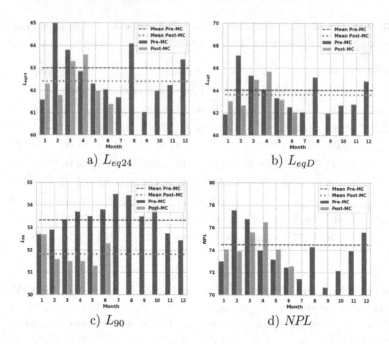

Fig. 5. Mean levels of noise analyzed here gropued by months. The red dashed and greed doted lines show the mean values for Pre-MC and Post-MC, respectively. (Color figure online)

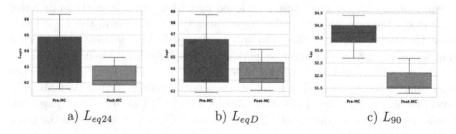

Fig. 6. Boxplots of the noise data metrics for both periods of time analized.

There is not a significant reduction of NPL (see Table 3). This is principally because this metric depends on L_{eq24} and the difference between L_{10} and L_{90}. On the one hand, there is not a significant difference in the L_{eq24}. On the other hand, both percentile noise levels are reduced during Post-MC. However, the reduction of L_{90} is grater, and therefore, the difference between them L_{10} and L_{90} increases. For example, if we subtract the mean values of L_{10} and L_{90} we get that for Pre-MC $64.53 - 53.46 = 11.07$ dBA and for Post-MC $63.88 - 51.82 = 12.06$ dBA.

Figure 7 illustrates the trend of some representative levels of sound (L_{eq24}, L_{eqD}, L_{90}, and NPL). According to the polynomial regression of grade 10 (black dashed line), there is a reduction of the equivalent levels of noise during the

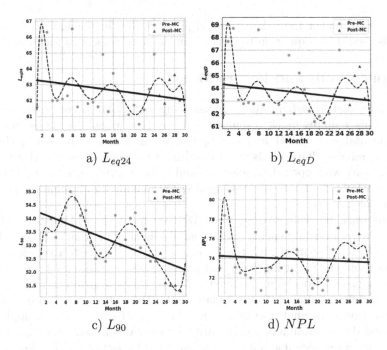

Fig. 7. Noise sensed linear regression. Red dots represents the data sensed during Pre-MC and green triangles the ones sensed during Post-MC grouped in months. The black line represents the general trend according to the lineare regression. (Color figure online)

months between 19 and 22. In turn, according to the linear regression (black line), the noise in MC is being reducing over the time with MC actions.

Finally, it is clear that the limitation of road traffic flows reduces all the different noise pollution metrics in MC, according to the sensed data.

4.3   Global Discussion

According to the analysis carried out, MC has reduced concrete pollutants in the air and in the sensed levels of noise. Specifically, regarding the air quality, the lowering of NO_2 is a very positive result. As we stated in Sect. 2, this is the component of pollution which affects health the most, increasing bronchitis, asthma and lung problems especially among the children and the older people. Besides, this is the component which lowering was specifically required to Spain by the EU. Accordingly, the reduction of this pollutant is extremely positive, not just having a positive effect for health but fulfilling so the international directions and so, avoiding the risk of fine.

Secondly, as the road traffic is the predominant source of noise pollution in urban areas, it was expected a reduction on all the levels of noise. This was proved to be true. However, and this is relevant, the levels of noise during the night are still higher than the threshold proposed by the Comunity of Madrid [3]. This should be a question to consider in the development of future actions.

5   Conclusions and Future Work

The quickness of the urbanization process brings new pollution problems, among others. This requires quick responses to create sustainable societies from an environmental, economical, and social points of view, as well to create inclusive spaces. A reliable diagnosis is key to address such challenges. Smart city initiatives, along with open data solutions and smart technologies have proved to be invaluable tools of analysis, helping decision making and leading to the best outcome for the city.

In this work, we evaluate data from ODP to evaluate the real impact of MC in terms of environmental benefits and accomplishment of international directives. Despite of the lifespan of MC, the measures proved to be effective addressing emission problems (reducing NO_2 and noise). These results may be used as a point to oppose the decision of removing MC by the new government.

The lack of use of open data standards in OPD and the poor documentation found hardeness the analysis capacity for this type of studies. For example, we have found data with different granularity for the same indicators (i.e., noise).

The future research lines are: (i) analysing the impact of MC not just in the downtown but in the whole city of Madrid (ii) new multivariable analysis taking into account new data (e.g., meteorological conditions); (iii) evaluating MC (or MC-like) measures considering new dimensions (such as, morbidity, economical impact, use of spaces, mobility behavioral changes); and (iv) studying effects on specific population groups (e.g., children and the elderly).

Acknowledgements. Irene Lebrusán has been partially funded by RCC Harvard program. Jamal Toutouh has been partially funded by European Union's Horizon 2020 research and innovation programme under the Marie Skłodowska-Curie grant agreement No. 799078. This research has been partially funded by the Spanish MINECO and FEDER projects TIN2017-88213-R (http://6city.lcc.uma.es) and TIN2016-81766-REDT (http://cirti.es). Universidad de Málaga, Campus Internacional de Excelencia Andalucía TECH.

References

1. Ayuntamiento de Madrid: Madrid Central - Zona de Bajas Emisiones (2018). https://tinyurl.com/y2jch2qb. Accessed 07 July 2019
2. Basner, M., et al.: Auditory and non-auditory effects of noise on health. Lancet **383**(9925), 1325–1332 (2014)
3. Counidad de Madrid: Compendio de Normativa de Ruido y Vibraciones (2004). http://www.madrid.org/bdccm/normativa/PDF/Ruidos%20y%20vibraciones/Compilacion/CPRUID.pdf. Accessed 7 July 2019
4. European Commission: Directive 2002/49/ec of the European parliament and the council of 25 June 2002 relating to the assessment and management of environmental noise. Official Journal of the European Union, L 189(18.07), 2002 (2002)

5. European Commission: Directive 2004/107/ec of the European parliament and of the council of 15 December 2004 relating to arsenic, cadmium, mercury, nickel and polycyclic aromatic hydrocarbons in ambient air. Official Journal of the European Union, L 23, 3–16 (2004)
6. European Commission: Directive 2008/50/ec of the European parliament and of the council of 21 May 2008 on ambient air quality and cleaner air for Europe. Official Journal of the European Union, L 152, 1–44 (2008)
7. European Environment Agency: Noise pollution is a major environmental health concern in Europe (2016). https://www.eea.europa.eu/themes/human/ noise. Accessed 7 July 2019
8. European Environment Agency: Air quality in Europe (2018). https://www.eea. europa.eu/publications/air-quality-in-europe-2018. Accessed 7 July 2019
9. European Environment Agency: Air quality in Europe: 2018 report (2018). https:// www.eea.europa.eu/publications/air-quality-in-europe-2018. Accessed 7 July 2019
10. Evans, G., Hygge, S., Luxon, L., Prasher, D.: Noise and its effects (2007)
11. Evans, G.W.: Child development and the physical environment. Annu. Rev. Psychol. **57**, 423–451 (2006)
12. Fotel, T., Thomsen, T.U.: The surveillance of children's mobility. Surveill. Soc. **1**(4), 535–554 (2003)
13. Lawton, M.P., Nahemow, L.: Ecology and the aging process (1973)
14. Ministerio de Agricultura y Pesca, Alimentación y Medio Ambiente: Evaluación de la Calidad del Aire de Espa na 2016 (2017). https://tinyurl.com/y2jch2qb. Accessed 7 July 2019
15. Palmgren, F., Berkowicz, R., Hertel, O., Vignati, E.: Effects of reduction of NO_x on the NO_2 levels in urban streets. Sci. Total Environ. **189–190**, 409–415 (1996)
16. Parajuli, A., Pojani, D.: Barriers to the pedestrianization of city centres: perspectives from the global north and the global south. J. Urban Des. **23**(1), 142–160 (2018)
17. Robinson, D.W.: The concept of noise pollution level. J. Occup. Environ. Med. **13**(12), 602 (1971)
18. Sobková, L.F., Čerticky̆, M.: Urban mobility and influence factors: a case study of prague. WIT Trans. Built Environ. **176**, 207–217 (2017)
19. Soni, N., Soni, N.: Benefits of pedestrianization and warrants to pedestrianize an area. Land Use Policy **57**, 139–150 (2016)
20. Steele, C.: A critical review of some traffic noise prediction models. Appl. Acoust. **62**(3), 271–287 (2001)
21. Tobon, M., Jaramillo, J.P., Sarmiento, I.: Pedestrianization and semi-pedestrianization: a model for recovery public space in the medellín downtown. In: MOVICI-MOYCOT 2018: Joint Conference for Urban Mobility in the Smart City, pp. 1–7 (2018)
22. Toutouh, J., Arellano, J., Alba, E.: BiPred: a bilevel evolutionary algorithm for prediction in smart mobility. Sensors **18**(12), 4123 (2018)
23. United Nations: World Urbanization Prospects: The 2018 Revision: key facts (2018). https://population.un.org/wup/Publications/Files/WUP2018-KeyFacts. pdf. Accessed 7 July 2019
24. Ward, S.V.: What did the Germans ever do for us? A century of British learning about and imagining modern town planning. Plan. Perspect. **25**(2), 117–140 (2010)

25. Witten, I.H., Frank, E., Hall, M.A., Pal, C.J.: Data Mining: Practical Machine Learning Tools and Techniques. Morgan Kaufmann, Burlington (2016)
26. World Health Organization: Ambient (outdoor) air quality and health (2018). https://www.who.int/en/news-room/fact-sheets/detail/ambient-(outdoor)-air-quality-and-health. Accessed 7 July 2019

Over-Voltage Protection for Pico-Hydro Generation Using PV Microinverters

Isabella Cristina Scotta[1,3](✉) , Gabriela Moreira Ribeiro[1,4] ,
Wellington Maidana[1,2] , and Vicente Leite[1,2]

[1] Instituto Politécnico de Bragança, Campus Santa Apolónia, Bragança, Portugal
{maidana,avtl}@ipb.pt
[2] Research Centre in Digitalization and Intelligent Robotics (CeDRI),
Bragança, Portugal
[3] Universidade Tecnológica Federal do Paraná,
Campus Toledo, Toledo, Paraná, Brazil
isahcs9@gmail.com
[4] CEFET/RJ, Campus Maracanã, Rio de Janeiro, Brazil
gribeiro.eletronica@gmail.com

Abstract. Innovative, low-cost, environmentally friendly and renewable resource-based solutions are emerging to meet growing global energy demand. Hydroelectric technology is quite old and mature. Despite its importance, it is associated with large plants, with environmental impact. On contrary, small-scale systems, called pico-hydro systems (up to 5 kW) are not yet explored. Anyway, the exploration of pico-hydro systems has been increasing consistently, from the first off-grid applications in remote places to distributed generation, with the injection of the generated energy in the main grid or microgrids. Very recently, there have been advances in grid connection of these small-scale systems, using off-the-shelf components. Indeed, pico-hydro systems can be connected to the grid using off-the-shelf components, namely photovoltaic inverters. Thus, grid-connected pico-hydro systems have gained an enormous potential in distributed production. However, in situations of over-power, or whenever the generator is under no load, there is a need for effective over-voltage protection, unlike photovoltaic systems. The goal of this paper is to propose an over-voltage protection circuit, designed to ensure the integration of low-power pico-hydro systems connected to the grid using conventional photovoltaic microinverters. Extensive tests were performed on an experimental platform using three microinverters easily found on the market and a low power generator (300 W) developed for small wind turbines. The experimental results, demonstrated the performance of the proposed over-voltage protection circuit in four different situations, presented in this work, thus avoiding irreversible damages of generators and microinverters, in the context of the above described grid connection approach.

Keywords: Microgrids · Distributed generation · Photovoltaic microinverters

© Springer Nature Switzerland AG 2020
S. Nesmachnow and L. Hernández Callejo (Eds.): ICSC-CITIES 2019, CCIS 1152, pp. 25–37, 2020.
https://doi.org/10.1007/978-3-030-38889-8_3

1   Introduction

The growing need for energy from renewable resources is undeniable today as a consequence of the increase in energy consumption, besides environmental commitments made by many countries to reduce greenhouse gases [3]. The new technologies to be developed for micro-generation based on green energy allow the creation of solutions that currently facilitate the electrification in developing countries [16], as well as promoting self-sustaining, growing systems in developed countries [5,11]. Distributed generation (DG), through different renewable resource plants, despite the low power, may contribute significantly to the increase in sustainability at the local and global levels [8,14].

According to [6], small hydropower plants can be considered one of the best methods for producing renewable energy, as long they are based on cheap, reliable, mature technologies and do not cause significant environmental changes where installed. Pico-hydro systems generate up to 5 kW [1] and have potential in meeting growing energy demand, once they allow widespread exploitation of small rivers, shallow water reservoirs, and wastewater [6,13].

Recent studies have shown the integration of low power wind generators with pico-hydro applications, in which they are connected to the grid through the use of photovoltaic (PV) inverters [9]. PV inverters are mature technologies widely available on the market. Its combination with a permanent magnet synchronous generator (PMSG) is an alternative for energy generation. Although PV inverters have been created to operate with PV modules, a PMSG and a bridge rectifier can be used as DC source, instead of those modules [9,10].

As is the case with large hydropower plants, in order to provide a stable voltage output, mechanical devices are generally used for water flow adjustments. Afterwards, the rotation of the turbine is controlled so as to reduce voltage and frequency deviation [15]. Hydraulic dynamics, with the seasonal variations of water flow, influence these parameters in a generation. The energy production efficiency is improved with turbines or water wheels performing at variable speed. Therefore, the characteristics of the generators and inverters require that they be integrated. Furthermore, to prevent damage to the electrical system, a protective circuit is required. Indeed, an over-voltage protection circuit is necessary to ensure that, during grid synchronization or disconnection and overpower generation, the generator does not damage the inverter [10].

This paper proposes a simple and low-cost over-voltage protection circuit that limits the rectified DC voltage of the generator by dissipating the energy in a power resistor or by short-circuiting the generator if over-power generation is detected. The reliability of the designed circuit is demonstrated with numerous tests carried out on a laboratory workbench and an experimental platform. The connection of low power PMSGs to the electrical grid through PV microinverters is also demonstrated.

2 Over-Voltage Protection

2.1 Integration Between Generator and PV Inverter

PV inverters, up to 5 kW, are widely diffused, have a competitive cost and are very widespread. There is also a significant set of manufacturers that provide a wide offer of generators, for that power range, namely for small wind turbines. Although the compatibility between PMSGs and PV inverters is not always guaranteed, their integration is possible by combining the safe operating areas of both, shown in Fig. 1.

Three parameters that establish the operating limits in which the inverter can operate, V_{DCmax}, I_{DCmax} and P_{DCmax} which are voltage, current and maximum power, respectively. In Fig. 2, the green lines represent the voltage and current characteristics of a generator after rectifying on the DC side, when it operates with constant speed. The brown area marks the safe operating area of the PV inverter [9].

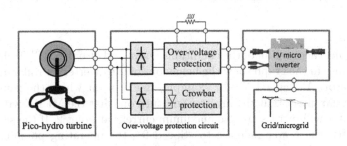

Fig. 1. Design topology for grid-connected pico-hydro systems.

To ensure the generator will work in the safe operating area of the inverter, certain conditions must be guaranteed. First, the no-load DC voltage of the generator, or the one imposed by the protection circuit, must be greater than the voltage $V_{PV_{start}}$ which enables the inverter to start operating. Also, the nominal power of the generator should be in the range of 0.4 P_{DCmax} to 1.0 P_{DCmax} of the inverter and the output DC voltage of the generator must be within the input voltage range of the inverter, thus less than V_{DCmax}. Finally, the rated current of the generator must be equal to or less than I_{DCmax}. Moreover, a current greater than P_{DCmax}/V_{DCmax} is recommended to ensure that the inverter will be able to process the available power without overloading the generator [10].

An over-voltage protection circuit is required to ensure the operation within the limits V_{DCmax} and P_{DCmax} allowed at the PV inverter input. Another important feature in PV inverters is their internal maximum power point tracking MPPT algorithm, which is the selection of a point of operation where the current and voltage pair allows the process of maximum power available from the connected power source. Unlike PV modules, generators have their maximum power point when their current approaches their rated value $I_{G_{DCrated}}$ [10].

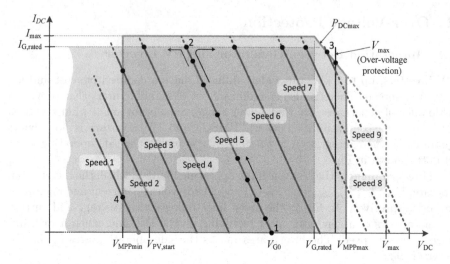

Fig. 2. Overlapping of the operating areas of PV inverter and generator. (Color figure online)

Taking into account all of the conditions above and also the MPPT algorithm, the green lines in the graph show the behaviour of the inverter for different speeds of a generator. At "Speed 5", for example, the point at which the generator is operating guarantees that the inverter will turn on, that the MPPT will start at point 1 and it will increase to the maximum current at point 2. If the speed and, consequently, the power increase to "Speed 9", the operating point is defined by point 3 and does not exceed this value, because at that point the protection comes into action and the excess energy is dissipated in the auxiliary resistor. In contrast, if the power and speed decrease to "Speed 1", the inverter operates at point 4, where there is the minimum voltage for which it can operate [10].

2.2 Over-Voltage Protection Circuit

This section presents an over-voltage protection circuit to limit the speed and, consequently, the output DC voltage of the generator. This is done by dissipating the energy in a power resistor or by short-circuiting the generator if the power is too high. The protection circuit is fundamental to ensure that the inverter will not be damaged and whenever the generator runs at no load. This can occur due to:

- Low power demand or high power delivered by the generator;
- Grid failure (e.g. due to frequency or voltage outside the limits) that turns off the inverter;
- The time required by the inverter for synchronization with the grid.

The protection circuit schematic is shown in Fig. 3. It is based on a step-down converter with a power MOSFET and a free-wheeling diode to dissipate the

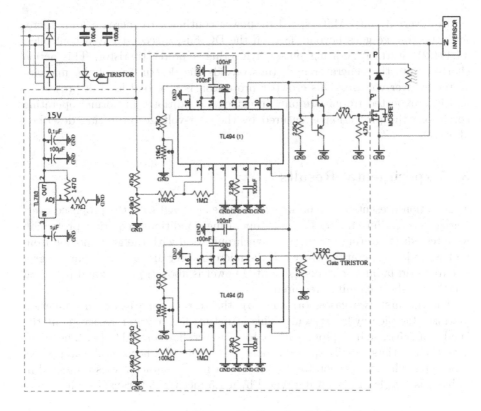

Fig. 3. Over-voltage protection circuit schematic.

energy in a power resistor. The control is performed by Pulse-Width-Modulation (PWM) using the PWM controller TL494(1). A voltage divider (at pin 1), with a 4k7 resistor and a 10k potentiometer, sets the threshold voltage for which the TL494(1) starts the generation of pulses. Another voltage divider (at pin 2) is used to measure the DC output voltage of the generator. The deviation between these two inputs is amplified by one of the two error amplifiers of the TL494. The error controls the generated duty-cycle. The resistor and capacitor connected to pins 5 and 6, respectively, set the switching frequency at approximately 4,54 kHz.

The microinverters used in this work have a V_{DCmax} of 50 V and the V_{MPP} is 40 V as it will be presented later. Therefore, upon reaching a voltage value equal to 45 V on the DC bus, the TL494(1) starts generating pulses with a duty-cycle proportional to the DC voltage. The MOSFET activates the part of the circuit that dissipates the energy in an external resistor R to avoid the no-load operation of the generator and, thus, limiting the DC output voltage. The power resistor must be sized to withstand the P_{DCmax} and at V_{DCmax}, hence:

$$R = \frac{V_{DCmax}^2}{P_{DCmax}}. \tag{1}$$

However, if the PMSG speed or power continues to increase and, therefore, the voltage goes beyond 48 V on the DC bus, a second PWM controller, TL494(2), starts generating pulses, triggering a power thyristor. This action short-circuits the generator and, thus, avoids the destruction of the microinverter by over-voltage. This crowbar protection is a second level of protection and it is expected to operate only in extreme conditions. In normal operating conditions the protection is ensured by the over-voltage protection described above.

3   Experimental Results

This section presents the experimental results achieved with the proposed over-voltage protection circuit. Different operating conditions requiring protection were tested: (a) during the inverter synchronization with the grid, moving from no load to load operation; (b) when the microinverter disconnects from the grid due to a grid failure; (c) when generated power is above P_{DCmax}; and (d) when the PMSG short circuit is required.

For the first two cases, (a) and (b), the test is done using an emulation platform for pico-hydro systems. This structure has a water reservoir, at the height of 3,5 m and 4 pipes with a total water flow of 40 l/s [4]. The pipes have their outlets equally spaced around the blades of a horizontal water wheel prototype. The wind generator 1 (gen. 1), with the characteristics presented in Table 1, is coupled to the water wheel by a 1:5 mechanical transmission.

Table 1. PMSG technical data.

Gen.	Speed (rpm)	V_{DC_0} (V)	V_{DC} (V)	I_{DC} (A)	P_{DC} (W)
1	300	45	28	10.7	300
2	630	30	24	12.5	300

In the third and fourth cases, (c) and (d), the tests were done on a workbench that has a three-phase induction motor driven by a conventional frequency converter. The PID macro, usually available in the frequency converters, was used to perform a closed-loop control of the shaft (mechanical) power of the generator. For these tests, it was used the wind generator 2 (gen. 2) presented in Table 1. This PMSG was directly connected to the shaft of the induction motor.

The microinverters presented in Table 2 were used in both experimental platforms.

3.1   Results Obtained with an Emulation Platform

As said above, an emulation platform for pico-hydro systems, consisting of a horizontal water wheel, was used for evaluation tests in real conditions. The

Table 2. Microinverter technical data [2,12] and [7].

Characteristic	Unit	Microinverter		
		1	2	3
P_{DCmax}	W	300	300	280
I_{DCmax}	A	11.5	9.5	10
V_{DCmax}	V	50	50	50
V_{DCmin}	V	20	18	22
$V_{MPPrange}$	V	24–40	20–40	28–40
P_{ACmax}	W	250	235	245

synchronization test (a) aims to show the performance of the protection circuit when the generator starts with no load and the microinverter initiates the synchronization procedure before connecting to the grid. At first, the generator is loaded by the protection circuit while waiting for the PV microinverter to be able to process the power generated by the turbine (water wheel). During this synchronization time the protection circuit operates and limits the voltage set point as designed. The energy is dissipated in a power resistor preventing damage of the PV microinverter.

During the start-up of the generator shown in Fig. 4(a), the microinverter sought to connect a few times. However, it was unsuccessful at first and the protection circuit actions were required. The microinverter of Fig. 4(b), connects the generator to the grid after about 15 s. The protection circuit operates during the last 5 s, limiting the DC voltage to 47,2 V. Both figures show the PWM operating as soon as the DC voltage reaches 45 V. For Fig. 4(c), the microinverter was very agile as it started and achieved the steady-state voltage value of approximately 28,8 V, even before the protection circuit was activated.

Similar to what occurs during grid synchronization, a grid failure causes the increase on generator voltage, unless the protection circuit limits the voltage. Test (b) is shown in Fig. 5, where the voltage, which was being maintained at an approximately constant operating point by the microinverters, passed to the value limited by the protection circuit, immediately after the grid failure simulation.

3.2 Results Obtained with a Work Bench

The over-power test (c), is performed with a generated power higher than the maximum input power of the microinverter. Figure 6 plots the power dissipated by the protection circuit in the resistive load and the power at the input of the microinverter. The tests were performed increasing the power. As soon as the input power of the microinverter reaches its limit, the protection circuit starts dissipating in the power resistor.

The crowbar test (d) was performed increasing the power until the voltage reached the value designed to short circuit the generator.

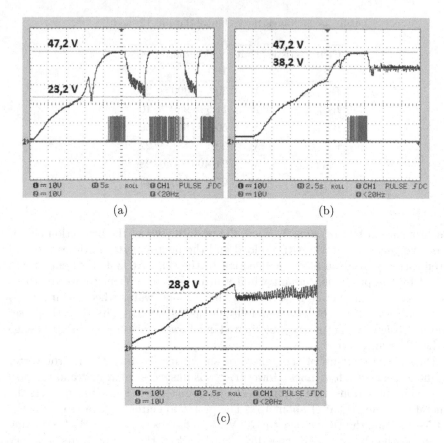

Fig. 4. Over-voltage protection circuit behaviour during generator start-up and grid synchronization tests with (a) Microinverter 1, (b) Microinverter 2 and (c) Microinverter 3.

Figure 7 illustrates the moment when the short-circuit occurs. First, PWM pulses (in blue) are generated by the over-voltage protection when the DC voltage reaches 45 V. Subsequently, when it catches up 47,2 V, the thyristor is turned on and the voltage falls drastically to a value corresponding to a voltage drop across the thyristor (2,4 V). The final value of short circuit current (for the maximum generated power) was 18 A.

4   Discussion

The evaluation results using a benchwork and real emulation platform proved the effectiveness of the protection circuit. Tests with the emulation platform, consisting of a horizontal water wheel, showed that the start-up of the generator (and water wheel) is slow enough for the Microinverter 3 to connect to the grid, even before the protection circuit action is required. Microinverter 2 connected

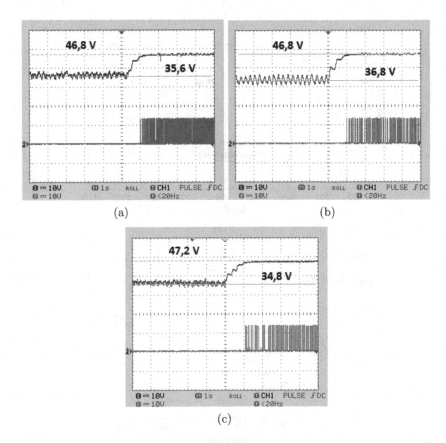

Fig. 5. Over-voltage protection circuit behavior in failure tests with (a) Microinverter 1, (b) Microinverter 2 and (c) Microinverter 3.

to the grid after about 15 s, but the action of the protection circuit was required during about 5 s to limit the voltage. Microinverter 1 took several seconds to connect to the grid. In this case, the protection circuit limited the DC voltage conveniently.

The performance of the protection was demonstrated when the DC voltage reached the value of 45 V and then limited it to 47,2 V, waiting for the Microinverters 1 and 2 connect the generator to the grid. After the starting transient all microinverters operated with a DC voltage defined by the MPP tracking algorithm (below the protection threshold) and the action of the protection circuit was terminated.

When simulating the grid failure, the protection circuit limited the DC voltage to 46,8 V with the first and second Microinverters and to 47,2 V with the third one. Once again, the developed circuit has proved effectiveness in protecting the devices.

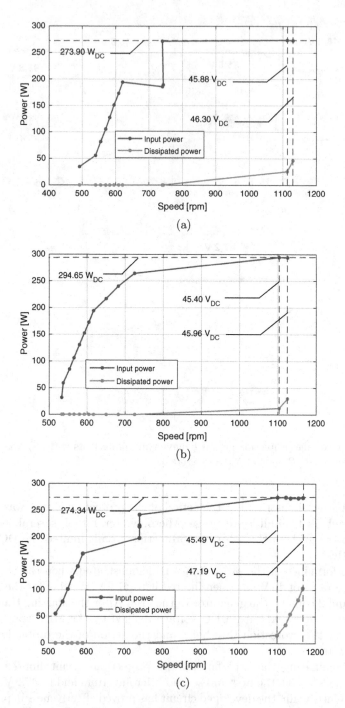

Fig. 6. Over-voltage protection circuit behaviour with over-power generation tests with (a) Microinverter 1, (b) Microinverter 2 and (c) Microinverter 3.

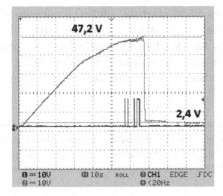

Fig. 7. Over-voltage protection circuit behaviour with a short-circuit test. (Color figure online)

Tests made on a workbench, showed that as the generator power increased, the speed and, therefore, the DC voltage also rose, as seen in Fig. 6. At a certain point, a P_{DCmax} value was reached and the microinverters were no longer able to process the generated power. In this case, the excess was dissipated in the auxiliary power resistor. Notably, the moment when maximum input power is reached, the resistor starts to dissipate. For all cases, the DC voltage protection threshold was approximately 45,50 V.

Moreover, when the generated power (and voltage) is too high, further protection is needed. This is done by short-circuiting the generator. During the test (d) it was demonstrated two protections (dissipation in the resistor and the short-circuit itself) working properly. The generator breaks and the speed is significantly reduced. The voltage in the DC bus is limited to the voltage on the thyristor. This additional protection prevents damage of the devices in extreme situations. In this situation, for the system to resume normal operation, operator intervention may be required. In effect, the thyristor will no longer turn off while there is voltage on the DC bus.

5   Conclusion

Small-scale pico-hydro systems are an interesting energy generation opportunity because they run 24 h a day. These systems can be easily exploited if standard technology widely available on the market is used, such as generators designed for small wind turbines and photovoltaic microinverters. The integration of this equipment, as distributed energy sources connected to the grid, is possible with the over-voltage protection circuit proposed and developed in this work. Experimental tests were performed for validation purposes, both in real context with a water wheel or on a workbench. The results demonstrated the usefulness and efficacy of the developed circuit. Two permanent magnet synchronous generators were connected to the grid using three different microinverters. The protection has proved to be effective in the expected situations:

during the turbine (generator) starting, while the microinverter is connecting to the grid; when the generator is at no load due to grid failures; and in cases of excessive power. Thus, the developed circuit effectively protects the generator against too high speeds and, consequently, it limits the DC voltage at the input of PV microinverters, whenever these are used for grid connection of pico-hydro turbines.

Acknowledgments. The authors would like to thank FCT (Foundation of Science and Technology, Portugal) for the financial support through the contract SAICT-POL/24376/2016 (POCI-01-0145-FEDER-024376), and to the partnership among IPB, CEFET/RJ and UTFPR in the teaching and research program.

References

1. Basar, M.F., Ahmad, A., Hasim, N., Sopian, K.: Introduction to the pico hydro power and the status of implementation in Malaysia. In: 2011 IEEE Student Conference on Research and Development, pp. 283–288, December 2011. https://doi.org/10.1109/SCOReD.2011.6148751
2. BeOn Energy Ltd., Portugal: Data Sheet: BeON 1 Microinverter, March 2019
3. European Commission: Novel carbon capture and utilisation technologies. https://ec.europa.eu/research/sam/pdf/sam_ccu_report.pdf#view=fit&pagemode=none. Accessed June 2019
4. Dalmarco, I., Araujo, P., Leite, V., Queijo, L., Lima, L.: Prototyping a horizontal water wheel for electricity generation in a small museum: the house of silk. In: I Ibero-American Congress of Smart Cities (ICSC-CITIES 2018), September 2018
5. Gaius-obaseki, T.: Hydropower opportunities in the water industry. Int. J. Environ. Sci. **1**(3), 392–402 (2010)
6. Hatata, A., El-Saadawi, M., Saad, S.: A feasibility study of small hydro power for selected locations in Egypt. Energy Strategy Rev. **24**, 300–313 (2019)
7. INVOLAR Corporation Ltd.: Installation and Operations Manual: INVOLAR MAC250 Photovoltaic Micro-inverter, 1.2 edn, August 2011
8. Lahimer, A., Alghoul, M., Sopian, K., Amin, N., Asim, N., Fadhel, M.: Research and development aspects of pico-hydro power. Renew. Sustain. Energy Rev. **16**(8), 5861–5878 (2012)
9. Leite, V., Couto, J., Ferreira, Â., Batista, J.: A practical approach for grid-connected pico-hydro systems using conventional photovoltaic inverters. In: 2016 International Energy Conference (ENERGYCON), pp. 1–6. IEEE (2016)
10. Leite, V., Ferreira, Â., Couto, J., Batista, J.: Compatibility analysis of grid-connected pico-hydro systems using conventional photovoltaic inverters. In: 2016 18th European Conference on Power Electronics and Applications (EPE 2016 ECCE Europe), pp. 1–9. IEEE (2016)
11. Leite, V., Figueiredo, T., Pinheiro, T., Ferreira, Â., Batista, J.: Dealing with the very small: first steps of a sicohydro semonstration project in an university campus. RE&PQJ **1**(10), 1305–1310 (2012)
12. GWL: Micro-inverters technical details and specifications, June 2019. https://www.ev-power.eu/Micro-Inverters-Tech/
13. Machado, M., et al.: Microturbinas em redes de abastecimento de água. Dissertação de mestrado, Universidade de Aveiro (2015)

14. Maidana, W., Leite, V., Ferreira, A., Bonaldo, J., Gonçalves, E., Batista, J.: Design of a self-sustainable system based on renewable energy sources for a small museum of science dissemination - the house of silk. In: III Congresso Ibero-Americano de Empreendedorismo, Energia, Meio Ambiente e Tecnologia - CIEEMAT 2017, Bragança, Portugal, July 2017
15. Mhlambi, B.A., Kusakana, K., Raath, J.: Voltage and frequency control of isolated pico-hydro system. In: 2018 Open Innovations Conference (OI), pp. 246–250, October 2018. https://doi.org/10.1109/OI.2018.8535603
16. Yah, N.F., Oumer, A.N., Idris, M.S.: Small scale hydro-power as a source of renewable energy in Malaysia: a review. Renew. Sustain. Energy Rev. **72**, 228–239 (2017)

Detecting Hot Spots in Photovoltaic Panels Using Low-Cost Thermal Cameras

Miguel Dávila-Sacoto[1](✉) iD, Luis Hernández-Callejo[2](✉) iD,

Víctor Alonso-Gómez[2](✉) iD, Sara Gallardo-Saavedra[2](✉) iD,
and Luis G. González[1](✉) iD

[1] Universidad de Cuenca, Campus Central, 010104 Cuenca, Ecuador
{miguela.davila,luis.gonzalez}@ucuenca.edu.ec
[2] Universidad de Valladolid, Campus Universitario Duques de Soria, 42004 Soria, Spain
{luis.hernandez.callejo,victor.alonso.gomez,
sara.gallardo}@uva.es

Abstract. One of the most important challenges to mitigate global climate change is to move towards replacing petroleum-based energy sources. In this idea, non-conventional renewable energy sources such as photovoltaic (PV) solar and wind power are the most used worldwide. In the case of the massification of PV solar generation systems due to its low cost, it has resulted in the use of large-scale supervision techniques that allow a quick and effective determination of the health status of its main components. This study, performs an analysis of the performance of different low-cost cameras for thermography. The analysis compares the accuracy of the thermal images obtained and the error is quantified by means of an image dispersion analysis in each of them. Three-dimensional meshes and contours figures are also made to determine the temperature of a faulty cell. The study shows that the performance obtained with low-cost cameras presents errors below 10% in costs and less than 0.015 USD/pixel.

Keywords: Thermography · PV panel · Low cost · Thermal camera · Image processing

1 Introduction

Thermography in PV panels is a technique that has been used in Operation and Maintenance (O&M) of PV solar generation systems for more than a decade [1]. It is used to determine hot spots in cells that can be originated as a result of cell deterioration or partial shading, and can compromise panel performance in a solar farm. Thermography is used to obtain representative images of temperature on the surface of solar panels, generally using high-resolution thermal cameras in order to obtain detailed information on the temperature of each part of the PV panel under study.

Nowadays most of the cameras used for thermography of solar panels are expensive, which is an inconvenience for the massification of this technology. However, there are low-cost thermal cameras in the market. Although they do not have the technical characteristics and advantages offered by the most sophisticated alternatives, they can be used

S. Nesmachnow and L. Hernández Callejo (Eds.): ICSC-CITIES 2019, CCIS 1152, pp. 38–53, 2020.
https://doi.org/10.1007/978-3-030-38889-8_4

for small-scale analysis providing information that allows initial actions to be taken in case of any anomaly observed.

This study shows the use of low-cost cameras for thermography, making measurements on solar panels under operation, detailing the most important features and emphasizing its cost. The analysis of the images obtained with both temperature tables and static images is carried out, and the corresponding temperature measurement error between cameras is obtained.

2 Thermal Cameras

2.1 Cameras Used in Thermography Studies

Thermal cameras capture the radiation emitted by an object [2], converting it into an image that represents the temperature pattern of the area of interest. The use of thermal cameras for analysis of equipment and machinery is known as thermography and is currently part of the non-invasive techniques to observe the temperature of an object [2]. Since last decade, the advance on new energy sources and especially the adoption of PV solar energy, mainly due to its rapid worldwide price reduction, has allowed the incorporation of techniques such as thermography that allows to identify failures in PV cells or in electrical connections [3–9], providing relevant information that facilitates the O&M of PV sites. However the equipment normally used is expensive. Table 1 shows the most important characteristics and costs of a set of thermal imaging cameras commonly used today.

Table 1. Features and prices of thermal cameras used in the thermographic analysis in PV panels.

Brand	Flir	Flir	Testo	Flir
Model	SC655	TAU2	870-2	i3
Thermal image quality (pixels)	640 × 480	640 × 512	160 × 120	60 × 60
Thermal sensitivity	<0.1 °C	<0.1 °C	<0.1 °C	<0.15 °C
Price (USD)	$26,990.00	$6,000.00	$2,528.00	$1,295.00
Price/resolution (USD/pixel)	0.0875	0.0183	0.1316	0.3597

Although the costs of the options presented in Table 1 are high, the resolution of the sensors is higher and allows detailed analysis. Regarding the relationship between cost and resolution, the most expensive options generally have a smaller cost per resolution ratio. Among them, the Flir TAU2 camera stands out with a lower cost per pixel.

2.2 Low-Cost Thermal Cameras

In the market, there are options of low-cost thermal cameras with technical characteristics suitable for its usage in thermography, in particular, those shown in Table 2. These are the cameras used in this paper.

Table 2. Features and prices of options for low-cost thermal cameras.

Brand	Caterpillar	Flir
Model	CAT s60	One Pro
Thermal image quality (pixels)	80 × 60	160 × 120
Thermal sensitivity	<0.15 °C	<0.15 °C
Price (USD)	$428.00	$388.92
Price/resolution (USD/pixel)	0.089	0.015

It is observed that the selected cameras have a similar price, below $500, which makes them easily accessible compared to others more expensive. In Fig. 1, images captured with the cameras under study are observed. They present similar behaviors, however, as expected, the one taken with the higher resolution camera (Flir One Pro) presents sharper or more defined edges.

(a)   (b)

Fig. 1. Thermal image of a PV panel captured by (a) FLIR One Pro camera, (b) Caterpillar Cat S60 camera.

3   Thermography with Low-Cost Cameras

The low-cost cameras in Table 2 were used to perform a thermographic analysis of the 35 kWp installation described in [10]. After manual inspection of 160 solar panels, two were found with anomalies identified as hot spots. One of these anomalies captured using the Flir One Pro camera and processed with the FLIR Tools software [11], in which measurement points were added, is shown in Fig. 2. Two points identified as T1 and T2 are observed with temperatures of 43.0 °C and 29.6 °C, respectively.

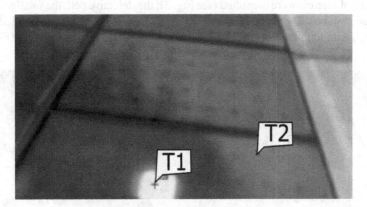

Fig. 2. Thermal image of a PV panel captured by a FLIR One Pro camera.

The FLIR One Pro camera and the Cat S60 embed into their images metadata corresponding to the temperature of each pixel. This information can be extracted with the thermal camera software and allows an analysis of the temperature at each point of the image, permitting the use of this information in the data processing software. Table 3 shows part of the metadata in Fig. 2 (rows and columns headers are only for reference).

Table 3. Metadata of Fig. 2, with Flir One Pro camera.

Row/column	Pixel [1, 2]	Pixel [1, 3]	Pixel [1, 4]	Pixel [1, 5]	Pixel [1, n]
Pixel [2, 1]	25.331	25.331	25.331	25.331	...
Pixel [3, 1]	25.338	25.338	25.338	25.338	...
Pixel [4, 1]	25.354	25.354	25.354	25.346	...
Pixel [5, 1]	25.376	25.376	25.376	25.369	...
Pixel [6, 1]	25.407	25.407	25.399	25.392	...
Pixel [7, 1]	25.437	25.437	25.43	25.422	...
Pixel [8, 1]	25.468	25.46	25.46	25.445	...
...	...	...	...	...	...

Other types of cameras display only an image that does not contain metadata, making necessary the use of image processing techniques that allow the temperature estimation to be determined based on the intensity of the color.

3.1   Thermal Image Analysis and Temperature Tables

First, was established a panel that showed considerable thermal variations, in which three points of interest were identified (see Fig. 3); the defective cell, the unaffected area and the junction box. Using the Flir One Pro camera, these points were identified as T1, T2, and T3, with temperatures of 51.3 °C, 35.3 °C, and 35.2 °C, respectively (Fig. 3a).

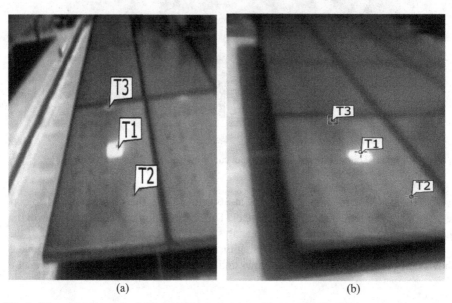

(a)   (b)

Fig. 3. Thermal image of a defective PV panel captured by (a) Flir One Pro camera (b) Cat S60 camera.

The temperature difference between the faulty cell and a different point on the panel in Fig. 3a, defined as $\Delta T = T1 - T2$, reaches 15.9 °C. The maximum temperature of the image under study is 52 °C. Studies indicate that 51.3 °C reached on the cell could be considered as a major fault [8], so short term maintenance is required. In addition, according to [4] the value obtained of ΔT indicates a "medium failure". On the other hand, Fig. 3b, captured with a Cat S60 camera, shows three points identified as T1, T2, and T3, with temperatures of 53.6 °C, 36.9 °C, and 38.4 °C, respectively. Here the temperature difference of points of interest reaches $\Delta T = 14.8$ °C between the faulty cell and a different point of the panel, with a maximum temperature of the image under study at 53.2 °C.

Using the temperature table obtained with Flir Tools tool, the thermal image (Fig. 4) was reconstructed as an intensity graph, where each pixel is given by Eq. (1):

$$pixel = (X\ position, Y\ position, temperature) \tag{1}$$

The intensity graph in Fig. 4 has the "appearance" of a grayscale image, however, it is not the result of applying a grayscale algorithm, but on the contrary, it is the direct graph of the pixel intensity information, that is, the graph of the temperature measured by the

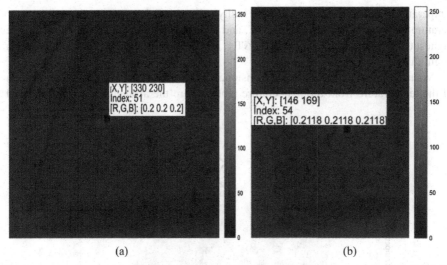

Fig. 4. Image reconstructed from the temperature table (a) Flir One Pro camera (b) Cat S60 camera.

thermal camera. This presents an important advantage because the exact temperature of each element in the image can be obtained without the need of any type of normalization or further processing.

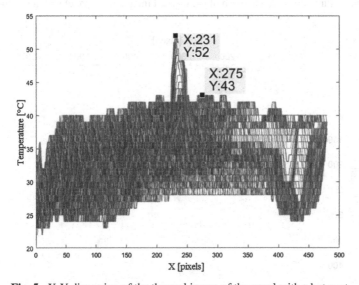

Fig. 5. X-Y dispersion of the thermal image of the panel with a hot spot.

From data in Fig. 4, an X-Y graph was made in Matlab® (see Fig. 5), where the dispersion of the temperature values is obtained. This allows identifying the maximum temperature value corresponding to the faulty cell, which shows the highest pixel temperature in that area, in this case, 52 °C, and a maximum temperature of 43 °C for the highest temperature area near the cell ($\Delta T = 9$ °C). According to [4] this could mean a "light failure".

Visualizing the data in a three-dimensional domain, Fig. 6, shows the representation of the temperature from the temperature table, where the arrangement of the thermal

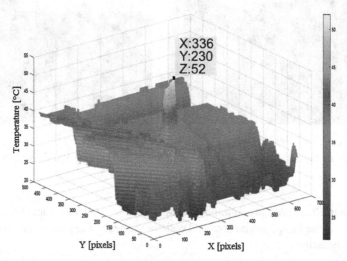

Fig. 6. A three-dimensional mesh of the thermal image of the panel with a hot spot.

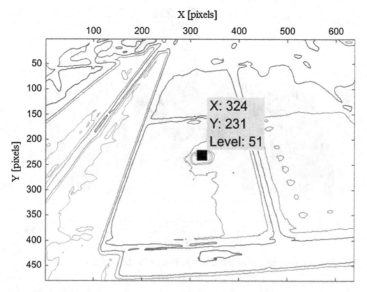

Fig. 7. The contour of the three-dimensional mesh of the thermal image.

image intensities can be observed. The mesh obtained allows to easily identify the hottest point of the image.

Performing a contour analysis, Fig. 7 shows the projection of the Z-axis (temperatures) of the three-dimensional function on a two-dimensional image, and it can be used as an edge detection approach.

3.2 Static Image Analysis

Because static images are common in low-cost cameras (without metadata), their analysis is studied to observe their validity in thermographic applications on PV solar panels. The static image is taken with its color map (sidebar that indicates the relationship between the color of the image and the temperature) to be able to have a reference of the temperature of each pixel without necessarily having the metadata, showing the maximum and minimum temperatures at the top and bottom of the bar (see Fig. 8). Through the tests performed it was observed that in the case of FLIR cameras these values do not correspond to the maximum and minimum recorded previously in the image. Here a maximum of 46 °C is observed, which does not agree with the 52 °C observed in the data in the temperature table.

Fig. 8. Static image obtained from a thermal camera with the color map on the left side.

In order to obtain the estimated pixel temperature, the image is initially converted to grayscale, and then the intensity values are normalized to find the new pixel value using Eq. (2):

$$Temperature_{pixel} = T_{min} + (T_{max} - T_{min}) \times Intensity \tag{2}$$

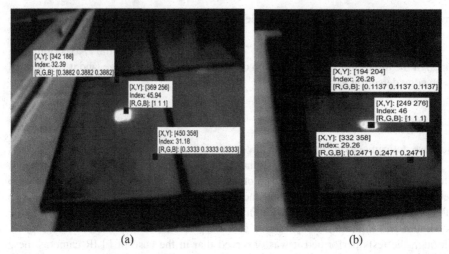

(a)   (b)

Fig. 9. Standard grayscale static image showing pixel temperature (a) Flir One Pro (b) Cat S60.

With this, a grayscale image is obtained, where the new pixel intensity value corresponds to a normalized temperature as shown in Fig. 9.

In the XY scatter plot shown in Fig. 10, the maximum pixel temperature can be found, however, there is a loss of details due to the normalization and the accuracy decreases due to the conversion of this type of image. It is also observed that the amplitude of the pixel values increases for areas other than the faulty cell and that there are more pixels with low temperatures.

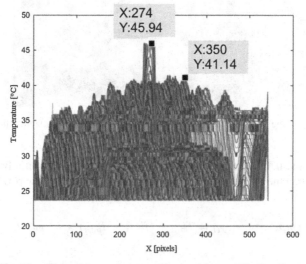

Fig. 10. Dispersion of the static image obtained from a Flir One Pro camera.

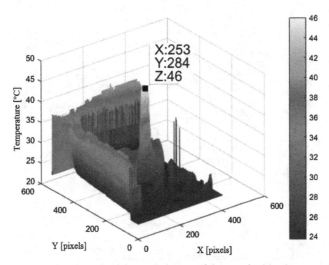

Fig. 11. A three-dimensional mesh of the static image of the panel with a hot spot obtained from the Cat S60 camera.

By repeating the procedure described above for the mesh graphic in the static image, Fig. 11, is obtained. A similar behavior of the thermal image is shown with the Cat S60 camera, with the difference in the maximum temperature achieved. In the same way, as in the dispersion, a greater amount of values is observed in the base of the graph within the lower temperatures of the image.

Finally, by repeating the contour of the mesh, Fig. 12a is obtained, where it is observed that, due to the normalization of the image, there are marked areas of the temperature gradient, which can make it difficult to use geometry identification algorithms in image processing. This variation between the different techniques is shown in Fig. 12b.

3.3 I-V/P-V Curves Analysis

The faulty PV modules under study are monocrystalline ATERSA A-250P of 250 Wp [12]. Figure 13a shows the I-V curves of the panel that has a hot spot and a panel without faults. The curves were captured with a Solmetric PVA-600 tracer [13]. It is observed that the voltage of the panel with failure falls at around 16 Vdc, showing a typical behavior of a damaged or "shaded" cell [14–17]. When reviewing the P-V curve of the panels (Fig. 13b), the decrease in the maximum power point is observed, obtaining a 25% less power in the panel with the hot point compared to a panel without failures.

3.4 UAV and Low-Cost Camera Tests

Inspections with low-cost cameras can be carried out with the help of remote-operated mobile systems. Further information about this kind of onboard thermal inspections can be found in [18] and [19]. In this research the behavior of the Cat S60 camera is tested. The camera was mounted on a DJI Mavic Pro drone (Fig. 14a) and used as proof of concept in order to verify that this camera can show the hot spot on the faulty panel. The

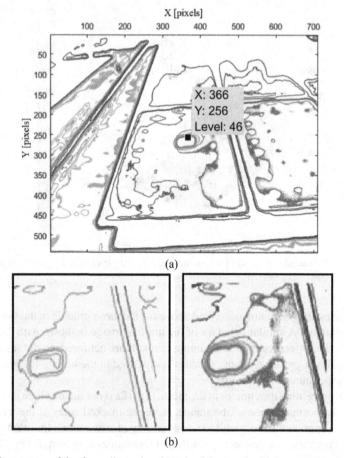

(a)

(b)

Fig. 12. The contour of the three-dimensional mesh of the panel with hot spot (a) obtained from the static image, (b) comparison between thermal image contour (left) and static image (right).

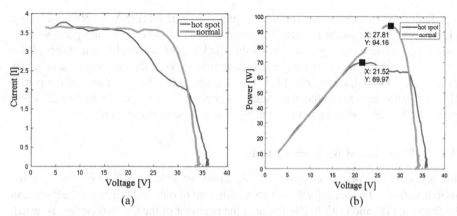

(a)   (b)

Fig. 13. Characteristic curves of the panel with failure and another without anomalies (a) I-V curves (b) P-V curves.

drone was flown at three meters above the panel, obtaining the image shown in Fig. 14b. It is noted that the hot spot in the image can be clearly identified. However, this camera does not deliver a heat map or a temperature table in video capture mode, so its use should be limited to manual hot spots detection.

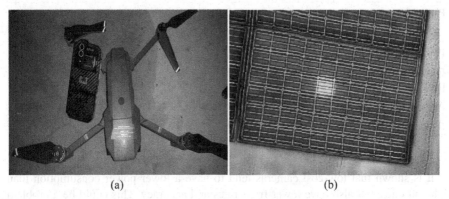
(a)   (b)

Fig. 14. Solar panel thermography with drone (a) Cat s60 thermal camera and DJI Mavic Pro drone (b) captured the image.

3.5   Technical Advantages of Low-Cost Thermal Cameras

Low-cost thermal cameras could be used for thermal inspection on small or mid-sized solar farms but considering their limitations. High-end or professional-grade thermal cameras are specifically designed to perform in challenging environments and record high-resolution images with high accuracy and confidence. General advantages of using professional thermal cameras include IP rating so using them in harsh environments is not a problem, higher framerate enabling smooth video analysis and included ethernet or industrial communication protocols.

On the other hand, low-cost alternatives are becoming widely used by hobbyists, students and contractors, while high-end cameras are used mainly by research institutes or by industries with large budgets. Some of the advantages of using low-cost thermal cameras include lower energy consumption (very important to embedded systems, or UAVs), standard and commercial communication protocols (USB) and wide community behind its use and development. The latter of these advantages for low-cost cameras is very important to independent researchers or too small research groups because when developing solutions or carrying out study cases, technical support is an important issue, especially if the camera manufacturer is from other country or speaks a different language than the user. With low-cost cameras (or nearly all low-cost solutions in hardware thanks to the open-source community), it is possible to find support within users. With high-end cameras users generally need to contact the manufacturer directly and wait for support or even pay for it.

Table 4 shows a technical comparison of 2 high-end thermal cameras and the 2 low-cost alternatives discussed in this document.

Table 4. Results.

Parameter	Low-Cost		High-End			
	Flir One Pro	Cat S60	Testo 870-2	Flir i3	Flir SC655	Flir Tau 2
Power [W]	1.1	1.2	2.3	1.6	24	1.3
Framerate [Hz]	8.7	8.7	9	9	50	60
Accuracy	±3 °C 5%	±5 °C 5%	±2 °C 2%	±2 °C 2%	±2 °C 2%	±2 °C 2%
IP grade	No	IP68	IP54	IP54	IP67	IP67

It is shown that low-cost cameras tend to have a lower power consumption than high-end ones, but also have lower framerates and accuracy. This could be a problem depending on the application. For example, if the research needs a real-time temperature monitoring system with instant readings, high-end cameras with high framerates are the best choice.

3.6 Results Comparison

Table 5 shows a comparison of the parameters obtained from the thermography analysis of both, the thermal image and the static image. It is observed that in the image analysis a relative error of 10.45% is obtained for the measured temperature of the faulty cell, and a relative error of 7.75% for ΔT between the cell and an adjacent panel point. For the analysis of the X-Y dispersion, an error of 46.67% is observed for the faulty cell, while for the mesh analysis there is a 11.54% error and for the three-dimensional contour a 9.80% error. This indicates that contour analysis and mesh analysis are better candidates than scatter analysis in image processing in cases where the temperature table is not available.

The errors observed in dispersion and contour analysis are less than 10%, so they can be used in the thermographic analysis by extrapolating the temperature [20]. Previous studies [21–23] show that the error can be improved with image processing techniques and neural networks. Table 6 shows a comparison of the cameras used and the limitations found according to on-site tests.

Table 5. Results.

Parameter	Thermal image	Static image	Absolute error	Relative error
T connection box	35.20 °C	32.39 °C	2.81 °C	7.98%
T panel	35.30 °C	31.18 °C	4.12 °C	11.67%
T faulty cell	51.30 °C	45.94 °C	5.36 °C	10.45%
ΔT faulty cell	16.00 °C	15.00 °C	1.24 °C	7.75%
Scatter				
T max faulty cell	52.00 °C	45.94 °C	6.06 °C	11.65%
T max adjacent area	43.00 °C	41.14 °C	1.86 °C	4.33%
ΔT faulty cell	9.00 °C	4.80 °C	4.20 °C	46.67%
Mesh				
T max faulty cell	52.00 °C	46.00 °C	6.00 °C	11.54%
Contour				
T max faulty cell	51.00 °C	46.00 °C	5.00 °C	9.80%

Table 6. Comparison of characteristics of low-cost thermal cameras

Camera	Flir One Pro	Cat S60
Temperature table	Yes	Yes
Connection	USB-C with Android/iOS smartphones	Included inside the smartphone
Weight	36.5 g	223 g
Outdoor use	No	No
Drone use	Yes (lighter)	Yes

4 Conclusions

This paper presents a description of the characteristics of low-cost thermal imaging cameras, emphasizing its cost/resolution relationship. It is observed that the analysis of thermography using low-cost cameras is viable considering the established errors, which can be less than 10%.

From the analysis of static images, it is shown that a three-dimensional contour is a valid tool with less than 10% error, which can be improved with artificial intelligence techniques and neural networks.

The thermal cameras used in this document cost 10% less than professional cameras (taking as reference a Flir TAU2), without compromising the detection of hot spots in PV panels, which allows these low-cost cameras to be used in thermographic studies considering the limitations in terms of its construction and its feasibility of outdoor use.

References

1. Usamentiaga, R., Venegas, P., Guerediaga, J., Vega, L., Molleda, J., Bulnes, F.G.: Infrared thermography for temperature measurement and non-destructive testing. Sensors (Switz.) 14(7), 12305–12348 (2014)
2. Battalwar, P., Gokhale, J., Bansod, U.: Infrared thermography and IR camera. Int. J. Res. Sci. Eng. 1(3), 9–14 (2015)
3. Ruggeri, E., Van Aken, B.B., Isabella, O., Zeman, M.: Electroluminescence and dark lock-in thermography for the quality assessment of metal-wrap-through solar devices. IEEE J. Photovolt. 8(5), 1174–1182 (2018)
4. Toledo, C., Serrano, L., Abad, J., Lampitelli, A., Urbina, A.: Measurement of thermal and electrical parameters in photovoltaic systems for predictive and cross-correlated monitorization. Energies 12(4), 668 (2019)
5. Santos, R.L., Ferreira, J.S., Martins Jr., G.E., de Souza, K.C.A., Sá Jr., E.M.: Low cost educational tool to trace the curves PV modules. IEEE Lat. Am. Trans. 15(8), 1392–1399 (2017)
6. Dhimish, M., Holmes, V., Mehrdadi, B., Dales, M., Mather, P.: PV output power enhancement using two mitigation techniques for hot spots and partially shaded solar cells. Electr. Power Syst. Res. 158(January), 15–25 (2018)
7. Amiry, H., et al.: Design and implementation of a photovoltaic I-V curve tracer: solar modules characterization under real operating conditions. Energy Convers. Manag. 169, 206–216 (2018)
8. Jaffery, Z.A., Dubey, A.K., Irshad, Haque, A.: Scheme for predictive fault diagnosis in photovoltaic modules using thermal imaging. Infrared Phys. Technol. 83, 182–187 (2017)
9. Salazar, A.M., Macabebe, E.Q.B.: Hotspots detection in photovoltaic modules using infrared thermography. MATEC Web Conf. 70, 10015 (2016)
10. Espinoza, J.L., Gonzalez, L.G., Sempertegui, R.: Micro grid laboratory as a tool for research on non-conventional energy sources in Ecuador. In: 2017 IEEE International Autumn Meeting on Power, Electronics and Computing, ROPEC 2017, vol. January 2018, pp. 1–7 (2018)
11. FLIR: FLIR Tools Thermal Analysis and Reporting (Desktop) | FLIR Systems. https://www.flir.com/products/flir-tools/. Accessed 11 Aug 2019
12. Atersa: Atersa A-250M datasheet, p. 1 (2019)
13. Solmetric: Solmetric PVA-600 PV Analyzer User's Guide
14. Garcia De La Cruz, P.: Trazador De Curvas V-I Para Seguimiento De Módulos Solares, no. Plan, p. 122 (1996)
15. Hemza, A., Abdeslam, H., Rachid, C., Aoun, N.: Simplified methods for evaluating the degradation of photovoltaic module and modeling considering partial shading. Meas. J. Int. Meas. Confed. 138, 217–224 (2019)
16. Quiroz, J.E., Stein, J.S., Carmignani, C.K., Gillispie, K.: In-situ module-level I-V tracers for novel PV monitoring. In: 2015 IEEE 42nd Photovoltaic Specialist Conference, PVSC 2015, pp. 1–6 (2015)
17. Kim, K.A., Seo, G.S., Cho, B.H., Krein, P.T.: Photovoltaic hot-spot detection for solar panel substrings using AC parameter characterization. IEEE Trans. Power Electron. 31(2), 1121–1130 (2016)
18. Gallardo-Saavedra, S., et al.: Aerial thermographic inspection of photovoltaic plants: analysis and selection of the equipment. In: 2017 Proceedings ISES Solar World Congress, IEA SHC 2017. International Conference on Solar Heating and Cooling for Buildings and Industry (2017). https://doi.org/10.18086/swc.2017.20.03
19. Gallardo-Saavedra, S., Hernández-Callejo, L., Duque-Pérez, O.: Image resolution influence in aerial thermographic inspections of photovoltaic plants. IEEE. Trans. Ind. Inform. 14, 5678–5686 (2018)

20. Zaaiman, W.: Solar irradiance and photovoltaic measurements from solar radiation to PV arrays (2012)
21. Tsanakas, J.A., Ha, L., Buerhop, C.: Faults and infrared thermographic diagnosis in operating c-Si photovoltaic modules: a review of research and future challenges. Renew. Sustain. Energy Rev. **62**, 695–709 (2016)
22. Koprowski, R.: Some selected quantitative methods of thermal image analysis in Matlab. J. Biophotonics **9**(5), 510–520 (2016)
23. Chine, W., Mellit, A., Lughi, V., Malek, A., Sulligoi, G., Massi Pavan, A.: A novel fault diagnosis technique for photovoltaic systems based on artificial neural networks. Renew. Energy **90**, 501–512 (2016)

Household Energy Disaggregation Based on Pattern Consumption Similarities

Juan Chavat$^{(\boxtimes)}$ (iD, Jorge Graneri, and Sergio Nesmachnow (iD

Universidad de la República, Montevideo, Uruguay
{juan.pablo.chavat,jgraneri,sergion}@fing.edu.uy

Abstract. Non-intrusive load monitoring allows breaking down the aggregated household consumption into a detailed consumption per appliance, without installing extra hardware, apart of a smart meter. Breakdown information is very useful for both users and electric companies, to provide an accurate characterization of energy consumption, avoid peaks, and elaborate special tariffs to reduce the cost of the electricity bill. This article presents an approach for energy consumption disaggregation in residential households, based on detecting similar patterns of recorded consumption from labeled datasets. The proposed algorithm is evaluated using four different instances of the problem, which use synthetically generated data based on real energy consumption. Each generated dataset normalize the consumption values of the appliances to create complex scenarios. The `nilmtk` framework is used to process the results and to perform a comparison with two built-in algorithms provided by the framework, based on combinatorial optimization and factorial hidden Markov model. The proposed algorithm was able to achieve accurate results, despite the presence of ambiguity between the consumption of different appliances or the difference of consumption between training appliances and test appliances.

1 Introduction

Electricity utilization in homes has shown an uninterrupted increase worldwide, as detailed in the World Energy Outlook report, prepared by the International Energy Agency [6]. The electric power demanded in 2050 is expected to be twice as much as that demanded in 2010 [11]. Under this premise, many investigations have been carried out to achieve an efficient use of electricity in factories, buildings, and homes.

One of the approaches implemented to achieve a more efficient use of electric energy in homes is based on encouraging users to have a behavior change, favorable to saving. The incentives for behavioral changes are derived from the analysis of electricity utilization. For this analysis, Non Intrusive Load Monitoring (NILM) techniques are applied.

NILM allows determining the energy consumption of individual devices that are turned on and off, based on the detailed analysis of the current and voltage of the total load, measured at the interface with the source of the load.

© Springer Nature Switzerland AG 2020
S. Nesmachnow and L. Hernández Callejo (Eds.): ICSC-CITIES 2019, CCIS 1152, pp. 54–69, 2020.
https://doi.org/10.1007/978-3-030-38889-8_5

This approach was developed to simplify the collection of energy consumption data by utilities, but it also has other applications. It is called non-intrusive to contrast it with techniques previously used to collect load data, which requires placing sensors on every appliance and, therefore, an intrusion on the user's energy consumption. In particular, NILM techniques are applied in residential households.

NILM uses only the aggregate signal to disaggregate the signal of each appliance, providing an easier way of generating detailed information about household energy consumption. The disaggregated information is useful to provide breakdown bill information to the consumer, schedule the activation of appliances, detect malfunctioning, and suggest actions that can lead a significant reduction in consumption (e.g., up to about 20% in some cases [12]), among other uses.

In this line of work, this article presents a first approach for solving the dissagregation problem by applying a simple algorithm for recognizing on/off appliances states using the aggregate consumption signal, and determine energy consumption patterns. The experimental evaluation of the proposed algorithm is performed over synthetic datasets, specifically built using real energy consumption data from the well-known UK-DALE repository [8]. Experiments are set to analyze the accuracy of the method varying the power consumption of appliances varies and generating complex scenarios including ambiguities between the power consumption of appliances. Experimental results are compared with two built-in methods of the nilmtk toolkit: Combinatorial Optimization (CO) and Factorial Hidden Markov Model (FHMM). Results shows that the proposed algorithm is able to achieve accurate results, accounting for an average of 0.95 on the F-score metric, in the most complex problem instances.

The proposal is developed within the project "Computational intelligence to characterize the use of electric energy in residential customers", funded by the National the Uruguayan government-owned power company (UTE) and Universidad de la República, Uruguay. The project proposes the application of computational intelligence techniques for processing household electricity consumption data to characterize energy consumption, determine the use of appliances that have more impact on total consumption, and identify consumption patterns in residential customers. The main contribution of this article is a simple approach to solve the problem of energy consumption dissagregation in residential households, conceived to be adapted to the main features of the Uruguayan system, and the experimental evaluation over a set of problem instances and the comparison with existing techniques.

The article is structured as follows. Section 2 presents the formulation of the problem addressed in the work. A review of the main related work is presented in Sect. 3. The proposed algorithms for solving the problem are described in Sect. 4. The experimental analysis is reported in Sect. 5. Finally, Sect. 6 presents the conclusions and the main lines of future work.

2   The Energy Consumption Dissagregation Problem

The problem consists of dissagregating the overall energy consumption of a house into the individual consumption of a number of appliances.

Consider a set of appliances available in a house $A = \{a_i\}, i = 1, \ldots, m$, and let x_t be the aggregate power consumption of the house at a given time slice t. x_t can be expressed as the sum of the individual power consumption x_t^i of each appliance in use in that time slice. The status of each time slice is indicated by the binary variable y_t^i, that takes value 1 when appliance i is ON and 0 when it is OFF. The simplest (binary) variant of the problem assumes just two possible values for the power consumption of each appliance, i.e., $x_t^i = c_i \times y_t^i$, that is to say that the power consumption of appliance i is constant and does not depend on the activity being performed by the appliance.

The total power consumption is described as a function $f \colon \{0,1\}^m \to R$ defined by the expression in Eq. 1.

$$x_t = f((y_t^1, y_t^2, \cdots, y_t^m)) = c_1 y_t^1 + c_2 y_t^2 + \cdots + c_m y_t^m \tag{1}$$

If function f is injective (one-to-one), the problem is trivial. Otherwise, the times series $\{x_t\}_{t \in T}$ must be studied in order to deduce from the variation of power consumption on time, the signatures of the individual appliances.

For instance, suppose the appliances are: fridge (power consumption 250 W), washing machine (2000 W), dish washer (2500 W), kettle (2500 W), and home theater (80 W). The aggregate power consumption is a non-injective function. There is ambiguity between the power consumption of dish washer and kettle, as defined by Eq. 2. The variation of the aggregate power consumption in time must be studied to deduce if the kettle or the dish washer is ON.

$$f((0,0,1,0,0)) = f((0,0,0,1,0)) = 2500 \tag{2}$$

Several attributes and patterns can be studied to solve ambiguities. In the previous example, additional information can be used to solve the ambiguity: e.g., the mean time of utilization of each appliance (it is a couple of minutes for kettle and longer than an hour for the dish washer). Other more sophisticated patterns can be detected to solve problem instances with more complex ambiguities.

3   Related Works

The analysis of the related literature allows identifying several proposals on the design and application of software-based methods for energy consumption dissagregation. The main related works are reviewed next.

Hart [5] presented the concept of Nonintrusive Appliance Load Monitoring (NALM). The author stated that the previously presented approaches on the subject had a strong hardware component, installing intrusively monitoring points in each household appliance connected to a central information collector. Hart proposed an approach based on using a simple hardware and complex software for the analysis, thus eliminating permanent intrusion in homes.

The model proposed by Hart considers that electrical appliances are connected in parallel to the electrical network and that the power consumed is additive (Eq. 3), where $a_i(t)$ represents the ON/OFF state of an appliance at time t.

$$a_i(t) = \begin{cases} 1 \text{ if appliance } i \text{ is ON at time } t \\ 0 \text{ otherwise} \end{cases} \qquad (3)$$

Multiphase loads with p phases are modeled as vectors of dimension p where each component is the load in each phase. The total charge of the vector is the sum of the p components. P_i is defined as a vector representing the power consumed by device i when it is turned on (Eq. 4), where $P(t)$ is the corresponding to time t, and $e(t)$ represents the noise or the recorded error for time t.

$$P(t) = \sum_{i=1}^{n} a_i(t).P_i + e(t) \qquad (4)$$

The proposed model involves solving a combinatorial optimization problem to determine vector $a(t)$ from P_i and $P(t)$, in order to minimize the error (Eq. 5).

$$\hat{a}(t) = \arg\min_a \left| P(t) - \sum_{i=1}^{n} a_i(t).P_i \right| \qquad (5)$$

However, the resulting combinatorial optimization problem is NP-hard and therefore computationally intractable for large values of n. Heuristic algorithms allow computing solutions of acceptable quality, but their applicability is limited because in practice the set of vectors P_i is not fully known, the value n is not fixed, and unknown devices tends to be described as a combination of those already known. Furthermore, a small variation in the measurement of $P(t)$ can cause large changes in $a(t)$, mistakenly predicting simultaneous on and off events.

In recent works, NILM has been treated as a machine learning problem, applying supervised and unsupervised learning methods. Supervised learning approach is based on a data set of the consumption of each circuit device and the aggregate signal, and the objective is to generate models that learn to disaggregate the signal of the devices from the added signal. The techniques most commonly applied in this approach are Bayesian learning and neural networks. The unsupervised approach seeks to learn signatures of possible devices from the aggregate signal without knowing a priori what devices are inside the circuit. Bonfigli et al. [2] presented a survey of the test data sets available to researchers and the main techniques used for the unsupervised NILM approach. The most used unsupervised learning techniques are those based on Hidden Markov Models (HMM), which define a number of hidden states in which the model can be moved, representing the operating conditions of the device (e.g., on, off and possible intermediate states) and an observable result, which depends on the real state that represents the analyzed consumption data.

Kelly and Knottenbelt [7] analyzed three deep neural networks for disaggregation in the NILM problem. The proposed neural networks had between one and 150 million trainable parameters, so large amounts of training data was needed. The data set used was UK-DALE. The approach consisted of training a neural network for each household appliance, taking as input a sequence of aggregate total consumption and returning as a result the prediction of the power demanded by the associated appliance. Three architectures of neural networks were studied: (i) long short-term memory (LSTM) recurrent neural network, suitable for working with data sequences because of its ability to associate the entire history of the inputs to an output vector; (ii) a self-coding for noise elimination (denoising autoencoder, dAE) that cleans the aggregate consumption signal to obtain only that corresponding to the target appliance; and (iii) a rectangle network to detect the start and end of the use of the target appliance, and its average power demanded at that time. The networks were trained using 50% of real data and 50% of synthetic data, generated with the signatures of the UK-DALE appliances using the nilmtk tool. Results were compared with CO and FHMM. The dAE and the rectangle networks outperformed the results of both CO and FHMM in F1 score, precision, proportion of total energy correctly assigned, and mean absolute error; while LSTM outperformed CO and FHMM in on/off appliances but was behind in multi-state appliances.

Several related works have used the nilmtk tool [1], a framework for NILM analysis implemented in Python that facilitates using multiple data sets by converting them to a standard data model. nilmtk implements algorithms for data preprocessing, statistics to describe the data sets, two disaggregation algorithms (CO and FHMM), and metrics for evaluation. Within the preprocessing algorithms are *downsample*, to normalize the frequency of consumption signals; and *voltage normalization*, to solve the problem of the variation of voltage between different countries [5], which implements a method to normalize the data and is able to combine different sets of household data from different countries.

Kolter and Johnson [10] introduced the REDD dataset and studied the performance of a FHMM algorithm for dissagregation using the available data. FHMM was evaluated using two weeks of data from five households, subsampled in ten-second intervals. Results showed that FHMM was able to disaggregate the total consumption, observing a clear degradation of the results when going from the prediction in the training set to the prediction in the evaluation set. The FHMM for the training set correctly classified 64.5% of the consumption, while for the evaluation set the correct classification was reduced to 47.7%. The authors posed the challenge of finding a way to combine REDD with the massive amount of untagged data generated daily by public energy service companies.

4   The Proposed Algorithm

This section describes the proposed algorithm to solve the problem of energy consumption disaggregation based on similar consumption patterns.

4.1   Algorithm Description

Function $f : \{0,1\}^m \to R$ gives the aggregate power consumption of a house for a set of appliances. A function $g : R^{2d+1} \to R^m$ is considered, where the positive number d determines a time neighbourhood for the predictions (Eq. 6).

$$(\hat{y}_t^1, \hat{y}_t^2, \cdots, \hat{y}_t^m) := g_{W,Z}(x_{t-d}^i, \cdots, x_t^i, \cdots, x_{t+d}^i) \tag{6}$$

In Eq. 6, $(\hat{y}_t^1, \hat{y}_t^2, \cdots, \hat{y}_t^m)$ is the estimated configuration of the set of house appliances. Function $g_{W,Z}$ has random elements; it is defined using the information of a training database $\{W, Z\} = \{w_t, z_t\}$ such that for $t = 1, \cdots, n$, $w_t \in \{0,1\}^m$, $z_t \in R$ and Eq. 7 holds.

$$z_t = f((w_t^1, w_t^2, \cdots, w_t^m)) \tag{7}$$

The parameters of function $g_{W,Z}$ are chosen empirically to maximize the sum given in Eq. 8, where A is the set of ambiguous configurations $A = \{y \in \{0,1\}^m / \exists y' \in \{0,1\}^m, y' \neq y, f(y') = f(y)\}$. This is equivalent to maximize the number of time slices $t \in T$ for which every appliance status is correctly detected.

$$\sum_{y_t \in A} \prod_{i=1}^m 1_{\{\hat{y}_t^i = y_t^i\}} \tag{8}$$

The proposed algorithm, named *Pattern Similarities* (PS), consists of two parts, training and testing (prediction), which are described next.

The output of the algorithm is y, the vector of disaggregated power consumption, computed using the following input:

- The vector x containing the aggregate power consumption of one house measured over a period of time with a certain time frequency.
- A training set z containing the aggregate power consumption of one or several houses measured over a period of time with the same time frequency as x.
- A training set w containing the disaggregated power consumption of the house (houses) described in z over the same period of time and with the same frequency as x is measured.
- The parameter δ that defines a power consumption neighbourhood.
- The parameter d that defines a time interval neighbourhood.
- The parameter H that separates high from low power consumption.

Algorithm 1 describes the processing on the training stage. The goal is to build an array (M_Z) with information relating each consumption record with its neighbour records. The information act as a feature of each appliance signature, for each sample. The main loop (lines 2–10) iterates over each sample in the training set. In each iteration step, the algorithm checks if the neighbour samples has similar consumption values to the currently analyzed sample (lines 4–8); if they have, then a counter is incremented. In the end, the array with the processed values is generated for each testing sample. That array is used in the testing stage to find samples whose consumption is similar to the sample being processed.

Algorithm 1. PS algorithm: training stage
___
1: $M_Z \leftarrow$ array of lenght Z
2: **for all** $z_i \in Z$ **do**
3:    counter $\leftarrow 0$
4:    **for all** $\{z_j \in Z : |j - i| < d\}$ **do**
5:       **if** $z_j > z_i - \varphi$ **then**
6:          counter $\leftarrow$ counter $+ 1$
7:       **end if**
8:    **end for**
9:    $M_Z[i] \leftarrow$ counter
10: **end for**
___

Algorithm 2. PS algorithm: testing stage
___
1: $M_X \leftarrow$ array of lenght X
2: **for all** $x_i \in X$ **do**
3:    counter $\leftarrow 0$
4:    **for all** $\{x_j \in X : |j - i| < d\}$ **do**
5:       **if** $x_j > x_i - \varphi$ **then**
6:          counter $\leftarrow$ counter $+ 1$
7:       **end if**
8:    **end for**
9:    $M_X[i] \leftarrow$ counter
10: **end for**
11: **for all** $x_i \in X$ **do**
12:    $I \leftarrow \emptyset$
13:    **for all** $z_j \in Z$ **do**
14:       **if** $|z_j - x_i| \leq \delta$ **and** $x_i > H$ **then**
15:          $I \leftarrow I \cup \{j\}$
16:       **end if**
17:       **if** $|I| \geq 1$ **then**
18:          $J \leftarrow \text{argmin}\{|M_Z(I(\cdot)) - M_X(i)|\}$
19:       **else**
20:          $J \leftarrow \text{argmin}\{|z(\cdot) - x(i)|\}$
21:       **end if**
22:       $k \leftarrow rand\{1, \ldots, length(J)\}$
23:       $y(i, \cdot) \leftarrow w(I(J(k)), \cdot)$
24:    **end for**
25: **end for**
___

Algorithm 2 presents the testing stage. The first loop (lines 1–10) is similar to the main loop in the training stage, but applied to the testing dataset. This loop builds an array (M_X) with the processed value of signature feature for each testing sample. It is used to compare with the array built into the training stage. The second loop (lines 11–26) iterates over each testing sample to find similarities with the samples of the training dataset. In line 13, each training sample is compared to the consumption of the sample being processed, if the difference between both is lower than a threshold (δ) and the testing sample have a consumption value greater than a minimum (H), it is added to set I, to be considered for next comparisons. If the set I is not empty, i.e., at least one training sample was found similar to the processing sample, the samples that minimize the difference between signature features (the difference between M_Z and M_X) are selected, and one of them is chosen randomly (line 18 and 22). If set I is empty, i.e., no training samples were found similar to the processing sample, the algorithm select the training samples that minimize the difference of consumption with the sample that is being processed, and one of them is chosen randomly (lines 20 and 22). Once the algorithm have found a similar training sample, it maps the consumption per appliance at the time of the training sample to the prediction results (line 23).

4.2 Implementation

A first version of the proposed algorithm was developed on Matlab, version 8.3.0.532 (R2014a), as a proof of concept. After that, it was re-implemented on python version 3, using **pandas** and **numpy**, which allows the implementation to be included as part of a pipe of execution in **nilmtk**. For this stage, several modifications were included in the metrics and utils files of the framework.

Two scripts were implemented for generating the synthetic datasets. The first script reads the UK-DALE dataset (HDF5 file), normalizes the values for the indicated houses and appliances, and builds a directory structure that contains metadata and the normalized data in CSV files. The normalization replaces all records over a given threshold by an indicated value, and set all other values to zero. The second script reads the directory structure and its content to generate a new HDF5 file with the synthetic dataset. In the resulting dataset, data have the same sample rate than in the original dataset, with the particularity that it does not present gaps, i.e., if original sample rate is six seconds, the generated dataset will have a record each six seconds. The gaps presented in the original dataset are filled by zeros. The algorithm implementation, the scripts for generating the datasets and the modified nilmtk files are available on a public repository (https://gitlab.com/jpchavat/nilm-scripts).

5 Experimental Analysis

This section presents the experimental analysis of the proposed algorithm. In the experiments, the algorithm was executed in a **nilmtk** pipeline of execution, using a synthetic dataset based on UK-DALE dataset as input. Results were compared with CO and FHMM algorithms executed in same settings.

5.1 Problem Instances and Datasets

The synthetic datasets used for the experiments are based on house #1 of the UK-DALE dataset, considering the following appliances: fridge, washing machine, kettle, dishwasher, and home theatre. These appliances are representative of devices that contribute the most to household energy consumption [14].

Four different instances were generated for the experimental analysis. All datasets were generated by downsampling the UK-DALE dataset period to 5 min. A *datetime* range limit was established for training and testing data. For training data, the limits were set from 2013-01-01 at 00:00:00 to 2013-07-01 at 00:00:00, while for the testing data the limits were set from 2013-07-01 at 00:00:00 to 2013-12-31 at 23:59:59. A threshold of minimum consumption was applied in the normalization, which was set to 5.0 W. This value allows discarding standby power consumption records. Instances were generated to analyze the efficacy of the proposed algorithm to solve different cases of energy consumption ambiguity. A description of each problem instance and the motivation of using it is provided next.

Instance #1. The generated dataset normalizes the consumption of each appliance using the median of maximum consumption per activation (i.e., periods of time in which an appliance remains in state ON). Outliers were filtered by lower and upper limits defined by the standard deviation. The generated dataset is used for training and testing. This instance aims at working with values close to the real ones but keeping constant consumption values over time.

Instance #2. The generated dataset normalizes the consumption values to generate ambiguity between the consumption of kettle and dish washer. The same dataset is used for training and testing the algorithms. This instance aims at testing how the algorithms solves the most basic case of ambiguity.

Instance #3. The dataset normalizes consumption values like instance #2, but including ambiguities between the sum of consumption of fridge, home theater, and washing machine with the consumption of the dish washer. The same dataset is used for training and testing the algorithms. This instance aims at studying how the algorithms solves a more sophisticated case of ambiguity.

Instance #4. The training dataset is the same than in instance #2; but a new dataset was generated for the testing step, introducing small variations in the consumption of every appliance, but the washing machine. For example, the consumption of the fridge was normalized to 260 instead of 250. This instance

Table 1. Normalized values per appliance for each instance

Instance	Appliance				
	Fridge	Washing machine	Kettle	Dishwasher	Home theater
#1 (testing, training)	117	3325	2390	2741	93
#2 (testing, training)	250	2000	2500	2500	80
#3 (testing, training)	300	1800	2200	2300	200
#4 (testing)	250	2000	2500	2500	80
#4 (training)	260	2000	2400	2600	70

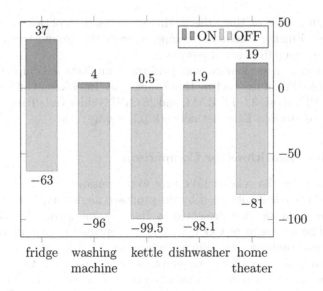

Fig. 1. Percentage of operating time of each appliance

aims at testing the algorithm in an scenario where testing appliances are similar but not equal to the appliances used for the training.

Table 1 reports the normalized value of the datasets used for training and testing for each instance, and Fig. 1 shows the percentage of records when each appliance is in state ON/OFF, which is the same for all the generated datasets.

5.2 Software and Hardware Platform

The nilmtk framework was used to implement the pipeline of execution for the experiments, as described in Fig. 2.

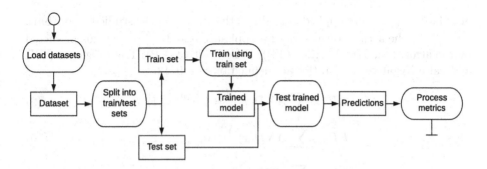

Fig. 2. Execution pipeline implemented in nilmtk

The first stage of the pipeline loads the dataset while the second splits the dataset into a training set and a testing set. The training set is used to train each algorithm and after that, the testing set is used to obtain the results of dissagregation. Finally, results are compared with the ground truth data (i.e. the test set) to compute a set of metrics.

The experimental evaluation was performed on National Supercomputing Center (Cluster-UY) infrastructure that counts with Intel Xeon-Gold 6138 nodes (up to 1120 CPU cores), 3.5 TB RAM, and 28 GPU Nvidia Tesla P100, connected by a high-speed 10 Gbps Ethernet network (cluster.uy) [13].

5.3   Baseline Algorithms for Comparison

Two methods from the related literature were considered as baseline for the comparison of the results obtained by the proposed algorithm: CO and FHMM.

The CO method was first presented by Hart [5], and included in the `nilmtk` framework. The approach of CO is to find the optimal combination of appliance states that minimises the difference between the total sum of aggregated consumption and the sum of the consumption of the predicted state on of appliances. CO searches for a vector $\hat{a}$ that minimises the expression on Eq. 5 Given the complexity of the CO algorithm, which is exponential in the number of appliances, it is not useful to address scenarios with a large number of appliances. The complexity of the CO algorithm is exponential in the number of appliances. Thus, it is not useful to address scenarios with a large number of appliances.

FHMM was introduced by Gharamani and Jordan [4]. Different variations of the original method were developed by Kim et al. [9] to solve the disaggregation problem. HMM are mixture models that encode historical information of a temporal series in a unique multinomial variable, represented as a hidden state; FHMM extends HMM to allow modeling multiple independent hidden state sequences simultaneously. FHMM scales worst than CO in scenarios with a large number of appliances.

5.4   Metrics for Results Evaluation

Standard metrics were applied to evaluate the efficacy of the studied algorithms. Let $x_i^{(n)}$ be the actual status series for appliance n and $\hat{x}_i^{(n)}$ the status predicted by the algorithm, True Positive (TP), False Positive (FP), True Negative (TN) and False Negative (FN) ratios are defined by Eqs. 9–12.

$$TP = \sum_i AND(x_i^{(n)} = 1, \hat{x}_i^{(n)} = 1) \tag{9}$$

$$FP = \sum_i AND(x_i^{(n)} = 0, \hat{x}_i^{(n)} = 1) \tag{10}$$

$$TN = \sum_i AND(x_i^{(n)} = 0, \hat{x}_i^{(n)} = 0) \tag{11}$$

$$FN = \sum_i AND(x_i^{(n)} = 1, \hat{x}_i^{(n)} = 0) \tag{12}$$

Five metrics are considered in the analysis:

- *precision* of the prediction, defined as an estimator of the conditional probability of predicting ON given that the appliance is ON (Eq. 13).
- *recall*, defined as the conditional probability that the appliance is ON given that the prediction is ON (Eq. 14).
- *F–Score*, defined as the harmonic mean of precision and recall (Eq. 15).
- *Error in Total Energy Assigned* (TEE), defined as the error of the total assigned consumptions (Eq. 16).
- *Normalized Error in Assigned Power* (NEAP), defined as the mean normalized error in assigned consumptions (Eq. 17).

$$precision = \frac{TP}{TP + FN} \tag{13}$$

$$recall = \frac{TP}{TP + FP} \tag{14}$$

$$F\text{-}Score = \frac{2 \times precision \times recall}{precision + recall} \tag{15}$$

$$\text{TEE}^{(n)} = \left| \sum_t y_t^{(n)} - \sum_t \hat{y}_t^{(n)} \right| \tag{16}$$

$$\text{NEAP}^{(n)} = \frac{\sum_t \left| y_t^{(n)} - \hat{y}_t^{(n)} \right|}{\sum_t y_t^{(n)}} \tag{17}$$

5.5 Results

Tables 2, 3, 4 and 5 report the results of the proposed algorithm (PS) and the baseline algorithms (CO and FHMM), on instances #1 to #4. All results were obtained using the following parameter configuration, set by a rule-of-thumb and empirical evaluation: $\delta = 100$, $d = 10$, $H = 500$ and $\varphi = 250$.

Results in Table 2 indicate that *PS* was able to accurately solve problem instances without ambiguity between power consumption of appliances. F-score values between 0.92 and 1.0 were obtained. Both *CO* and *FHMM* got F-score values around 0.6 for fridge and washing machine, around 0.3 for dish washer and home theater, and 0.04 (i.e., almost null) for kettle. In all cases, F-score values were lower than the obtained with *PS*.

Results in Table 3 indicate that F-score values of *PS* for appliances with ambiguities decreased up to 9%, while the rest of the F-score values remains similar to instance #1. Regarding the baseline algorithms, *CO* showed a decrease of 50% in the prediction of appliances with ambiguity, while results of *FHMM* remained similar to the ones computed for instance #1, with exception of the kettle (F-score decreased 66%).

Results in Table 4 indicates that the F-score values of *PS* decreased for washing machine (3%), dish washer (6%), and kettle (the worst value, 25% less than

Table 2. Results of CO, FHMM, and PS on instance #1

CO

Metric	Fridge	Washing machine	Kettle	Dishwasher	Home theater
TEE (kW)	292.18	2318.84	2767.39	6651.69	1118.64
NEAP	0.8663	0.7644	5.9284	2.6279	2.1975
Precision	0.8324	0.9863	0.7153	0.9758	0.8413
Recall	0.5584	0.4827	0.0228	0.2301	0.2814
F-score	0.6684	0.6481	0.0442	0.3724	0.4218

FHMM

Metric	Fridge	Washing machine	Kettle	Dishwasher	Home theater
TEE (kW)	306.46	3209.08	3399.42	5371.37	948.72
NEAP	0.8843	0.8367	6.8117	2.7134	2.3119
Precision	0.7576	0.9817	0.7810	0.9768	0.5799
Recall	0.5408	0.5078	0.0258	0.2377	0.2199
F-score	0.6311	0.6694	0.0500	0.3823	0.3188

PS

Metric	Fridge	Washing machine	Kettle	Dishwasher	Home theater
TEE (kW)	23.87	0.00	0.00	0.00	29.67
NEAP	0.0218	0.0000	0.0000	0.0000	0.1497
Precision	0.9839	1.0000	1.0000	1.0000	0.9409
Recall	0.9942	1.0000	1.0000	1.0000	0.9121
F-score	0.9891	1.0000	1.0000	1.0000	0.9263

Table 3. Results of CO, FHMM, and PS on instance #2

CO

Metric	Fridge	Washing machine	Kettle	Dishwasher	Home theater
TEE (kW)	2228.32	1701.36	5595.52	7206.13	685.29
NEAP	1.0053	1.5412	9.8478	3.0491	1.6285
Precision	0.6973	0.8271	0.6715	0.9807	0.7781
Recall	0.5123	0.2457	0.0111	0.1184	0.2907
F-score	0.5907	0.3789	0.0219	0.2113	0.4233

FHMM

Metric	Fridge	Washing machine	Kettle	Dishwasher	Home theater
TEE (kW)	1401.84	962.88	7904.24	5016.79	431.27
NEAP	0.9007	1.1175	13.2448	2.1841	1.7049
Precision	0.7687	0.9149	0.7007	0.9787	0.6649
Recall	0.5573	0.4790	0.0084	0.2379	0.2850
F-score	0.6461	0.6288	0.0166	0.3828	0.3990

PS

Metric	Fridge	Washing machine	Kettle	Dishwasher	Home theater
TEE (kW)	0.00	0.00	42.50	42.50	14.88
NEAP	0.0000	0.0000	0.1788	0.0473	0.1264
Precision	1.0000	1.0000	0.9416	0.9681	0.9460
Recall	1.0000	1.0000	0.8866	0.9843	0.9289
F-score	1.0000	1.0000	0.9133	0.9761	0.9374

Table 4. Results of CO, FHMM, and PS on instance #3

CO					
Metric	Fridge	Washing machine	Kettle	Dishwasher	Home theater
TEE (kW)	1690.42	2194.13	6298.06	6720.05	949.90
NEAP	0.9386	1.6483	12.1919	3.0818	1.7343
Precision	0.8217	0.8678	0.5876	0.9826	0.8432
Recall	0.5754	0.2400	0.0073	0.1212	0.3250
F-score	0.6768	0.3760	0.0145	0.2157	0.4692
FHMM					
Metric	Fridge	Washing machine	Kettle	Dishwasher	Home theater
TEE (kW)	2069.24	1655.52	6273.13	6895.43	1561.12
NEAP	1.1036	1.2927	12.1388	3.1483	2.0024
Precision	0.4318	0.9067	0.6387	0.9797	0.7645
Recall	0.4512	0.3677	0.0087	0.1380	0.2942
F-score	0.4413	0.5232	0.0171	0.2419	0.4249
PS					
Metric	Fridge	Washing machine	Kettle	Dishwasher	Home theater
TEE (kW)	4.50	82.80	15.40	89.70	13.60
NEAP	0.0221	0.0668	0.5000	0.1092	0.0377
Precision	0.9893	0.9771	0.7372	0.9266	0.9845
Recall	0.9886	0.9570	0.7566	0.9629	0.9780
F-score	0.9889	0.9670	0.7468	0.9444	0.9812

Table 5. Results of CO, FHMM, and PS on instance #4

CO					
Metric	Fridge	Washing machine	Kettle	Dishwasher	Home theater
TEE (kW)	2543.42	2239.86	5208.68	7414.75	637.84
NEAP	0.9819	1.7824	9.6185	3.0921	1.8408
Precision	0.6597	0.7653	0.6533	0.9826	0.7895
Recall	0.5202	0.1823	0.0121	0.1193	0.3205
F-score	0.5817	0.2944	0.0238	0.2128	0.4559
FHMM					
Metric	Fridge	Washing machine	Kettle	Dishwasher	Home theater
TEE (kW)	1829.65	699.35	8567.56	5080.58	560.53
NEAP	0.9218	1.1591	14.6967	2.2034	1.9148
Precision	0.7209	0.8403	0.6971	0.9797	0.6961
Recall	0.5453	0.4634	0.0083	0.2383	0.2931
F-score	0.6210	0.5974	0.0163	0.3834	0.4125
PS					
Metric	Fridge	Washing machine	Kettle	Dishwasher	Home theater
TEE (kW)	182.69	62.00	42.60	111.00	145.00
NEAP	0.0440	0.0142	0.3221	0.0821	0.2720
Precision	0.9985	1.0000	0.8066	0.9758	0.9666
Recall	0.9957	0.9860	0.8984	0.9787	0.9166
F-score	0.9971	0.9930	0.8500	0.9773	0.9409

for instance #1), increased for home theater (6%), and did not vary for fridge. *CO* decreased for washing machine (42%), kettle (67%), and dish washer (42%), compared with instance #1. F-score values for FHMM decreased for all the appliances (up to 66% for kettle), but the home theater (increased 33%).

Finally, results in Table 5 demonstrate that *PS* has a robust behavior when using different normalized datasets for training and testing steps. The F-score for *PS* was over 0.99 for fridge and washing machine, over 0.97 for dish washer, and over 0.94 for home theater. The lowest F-score value was obtained for kettle (0.85) With respect to instance #1, the F-score of the kettle decreased 15%. The rest of the appliances experienced a decrease/increase lower than 2%. For *CO*, F-score values decreased for all appliances but the home theater For *FHMM*, F-score values of fridge and dish washer varied less than 1.6% with respect to instance #1, and decreased for washing machine and kettle (up to 67%).

Overall, the proposed *PS* algorithm achieved satisfactory results for all the studied instances. Improvements on F-score were 60% over *CO* and 57% over *FHMM* in average, and up to 64% over *CO* in problem instance #4 and up to 60% over *FHMM* in problem instance #3. Furthermore, *PS* systematically obtained the lowest values of both TEE and NEAP metrics for all instances. Degraded results obtained for kettle in problem instances with ambiguity suggest that the lower percentage of operating time (0.5% for kettle) affects the results negatively and the more complex the dataset is, the more consumption samples are needed in the testing dataset.

6   Conclusions and Future Work

This article presented an approach to address the problem of household energy disaggregation. An algorithm based on pattern similarities was proposed. The experimental evaluation performed over realistic problem instance showed that, overall, the proposed algorithm is effective for addressing the problem of energy consumption disaggregation. Results can be applied to household energy planning by using intelligent recommendation systems [3].

The main lines for future work are related to study instances with different sample rates and noise in the power consumption, and extend the parameter analysis of the proposed algorithm. In addition, more sophisticated computational intelligent methods can be evaluated to solve the problem.

References

1. Batra, N., et al.: NILMTK: an open source toolkit for non-intrusive load monitoring. In: 5th International Conference on Future Energy Systems, pp. 265–276 (2014)
2. Bonfigli, R., Squartini, S., Fagiani, M., Piazza, F.: Unsupervised algorithms for non-intrusive load monitoring: an up-to-date overview. In: 15th International Conference on Environment and Electrical Engineering (2015)

3. Colacurcio, G., Nesmachnow, S., Toutouh, J., Luna, F., Rossit, D.: Multiobjective household energy planning using evolutionary algorithms. In: Iberoamerican Congress on Smart Cities (2019)
4. Ghahramani, Z., Jordan, M.: Factorial hidden Markov models. In: Advances in Neural Information Processing Systems, pp. 472–478 (1996)
5. Hart, G.: Nonintrusive appliance load monitoring. Proc. IEEE **80**(12), 1870–1891 (1992)
6. International Energy Agency: World Energy Outlook 2015. White paper (2015)
7. Kelly, J., Knottenbelt, W.: Neural NILM: deep neural networks applied to energy disaggregation. In: 2nd ACM International Conference on Embedded Systems for Energy-Efficient Built Environments, pp. 55–64 (2015)
8. Kelly, J., Knottenbelt, W.: The UK-DALE dataset, domestic appliance-level electricity demand and whole-house demand from five UK homes. Sci. Data **2**, 150007 (2015)
9. Kim, H., Marwah, M., Arlitt, M., Lyon, G., Han, J.: Unsupervised disaggregation of low frequency power measurements. In: SIAM International Conference on Data Mining, pp. 747–758. SIAM (2011)
10. Kolter, J., Johnson, M.: REDD: a public data set for energy disaggregation research. In: Workshop on Data Mining Applications in Sustainability, pp. 59–62 (2011)
11. Larcher, D., Tarascon, J.: Towards greener and more sustainable batteries for electrical energy storage. Nat. Chem. **7**(1), 19–29 (2015)
12. Neenan, B., Robinson, J., Boisvert, R.: Residential electricity use feedback: a research synthesis and economic framework. Electric Power Research Institute (2009)
13. Nesmachnow, S., Iturriaga, S.: Cluster-UY: high performance scientific computing in Uruguay. In: International Supercomputing Conference in Mexico (2019)
14. Orsi, E., Nesmachnow, S.: Smart home energy planning using IoT and the cloud. In: IEEE URUCON (2017)

A Hybrid Energy Storage System for Renewable-Based Power Plants

Francisco Díaz-González$^{(\boxtimes)}$, Francesc Girbau-Llistuella,
Mònica Aragüés-Peñalba, Cristian Chillón-Antón, and Marc Llonch-Masachs

Centre d'Innovació Tecnològica en Convertidors Estàtics i Accionaments
(CITCEA-UPC), Universitat Politècnica de Catalunya ETS d'Enginyeria Industrial
de Barcelona, C. Avinguda Diagonal, 647, Pl. 2, 08028 Barcelona, Spain
`francisco.diaz-gonzalez@upc.edu`

Abstract. This paper presents an hybrid energy storage system for the
integration of renewable-based power plants in power networks. A hybrid
energy storage system is defined as that able to integrate and maximize
the contribution of a heterogeneous grouping of storage systems. The services which this hybrid solution is able to perform are identified and then
related to a specific storage technology which have the best potential to
solve the issues created by the intermittent renewable generation. The
presented solution combines three different storage technologies, a lead-
acid battery pack, a flywheel and a set of supercapacitors. The description of the system is complemented by a study case, for the performance
analysis of the set of supercapacitors.

Keywords: Smart grids · Hybrid energy storage systems ·
Renewable-based power plants

1 Introduction

The installation of renewable generation presents a growing tendency worldwide over the last decades, being mainly motivated by the need for reducing the
dependency from fossil fuels and coal, as well as the required drastic decrease
of pollutant emissions. According to IRENA (International Renewable Energy
Agency) [1], at the end of 2019, global renewable generation capacity was 2351
GW, dominated by hydro (1172 GW), wind (564 GW) and solar (486 GW).
More than 80% of the new capacity that was built in 2018 came from solar and
wind installations. Therefore, it is clear wind and solar power plants play a key
role for contributing to the power system decarbonisation. However, their generation presents variability and uncertainty, which are a barrier to a constant
and predictable power output from this power plants. In this sense, Energy Storage Systems (ESS) can help to integrate large amounts of renewable generation.
Furthermore, energy storage can also provide a fast response to large variations
in demand.

S. Nesmachnow and L. Hernández Callejo (Eds.): ICSC-CITIES 2019, CCIS 1152, pp. 70–79, 2020.
https://doi.org/10.1007/978-3-030-38889-8_6

The services that energy storage systems can provide in grids with large penetration of renewable generation are described in [2]. They are classified in three categories in terms of power rating, energy rating and main type of beneficiary of the service. Small scale ESS (from a few tens of kW to a few MW in power and few tens of kWh to a hundreds of MWh in energy) is specially used for services for end-user or customer level. Mid scale ESS (from a few tens of kW to a few MW in power and few tens of kWh to a few MWh in energy) have applications for services at distribution level. Large scale ESS (from a few to hundreds of MW in power and time response up to several hours) are the ones that provide services to large scale renewable power plants.

The focus of this paper is on mid scale ESS and, in particular, on hybrid mid scale ESS. Hybrid ESS combine different energy storage technologies so as to benefit from the technical and economical advantages each one can offer depending on the response required in different operational situations. Depending on the type of battery selected, a large amount of energy can be available but with reduced power, or high power peaks for less time (low power); not both at the same time. Similarly, superconductors and flywheels offer high power peaks, but for a short time (low stored energy). The design of storage systems capable of offering good performance in power, energy, life expectancy, response times, ease of operation, scalability, reliability, security, etc., is possible through the concept of hybridization. Additionally, a hybridization can also allow lower costs and lower size for the ESS solution to be developed. For instance, a lead-acid battery supports instantaneous electrical currents of up to 100% of the nominal, without affecting dramatically the useful life of it. In contrast to lead-acid batteries, lithium-ion batteries (especially those of lithium-iron-phosphate) can exchange currents of up to ten times their nominal value for 30 s [3]. These maximum currents are even larger for supercapacitors [4]. Thus, hybrid solutions that provide high instantaneous currents can be configured without having to install in parallel a high number of batteries with low power performance, with the consequent reduction in cost and size.

In this study, a hybrid ESS is here proposed, which consists of a front-end inverter and three parallel DC/DC modules, each one integrating a different energy storage technology: electrochemical (lead-acid battery), electrical (supercapacitor) and electromechanical (flywheel). The objective of this device is to enable a large penetration of renewable generation in distribution grids, while guaranteeing the accomplishment of grid code requirements [7] and ensuring power quality in these networks. The paper is structured as follows. In Sect. 2, the type of services provided by ESS in combination with renewable based generation are detailed. Then, in Sect. 3, the conceptual design of the hybrid ESS is presented, explaining the advantages and drawbacks of the power electronics and energy storage technologies selected. The experimental characterization of the behavior of the supercapacitor is shown in Sect. 4. Finally, conclusions are drawn.

2 Services from Energy Storage in Renewable-Based Power Plants

ESS can provide numerous services to electrical networks. Literature on this matter is extensive [5,6], providing approaches from various perspectives, from the technology to the market sides.

The energy and power ratings of an ESS greatly determine the services it can provide in electrical networks. For instance, a flywheel cannot store large amounts of energy because it would imply to apply an unrealistic rotating disk. In addition to ratings, suitable services for ESSs are constrained by other inherent characteristics of the technology, such as cyclability, time response and ageing mechanisms. So each technology fits best for a particular catalogue of services.

In general terms, as introduced in [2], services can be classified in three main categories. A brief summary is offered in the following. The first category is that requiring small-scale ESSs. Energy storage here can be exploited to improve the self-consumption performance and to provide services to the end user. In this case, the storage device is installed at local residences or small facilities. Services in this regard can be that for maximizing self-consumption, off-grid operation of neighbourhoods and in synergy with demand management.

Small-scale storage devices can be sized here considering the local consumption and generation profiles and the desired service level. The size of these systems are in the scale of few kW to hundreds of kW in power and of few tens of kWh to hundreds of kWh (for community scale installations). Suitable ESSs for end user centered applications are mainly secondary batteries, specially lead-acid ones, because of their low cost; and progressively gaining momentum, lithium-ion ones, because of their great performance.

The second category of services is that requiring mid-scale ESSs. These technologies, aimed to be installed in low and medium voltage networks, will help to trigger vast deployment of distributed generation and electrical vehicles. In particular, services here include various keywords, such as power quality improvement, congestion alleviation in networks, and improvement of security of supply. Thus, these storages may provide services to the grid operator and end users.

The power and energy ratings for eligible energy storage systems in this category will depend on the type of customers willing to profit from these service. The power rating of the power electronic equipment will be in the range of a few tens kW to few MW. The energy storage capacity will depend on the interruption time allowed in the installation and is in the range of tens of kWh to few MWh and this depends on the time a grid congestion occurs and its severity, for instance. Thus, the most suitable storage technologies are secondary batteries and flow batteries. Also, short-term storages offering high cyclability and power ramp rates such as flywheels and supercapacitors are well addressed for power quality improvement related services.

Finally, the third category of services is that requiring large-scale ESSs. These technologies, aimed to be installed in large renewable power plants or primary substations may be operated to provide grid ancillary services and to improve the controllability of power flows within the power network. Grid ancillary services refer to the provision of primary and secondary power reserves, voltage control, power ramp-rate limitation and black start capability of power plants. In regard of the application of energy storage in renewable-based power plants, operational rules and related control algorithms should be explored according to the corresponding regulations, or namely grid codes. The applicable grid code regulation in Europe that determines the requirements for the grid connection of renewable-based power plants and the ancillary services they should provide is the European Commission Regulation 2016/631 of 14 April 2016 [7]. The controllability of power flows within the network, specifically refers to the time shifting and compensation of forecasting errors for renewables, thus facilitating the grid integration of such bulk renewable generation.

Usual capacity requirements for these services are between few MW to hundreds of MW in power. The most suitable technologies are compressed-air energy storage, pumped-hydro installations, hydrogen and secondary batteries, especially lithium-ion, lead-acid or sodium ones for systems rated at tens of MW. Flywheels, because of their easy scalability, enabling the realization of systems rated at tens of MW in power can be also suitable for these services.

3 The Hybrid Energy Storage Solution

The hybridization of ESSs permit to provide various services with a unique device. The proposed hybrid solution for the purposes of the present work, i.e. the grid integration of renewable-based power plants, is presented in this section.

The aim of the solution is to maximize the integration of renewable generation into the distribution grid. It has to contribute to the fulfillment of the grid code requirements for the renewable-based power plants, as well as those related to the participation in grid ancillary services. Moreover, it pursues the improvement of voltage waveform, compensating the slow variations, smoothing the fluctuations and eliminating the flicker generated by the intermittent generation.

The solution is designed as an hybrid energy storage system. The main idea behind the hybridization is to combine complementary storage systems for taking advantage of their strengths, and facilitate the renewable accommodation at a reasonable cost. Figure 1 depicts a conceptual scheme of the hybrid energy storage solution. In particular, the adopted solution is composed by a front-end inverter and three parallel DC/DC modules. Each one of these DC/DC modules integrates a different energy storage technology.

Figure 1 also presents the architecture of the solution. It is selected because it offers excellent performance in regard of efficiency, flexibility and fault tolerance, with the potentiality of configuring a solution with less volume than others architectures, according to a quantitative comparison realized in [8]. However, it also has the following limitations:

– The front-end inverter is a bottleneck. In other words, there is only a way to exchange power with the external grid, i.e. through the unique front-end

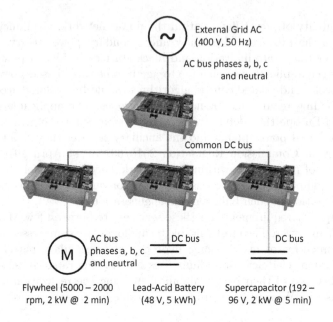

Fig. 1. Conceptual scheme of the hybrid energy storage solution.

inverter, therefore, the whole power of the solution is limited by the rated power of this inverter.

– The power electronics performance is higher when the output power reach the rated value. Therefore, if the inverter is oversized to cover the whole storage systems (or at least the highest storage system) rated power, the performance will be lower some occasions.

– The front-end inverter requires that the voltage of the common DC bus is at least $400\frac{2\sqrt{2}}{\sqrt{3}}$. It is really high voltage in comparison with the rated DC voltage of the storage systems, so the difference between them is notably large, and therefore, the duty will be veritably small and its range will be also short.

The particular hybrid energy storage system combines three different technologies: an electrochemical technology, a lead-acid battery; an electrical, a super-capacitor; and electromechanical technology, a flywheel. Following a short revision of technologies is performed.

The lead-acid batteries are featured by:

– Its reduced cost and hazard level.
– They can provide instantly a so high short-circuit current.
– They are used in stationary applications which do not require to cycle them many times, to estimate their state of charge, and to calculate their performance.
– In addition, there is a high complexity to estimate the previous points because the internal resistance is remarkably high (in comparison other battery technologies) which makes it difficult and extremely dependent of the current.

- It is not common find accurate BMS solutions in the market.
- Both power-weight and energy-weight ratios are typically lower than lithium batteries.

Flywheels and super-capacitors are two similar technologies which stores energy via inertia and voltage, respectability, both are characterized by:

- Their reduced cost and long life.
- They are faster technologies and are much more suitable for cycling than batteries.
- However, it is necessary to oversized them because it is not possible to operate them at the whole range. By way of example, the flywheel has to be able to supply 2 kW during 2 min. If it is presented the power curve for this flywheel (see Fig. 2) it is appreciated that it can only exchange 2 kW in the range between 2000 to 5000 rpm. Therefore, if it required to supply this power during 2 min, the flywheel will decrease its velocity from 5000 to 2000 rpm. Similarly, the super-capacitor has to be able to supply 2 kW during 5 min, so it will decrease its voltage from 192 V to 96 V.
- Their self-discharging is higher than batteries. As Fig. 2 it is appreciated that the flywheel operates at least 2000 rpm, so it is continuously rotating, therefore, it is always required and a small torque input in order to ensure that its angular velocity does not decrease from 2000 rpm. Similarly, it happens with the super-capacitors, so a small current is always required to avoid its completely discharge.
- In addition, in case of flywheel technology, the bearings are also a source of losses and can create problems.

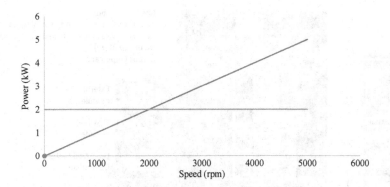

Fig. 2. Flywheel operation range. The power characteristic of the motor is under a constant torque condition.

As traditional energy storage system solutions, the proposed solution is composed by two main parts: (i) a so-called power plane; and (ii) a management plane. The power plane includes the components actually exchanging electrical power with the network. This plane defines how the system is connected, i.e. storage systems and power electronics are linked according to previous architecture. In turn, the management plane is composed by algorithms and related hardware managing the aforementioned system. In this sense, the management the front-end inverter is the responsible of maintaining the voltage in the common DC bus while the DC/DC modules exchanges power with the external grid, in order to provide the expected response. In this sense, apart from the implementation of grid services in the device, it is necessary to develop a power sharing algorithm that ensures the proper functioning of the whole system.

Finally, the Fig. 3 depicts the prototype designed. The whole power electronic solution is contained in the same cabinet, except from the storage units which are directly connected to it. Inside the cabinet, there is a holder for the modules. In this holder there are the four independent power converter which constitute the hybrid storage solution. The holder provides all the connections for the power and controls, in front of this holder, there is the control and measurement equipment. Finally, below the modules holder cabinet, there are all the power interconnections and the protection equipment.

4   Study Case: Experimental Characterization of Supercapacitors

After the presentation of the hybrid energy storage solution and the discussion of the complementarity of the storage technologies embedded into it, this section presents laboratory tests to characterize the supercapacitor modules.

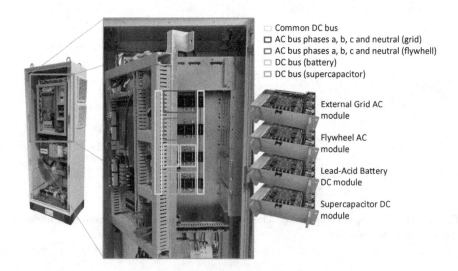

Fig. 3. Hybrid energy storage solution demo platform.

There are three supercapacitor modules connected in series from the manufacturer Maxwell Technologies, model BMOD0141 P064 B04 (see Fig. 4).

Fig. 4. The three supercapacitor modules connected in series. The maximum voltage is 192 V and the capacitance per each module is 141 F.

Supercapacitors are well suited for providing power during relatively short time (few minutes at most), accounting on low degradation. This way, they can be cycled hundreds of thousands times till reaching the end of life condition.

A test has been performed to the set of three supercapacitor modules connected in series to characterize the energy ratings and efficiency. Results are plotted in Fig. 5. The upper subplot presents the voltage per each of the three modules and the lower subplot depicts the driving current. As can be observed, the supercapacitors are charged from a minimum operating voltage of 30 V to the rated voltage per each of the modules (64 V), and then discharged back to the minimum state of charge. The following conclusions are derived from the test:

– Setting a minimum operating voltage for each supercapacitor module of 30 V and the maximum one to 64 V, and while charging at 20 A, the energy consumed in this process is 330 Wh. While discharging back to 30 V per module and, again, at constant current of 20 A, the energy provided is 318 Wh. Therefore, the round trip energy efficiency for the set of supercapacitor modules is

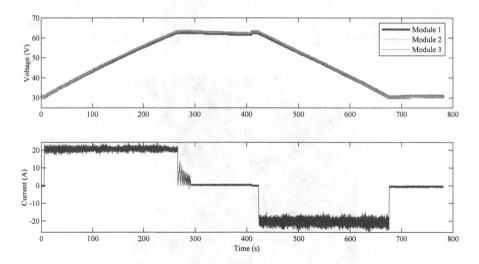

Fig. 5. The upper subplot presents the voltage per each of the three supercapacitor modules connected in series. The lower subplot shows the charge (positive) and discharge (negative) current for the test.

96.3%. This implies a small internal resistance for the cell, as determined by the manufacturer.

– The practical energy storage capacity of a supercapacitor is bounded by the minimum operating voltage, and this should be determined by the designer. Very low voltages, although admissible for the supercapacitors, are not practical. This is because excessive currents through the supercapacitors would be required to develop the required power.
– Negligible voltage unbalances among supercapacitor cells are experienced. This can be observed in Fig. 5, in the upper subplot: all three voltage profiles are almost identical. Such small voltage unbalances among different modules in series is a clear advantage of supercapacitors over batteries.

5   Conclusions

This paper presented a hybrid energy storage system for the provision of services in renewable-based power plants. The system is hybrid, since combining through a single power-electronics cabinet, three types of energy storage technologies: a lead-acid battery pack, a flywheel and a supercapacitor. The complementarity of the storage technologies trigger the provision of various services simultaneously, i.e. the provision of energy-based services through the battery, and power-based services by the management of the supercapacitor and the flywheel. The modularity of the power-electronics cabinet permit to operate differently each of the storage technologies, even triggering a power sharing among them if necessary. Complementing the description of the solution, one of the storage technologies embedded into the hybrid solution, the supercapacitor, has been tested in laboratory. Results derive a round trip efficiency of 96.3%, and minimum voltage unbalances among the modules connected in series. Such performance serve to identify supercapacitors as well suited for services requiring frequent charge and discharge.

Acknowledgments. This work was supported by the Ministerio de Economia, Industria y Competitividad (Spanish government), under the grant agreement number ENE2017-86493-R.

References

1. Renewable Capacity Statistics 2019. International Renewable Energy Agency (IRENA), March 2019. https://www.irena.org/publications/2019/Mar/Renewable-Capacity-Statistics-2019. Accessed July 2019
2. Díaz-González, F., Bullich-Massagué, E., Vitale, C., Gil-Sánchez, M., Aragüés-Peñalba, M., Girbau-Llistuella, F.: Services of energy storage technologies in renewable-based power systems. In: Nesmachnow, S., Hernández Callejo, L. (eds.) ICSC-CITIES 2018. CCIS, vol. 978, pp. 53–64. Springer, Cham (2019). https://doi.org/10.1007/978-3-030-12804-3_5
3. A123 Systems (2017) AMP20M1HD-A Prismatic Cell datasheet
4. Maxwell Technologies. BMOD0094 P075 B02 datasheet (2017). http://www.maxwell.com/
5. Díaz-González, F., Sumper, A., Gomis-Bellmunt, O.: Energy Storage in Power Systems. Wiley, Chichester (2016)
6. Energy Storage Association. Energy Storage, Case Studies (2000). http://energystorage.org/energy-storage/case-studies/delivering-100-commercial-reliability-aes-los-andes-battery-energy. Accessed June 2018
7. European Commission. Commission Regulation (EU) 2016/631 of 14 April 2016 establishing a network code on requirements for grid connection of generators (2016). https://eur-lex.europa.eu/legal-content/EN/TXT/?uri=OJ%3AJOL_2016_112_R_0001. Accessed June 2018
8. Díaz-González, F., et al.: D2.1 - Power electronics device design specifications and models for the architectures (2017). https://resolvd.eu/documents/. Accessed July 2019

LoRa-Based IoT Data Monitoring and Collecting Platform

Andres Felipe Fuentes[1]([envelope]) [iD] and Eugenio Tamura[2]([envelope]) [iD]

[1] Universidad Javeriana Cali – Cali, Carrera 109 No. 22-00, Cali, Colombia
andresf.fuentesv@unilibre.edu.co
[2] Pontificia Universidad Javeriana – Cali, Calle 18 No. 118-250, Cali, Colombia
tek@javerianacali.edu.co

Abstract. IoT (Internet of Things) refers to an integration concept of different communication systems used for connecting heterogeneous devices with constraints on processing, storage capabilities and power consumption to the Internet, with the purpose of data collecting for analysis and decision making about the measurements of data collected. This new paradigm can be applied in different fields to wirelessly measure variables through mobile devices, laptops and wireless devices having in mind restrictions in terms of battery lifetime, capacity, and cost. This paper describes the implementation of a flexible and low-cost monitoring and data collecting platform using sensors based on open hardware such as Arduino, interconnected through a LoRa network and a cloud-based data storage system developed using open source code. The main objective is to quickly collect different types of variables based on a flexible monitoring and collecting platform adaptable to different types of sensors which could be used in both rural and urban areas in applications that require long-range transmission and low energy consumption. In the future, research on the analysis of performance and improvement solutions will be carried out, as well as the use of other types of devices and protocols in order to compare performance and expand the field of implementation of the proposed platform.

Keywords: LoRa WAN · Wireless Sensor Networks (WSN) · Internet of Things (IoT) · Monitoring system · Web Services

1 Introduction

The fast development of IoT and WSN applications and its associated growth of connected devices, which is predicted to be in the order of billions for the coming years [1], make necessary to take advantage of flexible and scalable technologies that allow collection and storage of data from devices like sensors, that take information from the real world and send it to repositories for further processing, analysis and/or identification of patterns for making smart decisions in real-time or according to the required application.

© Springer Nature Switzerland AG 2020
S. Nesmachnow and L. Hernández Callejo (Eds.): ICSC-CITIES 2019, CCIS 1152, pp. 80–92, 2020.
https://doi.org/10.1007/978-3-030-38889-8_7

The application scenarios of IoT technologies include smart cities, smart agriculture, pollution monitoring, manufacturing automation, remote health care, and more [2]. These kind of applications demands a platform that allows the interconnection of devices and systems for collecting data from different types of sensors considering specific requirements such as long-range, low data rate, low energy consumption, and cost-effectiveness. Short-range radio technologies (e.g., ZigBee, Bluetooth) are not adapted for long-range transmission. The cellular communications (e.g., 2G, 3G, and 4G) can provide larger coverage, but energy efficiency is low. Therefore, in this scenario, Low Power Wide Area Network (LPWAN) characteristics offer a solution adaptable to the IoT applications requirements [3]. LPWAN is increasingly gaining popularity in industrial and research communities because of its low power, long-range, and low-cost communication characteristics. It provides long-range communication up to 10–40 km in rural zones and 1–5 km in urban zones [4]. An LPWAN example is LoRa, a wireless communication technology for long-range applications, whose use is rapidly increasing and could be considered a complement of Wi-Fi, Bluetooth, and Cellular.

In addition to the above, for IoT applications there exist different types of platforms for the interconnection of devices, and different types of protocols such as Constrained Application Protocol (CoAP) or Message Queue Telemetry Transport (MQTT) are used as well. These platforms have data acquisition and analytic components, device management components, integration components, and security components [5,6].

Consequently, when WSN are integrated with platforms of this type, it is necessary to identify the different layers that make up these architectures, classifying the components to determine the options that better fit the requirements of the problem, including the cost and a balance between performance, latency, energy efficiency, scalability, and implementation complexity.

Therefore, in order to understand how these platforms work, it becomes necessary to identify the different blocks that compose them. This paper analyzes the main components of an IoT platform including Sensing component, Communication component, Computation and Cloud component, and Services and Applications components [7].

Once the different components of an IoT platform are analyzed, a platform based on open source components is proposed. Using open hardware devices and using open source software allows faster combination of new integrated IoT solutions towards the development and implementation of different kind of applications [8]. The platform will be designed and implemented using the LoRa protocol [9] for communication between devices; also open hardware devices like Arduino are used as sensor devices. Besides, the data collection and storage platform is also based on open-source software, i.e., PHP and MySQL [10]. Thus, the integration of these components offer a low-cost platform for the quick development of IoT applications for data acquisition and can be adapted for use in applications like smart farming in rural areas where neither cellular coverage nor other networks are available.

2   Related Work

Since IoT has become a subject of research and development, new fields of application for domains such as health, mobility, agriculture or smart cities [11,12] have been increasing in an exponential manner. Hence, the demand for deploying these kind of systems has being grown lately. This trend implies a faster yet robust development of WSN-based systems in scenarios where different needs are constrained by hardware and software resources [13].

Shinde and Bhagat presented a paper on Industrial Process Monitoring Using IoT. In this paper, a basic platform of IoT is presented through which an industrial monitoring system is implemented using industry-standard protocols on IoT modules, and data conversion mechanisms for different industrial applications, which can also be used for monitoring different real-time applications in industries according to the requirements as well. The principal advantages of using a specific platform were modularity in system, scalability, adaptability, and ease of maintenance [14].

A LoRa-based renewable energy monitoring system is described by Choi, Jeong, and Park. This system is developed using open hardware and an overall platform of the implemented energy IoT monitoring system is showed, focusing on low-cost and quick-construction. The platform shown in this work could be adapted for different applications according to the needs [15].

On the other hand, works like [16] and [17] expose the development of IoT projects based on LoRa, where a specific platform is designed for each project. Both works expose the relevance of a platform for the development of IoT applications.

In the reviewed papers, the use of different kind of open hardware and open software, including wireless communication technologies such as LoRa, is frequent. Also is notorious that each project includes a platform scheme that classifies the functional structure of the hardware, software, and protocols used, as it becomes a fundamental aspect for understanding the IoT applications developed.

3   IoT Platform Components

An IoT platform is an integrated service that offers the necessary technologies to connect heterogeneous devices, such as sensors or actuators, to the Internet. Through an IoT platform, it is possible to interconnect several devices simultaneously, collect the information that these devices generate and manage each one of them.

In order to understand an IoT platform, it can be expressed in several layers such as (1) sensing layer, (2) communication layer, (3) computation and cloud layer, and (4) services and applications layer [5].

Sensing Layer. Different types of sensors, meters, actuators, and controllers are connected in this layer. The node sensors collect data including temperature, humidity, lightness, energy consumption. The controllers and actuators execute actions to generate some kind of effect on a process.

Communication Layer. This layer contains the IoT communication protocols for sending and receiving data. The different IoT devices use communication technologies such as Wi-Fi, ZigBee, NFC, BLE, LTE, LoRa, SigFox or NB-IoT. Usually, in a WSN configuration, the sensors collect the data and send it to a device configured as a gateway which sends the collected data to the Internet.

Computation and Cloud Layer. This layer stores and processes the raw data collected by the sensors. The Computation and Cloud Layer represents the computing and processing capacity of the IoT platform and interacts with the connected devices and the different data processing applications.

Services and Applications Layer. It has the function of exposing the different indicators resulting from the processing, analysis, and diagnosis of the data collected; it also performs as the user interface for monitoring, controlling and feedback data to WSN through the Communication Layer.

4   LoRa-Based IoT Data Platform Development

Thus, having in mind the different layers exposed above as components of an IoT platform, a design for the development of a LoRa-based IoT Data Platform, the main objective of this work, is proposed in Fig. 1. The proposed platform includes a layer that integrates the Sensing Layer and the Communication Layer, which is called the *Front Layer*. The Computation and Cloud Layer and the Services and Applications Layer, are integrated into a layer called *Back Layer*.

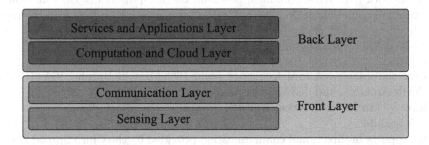

Fig. 1. Proposal of layers for an IoT Platform layer-based design [5]

Figure 2 depicts a diagram with a more detailed view of the components of the LoRa-based IoT Platform proposed in this paper.

For the implementation of the Front Layer, nodes that enable integration with sensors modules and include a LoRa radio (LoRa-Nodes in the following) are used. On the other hand, a gateway (LoRa-Gateway in the following) is

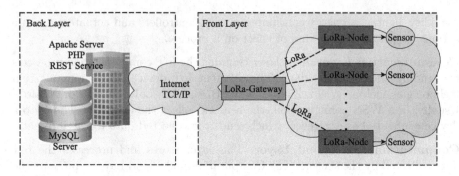

Fig. 2. Proposed LoRa-based IoT Platform

used to receive the data from LoRa-Nodes in order to send it to the Back Layer through the Internet using a TCP/IP stack.

The Back Layer, receives the data from the Front Layer and stores it in a Web Server and the data is exposed to the final users through a web application.

The description of the technologies chosen for the development of the IoT platform proposed in Fig. 2 are described below, indicating the advantages they offer regarding IoT applications, including battery efficiency, scalability, coverage, range, deployment, and cost.

LoRaWAN. LoRaWAN is an open standard communication solution, it is relatively new and became the focus of several research centers across the world. LoRa (Long Range) is a modulation technique that enables the long-range transfer of information with a low transfer rate [18].

A LoRaWAN network (Long Range Network Protocol) is a Low Power Wide Area Network (LPWAN) standard, based on battery-powered devices including bidirectional communication. The LoRaWAN specification ensures high interoperability between IoT devices, without the need for complex implementations [19].

LoRaWAN technology advantages are [20]:

1. Uses the unlicensed ISM frequency band (868 MHz in Europe, 915 MHz in North America, and 433 MHz in Asia).
2. Range 5 km (urban), 20 km (rural).
3. It is scalable.
4. It supports bi-directional communication provided by the Chirp Spread Spectrum (CSS).
5. Provides a high level of security due to encryption algorithms.
6. Maximum data rate 50 Kbps.

LoRa implements six spreading factors (SF7 to SF12) to adapt the data rate and range compensation. A higher spreading factor allows a longer range at the expense of lower data rate, and vice versa. The LoRa data rate is between 300 bps and 50 kbps depending on the spreading factor and channel bandwidth [3].

LoRa devices implement a sleep mode since most of the time they do not need to operate, thus increasing the battery life.

When comparing LoRa with other LPWAN technologies like SigFox or NB-IoT, each technology has advantages for IoT applications. Sigfox and LoRa offer lower-cost devices, with very long-range (high coverage), and very long battery lifetime. NB-IoT offer very low latency and high quality of service [3]. However, LoRa is the lower-cost device, with very long-range (high coverage) and very long battery lifetime.

Back-End Technologies. For the development of the Back Layer proposed, an integration of different technologies was done.

These technologies include development using Representational State Transfer (REST) services which is an interface between systems that uses the HTTP protocol to obtain data or generate operations on that data in several possible formats, such as XML and JSON [21]. REST services offer integration with heterogeneous devices, technologies, and systems, giving flexibility in the development of an IoT platform.

Other elements used for the development of the Back Layer were the MySQL database and the PHP language. PHP is oriented to the development of dynamic web applications with access to information stored in a database. In the PHP language, REST services can be developed by establishing subscription mechanisms in order to receive data from external applications and store them in a database, using their capabilities to connect with database engines like MySQL [14,22,23]. The PHP language can also be useful for the development of web pages in order to show data and information to the final user.

4.1 LoRa-Based IoT Monitoring and Collecting System Development

According to the design in Fig. 2, both the Front Layer and the Back Layer compose the architecture for the development of the LoRa-based IoT Monitoring and Collecting System, which is developed by integrating the technologies exposed above in the corresponding layer.

Front Layer. The Front Layer integrates the LoRa-Nodes and the LoRa-Gateway modules to collect data from different kinds of sensors and send it to the Back Layer. The Front Layer network is configured in a star network topology, where LoRa-Nodes do not have routing capabilities and each LoRa-Node message reaches the LoRa-Gateway in just one hop.

LoRa-Node. The core of the LoRa-Node is the LoRa32u4 II board, which is a light, low consumption, low-cost and commercially available board, based on the Atmega32u4 with 868 MHZ/915 MHz. It is a high-quality LoRa module, with transfer rates range between 0.018 kbps and 37.5 kbps and includes a USB LiPO battery charging circuit [24]. The LoRa32u4 II board can be used as both node or gateway and its architecture is similar to that of the Arduino UNO module.

This board includes the LoRaWAN Protocol library [25] and can be programmed with the Arduino IDE, including the LoRa library by BSFrance.

The LoRa-Node's main process is to take data from external sensor modules and send it directly to the LoRa-Gateway through a one-hop communication, calling the send API function from the LoRa protocol stack. The external sensor modules are connected to the LoRa32u4 II board through both Analog to Digital Converter or Digital Inputs provided in the board.

In order to maximize the battery life span a function that detects changes in the data that is being collected, is included in the main program, thus using the LoRA wireless module only when a change in a data collected magnitudes is detected.

Each LoRa-Node is configured with a unique identification (ID) to discriminate the origin of the messages in the LoRa-Gateway. The LoRa-Node's messages sent can include the ID, the collected data, the timestamp, the battery level and a sequential message number that allows detecting whether a message has been missed.

LoRa-Gateway. The LoRa-Gateway consists of two parts: (1) a LoRa32u4 II board configured like a sink node that receives the messages from every LoRa-Node connected to the network and (2) a mechanism developed in an Android-based application (App) running on a smartphone, that takes the messages received by the sink node and uploads them to the Back Layer.

The messages received from the LoRa-Nodes are taken by the sink node and are sent, via a serial USB interface [26], to an Android-based application (App) deployed in an Android-based mobile device. The data received in the LoRa-Gateway module is then sent to the Back Layer, through an Internet connection, using a REST service exposed by the Back Layer. The App decodes the messages sent from each LoRa-Node and packs them using a JSON format and the uplink messages exchange to the Back Layer is carried out by using the Volley library [27]. The App is developed in the Java language.

Regarding the LoRa modulation capability of the sink node, it can communicate simultaneously on different channels and can have on the same channel signals modulated with different modulation Spreading Factors [28]. In case of collisions, the strongest signal is decoded. Using this feature offers the possibility of increasing the number of sink nodes thus increasing the network's capacity [25].

For the IoT platform proposed, the LoRa network works on the European frequency band of 867–869 MHz.

Back Layer. The core of the Back Layer is a web application developed using PHP and MySQL. Additional languages as Javascript, Cascade Style Sheets (CSS), and libraries like JQuery and AJAX were used as well. To deploy the Back Layer web application an Apache HTTP server was configured on a Ubuntu server, including PHP and MySQL Server.

A REST service was developed in PHP, which receives and decodes the JSON encoded messages coming from the Front Layer. Once the message is decoded, a PHP function sends the message content to a MySQL database created to store the data using the LoRa-Node's ID that collected the data as a key together with the data collected and the timestamp.

Therefore, when the data is stored in the database, it is available to other PHP functions that create a web graphical user interface in order to show the collected data to the end user. At this moment, it is possible to create charts to make a graphical representation of data and show trends or create additional functions to process, transform and interpret data, even apply statistical formulas, data analytic algorithms or machine learning algorithms.

The Back Layer web application was developed in PHP using Object-Oriented Programming; no framework was used. Access from PHP functions to MySQL database is done through the PHP Data Objects (PDO) extension.

5   Experimental Results

In order to test the proposed IoT Data Monitoring and Collecting Platform, a simple prototype to collect data was mounted for the purpose of measuring soil moisture.

Three LoRa-Nodes and one LoRa-Gateway were utilized for this test. The FC-28 soil moisture sensor was used to collect humidity data. The FC-28 sensor can be connected to the LoRa-Node in two modes: analog mode and digital mode. For the test the analog mode was used; the sensor works in the range from 0–1023 (the higher the value, the more dry is the soil). Moisture is measured in percentage; then, the values are mapped from 0–100.

Figure 3 shows the deployed components for the experimental setup.

An FC-28 sensor is connected to the LoRa32u4 II board ADC input, in each LoRa-Node; see Fig. 3(B). A script written in C for the LoRa32u4 II board, takes the data from the ADC input and calls the LoRa API to send it as a message to the sink node in the LoRa gateway. A 3.7 V 3000 mA polymer Lithium-Ion battery is used as a power supply for the LoRa-Node.

The LoRa-Gateway sink node receives data from the three LoRa-Nodes and sends it to an Android-based Tablet through a serial connection using an OTG cable connector; see Fig. 3(A). The App running in the Android-based Tablet parses the messages received and formats them using JSON and sends them to the Back Layer. The App can show the data values collected by each LoRa-Node as well as the time that it was received; see Fig. 3(A).

On the other hand, the Back Layer receives the messages from the Front Layer, decodes the messages and stores the data in the MySQL database. A simple web page was developed in order to show a tabulation and a chart of the soil moisture data collected by each LoRa-Node; see Fig. 4.

Measurements for the proposed IoT Data Monitoring and Collecting Platform were done at different distances both in urban and rural environments. In urban conditions with medium dense buildings and no Line Of Sight (LOS) between the LoRa-Nodes and LoRa-Gateway, the communication range lies between 300 to 600 m. For the urban test, the LoRa-Gateway was located in

Fig. 3. Front Layer components. (A) Lora-Gateway, (B) Lora-Node, (C) Lora-Node on a cloudy day at 30 °C

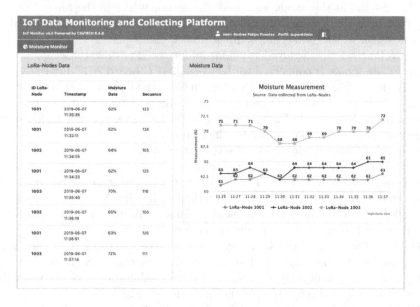

Fig. 4. Web page at the Back Layer to show the soil moisture data collected by each LoRa-Node

the Research Lab in the School of Engineering at Libre University Sectional Cali and the LoRa-Nodes around the campus. On the other hand, in a rural environment with Line Of Sight between the LoRa-Nodes and LoRa-Gateway, the communication range was from 600 m to 1.5 km. For the rural test LoRa-Nodes were placed in a sugar cane farm near Cali, Colombia, where there is no coverage for neither cellular nor other networks.

The setup values in the LoRa32u4 II module of the LoRa-Gateway and each LoRa-Node are listed in Table 1.

Table 1. Setup values in LoRa-Nodes and LoRa-Gateway.

LoRa module parameters	LoRa API function [29]
Power transmission: 20 dBm	`LoRa.setTxPower(17);`
Bandwidth: 125 kHz	`LoRa.setSignalBandwidth(125E3);`
Radio frequency: 868 MHz	`LoRa.begin(868E6);`
Coding rate: 4/8	`LoRa.setCodingRate4(8);`
Spreading Factor (SF): 7	`LoRa.setSpreadingFactor(7);`

On the LoRa32u4 II wireless module of each LoRa-Node, the Spreading Factor (SF) values were changed to 7, 9 and 12 and measurements were made at the same distances [28]. When the SF is increased, the package size will be reduced, resulting in higher power over the channel and a longer communication distance. The LoRa spreading factors for 125 kHz bandwidth are listed in Table 2.

Table 2. LoRa spreading factors for 125 kHz bandwidth

Spreading factor	Bit rate (bit/s)
7	5469
9	1758
12	293

The Data Rate column in Table 3, shows the configured values for SF and the Transmission Time column shows the time values that the data transmission takes, observed from the LoRa-Gateway. Messages with an SF equal to 7 take a transmission time of around 40–60 ms, depending on the size of the data. Messages with an SF equal to 9 take a transmission time of more than 164 ms and with an SF equal to 12 they take a transmission time of 1482 ms, more than 20 times the amount of time required to send the same message with SF set to 7.

As shown in Table 3, a higher SF has an enormous effect on battery life, which will be shorted around 20 times if SF 12 is used compared to SF 7.

Table 3. LoRa messages received by LoRa-Gateway using various spreading factors

Frequency	CR	Data rate	Transmission time	ID LoRa-Node	Message size
868.3	4/5	SF 7 BW 125	41.2	1001	12 bytes
868.3	4/5	SF 7 BW 125	61.7	1001	24 bytes
868.5	4/5	SF 9 BW 125	165.3	1002	17 bytes
868.5	4/5	SF 12 BW 125	1379.5	1003	24 bytes

6   Concluding Remarks

This paper proposes a platform for data collection and monitoring applicable to IoT projects based on LoRa, which is a wireless communication technology that is currently applied in the development of IoT [3]. The proposed platform brings a framework for the development of IoT projects by appropriating open hardware and software technologies, as well as low-cost components with a balanced performance.

In addition to the LoRa communication components, this work integrates different technologies, including Web Services and databases engines, for the storage and visualization of the data collected, with the aim of contributing to the development of different projects that require adoption and inclusion of mechanisms of this kind to enhance the use and interpretation of data coming from wireless sensor networks.

Although this work focuses its efforts on the definition of a basic platform for LoRa-based IoT systems, other types of communication schemes based on LPWAN technologies such as Sigfox or NB-IoT, could be used, in order to expand the proposed platform.

Eventually, in order to show the applicability of the LoRa-based platform proposed, an IoT application for moisture measurement is developed, where basic communication tests were carried out identifying the factors that affect the platform performance like LoRaś spreading factor.

In future works, it is possible to expand the number of nodes in the network to further analyze aspects of performance, latency and energy efficiency, as well as include different types of sensors for data collection, different LPWAN technologies, as well as the improvement of Web services for data analysis such as machine learning algorithms.

References

1. Lucero, S., et al.: IoT platforms: enabling the Internet of Things. IHS Technology white paper (2016)
2. Zanella, A., Bui, N., Castellani, A., Vangelista, L., Zorzi, M.: Internet of Things for smart cities. IEEE Internet Things J. **1**(1), 22–32 (2014)
3. Mekki, K., Bajic, E., Chaxel, F., Meyer, F.: A comparative study of LPWAN technologies for large-scale IoT deployment. ICT Express **5**(1), 1–7 (2019)

4. Centenaro, M., Vangelista, L., Zanella, A., Zorzi, M.: Long-range communications in unlicensed bands: the rising stars in the IoT and smart city scenarios. IEEE Wirel. Commun. **23**(5), 60–67 (2016)
5. Hejazi, H., Rajab, H., Cinkler, T., Lengyel, L.: Survey of platforms for massive IoT. In: 2018 IEEE International Conference on Future IoT Technologies (Future IoT), pp. 1–8. IEEE (2018)
6. Al-Fuqaha, A., Guizani, M., Mohammadi, M., Aledhari, M., Ayyash, M.: Internet of Things: a survey on enabling technologies, protocols, and applications. IEEE Commun. Surv. Tutor. **17**(4), 2347–2376 (2015)
7. Agrawal, S., Vieira, D.: A survey on Internet of Things. Abakós **1**(2), 78–95 (2013)
8. Mineraud, J., Mazhelis, O., Xiang, S., Tarkoma, S.: A gap analysis of Internet-of-Things platforms. Comput. Commun. **89**, 5–16 (2016)
9. LoRa Alliance. Lorawan regional parameters v1. 0. LoRa Alliance, Fremont, CA, USA (2016)
10. Rautmare, S., Bhalerao, D.M.: MySQL and NoSQL database comparison for IoT application. In: 2016 IEEE International Conference on Advances in Computer Applications (ICACA), pp. 235–238. IEEE (2016)
11. Wan, J., Tang, S.: Software-defined industrial Internet of Things in the context of Industry 4.0. IEEE Sens. J. **16**(20), 7373–7380 (2016)
12. Seungjun, Y., Hyojung, J.: Issues and implementation strategies of the IoT industry. In: 10th International Conference on Innovative Mobile and Internet Services in Ubiquitous Computing, pp. 503–508 (2016)
13. Fuentes Vasquez, A.F., Tamura, E.: From SDL modeling to WSN simulation for IoT solutions. In: Figueroa-García, J.C., Villegas, J.G., Orozco-Arroyave, J.R., Maya Duque, P.A. (eds.) WEA 2018. CCIS, vol. 916, pp. 147–160. Springer, Cham (2018). https://doi.org/10.1007/978-3-030-00353-1_13
14. Shinde, K.S., Bhagat, P.H.: Industrial process monitoring using IoT. In: 2017 International Conference on I-SMAC (IoT in Social, Mobile, Analytics and Cloud) (I-SMAC), pp. 38–42, February 2017
15. Choi, C.-S., Jeong, J.-D., Lee, I.-W., Park, W.-K.: LoRa based renewable energy monitoring system with open IoT platform. In: 2018 International Conference on Electronics, Information, and Communication (ICEIC), pp. 1–2. IEEE (2018)
16. Wydra, M., Kubaczynski, P., Mazur, K., Ksiezopolski, B.: Time-aware monitoring of overhead transmission line sag and temperature with LoRa communication. Energies **12**(3), 505 (2019)
17. Paredes-Parra, J.M., García-Sánchez, A.J., Mateo-Aroca, A., Molina-García, Á.: An alternative Internet-of-Things solution based on LoRa for PV power plants: data monitoring and management. Energies **12**(5), 881 (2019)
18. Sisinni, E., Carvalho, D.F., Ferrari, P., Flammini, A., Silva, D.R.C., Da Silva, I.M.D.: Enhanced flexible LoRaWAN node for industrial IoT. In: 2018 14th IEEE International Workshop on Factory Communication Systems (WFCS), pp. 1–4. IEEE (2018)
19. LoRa Technology. https://www.lora-alliance.org/what-is-lora/technology
20. Semtech, AN1200. Lora^{TM} modulation basics, application note, 22
21. Cheng, B., Zhao, S., Qian, J., Zhai, Z., Chen, J.: Lightweight service mashup middleware with REST style architecture for IoT applications. IEEE Trans. Netw. Serv. Manage. **15**(3), 1063–1075 (2018)
22. Jagadesh, M., Saravanan, M., Narayanan, V., Priya Vadhana, M., Logeshwaran, K.: Monitoring system in industry using IoT. In: 2019 5th International Conference on Advanced Computing Communication Systems (ICACCS), pp. 745–748, March 2019

23. Hans, V., Sethi, P.S., Kinra, J.: An approach to IoT based car parking and reservation system on cloud. In: 2015 International Conference on Green Computing and Internet of Things (ICGCIoT), pp. 352–354, October 2015

24. LoRa32u4   II.   https://bsfrance.fr/lora-long-range/1345-lora32u4-ii-lora-lipo-atmega32u4-sx1276-hpd13-868mhz-eu-antenna.html

25. Lavric, A., Popa, V.: Internet of Things and LoRa^{TM} low-power wide-area networks: a survey. In: 2017 International Symposium on Signals, Circuits and Systems (ISSCS), pp. 1–5. IEEE (2017)

26. Felipe Herranz felHR85. https://github.com/felhr85/usbserial

27. Yang, S., Hu, J.: Research and implementation of web services in android network communication framework volley. In: 2014 11th International Conference on Service Systems and Service Management (ICSSSM), pp. 1–3. IEEE (2014)

28. Sağır, S., Kaya, İ., Şişman, C., Baltacı, Y., Ünal, S.: Evaluation of low-power long distance radio communication in urban areas: LoRa and impact of spreading factor. In: 2019 Seventh International Conference on Digital Information Processing and Communications (ICDIPC), pp. 68–71, May 2019

29. Sandeep Mistry. https://github.com/sandeepmistry/arduino-lora

Sustainable Mobility in the Public Transportation of Montevideo, Uruguay

Silvina Hipogrosso[✉][iD] and Sergio Nesmachnow[✉][iD]

Universidad de la República, Montevideo, Uruguay
{silvina.hipogrosso,sergion}@fing.edu.uy

Abstract. Sustainable mobility is a very relevant approach within the novel paradigm of smart cities. This article presents an analysis of sustainable mobility initiatives recently developed in the public transportation of Montevideo, Uruguay. The case study is analyzed considering the main concepts from related works and well-known quantitative and qualitative indicators. Three initiatives are studied: electric bus, public bicycles, and electric scooters. They constitutes novel and promising ways for public transportation in the city. The reported results for each mean of transportation suggest that the first initiatives focus on specific sectors of the population and should be improved in order to extend their accessibility and affordability. Specific recommendations are formulated to develop and improve sustainable mobility in Montevideo.

Keywords: Sustainable mobility · Public transportation · Smart cities

1 Introduction

In modern cities, the participation of citizens in social, economic, and cultural activities requires people to travel, sometimes over long distances and involving long periods of time [8]. The ability of individuals to overcome the limitations imposed by distances and other mobility-related difficulties is critical to guarantee an active participation in city life [4].

Sustainable mobility is a subject that studies the development and use of means of transportation that are sustainable regarding several matters, mostly economic, environmental, and social [11]. Assessing sustainability and studying alternative means of transportation is very important considering that transportation largely contributes to environmental pollution with direct negative implications in health and quality of life of citizens. This is a relevant subject of study under the novel paradigm of smart cities [3].

Public transportation provides the most sustainable mean for mobility [21]. This is the case in Montevideo, Uruguay, where just a few initiatives to promote sustainable private mobility (e.g., electric vans for last mile distribution of people and goods [22]) have been developed recently.

In this line of work, this article presents a study of sustainable mobility initiatives recently developed in Montevideo, Uruguay. Three initiatives are studied:

© Springer Nature Switzerland AG 2020
S. Nesmachnow and L. Hernández Callejo (Eds.): ICSC-CITIES 2019, CCIS 1152, pp. 93–108, 2020.
https://doi.org/10.1007/978-3-030-38889-8_8

electric bus, public bicycles, and electric scooters, which are novel and promising ways for public transportation in the city. The main motivation of the study is to analyze and characterize the current reality regarding sustainable public transportation in Montevideo, in order to reduce problems in the city and redirect mobility towards a better sustainability.

Specific suggestions and recommendations are provided to develop and improve sustainable mobility in Montevideo.

The main contributions of this article are: (i) a review of the related literature about sustainable mobility and those proposals that can be developed in Montevideo; (ii) the analysis of current initiatives of sustainable mobility in the public transportation system of Montevideo regarding several quantitative and qualitative indicators; and (iii) the proposal of suggestions and recommendations to develop and improve sustainable mobility in Montevideo.

The article is structured as follows. Section 2 presents the main concepts related to sustainable mobility. A review of the main related work is presented in Sect. 3. The analysis of current initiatives in Montevideo is reported in Sect. 4. The suggestions and recommendations for developing and improving sustainable mobility in Montevideo are described in Sect. 5. Finally, Sect. 6 presents the conclusions and the main lines of future work.

2   Sustainable Mobility

Sustainability has been a major concern of society since the last decades of the XX century. In 1987, the Brundtland Report for the World Commission on Environment and Development introduced the term *sustainable development*, to define *"the development that meets the needs of the present without compromising the ability of future generations to meet their own needs"* [26]. This concept has become a paramount rule for modern sustainable mobility, a concept related to guarantee the movement of people with minimal environmental impact.

Several concepts are integrated in the sustainable mobility paradigm [2]. A new approach is proposed for designing and planning transportation systems, based on social processes, accessibility, reduction of motorized transportation, integration of people and traffic, and other factors oriented to consider mobility as a valued activity and regarding environmental and social concerns [17]. The World Business Council for Sustainable Development defined sustainable mobility as the ability of a society to fulfill requirements related to the movement of people without sacrificing fundamental human or ecological values [27].

Many researches on sustainable mobility focused on the impacts on environment, but recently, other aspects have also been analyzed, such as the relation with equity and the impact on economy, safety, health, and quality of life in general. In his regard, technology has been identified as one of the main tools that helps ensuring energy efficiency, using alternative and renewable energy sources, reducing contamination (e.g., pollutants emissions, noise, etc.), and provide environmental friendliness.

Furthermore, measures oriented to sustainable mobility put special emphasis on raising awareness and involving citizens, in order to foster a behavioural change. The ultimate goal is that citizens realize that means of transportation proposed by the sustainable mobility paradigm helps society, thus citizens choose to use more sustainable options by their own.

Specific indicators have been proposed and developed to study sustainable mobility in urban scenarios [7]. Furthermore, they have been applied to analyze different means of transportation in many cities around the world. Some of the main related works on the topic are reviewed on next section.

3 Related Work

Several means of transportation coexist and share the urban space in modern cities. These means are supposed to be well integrated and connected, in order to provide citizens with efficient and effective mobility [28]. However, administrators often apply traditional urban planning processes that only focus on few parts of the transportation system, instead of providing holistic plans accounting for all means operating in the city and including a comprehensive decision-making to consider indirect and interrelated impacts of the implemented solutions.

The approach that does not consider the city and transportation systems as a whole, leads to isolated actions that usually result in poor and inefficient policies, which fails to solve the main problems related to mobility.

Litman and Burwell [13] acknowledged the aforementioned issues and recognized that in order to achieve sustainability, transportation must be conceived from a broad point of view to consider energy efficiency, health, economic and social welfare, and other relevant aspects related to sustainable development.

A paradigm shift was proposed for rethinking transportation, in order to consider different integrated solutions to achieve sustainable transportation systems.

Sustainable urban mobility planning begins with designing a strategic plan for the community. Banister [2] put special emphasis on the participation of stakeholders in the planning process in order to involve them in the reasoning and implementation of specific initiatives for sustainable mobility. Several articles [7,12,25] studied indicators and methodological analysis as tools to evaluate the situation of sustainable mobility in cities, understand the evolution towards sustainable transportation systems, and evaluate the impact of selected solutions.

Indicators simplify complex phenomena and they often just provide hints of a specific issue or situation [16]. However, the combination of multiple indicators allows capturing different dimensions and aspects of sustainable mobility.

The main concepts about indicators and performance measurement for sustainable transportation were presented in the book by Gudmundsson et al. [7], focusing on the role and importance of quantitative and qualitative indicators for stakeholders (including decision-makers, planners, and operators).

A review of frameworks for assessing sustainability metrics and a proposal towards a framework for sustainability transportation were also presented. Two case studies were presented: European transportation and high speed rail in England.

Miller et al. [21] studied the role of public transportation regarding sustainability and reviewed articles that analyzed case studies of sustainable transportation. A set of recommendations were provided for developing and planning sustainable public transportation systems.

Rodrigues et al. [25] developed an index of sustainable urban mobility including several important features identified by Litman [14] for comprehensive and sustainable transport planning. The index is based on data obtained from planners and includes weights for different criteria, defined by experts. An application on the city of São Carlos, Brazil, demonstrated that the proposed index was relatively easy-to-compute and flexible enough to be applied to characterize sustainable mobility. The approach was extended by performing a multiple criteria decision analysis to determine variables that capture the main features of the reality in Brazilian cities concerning sustainable mobility. The analysis was performed over eleven cities in different states of Brazil. Several dimensions of sustainability were studied and results allowed identifying key elements to be used for proposing public policies for improving sustainable mobility.

Johnston [12] developed a comprehensive method for modeling the impacts of transportation, to be included in an integrated urban model of California. Several major transportation scenarios were studied, evaluating greenhouse gas emissions, economic welfare and equity, air pollution, Results of the analysis were reported as relevant to state and regional transportation plans.

The successful case of Bogotá, Colombia was studied by Lyons [15], focusing on the actions taken to address environmental protection and both, economic and social sustainability via a non automobile-centric approach. The integration between transportation planning and social planning was highlighted, especially for the case of new houses and open spaces that complemented transportation, restriction to vehicles during rush hours, and the TransMilenio BRT system. Several outcomes related to sustainability were reported and analyzed. The author concluded that the case study can be replicated in other developing countries in the path towards sustainable transportation.

In Uruguay, project URU/17/G32 "Towards a sustainable and efficient urban mobility system in Uruguay" was launched in 2017, as a joint effort of government and transportation companies. The main goals of the project are defining regulations for low carbon transportation systems, evaluating clean technologies (e.g., electric cars) in Montevideo, and promoting a cultural change towards sustainable transportation modes (e.g., bicycles). Other recent initiatives for studying and developing sustainable transportation in Montevideo are project MOVES [22], which aims at promoting an effective transition towards inclusive, efficient, and low-carbon urban mobility in Uruguay, and project 'Public transportation planning in smart cities' [24], funded by Fondo Conjunto de Cooperación Uruguay-México (2018–2019).

The research reported in our article constitutes a novel proposal for Uruguay and is oriented to the evaluation of current sustainable mobility initiatives in Montevideo, both included and not in the aforementioned project URU/17/G32.

4   Analysis of Sustainable Mobility Initiatives in Montevideo

This section describes and analyzes sustainable mobility initiatives that are operating in Montevideo through public or private transportation companies.

4.1   Sustainable Mobility Initiatives

Three sustainable mobility initiatives have been developed recently in Montevideo: electric bus, public bicycles, and electric scooters. The main details of each initiative are presented next.

Electric Bus (Pilot Plan). The main bus transportation company operating in Montevideo (CUTCSA, accounting for about two thirds of the market share and also of the buses operating in the city) has conducted tests of mobility using electric buses, with incentives and support from the Ministry of Energy and the City Hall of Montevideo. Since 2017, a pilot plan is in course, using one electric bus that operates rotatively in different lines to test the performance of this new mean of transportation. The company is working in a financing proposal to be evaluated for the Green Climate Fund in order to buy 100 electric buses and integrate them to the transportation system.

Public Bicycles. In 2015, the City Hall of Montevideo introduced a public bicycle system, called *Movete*, as part of the urban transportation system to promote green mobility and a healthy way to know the city, move to workplaces, or simply extend the accessibility of public transportation systems to final destinations. The service consists of a fleet of 80 bicycles spread in a network of eight automated stations, distributed from the Old City to the Center neighborhoods. Bicycles can be rented at one station and returned in another station in the coverage area. A card of the integrated Metropolitan Transportation System (STM) is required to rent a bicycle in Movete and people that do not own a STM card, e.g. tourists, can obtain it with no charge in the center office of Movete. Users cannot use the bicycle service for more than four hours per day. Public bicycle service is planning to expand the coverage area of operation in 2020, to include 60 stations and 600 bicycles in order to increase accessibility and promote active mobility.

Electric Scooters. The electric scooter is a new mode of urban transportation that has gained popularity all over the world as an alternative to driving. Electric scooters provides an environmentally friendly alternative for short journeys that are either too far to walk, or too close to drive a car, to be a cost-effective option. Three companies of electric scooter (Grin, Lime, and Movo) have been operating in Montevideo since 2018. The service provides a practical and easy way to use electric scooters: by simply downloading a mobile application and setting up a payment method, users have access to a network of scooters that they can use at any time. Electric scooters have GPS blue tracking, so users are never too far from picking up a electric scooter and they can leave it anywhere within the area where the service operates.

4.2 Indicators to Assess Sustainable Mobility

The analysis considers sustainable mobility indicators proposed by the World Business Council for Sustainable Development [27].

Indicators were separated in two groups; *quantitative indicators*, for which the available data in Montevideo allows computing a numerical value for the specific criteria, and *qualitative indicators*, for which only a qualitative analysis can be performed, since some of the relevant pieces of information are not available for the studied initiatives.

Quantitative Indicators. The quantitative indicator group includes: coverage, access to mobility service, affordability, and commuting travel time. The corresponding definitions are presented next.

Coverage. The coverage (cov) is defined as the ratio of the area covered by each sustainable mobility service (ci) and the total urbanized area of the city (ta), according to Eq. 1. The total urbanized area of Montevideo is considered to extend for $200\,km^2$. The scale for this indicator is straightforward, 0 correspond to 0% of coverage and 10 correspond to 100% of coverage.

$$cov = \frac{ci}{ta} \qquad (1)$$

Access to Mobility Service. Access to mobility service (am) is defined as the share of population with appropriate access to each service, according to Eq. 2, where nh is the number of citizens living in the city, and $PR(i)$ is the percentage of people living within $400\,m$ from a public transportation stop or from a possible renting point of a shared mobility system.

$$am = \frac{\sum_i PR(i)}{nh} = 1 - \frac{\overline{PR}}{nh} \qquad (2)$$

The methodology for calculation implies determining the percentage of people living within the service areas by using spatial data analysis. Service area are limited by a distance of $400\,m$ of a sustainable mobility service, which is considered as the maximum distance that a person considers to walk to use a public transportation service [1]. The scale for the am indicator is: 0 represents 0% of the population in the city and 10 represents 100% of the population.

Affordability of Sustainable Mobility Transportation. Affordability (af) is defined as the expenses on transportation made by persons as a percentage of their income. The calculation is based on the methodology by Carruthers et al. [5], considering the cost of performing 45 and 60 trips on each transportation mode and on existing socio-economic data. The indicator is computed for two different relevant social groups, considering the minimum income and the middle income per capita, according to values reported for 2019 by National Institute of Statistics, Uruguay (INE) [10].

The calculation method is described by Eq. 3, where nt is the number of trips, p is the cost of a single trip, and is is the income per capita.

The scale for the *af* indicator is: 0 indicates affordability index is over 35% and 10 indicates that is less than 3.5%

$$af = \frac{nt \times p}{is} \tag{3}$$

Commuting Travel Time. This indicator is defined as the average time spent by a person when travelling from origin to destination of a trip performed in the public transportation system. The methodology applied for calculation considers that: (i) (for bus) the average commuting travel time includes the time for a person to walk to the bus stop and the time waiting for the bus to arrive; persons are supposed to walk from the centroid of the zone and the average walking speed is assumed to be 5 km/h; (ii) (for bicycles) the average speed is 13.5 km/h and the average walking time to a bicycle station is 4 min (walking up to 400 m); and (iii) (for scooters) the average speed is 10 km/h and the walking time a person takes to find a scooter is less than 3 min.

Commuting travel times are computed for two relevant distances: (i) a *short travel* of 3 km, a reasonable distance for travels to nearby locations such as offices, shopping, education, etc. It is also the average travel distance for electric scooters, considering an average speed of 12 km/h; and (ii) a *medium distance* of 10 km, a reasonable average distance for travels to work, according to data from the urban mobility survey for Montevideo [20]. It is also the average travel distance on public transportation, considering an average bus speed of 13 km/h [23].

Two scales are considered for this indicator, for 3 and 10 km. Both considers as lower limit the time to travel the corresponding distance at the average human walking speed of 5 km/h, and as upper limit the time to travel the corresponding distance at the limit speed of bicycles and electric scooters (25 km/h). Thus, for the 3 km distance, 0 represent a trip duration of over 36 min and 10 represents a trip duration of 7 min; and for the 10 km distance, 0 represent a trip duration of over 2 h and 10 represents a trip duration of 24 min.

Qualitative Indicators. The qualitative indicator group includes: net public finance, energy efficiency, intermodal connectivity, intermodal integration, and confort and pleasure. The corresponding definitions are presented next.

Net Public Finance: Percentage of the cost of each mobility service that the government grants as subsidy to transportation companies.

Energy Efficiency: Energy consumption in public transportation, usually evaluated in oil equivalent. The efficiency indicator considers the total energy demand from clean (i.e., renewable) and non-renewable sources.

Intermodal Connectivity: Number of locations where users can change from one mode of transportation to another.

Intermodal Integration: Quality of the intermodal facilities between the different transport modes.

Comfort and Pleasure: Satisfaction perceived by citizens about comfort and pleasure of moving in the city using different transportation modes. Comfort and pleasure indicator is analyzed through access to information, quality of the service, and security.

4.3   Analysis and Results

This subsection reports the results of the study to characterize the sustainable mobility initiatives. The study applies a urban data analysis approach [18], accounting for relevant data from each initiative, obtained from public sources.

Quantitative Indicators

Coverage. The electric bus operated in several lines during 2017–2018. Table 1 summarizes the number of days of operation on the most relevant lines.

Table 1. Lines operated by the electric bus service in Montevideo (2017–2018)

Line	Days	Percentage
128	78	14.0%
142	16	2.9%
169	47	8.4%
180	303	54.4%
181/183 (circular)	45	8.1%
187	20	3.6%
Other lines	Less than 6 days	Less than 1%

According to the results in Table 1, the area considered to calculate the coverage of the electric bus service is the one corresponding to the buffer area defined by parallel segments located at 400 m of the most used lines routes: 128, 169, 180, and 181/183. For public bicycle, the coverage of the actual service and the projected coverage of the service are reported. The overall area for electric scooters is the one defined by the Grin service, which covers the area of service of the other two companies (Lime and Movo).

The area covered by each studied sustainable mobility initiative in Montevideo and the value of the *cov* indicator is reported in Table 2. Results were computed based on open data from each service.

The coverage maps for electric bus, public bicycles, and electric scooters services are presented in Fig. 1.

The analysis of the coverage indicator demonstrate that the area of service of each sustainable mobility initiatives is represents a small fraction of the total area of the city. The best coverage is for the electric bus service, which covers 25.7% of the city.

Table 2. Coverage and the *cov* indicator for sustainable mobility initiatives

Initiative	Area	Coverage	cov indicator
Electric bus	$51.4\,km^2$	25.7%	2.57
Public bicycle	$3.5\,km^2$	1.75%	0.175
Public bicycle (projected)	$13\,km^2$	6.5%	0.65
Electric scooter (Grin)	$23.5\,km^2$	11.75%	1.175
Electric scooter (Lime)	$15\,km^2$	7.5%	0.75
Electric scooter (Movo)	$7\,km^2$	3.5%	0.35
Electric scooter (overall)	$23.5\,km^2$	11.75%	1.175

Coverage results are somehow expected, as the studied initiatives are new and public bicycles were introduced mainly for tourist. For electric scooters, coverage is also limited to zones with highest income (coast area).

Overall, the three studied modes provides a service that covers an area of $67.6\,km^2$, which represents a 33.8% of the urbanized area of Montevideo, for a coverage index of 3.8. In conclusion, two thirds of the citizens who live in the urbanized area are not covered by these sustainable modes of transportation.

Access to Mobility Service. The population served by each service was computed by intersecting coverage areas with the population map and counting the total population in each zone.

The urban population of Montevideo is 1 305 082.

The electric bus service covers 429 269 citizens (32.9% of the population), accounting for the largest access index ($am = 3.29$). Public bicycles cover 86 917 citizens ($am = 0.67$) and the planned expansion is set to cover 193 368 citizens ($am = 1.48$). The electric scooters companies provides service to 285 445 citizens ($am = 2.19$). Overall, sustainable transportation modes cover 554 172 citizens (42.5% of the population, $am = 4.25$).

As a consequence, most of the urban population have no access to these sustainable modes of transportation.

Affordability of Sustainable Mobility. The affordability index was computed for the three studied transportation modes considering *short trips* with a length of 15 min (the most frequent travel duration for scooters) and long trips length of 45 min (the average time travelled in bus [20]).

Income per capita in Montevideo is USD 691 (middle) and USD 423 (minimum)(as of August, 2019, 1 USD = 37 Uruguayan pesos).

The cost of a standard ticket (allowing one transfer trip in one hour) in electric bus is 0.85 USD.

Electric scooters and public bicycles apply a time-based fare. The cost of using the public bicycles is 0 (free service) up to 30 min and after that, the rental cost is 0.74 USD for 30 min.

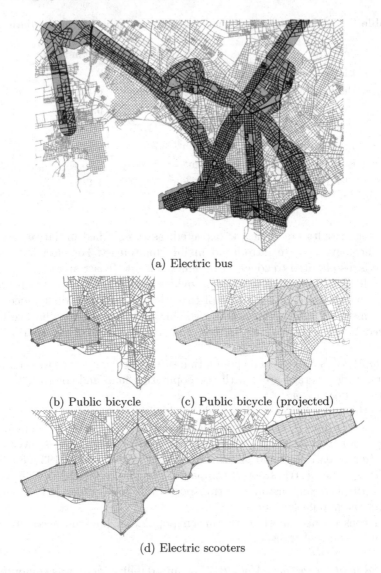

(a) Electric bus

(b) Public bicycle   (c) Public bicycle (projected)

(d) Electric scooters

Fig. 1. Coverage of sustainable mobility initiatives in Montevideo

The cost of a 15-min rent (average time of utilization) for the electric scooter is 2.1 USD and for one hour is 5.4 USD.

Table 3 reports the affordability index of each sustainable transportation mode for middle and minimum income people.

Results indicate that for 15 min, public bicycle has the maximum *af* value (10) for both income groups, since it is a free service. Affordability do not reduce significantly when considering 45 min trips. Buses are cheaper than scooters for both short and long periods of time. Furthermore, the *af* indicator for buses is the same, while electric scooters downgrade to $af = 0.0$ for one hour trips. Overall, public bicycle is the most affordable mode of transportation.

Table 3. af indicator for minimum and middle income in Montevideo

Income	45 trips			60 trips		
	Bus	Bicycle	Scooter	Bus	Bicycle	Scooter
Trip length: 15 min						
Minimum	9.1% (8.2)	0 (10.0)	22.7% (3.9)	12.0% (7.3)	0 (10.0)	30.2% (1.5)
Middle	5.5% (9.5)	0 (10.0)	13.9% (6.7)	7.3% (8.8)	0 (10.0)	18.5% (5.2)
Trip length: 45 min						
Income	45 trips			60 trips		
	Bus	Bicycle	Scooter	Bus	Bicycle	Scooter
Minimum	9.1% (8.2)	4% (9.8)	57.2% (0.0)	12.0% (7.3)	5.4% (9.4)	76.2% (0.0)
Middle	5.5% (9.5)	2.5% (10.0)	35.0% (0.0)	7.3% (8.8)	3.3% (10.0)	46.7% (0.0)

Commuting Travel Time. Table 4 reports the commuting travel times for distances of 3 km, 10 km, and from end-to-end (*EtoE*) of the coverage areas for each mobility service. Speed and average times for bus were computed according to the methodology by Massobrio and Nesmachnow [19], using the Open Street Map service, estimations of average speed, and public applications.

Table 4. Commuting travel times (minutes)

Bus			Bicycle			Scooter		
3 km	10 km	EtoE (17.3 km)	3 km	10 km	EtoE (3.5 km)	3 km	10 km	EtoE (17.5 km)
17.8	49.3	116.0	13.3	44.4	15.6	20.0	60.0	102.0

Results show that bicycle is the fastest option for both short and long distance, followed by the bus, and in third place the electric scooter. Differences between bicycle and bus reduce for 10 km. EtoE bus trips takes longer than traveling on scooter, so in between 10 and 17.5 km travels on scooter become faster than on bus. Overall travel times suggest that sustainable mobility modes do not allow traveling faster on the city.

4.4 Qualitative Indicators

Net Public Finance. Electric buses are benefited from three subsidies: a municipal contribution for students and retirees, fuel subsidy (from the Ministry of Transportation) and contributions to keep the price stable (from the Ministry of Economy and Finance). Furthermore, electric buses are granted a total of 100.000 USD to promote the substitution of 4% of diesel bus to electric.

The public bicycles service is completely financed by the city Hall of Montevideo to promote active and sustainable mobility. Electrics scooters do not received any subsidy as they are run by private companies.

Energy Efficiency. All the studied transportation modes use clean renewable energy. Public bicycle is the most efficient of the initiatives, since it does not requires energy of external sources. Electric buses provides a significant improvement over the current diesel vehicles regarding energy efficiency. They produce no CO_2 emissions and have an iron phosphate battery that consumes $100\,KWh$ each $100\,km$, which is a good rate for public transportation. Regarding electric scooters, the energy of operation represents a very low percentage of the total emissions generated (e.g., 4.7% according to the study by Hollingsworth for the city of Raleigh, North Carolina [9]). However, several other concerns arise, such as the non-clean energy required for collecting and distributing scooters, and the short life cycle of batteries, which can have negative environmental impacts.

Intermodal Connectivity. The studied sustainable mobility initiatives operate in a common area of $2.8\,km^2$ (with the projected expansion for bicycles, $7.3\,km^2$). Within this common area, public bicycles offer full connectivity with buses and scooters, since stations are located less than $100\,m$ of bus stops and scooters are available nearby. Electric scooters facilitates door-to-door mobility, allowing users to leave scooters anywhere within the operation area, thus providing a valid alternative for intermodal connectivity. Buses also allows intermodal connectivity, limited to the availability of bicycles or scooters near the bus stops.

Intermodal Integration. Even though the three transportation modes studied provides intermodal connectivity, the system lacks of intermodal integration. Each service focuses on their own operation, without facilitating integration with others: no information or route guidance is provided to users, terminal bus stations do not provide parking lots for public bicycles or scooters, etc. The only integration is regarding the payment method for buses and public bicycles, which can be paid using the same public transportation card (STM). All these facts are specific drawbacks for intermodal mobility. Overall, integration should be improved to provide efficient mobility.

Comfort and Pleasure. Available information of public buses is recognized as one of the best features offered to citizens, according to the recent mobility survey for Montevideo [20]. On the other hand, trip comfort (43,9%) and bus stop comfort (46.4%) were the worst rated attributes of the bus system.

Users have presented multiple claims about the poor service of Movete and bad conditions of the bicycles [6]. Furthermore, the city lacks of a proper infrastructure (e.g., exclusive lanes) for connecting stations of the system.

Finally, users perceive many benefits of electric scooters: they are easy to locate, ride effortlessly, dock-less, and can be parked anywhere. On the other hand, electric scooters are vulnerable to road risks, as they are driven on the same lane as automobiles, and are an uncomfortable mean of transportation with bad weather conditions.

5 Suggestions and Recommendations for Sustainable Mobility in Montevideo

This section provides some recommendations and suggestions that can be implemented in the city of Montevideo to promote sustainable mobility. Recommendations and suggestions are based on the review, analysis, and main results of the study of the three initiatives for public sustainable mobility.

One of the main facts from the analysis is that the initiatives for sustainable mobility are not widespread through the city, but provide a limited coverage and poor access to citizens. In this regard, one of the main recommendation is related to expand the coverage area, by introducing more bicycle stations, operating new lines of the electric bus, covering different routes or extending the routes offered, and expand the areas available to operate electric scooters. To improve coverage, more vehicles must be introduced and an articulated network of exclusive lanes, which will help to improve other indicators too.

Specific suggestions to increase accessibility are extending the bus and ciclying network and the electric scooters operation area by previously evaluating the real demand for each transportation mode via direct and indirect methods, e.g. mobility data analysis approach.

Other suggestion to increase accessibilty is to do a viability study in order to offer these mobility services to areas of lower social incomes.

Concerning affordability, the study demonstrated that electric bus is expensive and electric scooters are prohibitive for low-income citizens. In this regard, a specific suggestion for mobility services is to provide ticket packages for frequently users, offering a lower price and combination with other services, to facilitate intermodality. The public finance can be reviewed to contribute to affordability, mainly by redirecting the assistance to reduce operation and maintenance costs, to guarantee a lower ticket price.

Several suggestions are related to improve travel time, in order to provide more useful and efficient sustainable transportation systems.

In this regard, both city administration and transportation companies must focus on providing accurate information to citizens and guaranteeing a quick access to relevant information for travel planning. Electric bus should provide a high frequency service, by redesigning or updating existing timetables, and a better effort must be done in order to provide good synchronization between different bus lines.

For public bicycles and electric scooters, travel times are related to availability of vehicles and also on the available interconnection network, so specific improvements on the fleets size and on infrastructure can contribute in this regard.

To take advantage of the modal shift from diesel to electric buses to improve energy efficiency, smart planning of battery charge is needed, by properly locating charge stations in strategic points of the operation area or planning the use of external batteries. Electric scooters also need to review their operation efforts for collecting and distributing vehicles, which demands non-clean energy. A specific suggestion to improve efficiency is installing secure parking stations to charge scooters batteries while parked.

A certain recommendation to enhance sustainable mobility is to promote intermodal connectivity between transportation modes.

In this regard, services should work on providing real time data information (e.g., vehicles available, location, bus stops information, timetabling, etc.) and on installing shared stations for at least two services. A specific suggestion is to integrate the ticketing system, allowing users to share modes within a ride, maybe linked with the aforementioned offers to improve affordability.

In terms of comfort and pleasure, companies can offer a better quality service by improving the comfort of the vehicle, and particularly adopting security measures to guarantee safe travels. Bicycles and electric scooters can incorporate helmet to their service and buses can include seat belts for passengers. Related to the overall quality of experience, companies and city administration can improve access to information providing users with mobile applications, oriented to reduce walking time, waiting time, and the overall travel times.

6   Conclusions and Future Work

This article studied three recent sustainable mobility initiatives implemented in Montevideo, Uruguay. The study reviewed the main concepts of sustainable mobility from related work and analyzed the three modes of transportation (electric bus, public bicycles, and electric scooters) through quantity and qualitative indicators of sustainable mobility.

The results of the study indicate that the area of service of each sustainable mobility initiatives represents a small fraction of the total area of the city. Consequently, a significant part of the urban population have no access to these sustainable modes of transportation.

Public bicycle is not only the most affordable mode of transportation, but also the fastest and ecological option to travel for short and long distance. Electric bus is the second best option.

These two services have public finance, so the can keep a reasonable price or even reduce it.

Electric scooters have prohibitive prices for low income citizens.

On the other hand, the service quality of public bicycle is the worst of the three modes in terms of comfort and pleasure. Finally, although the three modes provides intermodal connectivity between them, there is a lack of intermodal integration between services.

Taking into account the result of the analysis, specific suggestions are provided in order to improve sustainable mobility in Montevideo.

The main lines for future work are related to extend the analysis by considering other sustainable mobility indicators and study best practices implemented on other cities in order to contribute to the improvement of urban sustainable mobility in Montevideo.

References

1. Atash, F.: Redesigning suburbia for walking and transit: emerging concepts. J. Urban Plann. Dev. **120**(1), 48–57 (1994)
2. Banister, D.: The sustainable mobility paradigm. Transp. Policy **15**(2), 73–80 (2008)
3. Barrionuevo, J., Berrone, P., Ricart, J.: Smart cities, sustainable progress. IESE Insight **14**(14), 50–57 (2012)
4. Cardozo, O., Rey, C.: La vulnerabilidad en la movilidad urbana: aportes teóricos y metodológicos. In: Foschiatti, A.M.H. (ed.) Aportes conceptuales y empíricos de la vulnerabilidad global, pp. 398–423. Editorial Universitaria de la Universidad Nacional del Nordeste (2007)
5. Carruthers, R.: Affordability of public transport. In: International Conference Series on Competition and Ownership in Land Passanger Transport, pp. 1–15 (2005)
6. El País: IMM licita 60 estaciones para 600 bicicletas en Montevideo, 24 June 2019. https://www.elpais.com.uy/informacion/sociedad/licitan-bases-bicicletas-montevideo.html. August 2019
7. Gudmundsson, H., Hall, R.P., Marsden, G., Zietsman, J.: Sustainable Transportation. STBE. Springer, Heidelberg (2016). https://doi.org/10.1007/978-3-662-46924-8
8. Harvey, D.: Social justice, postmodernism and the city. Int. J. Urban Reg. Res. **16**(4), 588–601 (1992)
9. Hollingsworth, J., Copeland, B., Johnson, J.X.: Are scooters polluters? the environmental impact of shareddockless electric scooters. Environ. Res. Lett. **14**(8), 1–10 (2019)
10. Instituto Nacional de Estadística, Uruguay: Ingresos de los hogares y de las personas. https://www.ine.gub.uy/gastos-e-ingresos-de-las-personas-y-los-hogares. August 2019
11. Jeon, C., Amekudzi, M.: Addressing sustainability in transportation systems: definitions, indicators, and metrics. J. Infrastruct. Syst. **11**(1), 31–50 (2005)
12. Johnston, R.: Indicators for sustainable transportation planning. Transp. Res. Rec. J. Transp. Res. Board **2067**(1), 146–154 (2008)
13. Litman, T., Burwell, D.: Issues in sustainable transportation. Int. J. Global Environ. Issues **6**(4), 331–347 (2006)
14. Litman, T.: Exploring the paradigm shifts needed to reconcile transportation and sustainability objectives. Transp. Res. Rec. **1670**(1), 8–12 (1999)
15. Lyons, W.: Sustainable transport in the developing world: a case study of bogota's mobility strategy. In: International Conference on Sustainable Infrastructure (2017)
16. Maclaren, V.: Exploring the paradigm shift needed to reconcile sustainability and transportation objectives. J. Am. Plann. Assoc. **62**(2), 184–202 (1999)
17. Marshall, S.: The challenge of sustainable transport. In: Layard, A., Davoudi, S., Batty, S. (Eds.) Planning for a Sustainable Future, pp. 131–147 (2001)
18. Massobrio, R., Nesmachnow, S.: Urban data analysis for public transportation systems. In: 2nd Iberoamerican Congress on Smart Cities (2019)
19. Massobrio, R., Nesmachnow, S.: Urban mobility data analysis for public transportation systems: a case study in Montevideo, Uruguay. Environment and Planning B: Urban Analytics and City Science (2019)
20. Mauttone, A., Hernández, D.: Encuesta de movilidad del área metropolitana de Montevideo (2017). https://scioteca.caf.com/bitstream/handle/123456789/1078/EncuestadeMovilidadMVD-documentocompleto-final.pdf. August 2019

21. Miller, P., de Barros, A., Kattan, L., Wirasinghe, S.: Public transportation and sustainability: a review. KSCE J. Civil Eng. **20**(3), 1076–1083 (2016)
22. Ministry of Industry, Energy, and Mining, Uruguay: Proyecto Movés: Movilidad urbana eficiente y sostenible (2017). https://www.miem.gub.uy/energia/proyecto-moves-movilidad-urbana-eficiente-y-sostenible. August 2019
23. Nesmachnow, S., Bana, S., Massobrio, R.: A distributed platform for big data analysis in smart cities: combining intelligent transportation systems and socioeconomic data for Montevideo, Uruguay. EAI Endorsed Transactions on Smart Cities, pp. 1–18 (2017)
24. Nesmachnow, S., Tchernykh, A., Cristóbal, A.: Planificación de transporte urbano en ciudades inteligentes. In: I Ibero-american Conference on Smart Cities, pp. 204–218 (2018)
25. Rodrigues, A., Costa, M., Macedo, M.: Multiple views of sustainable urban mobility: the case of Brazil. Transp. Policy **15**(6), 350–360 (2008)
26. United Nations General Assembly: Report of the world commission on environment and development: our common future (1987). http://www.un-documents.net/wced-ocf.htm. August 2019
27. World Business Council for Sustainable Development: Methodology and indicator calculation method for sustainable urban mobility. Technical report 978-2-940521-26-5 (2015)
28. Xiong, Z., Sheng, H., Rong, W., Cooper, D.: Intelligent transportation systems for smart cities: a progress review. Sci. China Inf. Sci. **55**(12), 2908–2914 (2012)

IPN Sustainability Program: Solar Photovoltaic Electricity Generation and Consumption Reduction

P. J. Escamilla-Ambrosio[1](✉) ⓘ, M. A. Ramírez-Salinas[1] ⓘ, O. Espinosa-Sosa[1],

G. Gallegos-García[1], M. Morales-Olea[2], and Luis Hernández-Callejo[3](✉) ⓘ

[1] Instituto Politécnico Nacional, Centro de Investigación en Computación, Mexico City, Mexico
pescamilla@cic.ipn.mx
[2] Fundación INBA A.C, Mexico City, Mexico
[3] Campus Duques de Soria, Universidad de Valladolid (UVa), C.P. 42004 Soria, Spain

Abstract. As part of the energy sustainability program intended to reduce the carbon footprint of the National Polytechnic Institute, solar photovoltaic electricity generation systems along with electricity consumption reduction actions have been implemented in three entities. These actions were implemented in accordance with recommendations defined by environmental committees and considering the diagnoses of baseline energy consumption. This work reports the quantification of the savings generated by the implementation of operational measures of technological substitution and solar photovoltaic electric power generation. The foregoing includes a process of identification of the baseline of electricity consumption, the replacement of infrastructure and equipment of high energy consumption with equipment of low consumption and environmental impact, as well as the installation of technology for the generation of electrical energy by renewable sources. Three solar photovoltaic systems were installed, replacement of luminaires, replacement of hand dryers and replacement of obsolete air conditioning equipment. It was found that on average the reduction in monthly electricity consumption is 31% with the consequent economic savings. Regarding the reduction of the carbon footprint, an impact on non-generation of tonnes of CO2 equivalent amount 37% quantified with reference to the generation before the implementation of the operational and power generation measures. This is equivalent to not having generated 18.31 tCO2e per month. This work describes the activities carried out and the methodology used to calculate the savings found, both in energy consumption, economic, and in reducing the carbon footprint.

Keywords: Energy sustainability · Photovoltaic system · Carbon footprint

1 Introduction

As part of the energy sustainability and carbon footprint reduction project at the National Polytechnic Institute (IPN, from Instituto Politécnico Nacional, in Spanish) [1], a pilot program was implemented in 3 instances: Computer Research Center (CIC, from Centro

© Springer Nature Switzerland AG 2020
S. Nesmachnow and L. Hernández Callejo (Eds.): ICSC-CITIES 2019, CCIS 1152, pp. 109–120, 2020.
https://doi.org/10.1007/978-3-030-38889-8_9

de Investigación en Computación, in Spanish), Center for Innovation and Technological Development in Computing (CIDETEC, from Centro de Investigación y Desarrollo Tecnológico en Cómputo, in Spanish) and Higher School of Computing (ESCOM, from Escuela Superior de Cómputo, in Spanish).

The project seeks to establish policies that facilitate the transition of the IPN education system to a sustainable development model, which promotes the incorporation of innovations and technological developments in the area of equipment, furniture and work instruments, to reduce the impact on the environment of its daily operation.

In this work technological substitutions and generation of electrical energy from a renewable energy source, which were implemented at 3 units of IPN, are presented. These actions aim to reduce the environmental impact, the carbon footprint and reduce the consumption and dependence of electricity generated by fossil fuels.

The information of the results generated from the initial approach and corresponding monitoring of the project is presented, as well as the analysis of the data generated through the activation of the technological platform refereed to as "Strategic System for Evaluation and Performance of Sustainability" (SEEDS, from Sistema Estratégico de Evaluación y Desempeño de la Sostenibilidad, in Spanish), implemented at CIC, CIDETEC and ESCOM buildings, which were equipped with the infrastructure that allows the use of alternative and sustainable energy.

CIC is located at Av. Juan de Dios Bátiz s/n esq. Miguel Othón de Mendizábal, Col. Nueva Industrial Vallejo, Mayor Gustavo A. Madero, C.P. 07738, Mexico City, Mexico. See Fig. 1. In its infrastructure CIC has a building with a total constructed area of 9,768.8 m^2, the property is 20 years old, it houses a total population of 383 users, the operation of the building is from Monday to Sunday, at a schedule of 07:00 am to 9:00 p.m., although it is an open-door building for its users, that is, it is functional 24 h a day, 365 days a year.

Fig. 1. Location and view of CIC.

CIDETEC is located at Av. Juan de Dios Bátiz s/n esq. Miguel Othón de Mendizábal, Col. Nueva Industrial Vallejo, Mayor Gustavo A. Madero, C.P. 07700, Mexico City, Mexico. See Fig. 2. In its infrastructure, CIDETEC has a building with a total constructed area of 2,563.26 m^2, the property is 12 years old, it houses an approximate population of 174 users, the operation of the building is from Monday to Sunday, at a schedule of

07:00 am to 9:00 p.m., although it is an open-door building for its users, that is, it is functional 24 h a day, 365 days a year.

Fig. 2. Location and view of CIDETEC.

ESCOM is located at Av. Juan de Dios Bátiz s/n Col. Nueva Industrial Vallejo, Mayor Gustavo A. Madero, C.P. 07738, Mexico City, Mexico. See Fig. 3. In its infrastructure ESCOM has 5 buildings with a total constructed area of 17,172.71 m^2, the property is 25 years old, has a total of 386 fixed users and 2800 variable users (students), the operation of the building is from Monday to Saturday, at 07:00 am to 10:00 pm.

Fig. 3. Location and view of ESCOM.

2 Baseline of Electricity Consumption and Replacement of Infrastructure

In order to determine the baseline of electricity consumption in the three units considered, the following actions were carried out: (a) activation of the SEEDS technology platform; (b) installation of an electrical energy consumption monitoring network; (c) replacement of infrastructure and equipment; (d) installation of PV electricity generation systems, and (e) quantification of energy, economic and environmental savings. These actions allowed monitoring the consumption of electrical energy through the installation of equipment for the measurement and processing of data, through a technological tool, which facilitated informed decision-making in the implementation of strategic projects that promote sustainable development.

2.1 Activation of the SEEDS Technology Platform

SEEDS is a software platform designed to support decision makers and administrators in the transition towards a model of sustainable development in organizations. Through programs developed for mobile and web environments, SEEDS allows to obtain the baseline of different sustainability variables, and evaluate performance in different intervention cycles. Furthermore, SEEDS allows entities the designing and monitoring of the effectiveness of improvement actions with respect to different sustainability variables, prioritizing the analysis of the consumption of electric energy and water usage, also as electricity energy generation. This software platform was installed in three instances of IPN in order to analyze and display information on the consumption of electricity and water, as energy generation, in real time, though an interactive web interface. The platform collects data through two systems:

1. Meters. The information is incorporated, from meters of electricity and water consumption, as electricity generation, in real time, to a database for processing and querying indicators in a web interface. This system has an API (Application Program Interface) to perform queries from other systems that have access permissions, for example, an Android application or other web system that request these data.

2. Logs. Module that allows to create logbooks with the information fields required to maintain a process of measuring the consumption of electricity and water, as well as electricity generation and the pattern of waste production.

SEEDS has a web interface for entering and consulting information. With the activation of SEEDS it was possible to integrate data that allow to know the pattern of resources consumption, in real time, identifying savings possibilities with the implementation of operational actions for the consumption of electric energy. By having data to define the quantification of electric power consumption, it was possible to establish indicators and goals related to the variables of sustainability based on a baseline of energy consumption. An example of the electricity consumption in a day at CIC, as registered in the SEEDS platform, is shown in Fig. 4.

2.2 Installation of the Electrical Energy Consumption Monitoring Network

The installed monitoring network had seven basic components, I. energy consumption meters, II. water consumption meters, III. analog transmission antennas, IV. systems for data acquisition, V. systems for information processing, VI. components for sending data and VII. Information display systems. The equipment that was installed in the entities seeks to innovate with the use of technological tools to facilitate decision-making in projects focused on saving resources and improving the quality of energy. The general architecture of the monitoring network is shown in Fig. 5. The first step consisted of the installation of the electricity and water meters in the general connections, in the cases that were necessary, transmitting and receiving antennas were enabled to send

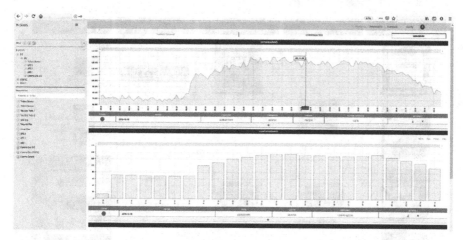

Fig. 4. Electricity consumption as registered in the SEEDS platform at CIC on 2018-12-18.

the information to the data acquisition system. These meters were then connected to the data acquisition system to enable the reception and sending of the electric and water consumption records; data is sent according to the type of connection available (ethernet, Wi-Fi or 3G). A screen in the local monitoring system was installed so that general users could monitor the consumption of electricity and water in real time.

2.3 Replacement of Infrastructure and Equipment

The installation of energy saving equipment in each of the IPN instances included several actions: replacement of high-energy consumption luminaires by low-energy consumption LED luminaires, replacement of high-energy consumption hand dryers with low-energy consumption hand dryers, replacement of obsolete and high-energy consumption air conditioning with low-energy consumption air conditioning system, installation of solar PV powered luminaries, among other actions. A summary of the actions carried out in each instance is given in Table 1. A view of some of the installed equipment is shown in Fig. 6.

2.4 Baseline of Electricity Consumption

The averaged electrical energy consumption (KWh) per day, per month and per year, at CIC, CIDETEC and ESCOM were obtained using data collected by the installed monitoring network and registered in the SEEDS platform. It should be mentioned that the data used correspond to a period of four months (November–December 2018 and January–February 2019). The results obtained are summarized in Table 2. As can be seen, the most power-hungry instance is CIC, this is mainly because this Centre host a Computing Site which is operational 24 h, the 365 days of the year.

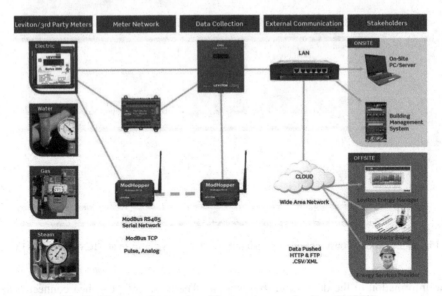

Fig. 5. Diagram of network architecture (source: Leviton, 2017 [2]).

Table 1. Summary of the replaced Equipment.

Instance	Replaced equipment	Quantity
CIC	Luminaire, hand dryers and air conditioning	2,048 LED luminaires 12 hand dryers 1 air conditioner
CIDETEC	Hand dryers, presence sensors, luminaires and smart bars	6 hand dryers 11 presence sensors 337 LED luminaires 30 smart bars
ESCOM	Solar LED luminaires, luminaires, photocells and time-curlers	441 PV luminaires 200 LED luminaires 50 photocells 50 timers

Fig. 6. Replacement of luminaries, PV luminaries and low consumption hand drier.

Table 2. Averaged, consumption.

Instance	Averaged daily consumption (KWh)	Averaged monthly consumption (KWh)	Averaged annual Consumption (KWh)
CIC	2,285	68,453	821,435
CIDETEC	276	8,279	99,348
ESCOM	1,383	41,341	496,094

3 Installation of Solar PV Electricity Generation Systems

In order to reduce the consumption of electric energy, and to reduce the carbon footprint, the company Greensun [3], carried out the design of the projects and performed the installation of three solar PV electricity generation systems, one in each of the instances considered (CIC, CIDETEC, ESCOM). Table 3 presents a summary of the Installed solar PV systems. Figures 7, 8, 9 show some views of the installed PV systems in each of the instances considered. The total power generation capacity considering the three FV systems is 126.72 KW, with a total of 352 PV panels and 7 inverters.

Table 3. Solar PV systems installed at CIC, CIDETEC and ESCOM.

Characteristic	CIC	CIDETEC	ESCOM
Generation power	66.96 KW	15.12 KW	44.64 KW
Number of PV panels, brand, power	186, Canadian Solar CS3U, 360 W	42, Canadian Solar CS3U, 360 W	124, Canadian Solar CS3U, 360 W
Number of inverters, brand, power	3, Fronius Symo, 22.7 KW	1, Fronius Symo, 15 KW	3, Fronius Symo, 22.7 KW
Daily average power generation	280.9 KWh	63.4 KWh	187.24 KWh
Annual power generation	102.52 MWh	23.14 MWh	68.34 MWh
Daily electricity consumption (SEEDS)	2,285 KWh	276 KWh	1,383 KWh
Percentage of demand covered	12.29%	22.97%	13.53%

4 Quantification of Savings

In this section the quantification of electricity savings, cost savings and reduction of carbon footprint are presented. These savings are due to the implementation of operational

Table 4. Quantification of carbon footprint reduction at CIC, CIDETEC and ESCOM.

Instance	Average monthly emissions before the implementation of savings measures (tCO2e)	Average monthly emissions after the implementation of savings measures (tCO2e)	Average monthly emissions reduction (tCO2e)	% Average monthly emissions reduction (tCO2e)
CIC	36.9	26.13	10.77	29.19
CIDETEC	4.44	1.86	2.58	58.11
ESCOM	20.78	15.82	4.96	23.87
TOTAL	62.12	43.81	18.31	37.06

Fig. 7. Solar FV system installed at CIC-IPN.

measures including PV electricity generation and technological replacement of energy-hungry equipment. These savings were calculated using data of electricity consumption corresponding to the months of November 2018, December 2018, January 2019 and February 2019. The quantifications of the electricity savings in each instance considered are shown in Table 4. The quantifications of the corresponding economic savings in each instance considered are shown in Table 5. Finally, the quantification of the reduction of the carbon footprint in each instance considered are shown in Table 6. Notice that in the case of the carbon footprint, values are obtained in tonnes of carbon dioxide equivalent (tCO2e) [4]. Also, it is necessary to specify that the carbon footprint and savings were calculated considering only the electricity consumption and electricity savings due to PV electricity generation and technology substitutions.

According to the data provided by the Energy Regulatory Commission (CER) of the Mexican Federal Public Administration as a regulatory body on energy matters and

Fig. 8. Solar FV system installed at CIDETEC-IPN.

Fig. 9. Solar FV system installed at ESCOM-IPN.

with the opinion of the Secretary of Environment and Natural Resources (SEMARNAT), established that the National Electric System Emission Factor for 2017 is 0.527 tonnes of CO2/MWh.

Hence, the calculation of the reduction in the number of tonnes of CO2 equivalent (tCO2e) is a direct function of the total electricity consumption of the IPN instances, specified in MegaWattsHora.

With the use of the monitoring network and through the SEEDS platform, the electricity consumption in MegaWatts/Month was obtained for the months of October, November and December 2018, as well as for the months of January, February and March of 2019, for the three instances considered (CIC, CIDETEC, ESCOM). In the months of April to December 2019, an average estimated consumption value of the previous months measured with the monitoring network was used and the savings obtained due to operational measures of technological substitution and energy generation were subtracted, this is:

$$CME = Average\ (CMA\_SMT) - AED\_LSAA - EGVPS \qquad (1)$$

where:
CME = Estimated Monthly Consumption
CMA_SMT = Previous Months consumption obtained through monitoring network
AED_LSAA = Estimated Savings LSAA Devices (Luminaires, Dryers, Air Conditioning)
EGVPS = Energy Generated Via Solar Panels

Table 5. Quantification of electricity savings at CIC, CIDETEC and ESCOM.

Instance	Average monthly consumption before the implementation of savings measures (KWh)	Average monthly consumption after the implementation of savings measures (KWh)	Average monthly savings in KWh	% Average monthly electricity savings
CIC	68,453	54,632.34	13,820.66	20.19
CIDETEC	8,279	3,551.76	4,727.24	57.1
ESCOM	41,341	34,177.92	7,163.08	17.33
TOTAL	118,073	92,362.02	25,710.98	31.54

Table 6. Quantification of economic savings at CIC, CIDETEC and ESCOM.

Instance	Average monthly cost for electricity consumption before the implementation of savings measures (MXN)	Average monthly cost for electricity consumption after the implementation of savings measures (MXN)	Average monthly economic savings in MXN	% Average monthly economic savings
CIC	68,453	54,632.34	13,820.66	20.19
CIDETEC	8,279	3,551.76	4,727.24	57.1
ESCOM	41,341	34,177.92	7,163.08	17.33
TOTAL	118,073	92,362.02	25,710.98	31.54

Table 6 shows the results obtained, which are also plotted in Fig. 10. The global savings are summarized in Table 7.

5 Conclusions

Derived from the analysis of the information collected by the installed monitoring network and using the SEEDS platform, it was possible to perform the quantification of the savings generated by the operational measures of technological substitution and the implementation of PV systems for the generation of electricity from a renewable energy source in three IPN units, reducing the environmental impact, the carbon footprint and also reducing the consumption and dependence of electricity generated by fossil fuels.

The quantifications made indicate an average monthly savings in consumption of 25,710.98 KWh, corresponding to 31.54% of the average monthly electricity consumption. In economic terms, this is equivalent to an average monthly savings for electricity consumption costs of $ 42,651.96 (MXN), equivalent to 35.45% of the average monthly

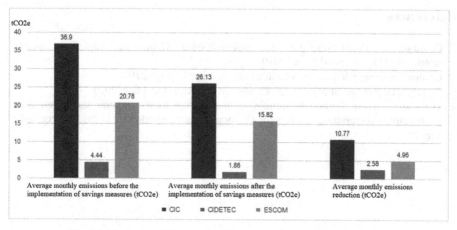

Fig. 10. Carbon footprint reduction at CIC, CIDETEC and ESCOM.

Table 7. Global savings at CIC, CIDETEC and ESCOM.

	Electricity consumption savings in KWh	Saving cost for electricity consumption in MXN	Reduction of emissions of tCO2
Overall monthly average savings	25,710.98	42,651.96	18.31
% Equivalent	31.54	35.45	37.06

total cost per electricity consumption in the three IPN instances. Finally, in terms of the reduction of the carbon footprint, expressed in the non-production of equivalent tonnes of CO2 (tCO2e), it corresponds to 18.31 tCO2e, which represent 37.06% of the total generation of tCO2e before the implementation of the measures of technological substitution and generation of electric energy from renewable sources.

The reduction in the consumption of electric energy, as well as the corresponding economic savings and reduction of equivalent CO2 emissions quantified so far, and whose measurement is maintained in the temporality specified in this work, gives the guideline to continue monitoring the information through the SEEDS platform installed in three IPN instances. It will be necessary to obtain the statistics to ratify that the operational measures of technological substitution and electricity generation provide substantial savings to IPN. If the trend of the figures obtained so far continues, then there will be enough information to recommend the route to improve the performance of other IPN instances by the gradual incorporation of technologies for sustainable development.

Acknowledgments. This work was supported by Fondo Sectorial CONACYT-SENER Sustentabilidad Energética, under project grant 264087.

References

1. Coordinación Politécnica para la Sustentabilidad Homepage, https://www.ipn.mx/sustentabilidad/. Accessed 1 Sept 2019
2. Leviton Homepage, https://www.leviton.com. Accessed 1 Sept 2019
3. Greensun Homepage, http://www.greensun.com.mx. Accessed 1 Sept 2019
4. The Carbon Trust: Carbon footprintin, online at https://www.carbontrust.com/resources/guides/carbon-footprinting-and-reporting/carbon-footprinting/#download-guide. Accessed 1 Sept 2019

Implementation of a Smart Microgrid in a Small Museum: The Silk House

Luís Guilherme Aguiar Figueiredo[1,3]([✉]) [iD], Wellington Maidana[1,2] [iD], and Vicente Leite[1,2] [iD]

[1] Instituto Politécnico de Bragança, Campus Santa Apolónia, Bragança, Portugal
guilhermeaguiar_f@hotmail.com, {maidana,avtl}@ipb.pt
[2] Research Center in Digitalization and Intelligent Robotics (CeDRI),
Bragança, Portugal
[3] Universidade Tecnológica Federal do Paraná, Cornélio Procópio, Paraná, Brazil

Abstract. Microgrids are an alternative approach for the supply of energy integrating decentralized power sources, electrical loads, energy storage, and management in a local grid. The system has the capability of power control and energy management using communications' network between all devices, and is known as smart microgrid. This paper presents the implementation of a smart microgrid in the Silk House, a museum dedicated to dissemination of science located in Bragança, Portugal. It was funded by the Foundation for Science and Technology of Portugal under the SilkHouse Project. The goal is to transform the House of Silk in a self-sustainable museum contributing to the dissemination of renewable sources and new technologies for future buildings in smart cities. This work presents the context and requirements for the microgrid and describes the implementation of the renewable sources (photovoltaic and pico-hydro) and the SMA Flexible Storage System based on Sunny Island and Sunny Home Manager. This work also presents and analysis the first operating results since the start of operation at the end of July 2019.

Keywords: Microgrids · Renewable sources · Energy management

1 Introduction

The worldwide need for more electricity results in a demand that grew at a rate of 2.9% in 2018, which is supplied by fossil fuels [1,2]. Despite this growth, the use of fossil fuels has been debated continuously, nowadays, for its consequences, such as 2% carbon emissions growth - the highest in seven years [1]. Environmental concerns related to these issues have been changing the behavior on the use of energy sources, which is increasingly adopting the use of renewable sources to generate electricity and supply the growing demand. Renewable sources lead to an increase in world power generation, with the growth of 14.5% [1].

The main primary sources of renewable energy, among the many available, are solar, wind, and hydro. The distributed generation of this energy brings environmental, technical, and economic benefits to the consumers and the distributions

© Springer Nature Switzerland AG 2020
S. Nesmachnow and L. Hernández Callejo (Eds.): ICSC-CITIES 2019, CCIS 1152, pp. 121–134, 2020.
https://doi.org/10.1007/978-3-030-38889-8_10

systems. Microgrids are a recent concept for the integration of renewable sources in the power grid.

A microgrid and the conventional distribution power system have basic differences [3]. The first has smaller generation capacity of the sources, the generated power is directly injected to the grid, and the sources are closer to the consumers. The concept of microgrid has several descriptions in the literature, but there is not a specific one adopted. In [3], a microgrid is essentially described as an active distribution network, because integrates distributed generation and different loads at the distribution voltage level. In [4] microgrid is described as an interconnected system of loads and a local generation that can operate independently of the power grid (off-grid) or is tied to it (on-grid). In short, microgrid is a distributed generation network, integrating renewable sources (or not), connected to loads (which are usually close to each other), with energy storage capacity, and with a management system (with higher or lower intelligence level), that can supply the electrical demand of a house, a building or a region. It may (or not) be connected to the conventional grid.

This paper presents the implementation of a smart microgrid in a small museum called Silk House. The microgrid integrates renewable sources, energy storage, and management system. It is connected to the main grid as an additional external source. The project aims to ensure the self-sustainability of the museum, in annual average terms. It will also be a showcase to spread to the society the use of local resources to produce renewable energy and the new technologies of microgrids for smart cities. The microgrid was installed, commissioned, tested, and is being monitored. The first results of its operation are shown and analyzed in this work.

2   Silk House

Silk House is part of the *Centro de Ciência Viva*, located in Bragança, in the north-eastern of Portugal. This place was used for dyeing silk in the 18th century and sometime later, during the 19th and 20th centuries was used as a mill. The Municipality of Bragança acquired the building in 1990 and restored it in 2006, maintaining the original constructive characteristics [5].

Nowadays, the place is a museum dedicated to the history of silk, with a permanent exhibit about it and to the dissemination of science, receiving about 11500 visitors per year. Exhibitions, lectures, and courses about several themes are frequent on-site.

The building is located in the historical center of the city, next to the Fervença river and conserves the historical architecture built of original stones. It has three levels, two galleries on the basement at river level, and a roof with ceramic tiles.

Before implementing the microgrid, the building's three-phase electrical system (400 V, 50 Hz) was powered by the mains, with a contracted power of 13.8 kW. The electrical loads are, basically, computers, monitors, multimedia projectors, heaters, air-conditioning system, a stereo system, and lighting. The regular operation of the museum is from Tuesday to Sunday, from 10 a.m. to 6 p.m.

It closes on Mondays, but some essential loads remain powered. The average daily consumption is 45 kWh in normal working days, and the annual average is about 16000 kWh [5].

3 Previous Microgrids Developed

The SilkHouse Project - Development of a smart microgrid based on renewable energy sources and a monitoring system for the House of Silk - is promoted by the Polytechnic Institute of Bragança (IPB), in cooperation with four other partners: Bragança Ciência Viva Center, Cávado e Ave Polytechnic Institute, Guarda Polytechnic Institute and the company JG Instalações Elétricas. The project is funded by the European Union through the Foundation for Science and Technology, supported by the Municipality of Bragança.

The SilkHouse project development started in 2017 with the first conceptual design [6]. The microgrid design took into account the analysis of two places of the building for the energy potential: the roof and the original galleries used by the former mill. They revealed viability for renewable energy generation using endogenous resources: solar irradiance and water, respectively. The roof is used to generate photovoltaic (PV) energy. The water and galleries are used to generate hydropower taking advantage of the proximity of a small dam already available in Fervença river [5]. Thus, the Silk House was provided with a smart microgrid by integrating both energy sources and energy storage in a microgrid with a management system. The renewable sources and storage system were size considering the annual energy consumption of the building [7].

The project uses SMA technology and is based on the Sunny Island inverters and Sunny Home Manager. Previous experience, with a small microgrid held in a laboratory of the School of Technology and Management of the IPB, demonstrated the feasibility and flexibility of this technology [8,9]. Based on these works and surveys aiming the application to the Silk House, it was designed the first schematic to the microgrid [6], as shown in Fig. 1. The following equipment composed the solution: three Sunny Island Inverters (SI), four Sunny Boy inverters (SB), one pico-hydro turbine, photovoltaic tiles, photovoltaic modules, battery bank, and an undefined control system [6].

The design was changed in a second phase. In fact, the use of PV tiles would be too expensive. On the other hand, tests achieved with 30 PV tiles (ZEP F10-U 9Wp) in the laboratory revealed the existence of shadow caused by the tiles themselves, in the morning and the afternoon [7]. Therefore, the project adopted high-efficiency PV modules instead of PV tiles.

Figure 2 presents the second microgrid design composed by: three Sunny Island inverters, five Sunny Boy inverters, one Sunny Home Manager 2.0, twenty four 2 V batteries blocks to form a 48 V battery bank, eighteen PV modules, a water wheel for electricity generation, a pico-hydro turbine, electrical board with protections, and breaking devices [7].

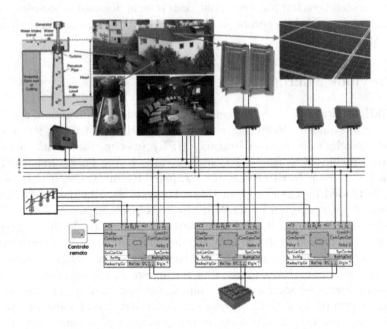

Fig. 1. First microgrid conceptual design [6].

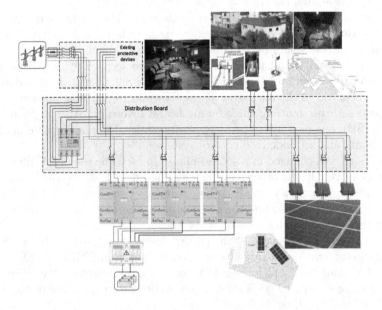

Fig. 2. Second microgrid conceptual design [7].

4   Microgrid Implemented

The microgrid implemented in the House of Silk has some specific requirements considered during the project development. The first one is that the museum is supposed to be self-sustainable. In other words, in annual average terms, the energy produced by the renewable sources must be equal to the energy consumed. Second, the electric grid must be an external energy source, but the energy injected into it must be zero. Hence, a third requirement is the energy storage in order to improve the self-consumption and self-sufficiency quotas [7,10]. Fourth, the generated energy from renewable sources - photovoltaic and pico-hydro - should use innovative solutions. Indeed, the pico-hydro embraces an innovative approach, which will use a PV inverter and a microinverter as the interface between turbines' generators and the microgrid [11,12]. Fifth, power management and monitoring system are required since this project is intended to be a permanent activity of the museum aiming the dissemination of the new technologies of microgrids for smart cities.

4.1   Silk House Microgrid

This section introduces the smart microgrid developed according to the above requirements. The microgrid integrates distributed generation (PV and pico-hydro), energy storage based on the battery bank, management, and monitoring system. It is three-phase (400 V, 50 Hz) microgrid to supply the House of Silk loads.

The smart microgrid is based on the SMA Flexible Storage System with battery-backup and increased of self-consumption [13]. It is composed by three Sunny Island 4.4M, three PV inverters Sunny Boy 1.5, one Sunny Home Manager 2.0, two SMA Energy Meter, three strings of six Panasonic's PV modules VBHN325SJ47, one 300 W horizontal water wheel to recover the historical heritage of the former mill, one low-head turbine (LH400 from PowerSpout), one PV microinverter, one PV inverter, a battery bank consisting of twenty four VRLA 2 V battery's blocks Sonnenschein's batteries A602/625 Solar, battery fuse, electrical panel, automatic transfer switch, and protections. Figure 3 presents a circuity overview of the smart microgrid implemented in the House of Silk and Fig. 4 shows the Silk House building with the PV modules installed and the microgrid devices. It is in full operation with the PV generation. By the time this work was written, the low-head pico-hydro system was being installed, and the water wheel was under construction.

The operation of the microgrid can be described as follows. The three-phase microgrid is the external electric grid whenever it is available. If the case of grid failure, the microgrid is established by the three Sunny Island (SI) 4.4M connected in a master-slave configuration. An automatic transfer switch is responsible by the external grid connection or disconnection [13]. The energy generated by the PV strings is injected into the microgrid, distributing the power by the three phases using three Sunny Boy 1.5.

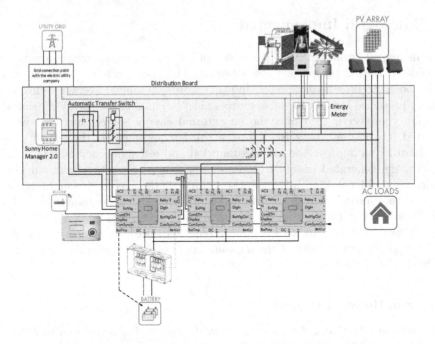

Fig. 3. Microgrid implemented in the Silk House.

Fig. 4. (a) Silk House, (b) Microgrid devices.

When the generation is higher than the consumption, the excess of energy is stored in the battery bank by the three bi-directional battery inverters, SI. These inverters use the batteries to control the power flow and, thus, to improve self-consumption [14]. The active power generated by the inverters connected to the PV strings is limited by frequency control [15], as better explained later. This happens whenever the generation is higher than consumption, the batteries are charged, and the energy fed into the external grid must be zero.

When the consumption is higher than the generation, the energy comes from the batteries and, if it is not enough, the remaining energy is purchased from the external grid to feed the loads. In case of grid failure, the microgrid is disconnected from the grid using the automatic transfer switch and starts working in stand-alone mode. In this operation mode, some hours of autonomy are available, but it strongly depends on the consumption, the generation, and the battery bank state of charge. In this case, some loads can be automatically disconnected.

4.2 Photovoltaic System

The photovoltaic system consists of three strings with six PV modules each and was installed on the roof with a slope of 12° and two shadowless areas. The first is oriented South and the second is oriented Southwest. Taking advantage of this, the PV strings were divided by these two roof surfaces to improve the distribution of PV generation throughout the day. One PV string is oriented South and the other two are oriented Southwest. In the morning, the Southern oriented string starts the generation before than the Southwestern oriented ones, allowing a higher production. In the afternoon, the Southwestern oriented strings will extend their generation longer. These orientations make possible to improve the distribution of photovoltaic generation throughout the day, adjusting it to the opening hours of the museum.

The modules chosen are from Panasonic, model VBHN325SJ47, series HIT with 19.7% efficiency [16]. The maximum power (P_{max}) is 325 W, and the maximum total to the system is 5.85 kW. Each string is connected to a SMA Sunny Boy 1.5-1 VL 40 (SB) PV inverter [17] which, in turn, is connected to one of three phases (L1, L2, L3). This inverter is compatible with the active output power control by the microgrid frequency control, as explained later.

4.3 Pico-Hydro System

The Silk House electric generation will be complemented, mainly in the winter periods, by two pico-hydro systems that are being installed. These systems are small-scale hydropower generation units up to 5 kW that converts the power of flowing water of a canal, river or stream in electricity [18]. These low power systems, but capable of producing energy 24 h a day, unlike what happened until a few years ago, it is possible to use permanent magnet synchronous generators, with variable speed, depending on the flow rate and head [19,20]. This happens because innovative results show that the energy produced can be harnessed using PV inverters, flexibly, and efficiently [19,20]. Furthermore, those generators and PV string inverters and micro-inverters are, nowadays, off-the-shelf and widely available components used in wind and photovoltaic applications.

The installation of the hydroelectric plant results from the proximity of the Silk House of the river Fervença, the existence of a small dam (less than 10 m) and the hydraulic infrastructure of the old mill, channels, and galleries, which has been conserved. On the one hand, the adopted solution preserves the building's architecture and, on the other, it recovers the building's historical heritage by installing a horizontal water wheel to produce energy in place of the former mill [7]. There are two galleries available. The first, at the upper level, was used to install the microgrid equipment. The other, where the mill was located, a 300 W horizontal water wheel and a 1.2 kW low-head turbine (LH400 from PowerSpout) are being installed. Two pipes were installed to capture water from the small dam and take it inside the gallery where the water wheel and turbine will be. The water is returned to the river 18 m downstream.

A PV microinverter from GWL Power [21] and a PV string inverter from Omnik, model Omniksol - 1.5k - TL2 [22], are used to connect the 300 W generator of the water wheel and the 1.2 kW generator of the low-head turbine to the microgrid, respectively. After extensive tests in the laboratory, the results show that the inverters presenting the best performance are not from SMA. Because of this, SMA Energy Meters must be used in order to account the energy produced by these renewable resources in microgrid energy management.

4.4 Microgrid Power Management

A smart system requires high-level control and a suitable communications' network. SMA technology has monitoring of the energy generated and also controls and regulates all the microgrid through a digital interface using the Internet portal Sunny Portal. The infrastructure should contain devices sharing the communications' network to turn the microgrid in a smart microgrid, being integrated into intelligent energy management.

SMA's devices have an integrated technology called Speedwire, which enables communication among each device used. It is a wired Ethernet communication for networks used in decentralized power generation, with a communication protocol optimized for PV systems [23]. The devices in this microgrid are connected to an Ethernet switch by UTP cables, which allows having Speedwire communication.

The Sunny Home Manager 2.0 (SHM) acts as a centralized energy manager in households with a PV system for self-consumption [24]. It receives data from other devices, as Sunny Boy and Sunny Island inverters and offers some functions which allow taking decisions about the microgrid.

The SHM carries out some important tasks [10], such as data collection of energy and power measured, energy monitoring via Sunny Portal presenting energy flows, energy management, dynamic limiting of the active power feed-in and support to self-consumption increase and its optimization.

The power management occurs when some decision of the microgrid is taken to control the generated energy. The SHM is capable of doing this and measuring the loads at the grid-connection point. This measure is presented in Sunny Portal, which also allows visualizing instantaneous data of the PV generation received via the integrated measuring device of the SB, the battery bank status connected to the SIs, and others SMA Flexible Storage System's devices connected to the local network.

An important parametrization of the microgrid is the limitation of active power supplied to the utility grid. This limit was set in 0 W (Zero Export), which means that the smart microgrid can not provide the generated energy to the utility grid and all the power should be stored or consumed by the microgrid loads (self-consumption system) [10].

When the generation is larger than the loads' consumption, efficient management is required of the microgrid power flow. The first step is to inject the excess power into the battery bank. If it is fully charged, the SI detects this situation and increases the frequency of the microgrid in order to limit the output power the SB inverters. The control strategy adopted by SMA called "frequency-dependent control of active power" to limit the power generated whenever it is excessive. The SI increases the frequency of the microgrid above the nominal value (50 Hz). The PV inverter must be compatible with this control. In this case, when they feel the frequency increase, they start to reduce the active output power out. If the frequency continues to increase, PV inverters further reduce its active power nearly to 0 W, as shown in Fig. 5. The SB inverters continue to monitor the frequency. When it decreases, they start increasing their active power linearly to the available value [25]. Figure 5 shows the active power control by frequency, and Table 1 shows an example of this frequency control.

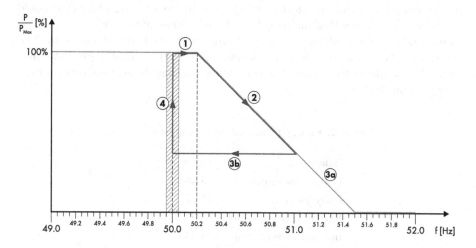

Fig. 5. Control of active power by frequency control [25].

Table 1. Example of the frequency values for the each positions in control of active power by frequency in Fig. 5.

Position	Stage	Frequency (Hz)
1	Normal operation	<50.2
2	Active power decreases linearly from maximum available power	>50.2
3a	Active power continues to decrease linearly up to 0 W	51.5 > Freq. > 50.2
3b	Frequency remains constant or returns to the nominal value PV inverter stops reducing active power	<51.5
4	Active power increases up to maximum available power	50.05

5   Analysis of Operation

This section presents the first results obtained immediately following the implementation and commissioning of the microgrid in the Silk House. Now, it is possible to see the microgrid operation by analyzing several data and graphics obtained via Sunny Portal. The smart microgrid with PV generation is in operation since the end of July. The operation with pico-hydro generation will be available during the next months, once it is being installed.

Figure 6 shows an energy balance, the temporal progress during the August 8th, 2019. The consumption graph shows when and from which sources the microgrid has been supplied with energy (photovoltaic, battery bank or utility grid). The generation graph shows when and how much energy was generated and how much is used for (direct consumption, battery charging, or greed feed-in).

On August 8th, 2019, the self-consumption rate was 100%, shown in Fig. 6, which means that all the energy generated was used on-site (for loads and battery-bank charging) and not fed into the utility grid as expected considering the requirements of this microgrid [26]. However, it should be noted that if the system allowed to feed into the utility grid, the self-consumption rate would be about 50–60% for this microgrid [7]. Direct consumption, which was 79%, corresponds to photovoltaic energy used directly in the loads. A minimum feed into the utility grid is inevitable and was 0.9 kWh feed-in. Table 2 presents some relevant data about the energy balance demonstrating the real operation of the microgrid on that day.

Table 2. Energy balance data of August 8th, 2019.

Balance	Energy (kWh)
Daily consumption	19.31
Daily yield	22.17
External energy supply	0.09
Internal power supply	19.22
Battery discharging	1.60
Battery charging	4.60
Direct consumption	17.62
Self-consumption	22.11

Figure 7 shows the production diagram of the three PV strings connected to the microgrid. It shows that the way they were installed, with different orientations, even though small, allows distributing better the energy generated throughout the day. It is worth mentioning this is important when the excess of power should be immediately consumed or stored, not supplied to the utility grid. The curves of SBs 2 and 3 show the PV generation prolongation between

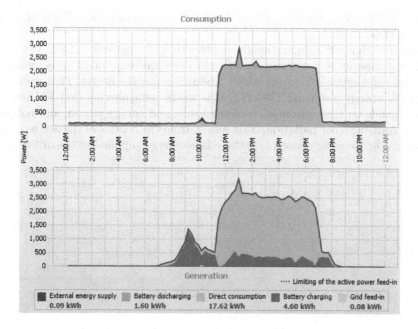

Fig. 6. Energy balance of August 8th, 2019.

6 p.m to 8 p.m., while the SB 1 generation is higher around 9 a.m. During the rest of the day, the generation was the same to the three SB, i.e., PV strings.

In addition, the operation of active power control adopted by the frequency of the microgrid is also evident, as the maximum power generation was not

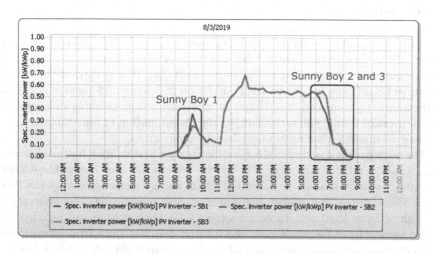

Fig. 7. Photovoltaic generation analysis of August 8th, 2019.

achieved. This was because of the fact that consumption was lower than an electric generation.

Figure 8 shows PV generation during the week of August 2–8, 2019. On Mondays, the museum is closed and therefore has less consumption. This is visible on the curve of August 5th, during which production was the lowest. That week, the three PV strings produced 255 kWh. It is worth remembering that PV generation depends on the consumption of the loads, and energy stored, and not just on the available solar radiation. This results from the control of the active power generated by frequency control, as there is no energy supplied to the utility grid.

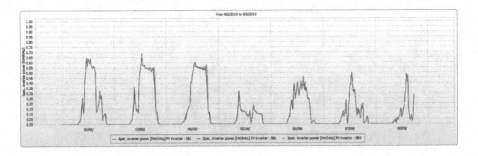

Fig. 8. Photovoltaic generation analysis during the week August 2–8, 2019.

An interesting data also available are the 174 kg avoided CO_2 during two weeks of operation. This information represents an avoided value of gas emissions into the atmosphere, given the operation of this building.

6   Conclusions

A smart microgrid was installed and commissioned in the Silk House. The Silk House of the Bragança Ciência Viva Center is a small museum dedicated to science dissemination located in Bragança, Portugal. It was carried out under the project SilkHouse funded by the Foundation of Science and Technology. This project aims to transform the House of Silk in a self-sustainable museum, in annual average terms, and contribute to the dissemination of renewable sources and new technologies for future buildings in smart cities.

The microgrid is based on SMA Flexible Storage System with battery-backup and increased self-consumption. The global system includes renewable energy generation, energy storage in a battery bank, energy consumption by the Silk House loads, power and energy management, and monitoring. The generation is obtained from local renewable resources: solar photovoltaic and pico-hydro, taking advantage of Fervença river and a small dam less than 10 m away. Pico-hydro systems are small-scale power plants (less than 5 kW). In the Silk House, they are a 300 W horizontal water wheel (to recover the historical heritage of a former mill) and a 1.2 kW low-head propeller turbine. These small plants are to be finished in the next months, and the rest of the microgrid was installed and commissioned and is in full operation since the end of July 2019. The microgrid is connected to the utility grid as an external source but not for power injection. This paper presented the microgrid implementation and analyzed the first results of its operation.

Acknowledgments. The authors would like to thank FCT (Foundation of Science and Technology, Portugal) for the financial support through the contract SAICT-POL/24376/2016 (POCI-01-0145-FEDER-024376); The Municipality of Bragança for its support; and the partnership between IPB and UTFPR (Federal University of Technology - Paraná) under the education and research program.

References

1. BP: BP Statistical Review of World Energy 2019. ed. 68. https://www.bp.com/content/dam/bp/business-sites/en/global/corporate/pdfs/energy-economics/statistical-review/bp-stats-review-2019-full-report.pdf. Accessed 26 Aug 2019
2. Fathima, H., Prabaharan, N., Palanisamy, K., Kalam, A., Mekhilef, S., Justo, J.J.: Hybrid-Renewable Energy Systems in Microgrids: Integration, Developments and Control. Woodhead Publishing (2018)
3. IRE Series: Microgrids and Active Distribution Networks. The Institution of Engineering and Technology (2009)
4. Farhangi, H.: Smart Microgrids: Lessons from Campus Microgrid Design and Implementation. CRC Press, Boca Raton (2016)
5. Maidana, W., et al.: Design of a self-sustainable system based on renewable energy sources for a small museum of science dissemination - the house of silk. III Congresso Ibero-Americano de Empreendedorismo, Energia, Ambiente e Tecnologia, 12–14 July 2017
6. Maidana, W.: Conceção de um Sistema Autossustentável para um Edifício de Divulgação de Ciência: A Casa da Seda. Master dissertation. Polytechnic Instute of Bragança, Bragança, Portugal (2017)
7. Silva, M., et al.: Designing innovative home energy systems for smart cities: the silk house project. Ibero-American Congress of Smart Cities (ICSC-cities2018), 26–27 September 2018
8. Leite, V., Ferreira, A., Batista, J., Couto, J.: Analysis of the operation of a microgrid with renewable distributed generation. III Congreso Iberoamericano sobre Microrredes con Generación Distribuida de Renovables, 1–2 December 2015
9. Leite, V., Ferreira, A., Batista, J.: On the implementation of a microgrid project with renewable distributed generation. I Congreso Iberoamericano sobre Microrredes con Generación Distribuida de Renovables, 23–24 September 2013
10. SMA: Planning Guidelines SMA Smart home - The System Solution for Greater Independence. http://files.sma.de/dl/1353/SI-HoMan-PL-en-51.pdf. Accessed 7 Aug 2019
11. Leite, V., Ferreira, Â., Couto, J., Batista, J.: Compatibility analysis of grid-connected pico-hydro systems using conventional photovoltaic inverters. In: 2016 18th European Conference on Power Electronics and Applications (EPE 2016 ECCE Europe), pp. 1–9. IEEE (2016)
12. Leite, V., Couto, J., Ferreira, Â., Batista, J.: A practical approach for grid-connected pico-hydro systems using conventional photovoltaic inverters. In: 2016 IEEE International Energy Conference (ENERGYCON), pp. 1–6. IEEE (2016)

13. SMA: Installation - Quick Reference Guide SMA Flxible Storage System with Battery Backup Function. ed. 3.3. https://files.sma.de/dl/20472/Ersatzstrom-IS-en-33W.pdf. Accessed 9 Aug 2019

14. SMA: Operating Manual - Sunny Island 3.0M/4.4M/6.0H/8.0H and Sunny Remote Control. ed. 3.3. https://files.sma.de/dl/17632/SI30M-44M-60H-80H-BE-en-33W.pdf. Accessed 9 Aug 2019

15. SMA: Planning Guidelines SMA Flexible storage system with battery-backup function. ed. 3.3. https://files.sma.de/dl/20472/Ersatzstrom-IS-en-33W.pdf. Accessed 7 Aug 2019

16. Panasonic: Photovoltaic module HIT VBHN330SJ47/VBHN325SJ47. https://eu-solar.panasonic.net/cps/rde/xbcr/solar_en/VBHN330_325SJ47_EN.pdf. Accessed 6 Aug 2019

17. SMA: Operating Manual - Sunny Boy 1.5/2.0/2.5. https://files.sma.de/dl/26198/SBxx-1VL-40-BE-en-13.pdf. Accessed 6 Aug 2019

18. Basar, M.F., Ahmad, A., Hasim, N., Sopian, K.: Introduction to the pico hydro power and the status of implementation in Malaysia. In: IEEE Student Conference on Research and Development, pp. 283–288 (2011)

19. Leite, V., Ferreira, A., Couto, J., Batista, J.: Compatibility analysis of grid-connected pico-hydro systems using conventional photovoltaic inverters. In: 18th European Conference on Power Electronics and Applications (EPE 2016 ECCE Europe), pp. 1–9 (2016)

20. Leite, V., Ferreira, A., Couto, J., Batista, J.: A practical approach for grid-connected pico-hydro systems using conventional photovoltaic inverters. In: IEEE International Energy Conference (ENERGYCON), pp. 1–6 (2016)

21. GWL: GridFree Micro AC Direct Inverter DC-AC 230V. https://www.ev-power.eu/docs/pdf/GWL/GWL-MAC230A-Spec.pdf. Accessed 25 Sept 2019

22. Omnik: User Manual - Installation/Operation Omniksol-1k-TL2, Omniksol-1.5k-TL2, Omniksol-2k-TL2, Omniksol-2.5k-TL2-S, Omniksol-3k-TL2-S. https://www.omnik-solar.com/ueditor/net/upload/file/20190122/UserManual_Omniksol-1k&1.5k&2k&2.5k&3k-TL2-S_EN_built-in%20card_V1.2_20190109.pdf. Accessed 25 Sept 2019

23. SMA: Technical Information - SMA Speedwire fieldbus. https://files.sma.de/dl/7680/Speedwire-TI-en-11.pdf. Accessed 7 Aug 2019

24. SMA: Operating Manual - Sunny Home Manager 2.0. ed 1.1. https://files.sma.de/dl/29870/HM-20-BE-en-11.pdf. Accessed 9 Aug 2019

25. SMA: Planning Guidelines - SMA Flexible Storage System with battery-backup function. ed 2.3. http://www.windandsun.co.uk/media/938530/sma-flexible-storage-system-with-battery-backup-planning-guidelines-v21.pdf. Accessed 9 Aug 2019

26. SMA: User Manual - Sunny Home Manager in Sunny Portal. https://files.sma.de/dl/15583/HoMan_Portal-BA-en-21.pdf. Accessed 8 Aug 2019

General Purpose I-V Tester Developed to Measure a Wide Range of Photovoltaic Systems

Bhishma Hernández-Martínez$^{(\boxtimes)}$ ⓘ, Sara Gallardo-Saavedra$^{(\boxtimes)}$ ⓘ,
Luís Hernández-Callejo$^{(\boxtimes)}$ ⓘ, Víctor Alonso-Gómez ⓘ,
and José Ignacio Morales-Aragonés ⓘ

University of Valladolid, Campus Universitario Duques de Soria, Soria, Spain
bhishma.hernandez@alumnos.uva.es, {sara.gallardo,
luis.hernandez.callejo,victor.alonso.gomez}@uva.es,
ziguratt@coit.es

Abstract. Within this paper it is proposed the design and development of an instrument with extended capabilities for photovoltaic (PV) devices I/V tracing. Commercial instruments that measure I-V curves from PV devices are suitable for a wide range of applications. However, more specific research and measurements require developing customized equipment. Custom-made development provides flexibility, and allows to implement tailored algorithms and to have accurate control of obtained information. Full control offers better flexibility for testing and extends the measurement possibilities. Designed I-V tester is capable to measure low voltages and manages very low resistance load to provide short circuit current values with voltages close to zero.

Keywords: I-V tracer · I-V tester · Measurement instrument · Arduino

1 Introduction

To date, cities have been consumers of resources (energy, water, food, etc.), but recently, under the concept of Smart City (SC), cities begin to be resource producers. In the case of energy, the SC is integrating renewable generation sources into existing infrastructure [1, 2].

In recent years, renewable systems are being integrated into electrical grids in a massive way. Specifically, renewable technology with the greatest boom and interest is PVs, and it is likely that the next few years will continue to be the most installed [3]. This trend is followed by cities, which will integrate PV technology into their spaces [4, 5].

But PV systems present problems. These problems can be caused in manufacturing, but most of them are caused by the operation of the system. As shown in [6], numerous problems occurred during the operation of the plant, so maintenance work is critical.

The detection of failures in PV systems is a very broad topic [7, 8]. For example, it is possible to use thermographic images for fault detection [9], or electroluminescence

© Springer Nature Switzerland AG 2020
S. Nesmachnow and L. Hernández Callejo (Eds.): ICSC-CITIES 2019, CCIS 1152, pp. 135–145, 2020.
https://doi.org/10.1007/978-3-030-38889-8_11

images [10]. However, the classic detection of loss of efficiency in a PV module is by means of instruments such as I-V plotter [11, 12].

Commercial I-V devices have some limitations, for example, they are not able to operate with very low currents and voltages. Therefore, these devices cannot make partial measurements within a module (set of cells embraced by a bypass diode) or a single cell. In this sense, this work presents the electronic architecture and software to have an I-V device capable of covering the lack of commercial devices.

2 Methodology and Resources

This section explains the current commercial I-V testers, their limitations found on field measurements and how developed I-V tester overcome those limitations. At the end of the chapter, it is presented some measurements that cannot be performed with commercial I-V tracers.

2.1 Commercial I-V Tester

PV testers allow field measurements of I-V Curve and determination of the main characteristic parameters both of a single module and of strings of modules for PV installations up to a maximum of 1500 V and 15 A. Some of them, manages an internal database of the modules, which can be updated at any time by the user and comparison between the measured data with the rated values allows immediately evaluating whether the string or the module fulfills the efficiency parameters declared by the manufacturer. I-V Curve can be adjusted also by decentralizing irradiation and temperature measurements by using an optional remote unit to measure reference temperature and irradiation. The display, once finishes the I-V Curve measurement, shows the measured parameters and compare it with the specifications declared by the PV module manufacturer.

2.2 Commercial I-V Tester. Specifications

Table 1 represents some of the main useful parameters measured by PV testers. The majority of PV modules could be analyzed accordingly.

Information provided by PV tester corresponds with raw information. Information measured is used to be analyzed to obtain further conclusions on PV research. Figure 1 PV module measured with PV tester Fig. 1 represents information obtained from the standard PV module measured on a field installation. Full I-V curve is shown, and short circuit current (Isc), open circuit voltage (Voc) and maximum power (Pmax) can be inferred.

2.3 Commercial I-V Tester. Limitations

PV modules are composed of different cell string layout. Different cells configurations provide electrical characteristics that the PV modules datasheet specify.

Detailed measurements of different systems and cell configurations are needed to understand some PV module failures. In this situation is when instrument limitation appears. Usually, a minimum input voltage of 15 V is required, and this value, limits

Table 1. Typical parameters of PV modules tester.

Symbol	Description	Range	Resolution
Pmax	Maximum nominal power of a module	50–4800 W	1 W
Voc	Open circuit voltage	15–99.99 V	0.01 V
		100–320.0 V	0.1 V
Vmpp	Voltage on point of maximum power	15–99.99 V	0.01 V
		100–320.0 V	0.1 V
Isc	Short circuit current	0.5–15 A	0.01 A
Impp	Current on point of maximum power	0.5–15 A	0.01 A

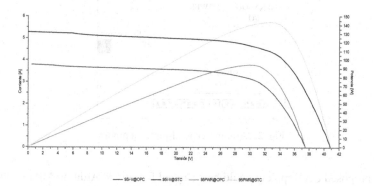

Fig. 1. PV module measured with PV tester.

measurements to full PV module. Therefore, the instrument does not provide capability to measure one PV string independently, which usually presents a voltage under this minimum value.

In some situations, is important to increase the level of detail and measure cell by cell. This is the most restrictive situation. PV cell electrical specifications are around 10 A and 0.6 V. Hence, the measuring instrument should be compliant with very restrictive electrical requirements. There are no instruments that could cover module measurements, string measurements and cell measurements at the same time.

Another important limitation is the I-V tester specifications. In most situations, algorithms used to measure and process measurements are not public. It becomes a limitation when an investigator needs to understand testing process from end-to-end and needs to have a full understanding of results obtained.

2.4 General Purpose I-V Tester

In order to overcome measurement limitations and to continue with researching and results, it was decided to develop a customized I-V tester to extend measurement needs. The instrument was developed based on Arduino platform.

Using open hardware and open software platforms, provide us well-documented information to grow the new functionality that was needed. It was decided to design a new layer for Arduino M0 motherboard. Arduino PCB provides a connector to be used as link between boards which parameters are standard. Common connectivity provides needed functionality and a simple method for scale designs.

Figure 2 presents the connectivity that most of Arduino devices have as general-purpose connectivity provided for user applications. Connectors are placed to ensure Pokayoke usability in order to avoid mistakes once the user-created layer (or skin) is placed.

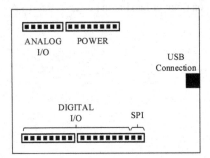

Fig. 2. Arduino general-purpose pinout.

The proposed development could be designed for simple Arduino M0 motherboard and used in other motherboards with more peripherals like Ethernet connectivity, SD memory card or Bluetooth.

Figures 3 and 4 show two motherboard that use same connector with same functionality but, providing different hardware solution. Different blocks represented show

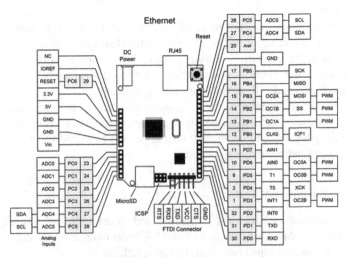

Fig. 3. Arduino ethernet.

the functionality available on each accessible pin: Ground connection (GND), analog to digital conversion (ADCx), digital pins and their functions (Pxyy, x = port name, yy = port number, PWM, Serial, SPI and I2C digital communications, etc.).

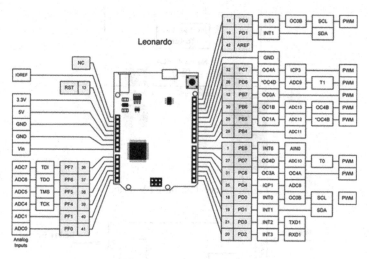

Fig. 4. Arduino leonardo.

If needed, the compatibility provided for the same platform, simplify changing the motherboard from one to other with different specifications.

2.5 General Purpose I-V Tester. Specifications

Numatia is the code name used for the general purpose I-V tester developed. Before design, the instrument is very important to define the characteristics and limitations that it should meet. In Numantia's case, two different inputs were defined.

First input used to measure high power elements up to 600 W (60 V@10 A). It is a useful input to characterize PV modules or strings that could be on those PV modules. It covers a big dynamic voltage range from 0 V to 60 V ensuring sensibility between measurements below 60 mV.

The second input is defined for low voltage and high current cells up to 10 W (1 V@10 A). This input needs to ensure a low resistance to ensure the capability to measure Isc with accuracy. To measure cells it should ensure a low resistance on fill measurement system due to a low voltage provided by standalone PV cells. The instrument provides by design on full measurement path the resistance lower than 5 mΩ.

Measure information is sent to the laptop through USB connection provided by Arduino that can manage ADC and DAC that system needs to configure to provide different measurements. Figure 5 represents topology that measurement system has.

The procedure used to measure I-V curve is based on variable resistor obtained configuring the MOSFET gate voltage. It was selected a low channel resistor to ensure reducing loses due to measurement system itself. Figure 6 represents the simplified block diagram of the custom I-V tracer.

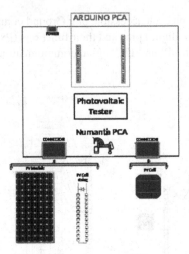

Fig. 5. General purpose PV tester.

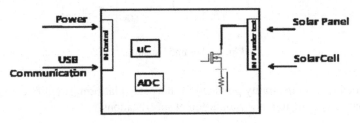

Fig. 6. General purpose PV tester block diagram.

2.6 General Purpose I-V Tester. Software and Hardware Configuration

Hardware devices defined to be involved on measurement system are critical. Instrument performance will depend on the quality and specifications of each component.

By definition, the MOSFET channel resistance is a maximum of 1.9 mΩ. The shunt resistor selected is different for both systems. To measure high power PV devices is used a 200 mΩ shunt resistor. However, to measure PV cells, it was needed to use 2 mΩ shunt resistor. Thanks to using different shunt resistors for different measurements it is obtained the capability to measure wide range of PV systems using same device and procedure.

Code is the second important part of the design. Arduino's open-source provides us the capability to do fast developments and test design instrument performance. In the specific case of I-V tracer is important to include in the code a few different variables in order to calibrate full system. We have obtained positive results using one constant to adjust the gain that electronics provide and second variable to remove offset. Using both constants defined at the beginning of the microcontroller firmware, instrument provides a high accuracy value.

All measurements are radiometric, it means that are linearly dependents on the power used to supply instrument. Power provided by USB is very stable, but there is uncertainty around exact value. The system could use USB batteries that could have voltage drift during full measurement procedure. To overcome this limitation, we define a double voltage cross-check. We measure power supply using Arduino and the voltage reference it has. The ADC in the instrument has one channel used to measure their own voltage as well. Both voltages are compared and use to adjust measures.

Figure 7 represents graphically how to adjust measure value to obtain better approach to real measures removing undesired effect from own measurement process.

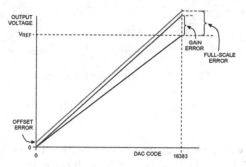

Fig. 7. Gain and offset.

Figures 8 and 9 presents the hardware-implemented for developed I-V tester and the user interface design to facilitate measurements and user interaction on testing procedure.

Fig. 8. Numantia PCA photo.

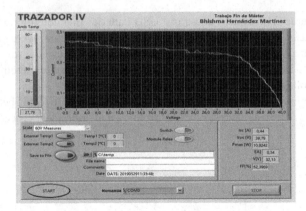

Fig. 9. User interface for I-V tester.

3 Results

Field measurements were performing on a monocrystalline PV module which specifications are P = 175 W, Voc = 44.35 V, Isc = 5.35 A. It is a monocrystalline PV module, it composes by 3 different strings with 24 PV cells each.

The main results obtained are summarized in Table 2. The differences in values obtained with both instruments come due to different irradiation values registered during both measurements.

Table 2. PV module field measurement using commercial I-V tester and developed I-V tester

	Voc[V]	Isc[A]	Pmax[W]	Irradiation[W/m^2]
Develop I-V tester	42.19	4.25	63.2	739
Commercial I-V tester	37.91	4.2	59.84	718

Figures 10 and 11 present the field failure PV failure measurement result. It is seen reviewing detail I-V curves a failure in some string. The shape obtained on both I-V measurements demonstrates good performance of developing I-V tracer has to compare with commercial calibrate instrument. Similar peaks and valleys are measured providing similar figures.

To improve PV module performance is needed to fully understand behavior that PV module is providing and their failure modes. Investigations will prove improvements and weaknesses that will be implemented in future manufacturing procedures.

By means of the developed instrument, we obtained the different string measurements that are present in Figs. 12, 13 and 14. Is not possible to present string measurements to be compared due to limitation that commercial instrument has. Using those measurements, there is new information from field that could use on current investigations.

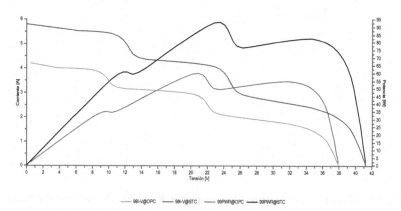

Fig. 10. Failure PV module measured with PV tester.

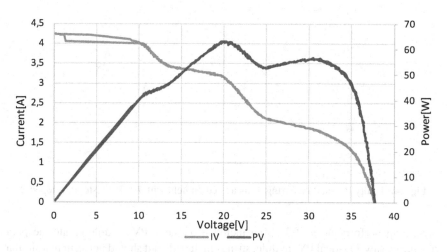

Fig. 11. Faulty PV module measured on field with I-V PV tester developed.

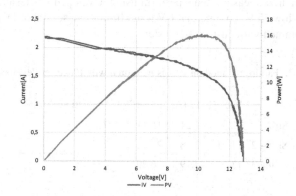

Fig. 12. Faulty PV module (string 1) measured on field with I-V PV tester developed

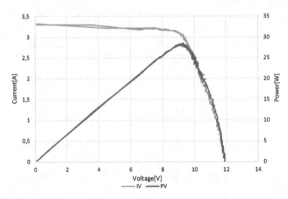

Fig. 13. Faulty PV module (string 2) measured on field with I-V PV tester developed

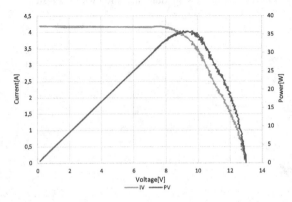

Fig. 14. Faulty PV module (string 3) measured on field with I-V PV tester developed

Different performances of 3 string included on same PV module create the poor performance saw. On ideal PV module, strings included on it should perform in a similar way. Represent values obtain on 3 different string and the big variation they have.

Table 3 summarize measurements perform using developed I-V tester. Due to open circuit voltage below 15 V (commercial I-V tester limitation, see Table 1), the table only reflects result obtained with custom I-V tester.

Table 3. Failure PV module strings measured with PV tester developed.

	Voc[V]	Isc[A]	Pmax[W]	Irradiation[W/m²]
String 1	12.9	2.21	16.11	718
String 2	11.91	3.28	28.14	723
String 3	13.5	4.19	36.20	724

4 Conclusions

The new custom instrument developed helps the research group to go further on field PV module failure analysis and to obtain new values for future studies.

Minimum voltage limits from commercial instruments are overcome, and brig new capability on field measurements to analyze PV panels, PV string and PV cells. Having information from all components represents the advantage of handling full functionality from all components.

It is valued very positively the flexibility provided by a tailored instrument in terms of the capability to modify algorithms and hardware for investigation requirements. To have full control over instrument functions and specifications facilitates adapting test procedures to different working conditions and enlarge the usability that it has.

Acknowledgments. The authors thank the CYTED Thematic Network "INTELLIGENT CITIES FULLY INTEGRAL, EFFICIENT AND SUSTAINABLE (CITIES)" n° 518RT0558. In addition, the work has been possible thanks to the "DOCTOR-PV" project Ref.: RTC-2017-6712-3, which has been funded by the "Ministry of Industry, Economy and Competitiveness, State R + D + i Program Oriented to the Challenges of the Society (Collaboration Challenges)".

References

1. Brenna, M., et al.: Challenges in energy systems for the smart-cities of the future. In: 2012 IEEE International Energy Conference and Exhibition (ENERGYCON), Florence (Italy), 9–12 September 2012 (2012)
2. Al-Nory, M.T.: Optimal decision guidance for the electricity supply chain integration with renewable energy: aligning smart cities research with sustainable development goals. IEEE Access **7**(May), 74996–75006 (2019)
3. Hernández-Callejo, L., Gallardo-Saavedra, S., Alonso-Gómez, V.: A review of photovoltaic systems: design, operation and maintenance. Sol. Energy **188**(August), 426–440 (2019)
4. Olowu, T.O., Sundararajan, A., Moghaddami, M., Sarwat, A.I.: Future challenges and mitigation methods for high photovoltaic penetration: a survey. Energies **11**(7), 1782–1814 (2018)
5. Gercek, C., Reinders, A.: Smart appliances for efficient integration of solar energy: a dutch case study of a residential smart grid pilot. Appl. Sci. **9**(3), 581–595 (2019)
6. Gallardo-Saavedra, S., Hernández-Callejo, L., Duque-Pérez, O.: Quantitative failure rates and modes analysis in photovoltaic plants. Energy **183**(September), 825–836 (2019)
7. Ashwini, P., Geethanjali, P.: Parameter estimation for photovoltaic system under normal and partial shading conditions: a survey. Renew. Sustain. Energy Rev. **84**(March), 1–11 (2018)
8. Mellit, A., Tina, G.M., Kalogirou, S.A.: A survey. Renew. Sustain. Energy Rev. **91**(August), 1–17 (2018)
9. Gallardo-Saavedra, S., Hernández-Callejo, L., Duque-Pérez, O.: Technological review of the instrumentation used in aerial thermographic inspection of photovoltaic plants. Renew. Sustain. Energy Rev. **93**(October), 566–579 (2018)
10. Deitsch, S., et al.: Automatic classification of defective photovoltaic module cells in electroluminescence images. Sol. Energy **185**(June), 445–468 (2019)
11. Szabo, R., Gontean, A.: Photovoltaic cell and module I-V characteristic approximation using Bézier curves. Appl. Sci. **8**(5), 655–678 (2018)

Short Term Load Forecasting of Industrial Electricity Using Machine Learning

Rodrigo Porteiro[1]([☒]), Sergio Nesmachnow[2]([☒]), and Luis Hernández-Callejo[3]([☒])

[1] UTE, Montevideo, Uruguay
rporteiro@ute.com.uy
[2] Universidad de la República, Montevideo, Uruguay
sergion@fing.edu.uy
[3] Universidad de Valladolid, Valladolid, Spain
luis.hernandez.callejo@uva.es

Abstract. Forecasting the day-ahead electricity load is beneficial for both suppliers and consumers. The reduction of electricity waste and the rational dispatch of electric generator units can be significantly improved with accurate load forecasts. This article is focused on studying and developing computational intelligence techniques for electricity load forecasting. Several models are developed to forecast the electricity load of the next hour using real data from an industrial pole in Spain. Feature selection and feature extraction are performed to reduce overfitting and therefore achieve better models, reducing the training time of the developed methods. The best of the implemented models is optimized using grid search strategies on hyperparameter space. Then, twenty four different instances of the optimal model are trained to forecast the next twenty four hours. Considering the computational complexity of the applied techniques, they are developed and evaluated on the computational platform of the National Supercomputing Center (Cluster-UY), Uruguay. Standard performance metrics are applied to evaluate the proposed models. The main results indicate that the best model based on ExtraTreesRegressor obtained has a mean absolute percentage error of 2.55% on day ahead hourly forecast which is a promising result.

1 Introduction

Decision making in the energy sector was historically supported by information that allows predicting, with certain degree of uncertainty, the variables that affect these decisions [8,22]. Much of the useful information is related to natural variables (e.g., temperature, wind speed, humidity). Other information is related to the energy consumption profile of users. In recent years, the sources of energy generation have diversified in the world. Many renewable sources that are directly related to natural variables have been incorporated [16].

All of aforementioned issues implies that for making decisions is necessary to take into account a large number of stochastic variables, to ensure that they are feasible/optimal from the economic point of view. The increase in complexity

© Springer Nature Switzerland AG 2020
S. Nesmachnow and L. Hernández Callejo (Eds.): ICSC-CITIES 2019, CCIS 1152, pp. 146–161, 2020.
https://doi.org/10.1007/978-3-030-38889-8_12

associated with the number of variables to be considered is mitigated by two factors. On the one hand, the sources of data on the variables have multiplied, since many technological components of measurement have emerged in all disciplines and the hardware infrastructure that supports these components has developed strongly. On the other hand, multiple new uses for energy have emerged.

The new reality presents the challenge of developing new tools that allow taking advantage of available data as much as possible. Classic statistical models that were always useful for making predictions have clear limitations in this new context. Computational intelligence algorithms have shown in recent years to perform excellently for forecasting in different areas [11,13,15]. These methods are able to learn the most relevant features of the data to be taken into account in order to provide a precise forecast, thus providing excellent results by excluding information of little relevance and considering the most relevant one.

In this line of work, this article presents the application of several prediction algorithms based on computational intelligence to forecast the electricity demand of an industrial pole for the next hour. The modeled scenario is based on historical demand data of an industrial pole in Spain from 2014 to 2017. From the study and comparison of the results of the algorithms developed for the next hour, a model is constructed to forecast the next 24 h. This model is based on optimizing the algorithm that presented the best results for the one hour forecast and extending it to 24 h forecast. The major contributions of this research are: (i) the evaluation and comparison of computational intelligence models applied to forecasting the demand of an industrial pole in Spain, and (ii) the optimization of the model using the infrastructure of the National Supercomputing Center, in Uruguay.

The article is organized as follows. Section 2 presents the formulation of the day ahead forecasting problem and a review of related works. Section 3 describes the proposed approach to solve the problem proposed. Section 4 presents Experimental Analysis of the problem. In Sect. 4.5 analysis of the best method and extension to 24 h load forecast is presented. Finally, Sect. 5 formulates the main conclusions and lines for future work.

2   Load Forecasting

This section introduces the load forecasting problem, describes forecasting techniques, and reviews related works.

2.1   General Considerations

The load forecasting problem is usually approached applying mathematical methods using historical data to predict the demand of electric power. In general, there is no method that can be used in all types of load forecasting. Thus, an appropriate method must be found for each load profile. Using historical data of a particular load profile is common in practice to determine the most effective algorithm. Electric load forecasting can be classified by time horizon to forecast:

(i) ultra short-term load forecasting: up to a few minutes ahead; (ii) short-term load forecasting: up to few days ahead; (iii) medium-term load forecasting: up to few month ahead; and long-term load forecasting: years ahead. Different techniques are applied when considering each time horizon. This work focuses in short-term load forecasting using historical data.

The energy management and operation of grids becomes highly difficult and uncertain, particularly when new technologies were incorporated. The power demand of end customers is versatile and is changing on hourly, daily, weekly, and seasonally basis. Hence, there is a real need of developing a model for precise and accurate forecasting at different time horizons, depending on the management goals. Day ahead hourly power load prediction is considered a short term forecasting problem, and it is very important to develop very precise models for solving this particular problem.

This work focuses on industrial power consumption. Residential (domestic) power profiles are usually very variable, mainly dependent on the time of the day and the day of the week, but it also dependent on occasional vacations and other particular factors. On the other hand, industrial users power profile tends to be more stable due to the needs of the industrial process itself.

There are two classes of forecasting models for predicting power profile: statistical and physical models. The main purpose of both classes of models is to predict the power profile at a future time frame. Statistical models can be built for time series analysis. Computationally, statistical models are less complex than physical models and are suitable for short term prediction. Physical models are based on differential equations for relating the dynamics of the environment and generally are applied for long term forecasting. In the present work, statistical models are selected for short term forecasting due to their very good prediction accuracy and lower complexity.

2.2 Problem Formulation and Strategies

Relation Between One Hour and 24 Hour Forecasting. The main goal of the study reported in this article is to apply computational intelligence methods to develop a model for electricity load 24 h ahead forecasting. When historical data are available with hourly frequency is natural to develop a model that predicts next hour. From that model, a multi-step time forecasting model can be constructed, in this case 24 steps in the future.

Four strategies are typically applied for multi-step forecasting starting from a one-step model:

- *Direct strategies* develop a different model for each time step to be predicted. Assuming past observations of the variable to be predicted are used, this strategy implies, in case of 24 steps, developing 24 models with the structure defined in Eq. 1, where $pred_t$ is the prediction of time t value and obs_t is the observed value at time t.

$$pred_{(t+1)} = model_1(obs_t, obs_{(t-1)}, ..., obs_{(t-n)})$$

$$pred_{(t+2)} = model_2(obs_t, obs_{(t-1)}, ..., obs_{(t-n)}) \tag{1}$$

$$...$$

$$pred_{(t+24)} = model_{24}(obs_t, obs_{(t-1)}, ..., obs_{(t-n)})$$

Unfortunately, a direct strategy implies developing a model for each time step to be predicted and consequently is very expensive computationally. In addition, temporary dependencies are not explicitly preserved between consecutive time steps.

– *Recursive strategies* apply a one-step model (recursively), multiple times. The predictions for previous time steps are used as input for making a prediction on the following time step. The structure to develop for a recursive strategy is presented in Eq. 2.

$$pred_{(t+1)} = model_1(obs_t, obs_{(t-1)}, ..., obs_{(t-n)})$$

$$pred_{(t+2)} = model_1(pred_{(t+1)}, obs_t, obs_{(t-1)}, ..., obs_{(t-n+1)}) \tag{2}$$

$$...$$

$$pred_{(t+24)} = model_1(pred_{(t+23)}, pred_{(t+22)}, ..., pred_{(t+1)}, obs_{(t-n+23)})$$

In this strategy predictions are used instead of observations. A single model is trained, but the recursive structure allows prediction errors to accumulate and the performance of the model can quickly degrade as the time horizon increases.

– *Hybrid strategies* combine the previously described to get benefits form both methods. A separate model is constructed for each time step to be predicted. Each model may use the predictions made by models at prior time steps as input values. For example, using all known prediction, a hybrid strategy produces the structure in Eq. 3.

$$pred_{(t+1)} = model_1(obs_t, obs_{(t-1)}, ..., obs_{(t-n)})$$

$$pred_{(t+2)} = model_1(pred_{(t+1)}, obs_t, ..., obs_{(t-n)}) \tag{3}$$

$$...$$

$$pred_{(t+24)} = model_1(pred_{(t+23)}, pred_{(t+22)}, ..., obs_t, ..., obs(t-n))$$

– *Multiple output strategies* develop a model that has as output all time steps to be predicted (in this case 24). Multiple output models are more complex as they can learn the dependence structure between inputs and outputs as well as between outputs. For this reason, they are slower to train and require more data to avoid overfitting. Equation 4 shows the corresponding structure.

$$pred_{(t+1,...,t+24)} = model_1(obs(t), obs(t-1), ..., obs(t-n))$$ (4)

In this work, hybrid strategies are applied for solving the forecasting problem.

One Hour Forecasting Model Training. Section 2.3 reviews different approaches and methods for short term load forecasting. This work explores the use of machine learning techniques, mainly those based on model ensembles. Feature selection is commonly applied in this kind of problems due to several reasons. Simpler models are easier to interpret, and have shorter training times. Also, the size of the model using less features is smaller, mitigating the *curse of dimensionality* [3]. But the main reason to apply feature selection is to reduce overfitting, enhancing generalization of the model to unseen data.

Once established the strategy to extend the next hour forecasting models to twenty four hours model, the main issue is to obtain the best possible model for the next hour. With this purpose, standard steps are taken: (i) data gathering, (ii) data preparation, (iii) choosing a model, (iv) training, (v) evaluation, (vi) parameter tuning, and (vii) testing. Each of these steps is described in detail in Sect. 3.

Complete Model. After obtaining a one hour model with optimized parameters, it is trained for the next hour taking all steps mentioned. Thus, 24 h different instances of this model are trained, one for each of the next 24 h. Then, the hybrid strategy described in Eq. 3 is applied to build a 24 h forecasting model. The complete model is evaluated on testing data and results are reported.

2.3   Related Works

Several methods support electricity demand forecasting, applying short, medium and long-term predictions. These methods are classified in statistical models and machine learning models. This work focuses on short-term load forecasting using machine learning.

Most used forecasting techniques include auto regressive models (AR), moving average models (MA), auto regressive moving average models (ARMA) and auto regressive integrated moving average (ARIMA) models [24]. These kind of models are easy to implement. ARIMA models for short term load forecasting were initially proposed by Hagan and Behr [12]. Taylor and McSharry [26] compared different ARIMA implementations using load data from multiple countries. Linear regression technique was described by Dudek [10]. However, linear models are inadequate to represent the non-linear behavior of electricity load series and fail to predict the accurate future demand values. Thus, their forecasting accuracy tends to be poor.

Several studies have been conducted on short-term load forecasting using non-linear models. For example, Do et al. [9] described a model for predicting hourly electricity demand considering temperature, industrial production levels, daylight hours, day of the week, and month of the year to forecast electricity consumption. Results suggested that consumption is better modeled considering each hour separately. In our work, this strategy is developed and applied. Son and Kim [25] proposed a method based on support vector regression preceded by feature selection for the short-term forecasting of electricity demand for the residential sector. For feature selection, twenty influential variables were considered and the quality of the model improved substantially.

Peak load estimation is also crucial to determine future demand, in order to assist future investment decisions [21]. In this article, the decision to consider ensemble models was taken based in the work presented by Burger and Moura [5], who applied a gated ensemble learning method for short-term electricity demand forecasting and showed that the combination of multiple models yielded better results than the use of a single model. Silva [23] presented a complex feature engineering to build gradient boosted decision trees and linear regression models for wind forecasting; in our work several similar ideas were developed for demand forecasting. De Felice et al. [7] applied several separate models for each hourly period. Each of those models measure variations in electricity demand based on multiple variables.

The analysis of the related works allowed to conclude that two main issues impact on the forecasting capabilities and the results quality: the model itself and other preparation and pre-processing techniques. Several works applied techniques like data normalization, filtering of outliers, clustering of data or decomposition by transformations [1, 2, 6, 14] in order to improve the results. In our research, several data preparation techniques are applied for building a robust approach for short term energy utilization forecasting. Next section describes the proposed approach.

3 The Proposed Approach for Day Ahead Industrial Load Forecasting

This section describes the proposed approach to solve the day-ahead electricity load forecasting for an industrial pole in Spain, applying the strategies described in Sect. 2.2.

3.1 General Approach

Data Description, Data Preparation, and Metrics. The analysis reported in this article considers historical hourly energy consumption data from an industrial pole in Spain. This data was collected between January 2014 and December 2017. The dataset studied in the research is formed by industrial energy consumption measurements. Each measurement is composed of:

- *Year* (integer), representing the year on which the measure was taken.
- *Month* (integer), indicating the month on which the measure was taken.
- *Day* (integer), indicating the day on which the measure was taken.
- *Hour* (integer), indicating the hour on which the measure was taken.
- *Dayofweek* (integer), indicating the day on which the measure was taken.
- *Workingday* (boolean), indicating whether the measure was taking in a working day or not.
- *Useful* (boolean), indicating whether the measure is valid.
- *Demand* (float), indicating the real power measured.

The data preparation consists in replacing useless measures or outliers using information from neighboring hours. A few useless measures and outliers were found (less than 0.0001%), and none of this measueres corresponded to consecutive hours. Thus, useless measures were replaced with the average measure of the previous and next hour. Outliers were replaced by the value of the mean of the measures plus 3 standard deviations. A measure is considered an outlier when its signed number of standard deviations by which is above the mean value of what is being measured is greater than 3. Feature standardization was applied to avoid scale problems. Finally, from the dataset, new features were generated associated with past demand measures to train the models. In particular, the last 48 measures were considered for each record to capture at least two days of consumption pattern directly in the features.

Several visualization analysis were performed to gain an intuitive insight of the information contained in each feature. The most relevant fact confirmed in this preliminary analysis was the daily periodicity of the demand value. The correlation diagram shown in Fig. 1 presents the high correlation between actual demand and the demand of the same hour of two days before. Data preprocessing was performed using pandas library [18]. The dataset from 2014 to 2017 was extended to include all lag features of the last 24 past hours. The training set included all data from 2014 to 2016, and the testing set included data from 2017. A linear regression model M_{sim} was trained using the sklearn toolkit [20], configured with default parameters as benchmark model. New training and test datasets were produced keeping only the relevant features, according to the analysis performed to determine the relative importance of each feature.

Three standard metrics were used for evaluation: Mean absolute percentage error (*MAPE*, Eq. 5), root mean square error (*RMSE*, Eq. 6) and mean absolute error (*MAE*, Eq. 7); $real_i$ represents the measured value for $t = i$, $pred_i$ represents the predicted value and n represents the predicted horizon length.

$$MAPE = 100 \times \frac{\sum_{i=1}^{n} \left| \frac{real_i - pred_i}{real_i} \right|}{n} \tag{5}$$

$$RMSE = \sqrt{\frac{\sum_{i=1}^{n} \left(real_i - pred_i\right)^2}{n}} \tag{6}$$

$$MAE = \frac{\sum_{i=1}^{n} |real_i - pred_i|}{n} \tag{7}$$

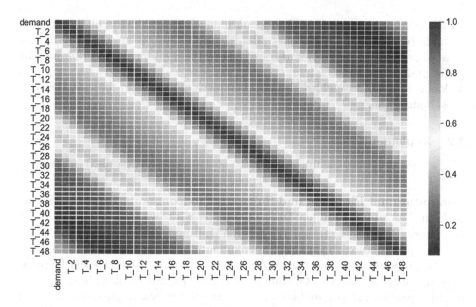

Fig. 1. Correlation diagram between actual demand and 48 last demand measures

Training One Hour Ahead Forecasting Models. Once all data was prepared for model training, a four-step procedure was applied for training and evaluation. The four steps are:

1. Training and test sets were generated in a 3:1 proportion. In this case, the training set considered data from 2014 to 2016 and the test set considered data from 2017.
2. A simple base model was trained for benchmarking. Using the trained model, a recursive feature elimination process was performed. The ten most important features are preserved.
3. Several models were trained and compared with the benchmark model.
4. The best model according to *MAPE, RMSE* and *MAPE* metrics was chosen.
5. An optimization of hyperparameters of the best model was performed using grid search techniques.

Finally, the best model found with the optimized hyperparameters was used as a reference to train the 24 h forecasting model.

Twenty Four Hour Model. The best model configured with the best hyperparameters obtained in the previous step, was used to generate twenty four models $M_1, M_2, ..., M_{24}$ to forecast day ahead hours, applying the following procedure:

1. Training and test sets were generated in a 3:1 proportion. the training set considered data from 2014 to 2016 and the test set considered data from 2017.

2. Model M_i was trained using y_i as output, where y_i consists of the demand value corresponding to i hours ahead, and input X is enriched for models $M_i, i > 2$ with a new column consisting of the $i - 1$ prediction obtained by the trained model M_{i-1}
3. Models M_i are assembled to get a complete model M to forecast the next 24 h altogether.

3.2   Implementation

This section describes the implementation of the approach described in Sect. 3.1.

Computational Platform and Software Environment. Experiments were performed in an HP ProLiant DL380 G9 server with two Intel Xeon Gold 6138 processors (20 cores each) and 128 GB RAM, from the high performance computing infrastructure of National Supercomputing Center Cluster-UY [19].

The proposed approach was implemented in Python. Several scientific packages were used to handle data, train models and visualize results. Used packages included pandas, sklearn, and keras. A generic module was implemented to train various type of models following a pipeline processing. Parameter tuning of the studied models were performed using RandomizedSearchCV and GridSearchCV modules from sklearn. The main details of the implementation of the studied models are provided in the following subsections.

Implementation of One Hour Model. Data preprocessing was already described in Sect. 3.1. All one hour models described in this section use a training set containing data from 2014 to 2016 and a test set containing data from 2017.

Base Model: Linear Regression. A linear regression model was trained to be used as benchmark for the results comparison. A recursive feature selection strategy [4] was also applied on this model to determine the most important features (the rest of features were removed from the dataset).

Ten features were selected based on their relative importance:

– T_1, T_2, T_{24}, T_{25}: demand values lagged.
– *workingday*: flag indicating whether the day of measured value is a working day
– *month*: month on which the measure was taken.
– *hour*: hour of the day on which the measure was taken.
– *dayofweek*: day of the week on which the measure was taken.
– *day*: day of month on which the measure was taken.
– *year*: year on which the measure was taken.

The most relevant past demand values are T_1, T_2, T_{24}, and T_{25} because the current demand is highly correlated with the immediate past demands and also with the demands of the previous day at the same time due to the daily periodicity. The full analysis is presented and discussed in Sect. 4.1.

Selection of the Best Method. Seven regression models were trained including the base model considering the ten most important features, and default parameters, using the scikit-learn API [4]: Linear Regression, MLP, Extra Trees, Gradient Boosting, Random Forest, K-Neighobors and Ridge. These models were evaluated using the *MAPE* metric and the linear regression model was used to determine a baseline performance value. The most accurate method was chosen for further evaluation (this method is called M_{best}).

Optimization of the Best Method. Parameter search techniques were applied to optimize a model based on the best method obtained (M_{best}). The model M_{best} trained with default parameters was optimized using two standard sklearn tools:

- GridSearchCV: The user specify a parameters grid selecting a discrete set of values for each parameter and a model. The tool trains the model in each point of the multidimensional grid generated and finds the best parameters setting according to a predetermined metric.
- RandomizedSearchCV: The user specify a parameter probability distribution and the number of points that must be draw. The tool samples according to the distribution and train the model in each of this points. Then finds the best parameters setting according to a predetermined metric.

The best parameter set obtained for M_{best} results in an optimal model M_{opt}. The main details of the implementation of the complete model based on M_{opt} are described in the next subsection.

3.3   Implementation of the Complete Model

Model M_{opt} was optimized for predicting the next hour and used for predicting any of the following 24 h to build the complete model. This decision was adopted assuming that the forecasting quality of the parameter setting obtained in the previous phase is independent of the hour used as output.

To build the complete model, 24 instances of the optimized model M_{opt} were trained. These instances are called $M_{opt,i}$, defining the model trained to forecast the i_{th} hour ahead. The output y_i used to train the model consisted in the demand value for the i-th hour ahead. For $i > 2$, the input X_i is enriched with a new set of columns consisting of all predictions obtained by models $M_{opt,1}, ..., M_{opt,i-1}$. Equation 8 describes the hybrid strategy applied to M_{opt}.

$$pred_{(t+1)} = M_{opt,(t+1)}(obs_t, obs_{(t-1)}, ..., obs_{(t-n)})$$

$$pred_{(t+2)} = M_{opt,(t+2)}(M_{(t+1)}, obs_t, ..., obs_{(t-n)})$$

$$(8)$$

$$...$$

$$pred_{(t+24)} = M_{opt,(t+24)}(M_{(t+23)}, M_{(t+22)}, ..., obs_t, ..., obs(t-n))$$

The complete model M_{opt} is computed by Eq. 9. Output of the model is a 24 valued vector, one prediction for each hour.

$$M_{opt}(t) = (pred_{(t+1)}, pred_{(t+2)}, ..., pred_{(t+24)})$$ (9)

4   Experimental Analysis

This section presents the results of the experimental analysis of the proposed computational intelligence methods for day ahead industrial electricity load forecasting.

4.1   Recursive Feature Elimination

A feature selection analysis was performed using the recursive feature elimination tool in sklearn. A model and a number of features are selected, and the tool works by recursively removing features and building a new model (of the type selected) on those remaining features. The accuracy of the new model is used to identify the features or combination of features that contribute the most to predicting the target attribute. The recursive feature selection tool was applied over the linear regression method described in Subsect. 3.2 and studying up to ten features. Figure 2 presents the results of the analysis, reporting the relative importance of the ten most important features.

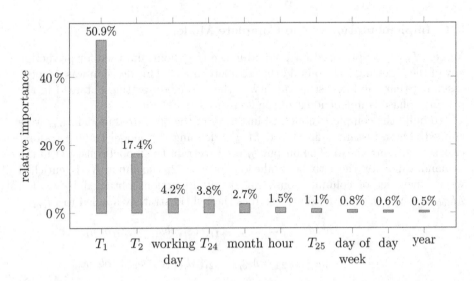

Fig. 2. Relative importance of most important features (percentage values)

4.2 Experimental Results on Preliminary Models

Performance metrics defined in Sect. 3.1 were used to evaluate implementation of one hour models as described in Sect. 3.2. Table 1 reports the obtained results for the studied forecasting models. The best results are reported in cells with green background. Results reported in Table 1 indicate that three methods achieved the best results regarding the analyzed metrics. Focusing on *MAPE*, Extratreesregressor improved over MLP by 4.16% and over RandomForest by 6.54%. Additionally, the training time of Extratreesregressor was approximately three times shorter than RandomForest and six times smaller than MLP. Overall, Extra-TreesRegressor was the most effective model for forecasting the next hour, outperforming all the other methods regarding the three standard metrics studied. According to this result, ExtraTrees was selected as the best method for showing the best performance and a low training time. $M_{best} = ExtraTreesRegressor$.

Table 1. Results for each regression method.

Regression method	MAE	MAPE	RMSE	Score	Time (s)
LinearRegression	127.63	3.60	176.00	0.96	1.72
Ridge	127.63	3.60	176.00	0.97	0.09
KNeighbors	180.54	5.03	253.20	0.93	0.07
RandomForest	180.20	3.21	151.54	0.98	3.1
GradientBoosting	121.97	3.38	166.17	0.97	1.99
MLP	111.08	3.13	154.23	0.97	6.21
ExtraTrees	**105.44**	**3.00**	**148.61**	**0.99**	**1.2**

4.3 Parameter Tuning

Parameter tuning techniques described in Sect. 3.2 were applied on the best model M_{best}. The following grid was generated as input for both studied techniques: *n_estimators*: [10, 50, 75, 100, 150], *max_features*: [auto, sqrt, log2], and *max_depth*: [50, 100,150, 200, 250]. GridSearchCV achieved the best results. The best parameter setting found by the algorithm was *n_estimators* = 50, *max_features* = auto and *max_depth* = 250, improving 14% on the *MAPE* results over the second best configuration.

4.4 Experimental Results After Parameter Tuning

Table 2 reports results of the *ExtraTreesRegressor* model before and after parameter tuning. The best results are highlighted (cells with green background).

Results show that the numerical results improved considerably for the three studied metrics. In particular, *MAPE* reduced from 3.00% to 1.79%. The performance improvement just demanded a negligible increase on training time increases after parameter tuning from 1.2 s to 1.7 s.

Table 2. Comparative results of ExtraTrees before and after parameter tuning.

Regression method	MAE	MAPE	RMSE	Score	Time (s)
ExtraTrees before tuning	105.44	3.00	148. 61	0.99	1.2
ExtraTrees after tuning	**87.52**	**1.79**	**111.08**	**0.99**	**1.7**

4.5   Experimental Results of the Complete Model

The forecast accuracy of the final model was validated by applying a metric that extends *MAPE*. Let $MAPE_h$ be the *MAPE* value for a predicted horizon h, the extension of *MAPE* to the complete testing set is defined by Eq. 10.

$$MAPE_{tot} = \frac{\sum_{i=1}^{k} MAPE_h}{k} \tag{10}$$

Table 3 reports the results for each of the 24 models. The expected behaviour is that the models trained for highly correlated hours in the future respect to the current hour, perform best. This fact is due to predictability, and it s enhanced when the correlation between input features and predicted values is higher. According to Fig. 1, highly correlated demand values correspond to the immediately preceding hours and from the same hours of the day before.

Analyzing the obtained results for the $MAPE_{tot}$ metric for each one of the 24 hourly models, the performance got worse from $i = 1$ to $i = 17$ and then improved from $i = 18$ to $i = 24$. These results show that highly correlated demand values performed better, as expected.

Table 3. $MAPE_{tot}$ score for each $ET_{opt,i}$ single hour model.

					hour						
	1	2	3	4	5	6	7	8	9	10	11	12
$MAPE_{tot}$	1.79	1.84	1.90	1.97	2.09	2.19	2.39	2.52	2.68	2.75	2.80	2.86

					hour						
	13	14	15	16	17	18	19	20	21	22	23	24
$MAPE_{tot}$	2.93	3.02	3.05	3.08	3.09	3.02	2.88	2.77	2.63	2.49	2.32	2.17

Finally, the complete model ET_{opt} was applied. A day-ahead hourly forecast load curve was generated for each time window for the testing set and the $MAPE_{tot}$ value was calculated.

The final result for the complete model was $MAPE_{tot} = 2.55\%$. This result implies that the model obtained for the day ahead demand forecasting of the industrial pole analyzed incurs in an error that is considered very low for most of the studies that rely on these types of models [13,15]. Figure 3 presents an example of the real demand curve and the predicted demand curve using the best model, for the testing set considered in the experiments.

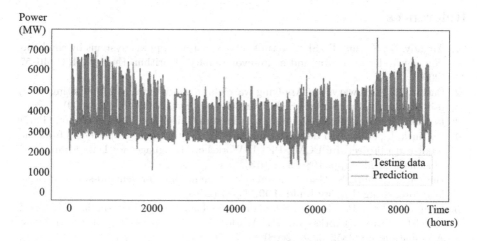

Fig. 3. Predicted demand and testing data curves

5   Conclusions and Future Work

This article presented an approach to address the problem of day ahead electricity load forecasting. Several machine learning models was presented and studied for next hour forecasting. Recursive feature selection was applied to select most relevant features to train the studied models. After a comparative evaluation, the best model was optimized using random search and grid search techniques. With the optimized model for single hour prediction, an hybrid strategy (direct and recursive) was applied to build a complete day ahead electricity load hourly forecasting model.

An extension of $MAPE$ metric was used to evaluate this complete model for the testing set, obtaining a value of $MAPE_{tot} = 2.55\%$. This result shows that the proposed algorithm is effective for addressing the problem of day-ahead industrial demand forecasting.

The main lines for future work are related to extend the analysis to other data sets of industrial poles with different demand profiles, and apply the proposed approach to residential demand forecasting, including other relevant features (e.g., related to weather, such as temperature, humidity, and wind speed, which have impact on residential demand [17]). Deep learning techniques (e.g., recurrent/long-short term memory neural networks) should be considered for future work, since they can provide accurate results in scenarios that are difficult for other simpler methods, i.e. when handling large volumes of historical data.

References

1. Amjady, N., Keynia, F.: Short-term load forecasting of power systems by combination of wavelet transform and neuro-evolutionary algorithm. Energy **34**(1), 46–57 (2009)
2. Bashir, Z., El-Hawary, M.: Applying wavelets to short-term load forecasting using pso-based neural networks. IEEE Trans. Power Syst. **24**(1), 20–27 (2009)
3. Bellman, R.: Dynamic Programming. Princeton University Press, Princeton (1957)
4. Buitinck, L., et al.: API design for machine learning software: experiences from the scikit-learn project. In: ECML PKDD Workshop: Languages for Data Mining and Machine Learning, pp. 108–122 (2013)
5. Burger, E., Moura, S.: Gated ensemble learning method for demand-side electricity load forecasting. Energy Build. **109**, 23–34 (2015)
6. Chen, Y., Luh, P., Rourke, S.: Short-term load forecasting: similar day-based wavelet neural networks. In: 7th World Congress on Intelligent Control and Automation, pp. 3353–3358 (2008)
7. De Felice, M., Alessandri, A., Ruti, P.M.: Electricity demand forecasting over italy: potential benefits using numerical weather prediction models. Electr. Power Syst. Res. **104**, 71–79 (2013)
8. Diniz, A., Costa, F., Maceira, M., dos Santos, T., Dos Santos, L., Cabral, R.: Short/mid-term hydrothermal dispatch and spot pricing for large-scale systems-the case of Brazil. In: Power Systems Computation Conference, pp. 1–7 (2018)
9. Do, L., Lin, K.H., Molnár, P.: Electricity consumption modelling: a case of germany. Econ. Model. **55**, 92–101 (2016)
10. Dudek, G.: Pattern-based local linear regression models for short-term load forecasting. Electr. Power Syst. Res. **130**, 139–147 (2016)
11. Fan, S., Chen, L., Lee, W.J.: Machine learning based switching model for electricity load forecasting. Energy Convers. Manag. **49**(6), 1331–1344 (2008)
12. Hagan, M., Behr, S.: The time series approach to short term load forecasting. IEEE Trans. Power Syst. **2**(3), 785–791 (1987)
13. Karrthikeyaa, S., Vijayaraghavan, V.: A two-fold machine learning approach for efficient day-ahead load prediction at hourly granularity for NYC. In: Advances in Information and Communication, vol. 2, p. 84 (2019)
14. Kim, C., Yu, I., Song, Y.: Kohonen neural network and wavelet transform based approach to short-term load forecasting. Electr. Power Syst. Res. **63**(3), 169–176 (2002)
15. Lahouar, A., Slama, J.: Day-ahead load forecast using random forest and expert input selection. Energy Convers. Manag. **103**, 1040–1051 (2015)

16. Lazos, D., Sproul, A., Kay, M.: Optimisation of energy management in commercial buildings with weather forecasting inputs: a review. Renew. Sustain. Energy Rev. **39**, 587–603 (2014)
17. Luján, E., Otero, A., Valenzuela, S., Mocskos, E., Steffenel, L., Nesmachnow, S.: An integrated platform for smart energy management: the CC-SEM project. Revista Facultad de Ingeniería (2019)
18. McKinney, W.: Data structures for statistical computing in python. In: Proceedings of the 9th Python in Science Conference, pp. 51–56 (2010)
19. Nesmachnow, S., Iturriaga, S.: Cluster-UY: scientific HPC in Uruguay. In: International Supercomputing in Mexico (2019)
20. Pedregosa, F., et al.: Scikit-learn: machine learning in python. J. Mach. Learn. Res. **12**, 2825–2830 (2011)
21. Qamber, I.: Peak load estimation studies in several countries. Electr. Power Syst. Res. **1**(2) (2017)
22. Resende, L., Soares, M., Ferreira, P.: Electric power load in Brazil: view on the long-term forecasting models. Production **28**, 83–99 (2018)
23. Silva, L.: A feature engineering approach to wind power forecasting: GEFCom 2012. Int. J. Forecast. **30**(2), 395–401 (2014)
24. Soliman, A., Al-Kandari, A.: Electrical Load Forecasting: Modeling and Model Construction. Elsevier, Amsterdam (2010)
25. Son, H., Kim, C.: Short-term forecasting of electricity demand for the residential sector using weather and social variables. Resour. Conserv. Recycl. **123**, 200–207 (2017)
26. Taylor, J., McSharry, P.: Short-term load forecasting methods: an evaluation based on European data. IEEE Trans. Power Syst. **22**(4), 2213–2219 (2007)

Potential for Thermal Water Desalination Using Microgrid and Solar Thermal Field Energy Surpluses in an Isolated Community

Jesús Armando Aguilar-Jiménez[1](✉) (iD), Nicolás Velázquez[1], Ricardo Beltrán[2],
Luis Hernández-Callejo[3](✉), Ricardo López-Zavala[1,4],
and Edgar González-San Pedro[1,4]

[1] Center for Renewable Energy Studies, Engineering Institute,
Autonomous University of Baja California, Mexicali, Mexico
a1116072@uabc.edu.mx
[2] Advanced Materials Research Center, Chihuahua, Mexico
[3] Department of Agricultural Engineering and Forestry, University of Valladolid (UVA),
Campus Universitario Duques de Soria, 42004 Soria, Spain
luis.hernandez.callejo@uva.es
[4] Faculty of Engineering, Autonomous University of Baja California, Mexicali, Mexico

Abstract. In this work, we present the study of seawater desalination potential using the energy surpluses of a microgrid based on renewable energies and a thermosolar absorption cooling system, installed in the isolated community of Puertecitos, Mexico and its primary school, respectively. Given the profile of electricity demand of the community in winter and the non-need for air conditioning, both systems can be used for the desalination of seawater, a resource greatly needed in the region because of the scarcity that is presented. Using the software TRNSYS and Aspen Plus, the simulation of the generating systems was carried out, activating a multiple-effect seawater desalination system during a typical week of February with measured data of electrical consumption. The results show that, with the energy available from both systems, it is possible to desalinate 2,500 kg/day of water with a thermal consumption of 25 kW, during 6 h daily operation. The electrical energy supplied by the microgrid contributes four times more to the desalination of water than the thermal solar field. With this production, it is possible to satisfy the basic requirements of hygiene, hydration and food for 25 people.

Keywords: Microgrid · Solar energy · Desalination · Isolated community

1 Introduction

Water scarcity is a global problem that has taken on great importance among public and private institutions. The United Nations incorporates it in the Sustainable Development Goal 6, mentioning that this resource, in sufficient quantity and quality, is essential for all aspects of life [1]. The decline in the availability of this resource is the result of several

© Springer Nature Switzerland AG 2020
S. Nesmachnow and L. Hernández Callejo (Eds.): ICSC-CITIES 2019, CCIS 1152, pp. 162–175, 2020.
https://doi.org/10.1007/978-3-030-38889-8_13

factors, such as the increase in world population, living standards and the pollution of water deposits; projections estimate that they will reach critical levels within the first half of this century [2]. It is for this reason that the efforts of scientists should be directed towards solving this problem, proposing new technologies that are more efficient, use renewable energies and can be applied in regions where there is a shortage of water.

The only methods to increase water supply are through desalination and reuse [3]. Of these two, seawater desalination offers a virtually unlimited and consistent supply of high quality water [4]. Desalination uses large amounts of energy to remove pure water from a salt water source [5]. Kalogirou [6] estimated that the production of 1,000 m^3 per day of fresh water requires 10,000 tons of oil per year. This is significant if the price of energy is expensive and populations with water needs cannot afford it.

The integration of desalination processes to solar concentration plants is today the best alternative to solve simultaneously the problems of water scarcity and exhaustion of fossil fuels [2]. Furthermore, if we relate that the regions where water is needed present a good solar resource and, in addition, can be found close to the sea, it becomes an attractive and sustainable combination. Using solar energy, the desalination process can be carried out in two ways, using electrical energy in reverse osmosis equipment, or thermally in multiple-stage flash (MSF), multiple-effect desalination (MED) or humidification/dehumidification systems [7, 8]. Although MSF systems predominate in the market [9], MED technology has improved and now has efficiency levels higher than MSF [10].

Numerous works have been carried out seeking to make desalination processes more efficient by using renewable energies as the source of activation, in which the studies carried out on the Almeria Solar Platform with a 14-effect solar MED system are highlighted [11–14]. López-Zavala et al. [15] proposed the coupling of an absorption cooling system to a desalination system through internal energy integration. With that configuration, the cooling system was 19.44% more efficient, while producing 838 L/day of fresh water with the same amount of energy supplied. Mata-Torres et al. [16] analyzed energetically the coupling of a MED system with a Rankine cycle for the simultaneous production of water and electrical energy, finding that largest MED plant sizes achieve the lowest unit exergy cost of electricity and water under all the conditions evaluated.

On the other hand, seawater desalination systems have been analyzed and implemented in isolated regions being activated with renewable energies [17–19]. Astolfi et al. [20] mention that solar power plants and desalination units can be integrated synergistically as long as their programming is optimized by an advanced energy management system. They also conclude that the combination of two solar plants, such as photovoltaic (PV) and thermal, allows to take advantage of the characteristics of both; the first for its low costs of electricity production during periods of high insolation, while thermal systems extend the hours of operation using thermal energy storage.

Puertecitos, Mexico, is a coastal community isolated from the national electricity grid that has generators based on renewable energy. However, in the region there is a serious problem with access to fresh water, a service that is in high demand among the population due to the low quality of life. For this reason, this paper presents a study of the potential for desalination of seawater in the community by means of a multi-effect desalination system, using the energy capacity during the winter season of the generators installed, a period in which they are partially or completely stopped. This is intended to satisfy the basic requirements of clean water to the maximum possible number of residents, improving their quality of life and taking advantage of the energy waste of the renewable energy systems of the community.

2   Renewable Energy Systems Installed in the Community

The community of Puertecitos is located in the state of Baja California, Mexico. (30°21′19.7″ N, 114°38′26.3″ W) and it's a village isolated from the national power grid. It has a variable number of residents, mainly due to weather conditions, availability of public services and fishing seasons, the latter is the predominant work activity.

Since it does not have electricity service, the Autonomous University of Baja California designed and installed a microgrid based on renewable energy to meet basic requirements, such as conservation of perishable foods, public lighting and air conditioning of spaces [21]. This system has 55.2 kW of photovoltaic modules, a 5 kW wind turbine, a 75 kVA diesel generator and a 522 kWh lead-acid battery bank, as shown in Fig. 1.

Fig. 1. Microgrid of the community of Puertecitos, Mexico.

In the same community of Puertecitos there is a primary school for the children who live there. This consists of four classrooms, where one is dedicated to preschool. However, the school suffers from a high rate of academic desertion due to the factors mentioned above, together with the high environmental temperatures present in the summer, which make it impossible to give classes under suitable comfort conditions. Since they did not have air conditioning systems or the economic resources to acquire them, besides not being able to pay the price of electricity from the microgrid, an absorption cooling system activated by solar thermal energy was installed [22], seeking that the school has the necessary comfort conditions for students to carry out their activities properly, reducing academic desertion or eventually leaving the community for lack of basic education. The system consists of a field of solar thermal collectors with 110.25 m^2 of caption area, which store thermal energy in a tank of 12 m^3 of capacity for subsequent use in an absorption water cooling machine of 35 kW, as shown in Fig. 2.

Fig. 2. Thermosolar absorption cooling system of 35 kW capacity installed in the primary school of Puertecitos, Mexico.

2.1 Operation in Winter Season

The climate in the community of Puertecitos differs greatly depending on the season. In the winters temperatures can reach close to 0 °C, while summers record temperatures in the order of 45 °C, with peaks of up to 50 °C in the shade. This causes a very different profile in the demand for electricity between these seasons. In the summer, when there is a need for air conditioning due to high temperatures, community demand can be up to five times greater than expected in winter. When dimensioning a system for the production of electrical energy, the problem of determining the appropriate size of the plant occurs; if the community's demand for summer is taken as a reference, the plant will be oversized for the winter period; on the other hand, if it is dimensioned with the winter demand, it will be very limited for the electrical needs of the hot months. The sizing study must contemplate a cost-benefit analysis between demand and production and storage capacity, including different generators and energy storage systems.

Figure 3 shows the predicted electricity demand of the community studied, based mainly on a socioeconomic study carried out on the population and extrapolated to a total of 20 houses, providing enough energy to have an acceptable quality of life [21]. During the first months of the year there is a demand of no more than 15 kW, mainly for public lighting, refrigerators, domestic lighting and entertainment. However, as ambient temperatures rise, forecasted demand tends to rise to a peak of around 60 kW in August, mostly due to the use of air-conditioning equipment to deal with high temperatures. During the months of September to December demand returns to its lowest levels. It was decided to install a 60 kW electrical system based on renewable energy and the energy shortfall during the critical months was covered by the diesel generator. In this way, a greater amount of economic resource could be allocated to a larger energy storage system. This resulted in a shortage of electricity for a short period of time per year, remedied with conventional energy, while the remaining time there is an excess of energy production by photovoltaic and wind generators.

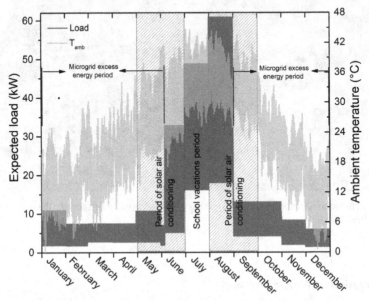

Fig. 3. Annual variation of the electric demand forecast for the community of Puertecitos and ambient temperature, where the periods of excess production of electric energy and use of the thermosolar absorption cooling system of the primary school are indicated.

On the other hand, the community primary school's thermosolar absorption cooling system has something similar to its operation. The need for air conditioning in the classrooms due to the region's high temperatures is present in the May-June and August-September periods, since July is considered a vacation period, as shown in Fig. 3, so the system will operate alone for four months of the year. During the remaining eight months there is no specific work defined, wasting the heating capacity of the solar field or the air conditioning of the absorption machine.

2.2 System for the Use of Energy Surpluses and Seawater Desalination

In the region there is a serious problem for the acquisition of clean water. The easiest way to obtain this resource is in a well 32 km away from the community, which is also overexploited and with high salinity indexes. In a direct questioning with the population of Puertecitos, they defined clean water as the second most desirable service in the community, only after electricity and even more desired than public health or safety services.

Taking into account the above, and seeking to take advantage of existing facilities in the community, such as the microgrid and field of solar thermal collectors, without affecting their main functions (meet the electricity needs and air conditioning of the classrooms of the school, respectively), it is proposed to evaluate the capacity of desalination of seawater in Puertecitos using surplus electricity from the microgrid and field of solar collectors during the periods mentioned above. In this way, the technical feasibility would be analyzed to provide this basic service so required in the region, without altering the current operation of the plants.

Figure 4 presents the schematic diagram of the proposed seawater desalination system in the community. During the months in which the energy storage batteries are at their maximum capacity, the instantaneous electric demand of the community is being satisfied and there is still plenty of energy, this will be used to activate electrical resistances inside the thermal energy storage tank (TEST) of the thermosolar cooling system, converting electrical energy into thermal energy and transferring it to the TEST. The field of solar thermal collectors, during the months when there is no need to cool the classrooms of the school, will be working to increase the thermal energy of the TEST. With the energy supplied by the two systems, a MED system will be activated.

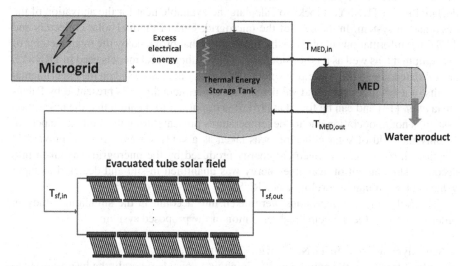

Fig. 4. Schematic diagram of the proposed system for the desalination of seawater using the surplus energy of the microgrid and thermosolar cooling of the community of Puertecitos.

3   Methodology

For the feasibility analysis of the proposal, the TRNSYS software was used to simulate the solar heating and microgrid systems, while Aspen Plus was used for the MED system. TRNSYS has a library of "types" programmed with mathematical models validated from a great amount of equipment, among them renewable technologies such as photovoltaic modules and solar collectors, which, interconnected with other programmed control modules or other processes, form a system that can be analyzed in a semi dynamic state. The advantage of this software is that it can use meteorological databases typical of the locality of study, so the analysis is carried out under more real operating conditions, subject to environmental variations, such as temperature, radiation and wind speed, among others.

The microgrid, solar collectors' field and storage tank, as well as the dynamics of control and operation of the general system, were simulated in TRNSYS since their performance depends directly on solar radiation conditions and temperatures, in addition to being also used as references for decision making regarding the operation of the global system. The meteorological information used in the simulation study represents a typical year, based on average measurements over the last 10 years. On the other hand, the MED system is simulated in Aspen Plus software due to its advantages in terms of databases of thermodynamic properties and heat transfer of a large number of substances, which facilitate the resolution of mathematical models used in their blocks, representative of physical and chemical processes.

The characteristics of the systems installed in the Puertecitos community, as well as those of the proposed MED system, are presented in Table 1. This information is declared in the TRNSYS blocks to calculate the available heat for the activation of the desalination system. In the case of the microgrid, field of thermal solar collectors and TEST, the information supplied to the simulator is that provided by the manufacturer of the equipment, as well as it is considered that the mathematical models used in TRNSYS are validated. The MED system developed in Aspen Plus was based on the experimental results of a 14-effect plant and validated with experimental results presented by Palenzuela et al. [13] and can be found at [15]. It is important to mention that the absorption system is not in operation due to the temperatures present during the simulation period, so only the field of solar collectors was taken as a study system. Also, as previously mentioned, the excess of electrical energy produced by the microgrid was taken into account. The amount of available energy was quantified in-situ and declared as input values in the simulator developed in TRNSYS.

The following considerations were taken into account in the simulation study in order to simplify the mathematical resolution of the proposed system:

- Semi-dynamic state in TRNSYS with simulation periods of 25 min.
- No heat loss from the equipment or piping was considered, only the heat transfer to the environment due to the temperature difference of the TEST and the solar collector field.
- Pressure drops in equipment and pipes were not considered.
- Since there is no direct link between the TRNSYS software and Aspen Plus, they were analyzed separately.
- The MED system was dimensioned based on the maximum usable thermal load of the TEST, looking for an operation for defined periods of time.

Table 1. System characteristics

Solar collector	
Brand/model	Suntask/SHC24
Collector type	Evacuated tube with CPC reflector
Number of tubes	24
Aperture area	4.41 m^2
Optical efficiency (a_0)	0.668
First order efficiency coefficient (a_1)	1.496 W/m^2*K
Second order efficiency coefficient (a_2)	0.005 W/m^2*K^2
Fluid	Water
Mass flow	0.02 kg/s*m^2
Number in series	5
Number of loops	5
Thermal energy storage tank	
Volume	12 m^3
Height	2.5 m
Material	Fiberglass
Insulation thickness	0.025 m
Loss coefficient	1.4 W/m^2*K
Fluid	Water
Microgrid system	
Brand/model	Solartec S72MC6-300
Power	300 W
Number of modules	184
Wind generator	5 kW
Inverter	Kehua 100 kVA
Controller	Kehua SPC348150-M
Batteries	2 V, 1,500 Ah each
Number of batteries	172 connected in serie
Diesel generator	75 kVA
Multiple-effect desalination system	
Number of effects	14
Thermal energy input	25 kW
Top brine temperature	70 °C
Condensation temperature	35 °C
Fresh water production	2,490 kg/h

4 Results

In order to carry out the feasibility study of seawater desalination with the excess energy of the microgrid and the entire solar heater field, a week of February was considered (period of 750–885 h per year) where the environmental conditions of radiation and temperature allow a stable operation of the system, as can be seen in Fig. 5. As it is a winter week, the present temperature allows the air conditioning systems to be switched off, both the school's thermosolar absorption and the domestic electrical systems, which is why an energy surplus is expected from the microgrid and the availability of using the school's collector field for the desalination of seawater. However, the global solar radiation available does not exceed 700 W/m^2 and the hours of use of the resource are less than would be expected in summer, reducing the amount of solar energy that can be acquired during the day.

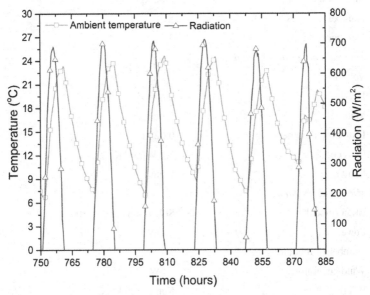

Fig. 5. Variation of ambient temperature and global radiation in the region of study during a week in February.

Figure 6 presents the operating dynamics of the Puertecitos community microgrid, as well as the electrical demand profile and the electrical energy surplus. This information corresponds to data measured in the community during the aforementioned analysis period. It can be seen that, during the whole week studied, there is a surplus of electrical energy due to low-demand. The first day begins with the state of charge (SOC) of the storage system in the order of 0.8, due to the discharge of the same during the night; as the solar resource increases and the production of the photovoltaic field satisfies the instantaneous demand of the community, the excess energy is used to charge the batteries to their maximum. When the storage system reaches a SOC of 1.0, the electrical surplus is used to activate the electrical resistances within the TEST.

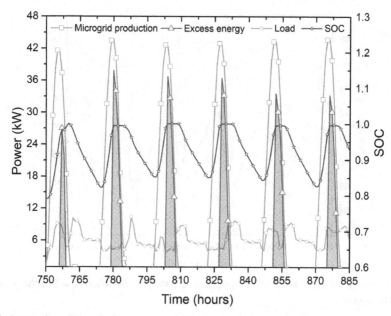

Fig. 6. Dynamics of electrical energy production by the microgrid, excess of energy due to the low demand of the Puertecitos community and SOC of the batteries of the system.

On the first day, due to the community's demand profile, a maximum of 27 kW of transferred energy was obtained for only a short period of time, giving a total of 49 kWh of harnessed energy. However, the rest of the days, after fully charging the battery bank, potencies in the order of 38 kW were reached, equivalent to an average daily energy of 96 kWh, the result of integrating the instantaneous power during the period of time presented, represented by the shaded area under the curve. It should be noted that, being winter season, the storage system in batteries does not fall below 0.8 of its SOC during the night period, allowing the use of excess energy for the desalination of seawater.

On the other hand, the field of thermal solar collectors of the cooling system is available in its entirety to be used as a medium for the activation of the MED system, together with the energy coming from the microgrid. Under the environmental conditions mentioned above, Fig. 7 shows the behavior of the solar thermal collection system during the analysis week. The output temperature of the solar field, $T_{out,sf}$, is directly influenced by the input temperature, $T_{in,sf}$, and the available solar radiation, and indirectly related to the temperature of the TEST. This can reach 95 °C during the solar mid-day, which is the set point defined as the maximum operating limit. The decrease in $T_{in,sf}$ is due to the fact that the solar heating system is not in operation for the night period. The thermal power supplied by the collector field increases with respect to the increased solar radiation, having a maximum of up to 35 kW at mid-day. This energy is transferred in its totality to the TEST to be used by the MED system.

Given the amount of energy available, both from the excesses of the microgrid and the collector field, Fig. 8 shows the production of clean water calculated by the proposed system. The MED will run for a period of 6 h daily, starting at 9:00 and ending at 15:00, as

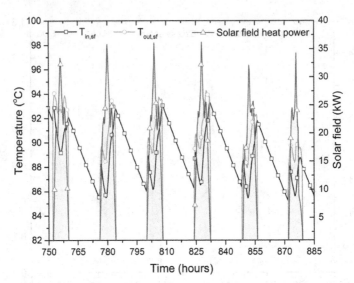

Fig. 7. Behavior of the solar thermal system of the Puertecitos school used in the seawater desalination system.

this allows a programmed operation throughout the week without affecting the operating temperature and TEST conditions, as well as using only the daily energy supplied by the generators. On the other hand, if you have a longer daily operation, the system will not be able to return to the initial conditions of temperature and stored energy of the TEST, affecting the quality of the energy and the subsequent days of operation. Using the energy of the two systems, it is possible to produce 414 kg/h of desalinated water during the 6 h a day, using 25 kW as thermal energy to activate the MED, giving a total of approximately 2,500 kg per day and a weekly accumulated of 17,500 kg.

It also presents the scenario in which only the solar field is available, without considering the electrical surpluses of the microgrid. For this case, during the same period of operation, it is possible to use a constant thermal power of 12 kW without negatively influencing the conditions of the TEST and, for a new capacity and design of the MED, it is capable of producing approximately 1,183 kg daily of desalinated water with a weekly accumulated of 8,305 kg. This results in a 52.5% reduction in water desalination when using only the thermal solar field, or seen in another way, the electrical excesses of the microgrid contribute two times more to the production of desalinated water than the entire solar collector field. Considering the recommendations of the World Health Organization [23], the quantity of 2,500 kg/day of desalinated water can satisfy the basic needs of food, hydration and hygiene of 25 residents of the community of Puertecitos, while using only the energy of the solar field satisfies the water requirements for 5 residents.

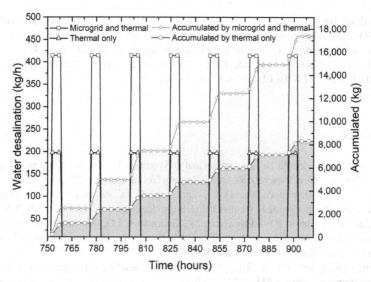

Fig. 8. Production rate of desalinated water and accumulated during the week of analysis.

5 Conclusions

A study was conducted to determine the potential for seawater desalination in the isolated community of Puertecitos, Mexico, using a multi-effect thermal desalination system to provide this scarce service in the region. This population has a microgrid based on renewable energy and, given that the profile of demand differs greatly depending on the seasonal season, we seek to take advantage of excess electricity in the winter period. In addition, a field of thermal solar collectors belonging to an absorption cooling system installed in the primary school of the community is available, which for eight months is without use because no air conditioning is needed in the classrooms.

Considering a week in February as the study period, the system was simulated using the TRNSYS and Aspen Plus software, based on the profile of electricity demand measured in the community, and the following was found:

- Using the energy surplus of the microgrid and the entire solar thermal field, it is possible to desalinate water using a MED system with a production of 2,500 kg/day.
- The thermal consumption of the MED system is 25 kW, being possible to maintain its operation for 6 h/day, during the period from 9:00 to 15:00.
- Using both generators, a weekly production of approximately 17,500 kg of water is obtained, while using only the field of solar collectors this decreases to 8,305 kg weekly.
- The excess energy of the microgrid contributes two times more to the desalination of water than the solar thermal field.
- According to the World Health Organization, it is possible to meet the basic hygiene, hydration and nutritional needs of 25 people with calculated water production.

Acknowledgments. The authors acknowledge CONACYT-SENER-SUSTENTABILIDAD ENERGÉTICA for the support received through the project P09 of CEMIE-Solar as well as a graduate scholarship for J. Armando Aguilar-Jiménez. The authors also acknowledge the CYTED Thematic Network "CIUDADES INTELIGENTES TOTALMENTE INTEGRALES, EFICIENTES Y SOSTENIBLES (CITIES)" no 518RT0558.

References

1. Nations, U.: Sustainable Development Goal 6 Synthesis Report on Water and Sanitation. United Nations, New York (2018). https://doi.org/10.1126/science.278.5339.827
2. Palenzuela, P., Alarcón-Padilla, D.-C., Zaragoza, G.: Concentrating Solar Power and Desalination Plants. Springer, Cham (2015). https://doi.org/10.1007/978-3-319-20535-9
3. Shannon, M.A., Bohn, P.W., Elimelech, M., Georgiadis, J.G., Marĩas, B.J., Mayes, A.M.: Science and technology for water purification in the coming decades. Nature **452**, 301–310 (2008). https://doi.org/10.1038/nature06599
4. Phillip, W.A., Elimelech, M.: The future of seawater desalination: energy, technology, and the environment. Science **333**, 712–717 (2011)
5. Qiblawey, H.M., Banat, F.: Solar thermal desalination technologies. Desalination **220**, 633–644 (2008). https://doi.org/10.1016/j.desal.2007.01.059
6. Kalogirou, S.A.: Seawater desalination using renewable energy sources. Prog. Energy Combust. Sci. **31**, 242–281 (2005). https://doi.org/10.1016/j.pecs.2005.03.001
7. Valero, A., Uche, J., Serra, L.: La desalación como alternativa al plan hidrológico nacional., Zaragoza (2001)
8. Tariq, R., Sheikh, N.A., Xamán, J., Bassam, A.: An innovative air saturator for humidification-dehumidification desalination application. Appl. Energy **228**, 789–807 (2018). https://doi.org/10.1016/j.apenergy.2018.06.135
9. IDA: Worldwide Desalting Plants Inventory (2006)
10. Zheng, H., Zheng, H.: Solar desalination system combined with conventional technologies. In: Solar Energy Desalination Technology, pp. 537–622. Elsevier (2017). https://doi.org/10.1016/B978-0-12-805411-6.00007-5
11. Chorak, A., Palenzuela, P., Alarcón-Padilla, D.C., Ben Abdellah, A.: Experimental characterization of a multi-effect distillation system coupled to a flat plate solar collector field: Empirical correlations. Appl. Therm. Eng. **120**, 298–313 (2017). https://doi.org/10.1016/j.applthermaleng.2017.03.115
12. Palenzuela, P., Alarcón-Padilla, D.C., Zaragoza, G.: Experimental parametric analysis of a solar pilot-scale multi-effect distillation plant. Desalin. Water Treat. **57**, 23097–23109 (2016). https://doi.org/10.1080/19443994.2016.1180481
13. Palenzuela, P., Hassan, A.S., Zaragoza, G., Alarcón-Padilla, D.C.: Steady state model for multi-effect distillation case study: plataforma Solar de Almería MED pilot plant. Desalination **337**, 31–42 (2014). https://doi.org/10.1016/j.desal.2013.12.029
14. Chorak, A., Palenzuela, P., Alarcón-Padilla, D.-C., Abdellah, A.B.: Energetic evaluation of a double-effect LiBr-H2O absorption heat pump coupled to a multi-effect distillation plant at nominal and off-design conditions. Appl. Therm. Eng. **142**, 543–554 (2018). https://doi.org/10.1016/J.APPLTHERMALENG.2018.07.014
15. López-Zavala, R., et al.: A novel LiBr/H2O absorption cooling and desalination system with three pressure levels. Int. J. Refrig **99**, 469–478 (2019). https://doi.org/10.1016/J.IJREFRIG.2019.01.003

16. Mata-Torres, C., Zurita, A., Cardemil, J.M., Escobar, R.A.: Exergy cost and thermoeconomic analysis of a Rankine Cycle + Multi-Effect Distillation plant considering time-varying conditions. Energy Convers. Manag. (2019). https://doi.org/10.1016/j.enconman.2019.04.023

17. Kershman, S.A., Rheinländer, J., Gabler, H.: Seawater reverse osmosis powered from renewable energy sources - Hybrid wind/photovoltaic/grid power supply for small-scale desalination in Libya. Desalination (2003). https://doi.org/10.1016/S0011-9164(02)01089-5

18. Kyriakarakos, G., Dounis, A.I., Rozakis, S., Arvanitis, K.G., Papadakis, G.: Polygeneration microgrids: a viable solution in remote areas for supplying power, potable water and hydrogen as transportation fuel. Appl. Energy. (2011). https://doi.org/10.1016/j.apenergy.2011.05.038

19. Bognar, K., Blechinger, P., Behrendt, F.: Seawater desalination in micro grids: an integrated planning approach. Energy. Sustain. Soc. 2, 1–12 (2012). https://doi.org/10.1186/2192-0567-2-14

20. Astolfi, M., Mazzola, S., Silva, P., Macchi, E.: A synergic integration of desalination and solar energy systems in stand-alone microgrids. Desalination 419, 169–180 (2017). https://doi.org/10.1016/j.desal.2017.05.025

21. Aguilar-Jiménez, J.A., Velázquez, N., Acuña, A., Cota, R., González, E., González, L., López, R., Islas, S.: Techno-economic analysis of a hybrid PV-CSP system with thermal energy storage applied to isolated microgrids. Sol. Energy 174, 55–65 (2018). https://doi.org/10.1016/j.solener.2018.08.078

22. Aguilar-Jiménez, J.A., Velázquez, N., López-Zavala, R., González-Uribe, L.A., Beltrán, R., Hernández-Callejo, L.: Simulation of a solar-assisted air-conditioning system applied to a remote school. Appl. Sci. 9, 3398 (2019). https://doi.org/10.3390/app9163398

23. Bartram, J., Howard, G.: Domestic Water Quantity, Service Level and Health. World Health Organization (2003). https://doi.org/10.1128/JB.187.23.8156

Electric Microgrid in Smart Cities: CEDER-CIEMAT a Case Study

Luis Hernández-Callejo[1]([✉]), Oscar Izquierdo Monge[2]([✉]), and Lilian J. Obregón[1]

[1] University of Valladolid, Campus Universitario Duques de Soria, Soria, Spain
luis.hernandez.callejo@uva.es, liliancitaobregon@gmail.com
[2] CEDER-CIEMAT, Autovía de Navarra A15 sal. 56, 42290 Lubia, Soria, Spain
oscar.izquierdo@ciemat.es

Abstract. The increase in the penetration of renewable generation sources is fundamental in Smart Cities. But these renewable sources can be integrated with distributed electrical storage and intelligence for the management of all assets through electric microgrids. Therefore, these new generation and consumption environments will be present in the Smart City. In this sense, this paper presents one of the most versatile and interesting electric microgrid that exists today, specifically the microgrid of the Center for the Development of Renewable Energies (CEDER) located in Soria (Spain).

Keywords: Electric microgrid · Smart city · Energy efficiency · Sustainability

1 Introduction

As it appears in [1], a *Smart City* (*SC*) is a sustainable urban environment, which tries to provide a high quality of life to its residents, for which it requires an optimal management of resources. Therefore, one of the main challenges of the *SC* will be to carry out an optimal and efficient management of the available resources.

Therefore, it is possible to say that the *SC* is faced with a challenge similar to that of micro-networks, specifically the management of existing assets [2]. In the case of the microgrid, these assets are: *Distributed Generation* (*DG*), distributed electrical storage and loads. These elements also appear in the scenario of the *SC*, so it must face a problem similar to that of the microgrid.

One of the benefits of the electric microgrid is its guarantee of efficiency and sustainability in the global network infrastructure. In this sense, in [3] it is shown how microgrids can be the future of cities in Europe and, therefore, throughout the world.

Other authors [4] focus on the importance of the integration of the electric microgrid in the SC in distributed electrical storage. The storage not only seen as support elements to the renewable *DG*, but as an integrating and agglutinating element of the electric vehicle.

The *SC* presents another great challenge, its management. When talking about management, not only must we think about the elements described as members of a microgrid, but also the circulation [5], parking [6, 7], infrastructures [8], etc.

© Springer Nature Switzerland AG 2020
S. Nesmachnow and L. Hernández Callejo (Eds.): ICSC-CITIES 2019, CCIS 1152, pp. 176–184, 2020.
https://doi.org/10.1007/978-3-030-38889-8_14

In the case of the microgrid, management mainly focuses on distributed resources (generators and storage) [9, 10]. This management is independent of whether the microgrid is designed in alternate or continuous [11, 12].

What it can affirm is that the electric microgrids will be part of the SC, for which the management of those will be their responsibility [13]. This coexistence makes it interesting that there are microgrid test environments, since the integration of these in the SC will depend on the degree of control and management of the microgrids.

Numerous are the test scenarios in electric microgrid environments, both real and simulated. However, the authors have selected a special environment in Spain, as it has special conditions in terms of DG elements and distributed electrical storage, which makes this environment likes a unique microgrid.

After this introduction the publication is as follows: Sect. 2 presents the selected microgrid environment; Sect. 3 lists the objectives that are intended to be covered by this electrical microgrid; and Sect. 4 ends with some conclusions and future work to be able to develop in this test scenario.

2 Test Scenario: CEDER-CIEMAT

As already mentioned, there are many scenarios in the world based on electric microgrids [14]. Some of these environments are based on simulation, others on emulation, but the vast majorities are real environments.

Without underestimating the simulated and emulated scenarios, it is in the real environments where the validation of the hypotheses takes a decisive character. The transition from simulated/emulated models to the real world is critical and fundamental, since this is where most of the problems or restrictive situations that are over- looked in computational environments appear.

In this sense, this work is centered on a scenario with electric microgrid, which undoubtedly represents one of the most interesting locations found in the literature. Specifically, we are talking about the Center for the Development of Renewable Energies (CEDER) of Lubia (Soria - Spain), created in 1987 as a national center for the re- search and development of renewable energies. CEDER presents a microgrid on a real scale, and this facility is in Castilla y León, and is owned by the Center for Energy, Environmental and Technological Research (CIEMAT), Public Research Organization, currently under the Ministry of Economy, Industry and Competitiveness.

As will be seen later, CEDER is an ideal environment for the validation and experimentation of the application and integration of DG, electrical storage, power electronics and intelligence technologies applied to the operation and control of electric microgrids. All the elements that make up the microgrid (substation, transformers, DG, storage, loads, etc.) of CEDER are owned by CIEMAT, allowing any type of maneuver and operation.

Figure 1 shows an area image of the entire CEDER complex. The research center is deployed in some 640 ha, where, as already said, there is a real microgrid, operated and managed in real time, and where the charges and generators are real, and its operation has consequences on the energy flow of the microgrid.

Fig. 1. Aerial image of CEDER. The center is located on 640 ha of land. Courtesy of CEDER.

CEDER has a medium voltage grid (15 kV) and 8 transformation centers can be identified, which adjust the voltage from 15 kV to 400 V three-phase low voltage. CEDER has a contracted power of 115 kW, and the distribution company supplies electrical power at a voltage level of 45 kV which, through a transformer at the entrance to the center, is conditioned to 15 kV. The input transformer element is 45/15 kV and 1,000 kVA. Next, the center deploys a medium voltage network of about 3 km, interspersing transformation centers to supply low voltage to the consumptions and generators.

All *DG* elements, distributed electrical storage and loads, are connected at low voltage. With regard to demand, the center presents different consumption profiles, which are similar to those that can be found in an industrial environment, in the service sector or even in the domestic sector.

2.1   Elements of *Distributed Generation*

As it could not be otherwise, a microgrid must integrate elements of *DG*, therefore, CEDER presents an interesting variety of these elements, besides being all of them renewable. The electric microgrid installed in CEDER presents the following *DG* elements:

- Wind generation systems: horizontal axis and leeward wind turbine with 50 kW of installed capacity. In addition, it integrates a wind turbine with a hori zontal and windward axis with 3.5 kW of installed capacity.
- Photovoltaic generation system: the center integrates 6 photovoltaic systems. The first installation consists of 16 kW distributed in 64 monocrystalline panels of 250 W each, connected to a three-phase inverter of 15 kW. A second roof system consisting of 80 panels of monocrystalline silicon, distributed in 5 arrays connected in parallel, where each array, consists of 16 panels connected in series each, to make a total of 12 kW of power and connected to an inverter three-phase of 10 kW. The third system is another installation on roof of 12.6 kW in 54 monocrystalline photovoltaic panels of two

different brands, there are 36 of the brand LDK of 230 W and another 18 of the brand SACLIMA of 240 W, all of them connected to a three-phase inverter of 10 kW in 3 series of 18 panels each. A fourth roof installation of 23 kW is divided into two groups of modules, which form a first series of 84 and another of 154 modules, forming a total of 238 thin-film panels of 97 W per panel, distributed in 17 series of 14 panels each, feeding a three-phase inverter of 20 kW. The fifth installation (5.04 kW) is on ground distributed in 24 polycrystalline panels of 210 W each. The sixth installation is on roof, divided into three blocks (one of 48, another of 30 and another of 48 modules), to form a set of 126 polycrystalline photovoltaic modules of 310 W, connected to 2 three-phase inverters of 20 kW.

- Microcentral hydraulics with Pelton turbine (Fig. 2) and three-phase asynchronous generator coupled directly to the impeller of the turbine, with maxi- mum electrical power generated 40 kW. The installation is completed with a bank of capacitor banks to compensate the power factor of the installation. The system is controlled by means of a system of supervision, control and acquisition of its own data, with instructions for active power and regulation through flow through injectors.

Fig. 2. Pelton hydraulic microcentral installation. Courtesy CEDER.

2.2 Distributed Electrical Storage Elements

Achieving a balance in power in a microgrid is necessary. In order to achieve this, it is imperative that the *DG* elements are supported with distributed electrical storage. In this sense, CEDER integrates different storage technologies, which make the center a flexible environment for demand management. The electric microgrid installed in CEDER presents the following elements of distributed electrical storage:

- Mechanical storage: associated to the hydraulic microcentral, the center has 3 water reservoirs (2.000 m^3 and 70 m head) and a hydraulic pumps system by means of two centrifugal pumps of 18 kW of power each, which can be managed independently.
- Pb-acid storage: the center also integrates electrochemical storage through three banks of Pb-acid batteries. There are 3 batteries banks: The first bank is composed of 150 elements (2 V) and with capacity of 1080 Ah (C120), the second has 120 elements (2 V) and 765 Ah (C120) and the third one 24 elements (2 V) and 660 Ah (C120).
- Lithium-ion storage: they also integrate another electrochemical storage technology, specifically a lithium-ion battery with a capacity of 2 × 50 Ah. Figure 3 shows the Li-ion battery bank and its corresponding bi-directional inverter.

Fig. 3. Lithium-ion battery and bi-directional inverter. Courtesy CEDER.

2.3 Existing Demand

A microgrid must be completed with charges, which will request energy to perform its functions (motors, lighting, boilers, laboratories, etc.). To guarantee the supply of said loads, or at least of the priority ones, will be the responsibility of the manager of the microgrid.

In this sense, CEDER has loads that must be fed. In addition, these loads are what allow the day to day operation of the center, or in other words, the different buildings that make up the center are those that demand energy for its operation.

In addition, these real charges have different consumption patterns, so some facilities behave as an industrial environment, while others do so as a domestic consumer or the service sector. In this way, the microgrid has different consumption profiles, which will allow different adjustments to generation and storage, based on the varied behavior of the existing demand.

3 Monitoring of Microgrid

The control center of CEDER is in charge of monitoring the entire microgrid. All the loads (buildings and installations) of CEDER are connected to this centralized man- ager by means of ethernet technology, so that the data can be sent and received at any point of the center, to be processed in a decentralized way later. The monitoring also reaches the *DG* elements and distributed electrical storage.

To fulfill this purpose of monitoring, CEDER has a total of 53 single-phase and three-phase smart meters, and 9 data concentrators to record the measurements taken by them. Each transformation center integrates a data concetrator, and those with a dou- ble transformer incorporate a second data concentrator, in master-slave configuration. Smart meters obtain current and voltage data, active power, reactive power in the four quadrants, bidirectional active energy, reactive energy in the four quadrants and instan- taneous power factor. All mentioned devices incorporate communications technology through *PoweRline Intelligent Metering Evolution* (*PRIME*). Figure 4 shows a display of three-phase smart meters and a data concentrator of a transformation center.

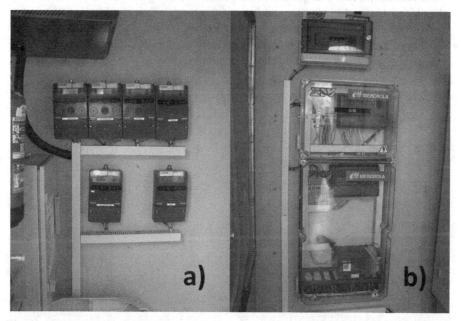

Fig. 4. (a) Smart meters for the measurement of consumption and *DG*; (b) Data concentrator in transformation center to monitor smart meters in low voltage.

4 Objectives of the CEDER-CIEMAT Electric Microrgrid

The main objective of the micro-network of CEDER is to approach the energy sustainability. For this, it is essential to integrate sources of renewable generation, small- scale
and as *DG*, and in this way reduce the dependence on foreign energy.

In addition, the communications displayed in CEDER allow achieving clear
objectives, namely:

- Monitoring: thanks to the advanced measurement it is possible to monitor the network
  topography, as well as its evolution over time through web services and specific
  software. In addition, it is possible to analyze the evolution of the different roles of the
  devices that make up the measure (smart meter and data concentrator), availability of
  the network, availability of smart meters, registered/deregistered devices and operation
  of the protocol *PRIME*.
- Intelligent measurement and management: the data coming from the measure are
  sent daily through scheduled tasks through web services implemented in the data
  concentrators. In this way, the data concentrators interrogate the smart meters of their
  subnet to obtain the specified information. The information is sent, in xml files, via
  FTP to the control center, where they are stored in data- bases. This information can
  be used for multiple offline processes: verification of simulations, training of models
  for predicting electricity demand or renewable generation, design of consumption and
  generation patterns, etc.
- Demand management: by comparing the tariff and electricity bills of CEDER with
  simulated tariffs and load profiles, it is possible to design behavior pat- terns with
  the objective of reducing costs and improving energy efficiency. Figure 5 shows the
  measurement of different buildings of the CEDER.
- Quality of service (noise and interference): from a communication perspective, in an
  electrical microgrid a reliable means of communication is necessary for proper data

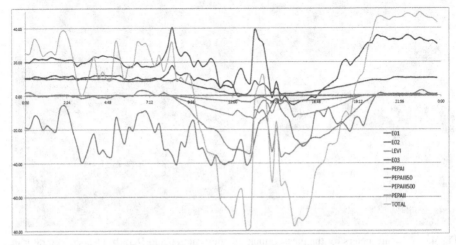

Fig. 5. (a) Daily consumption data collected

management. In this case, the electrical cable can be affected by interferences, which can cause alterations in the configuration of the network, as well as loss of data and the impossibility of controlling remote devices.

5 Conclusions and Future Jobs

The integration of renewable generation sources is a reality today. The integration is present in all the levels: transport and distribution in the electrical grids, and in the *SC*. In addition, the *SC* is also an integrator of the new paradigm that supposes the electric microgrid, being this in turn a *DG* integrator (renewable or not), distributed electrical storage and intelligence.

In this sense, the existence of demonstration environments and technology validators are crucial in the technological development. Electric microgrids position themselves as integrating spaces of different technologies, and of very different areas (energy, communications, systems, social, etc.).

This work has presented the electric microgrid of CEDER, located in Soria (Spain), which can be considered one of the most complete of the real microgrids in the world, mainly due to its great variety of *DG* and storage technologies.

Based on a very efficient and robust communications and monitoring layer, CEDER's microgrid effectively manages all its assets under its responsibility. In addition, this demonstration environment allows the addition of any other *DG* or storage element, since the CEDER dimensions allow it.

CEDER is presented as a perfect test scenario for the validation of electric microgrid technologies. The multiple possibilities that this environment allows, positions this microgrid as one of the most interesting in the world.

Acknowledgement. The authors thank the CYTED Thematic Network "CIUDADES INTELIGENTES TOTALMENTE INTEGRALES, EFICIENTES Y SOSTENIBLES (CITIES)" n° 518RT0558.

References

1. Calvillo, C.F., Sánchez-Miralles, A., Villar, J.: Energy management and planning in smart cities. Renew. Sustan. Energy Rev. **55**, 273–287 (2016)
2. Hernández-Callejo, L., Mirez, J., Horn, M., Bonilla, L.M.: Simulation of direct current microgrid and study of power and battery charge/discharge management. Dyna **92**, 673–679 (2017)
3. Schmitt, L., Kumar, J., Sun, D., Kayal, S., Mani Venkata, S.S.: Ecocity upon a hill: microgrids and the future of the Europeai city. IEEE Power Energ. Mag. **11**(4), 59–70 (2013)
4. Coelho, V.N., Coelho, I.M., Coelho, B.N., de Oliveira, G.C., Barbosa, A.C., Pereira, L., de Freitas, A., Santos, H.G., Ochi, L.S., Guimaraes, F.G.: A communitarian microgrid storage planning system inside the scope of a smart city. Appl. Energy **201**, 371–381 (2017)
5. Mwasilu, F., Justo, J.J., Kim, E.-K., Do, T.D., Jung, J.-W.: Electric vehicles and smart grid interaction: a review on vehicle to grid and renewable energy sources integration. Renew. Sustan. Energy Rev. **34**, 501–516 (2014)

6. Giuffre, T., Siniscalchi, S.M., Tesoriere, G.: A novel architecture of parking management for smart cities. Procedia Soc. Behav. Sci. **53**, 16–28 (2012)
7. Barone, R.E., Giuffre, T., Siniscalchi, S.M., Morgano, M.A., Tesoriere, G.: Architecture for parking management in Smart cities. IET Intel. Transp. Syst. **8**(5), 445–452 (2014)
8. Al-Hader, M., Rodzi, A.: The smart city infrastructure development & monitoring. Theor. Empirical Res. Urban Manag. **4**(2), 87–94 (2009)
9. Katiraei, F., Iravani, M.R.: Power management strategies for a microgrid with multiple distributed generation units. IEEE Trans. Power Syst. **21**(4), 1821–1831 (2006)
10. Zhou, H., Bhattacharya, T., Tran, D., Terence, T.S., Khambadkone, A.M.: Composite energy storage involving battery and ultracapacitor with dynamic energy management in microgrid applications. IEEE Trans. Power Electron. **26**(3), 923–930 (2011)
11. Chen, Y.-K., Wu, Y.-C., Song, C.-C., Chen, Y.-S.: Design and implementation of energy management system with fuzzy control for DC microgrid systems. IEEE Trans. Power Electron. **28**(4), 1563–1570 (2013)
12. Nejabatkhah, F., Li, Y.W.: Overview of power management strategies of hybrid AC/DC microgrid. IEEE Trans. Power Electron. **30**(12), 7072–7089 (2015)
13. Hernández, L., Baladrón, C., Aguiar, J.M., Calavia, L., Carro, B., Sánchez-Esguevillas, A., Cook, D.J., Chinarro, D., Gómez, J.: A study of the relationship between weather variables and Electric power demand inside a Smart grid/Smart world framework. Sensors **12**(9), 11571–11591 (2012)
14. Hernández, L.: Microrredes Eléctricas: Integración de generación renovable distribuida, almacenamiento distribuido e inteligencia. Garceta Grupo Editorial (2018)

Monthly Characterization of the Generation of Photovoltaic Arrays. Microgrid Case CEDER, Soria, Spain

Raúl A. López-Meraz[1]([⊠]) [iD], Luis Hernández-Callejo[2]([⊠]) [iD],
Luis Omar Jamed-Boza[1] [iD], and Víctor Alonso-Gómez[2] [iD]

[1] Universidad Veracruzana, Circuito Universitario Gonzalo Aguirre Beltrán s/n,
91000 Xalapa, Mexico
meraz_raul@hotmail.com, lojb33@gmail.com
[2] Universidad de Valladolid, Campus Universitario Duques de Soria s/n, 42004 Valladolid, Spain
{luis.hernandez.callejo,victor.alonso.gomez}@uva.es

Abstract. The implicit difficulties (resources and intermittent generation) of renewable energies prevent their insertion with greater security and reliability in electricity networks. However, as the priority of favoring environmental issues and represent one of the main axes of the electricity sector, it is essential to make efforts that characterize the behavior of the effective production of photovoltaic systems in real applications. In this way, the objective of this article is to propose a methodology where the monthly profile of future facilities is estimated. To this end, the received solar radiation (based on the Gamma probability distribution) is modeled along with the generation of seven photovoltaic arrays of different technology, connected to the microgrid of the Center for the Development of Renewable Energies (CEDER), belonging to the Center of Energy, Environmental and Technological Research (CIEMAT), located in Soria, Spain. The measurement of the solar resource was made with a Baseline Surface Radiation Network, and the injection of photovoltaic power to the microgrid was acquired with the help of smart meters. The verification of the procedure was carried out with simulations in Matlab and the statistical analyzes were confirmed with the JMP software. The results may be helpful in sizing a backup model and will collaborate in the proper management of the case study energy.

Keywords: Gamma distribution · Microgrid · Radiation · Simulated power

1 Introduction

In recent years, humanity demands a large amount of electricity; Latin America, for example, has a growth rate of 5% [1, 2]. The use of raw materials, the cornerstone of technical progress in the middle of the twentieth century, to satisfy consumption contributes to the erosion of nature and to promote anthropogenic climate change. In this scenario, renewable energies are incorporated as a new actor trying to cover what society requests in a less polluting way.

© Springer Nature Switzerland AG 2020
S. Nesmachnow and L. Hernández Callejo (Eds.): ICSC-CITIES 2019, CCIS 1152, pp. 185–198, 2020.
https://doi.org/10.1007/978-3-030-38889-8_15

There are essentially two schemes where renewable production is present. The first, distributed energy resources (DER), includes different aspects such as generation, storage and demand response. On the other hand, the new paradigms and the latest developments in the electricity sector are based on the introduction of distributed generation (DG), which is a philosophy where energy is not produced exclusively in large centralized plants, but also in smaller locations taking advantage of local conditions in order to minimize transmission/distribution losses, as well as optimizing production and consumption. This represents an opportunity for renewable energies, where elements such as photovoltaic panels and wind turbines, scattered throughout the network, supply installations on-site or sell energy depending on their generation/consumption conditions [3]. Consequently, according to data from the European Commission, DG penetration into the European network is estimated to be around 20–25% of the total generation by 2020, and by 2030 this figure will be set at 30–35%.

However, electricity generation based on renewable resources, mainly wind and solar, has highlighted additional challenges in the management of the electricity system, primarily due to the dispersion of this type of generators, the energy of changing output and to the inefficient coordination of the conditions of the electrical grid. These complications have created technical obstacles such as energy management, architecture design of electrical systems, voltage and frequency support, means of protection and low voltage aspects [4]. They also increase the computation difficulty due to the more complex and asymmetrical probability distributions associated with the intermittent plant [5]. In addition, given the considerable number of plants, there is the challenge of obtaining energy production data in real-time [6]. Other relevant issues are the difference, in statistical terms, between the availability of intermittent source resources and conventional generation, as well as the contribution that oscillating production can make to satisfy the peak demand of the system while maintaining its reliability [7].

Complications caused by photovoltaic generation are dependent on solar radiation, promoting the interest of different studies to find a probability model that best fits your measurement. Thus, [8] performs a radiation analysis in Taiwan with Weibull distributions, logistics, Normal and logNormal without detecting bimodal behavior. Also, in [9] they claim that the variation in radiation does not follow bimodal behavior. In addition, the study of the behavior of global radiation in the M'Sila region (Algeria) is developed in [10], using 6 individual frequency distributions finding that the Weibull distribution best matches the measured data for all months, that is, they did not find a bimodal fit either. On the other hand, [11, 12] argue bimodal performance in the distribution of radiation observations, [13] they analyze solar radiation records and similarly detect bimodal behavior in the distribution of data for intervals less than 60 min.

Given the importance of photovoltaic generation, this work attempts to approximate the quantification of the real power supplied from photovoltaic arrays (PVA) to the microgrid of the Center for the Development of Renewable Energies (CEDER) belonging to the Center for Environmental and Technological Energy Research (CIEMAT) located in Soria, Spain. The analysis focuses on modeling, on a monthly basis, the radiation with the Gamma probability distribution and, at the same time, finding relationships between it and the individual production in days with the best solar resource finding the profile of each PVA. The text is structured as follows: Sect. 2 describes the components of the case study and methodology used to model the radiation and determine the association functions between the solar resource and the PV power, the following part, with the help of the software JMP version 2.0, shows the results of the monthly radiation characterization and the reasons that represent the behavior of the Afvs are found to estimate the monthly power achieved by the solar array, the verification of the proposed has been achieved with the simulation in Matlab 2005a. Finally, the most relevant conclusions are presented.

2   Materials and Methods

In order to facilitate the understanding of the methodology developed and the variables involved in it, Fig. 1 shows the corresponding flow chart. Lines below deepen these sections.

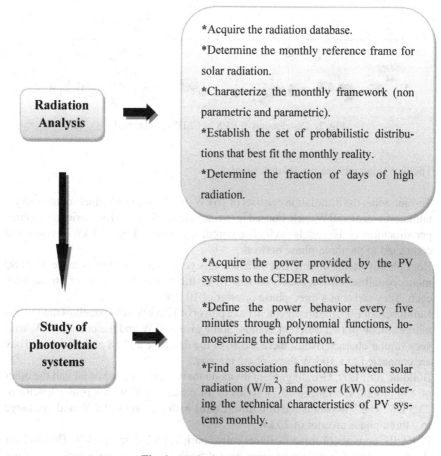

Radiation Analysis

*Acquire the radiation database.

*Determine the monthly reference frame for solar radiation.

*Characterize the monthly framework (non parametric and parametric).

*Establish the set of probabilistic distributions that best fit the monthly reality.

*Determine the fraction of days of high radiation.

Study of photovoltaic systems

*Acquire the power provided by the PV systems to the CEDER network.

*Define the power behavior every five minutes through polynomial functions, homogenizing the information.

*Find association functions between solar radiation (W/m^2) and power (kW) considering the technical characteristics of PV systems monthly.

Fig. 1. Methodological flow chart.

2.1 Case of Study

Of all the manageable components of CEDER's microgrid, this work focuses on a photovoltaic generation whose total peak power is of 78 kW. As shown in Fig. 2, the PVAs are assembled into five generation groups [14], three of them are on roofs and the rest are at floor level.

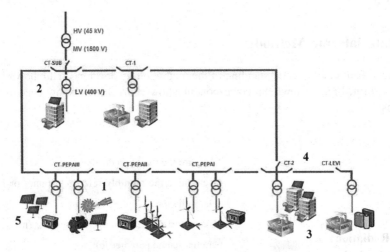

Fig. 2. Distribution of RES in CEDER microgrid.

The five solar sets are briefly described.

1. Turbine zone: the installation consists of 16 kW distributed in 64 panels of monocrystalline silicon of 250 W each, housed in two structures, forming four series (two series per structure) of 16 panels each. The output is connected to a 15 kW inverter and connected to the three-phase network.
2. Roof photovoltaic building E01 Arfrisol: this generator of 12 kW is made up of 80 monocrystalline silicon panels of 150 W, distributed in five series of 16 modules each. They arrive at a three-phase inverter of 10 kW.
3. Building roof E03: the arrangement has a power of 12.5 kW in 54 panels of monocrystalline silicon of two different brands. Some give 230 W and the other 240 W, with very similar characteristics, there are 36 of the first type and 18 of the second. They are connected to a 10 kW three-phase inverter.
4. Building roof E09, Grinding: plant divided into two groups, one of 84 and the other of 154 modules, arranged in 17 series of 14 panels each, with a peak capacity of 23.5 kW. The 238 panels are thin film (CdTe) with a power of 97 W and discharge to a three-phase inverter of 20 kW.
5. PEPA III: consists of three facilities called park 1, park 2 and park 3. They deliver their generation to single-phase inverters of 5 kW, connecting each park to a phase. Structures 2 and 3 are the same. Park 1: consists of 24 modules of polycrystalline silicon distributed in four series of 6 panels, its peak power is 5 kW. Parks 2 and

3: generators of 32 modules of monocrystalline silicon of 140 W, grouped in four series of 8 panels, providing a maximum power of 4.5 kW.

The measurement of the solar radiation in situ was made with a Baseline Surface Radiation Network (BSNR), being the period recorded from May 30, 2012 to March 3, 2015, in total 442,905 records of 5 min. The monitoring of the power injection produced by the photovoltaic plants to the CEDER network was done through intelligent meters, their acquisition is exported to a database formed at different granularity, 5 min and hourly, respectively. The correspondence between the measuring equipment and its respective PVA is presented in Table 1.

Table 1. Smart Meters with your generation plant.

Smart Meter	PV generator	Meter	PV generator
AE1037	Park 1	AE2005	E03
AE1038	Park 2	AE2010	Turbine zone
AE1044	Park 3	AE4360	E09 grinding
AE2000	E01 Arfrisol		

2.2 Radiation Modeling

Gamma Distribution

Since the behavior of a random variable is described by its probability distribution the closest to the measured monthly radiation was sought. Among the most useful for representing atmospheric parameters is Gamma, which is suitable for modeling when bias, positive asymmetry and time is involved. Such environmental measures include precipitation, wind speed and relative humidity, all restricted by a physical limit.

In short, the Gamma distribution is the one where the random variable occurs α times until there is a certain event [15]. Its density function is given by:

$$f(x) = \begin{cases} \frac{1}{\beta^\alpha \Gamma(\alpha)} x^{\alpha-1} e^{\frac{-x}{\beta}}, & \text{for } x > 0;\ \alpha, \beta > 0 \\ 0 \end{cases} \tag{1}$$

Where α is the shape parameter and β the scale parameter. When large values of α occur, distributions result in less bias and a shift in the probability of density to the right. For very large values of α ($50 < \alpha < 100$) the distribution approximates, in its form, the normal. The parameter β "extends" or "squeezes" the function to the right or to the left, when β is large the curve is more elongated [16]. The main cases of this distribution are as follows: with $\alpha < 1$ it is strongly skewed to the right. For $\alpha < 1$ the function cuts the vertical axis in $1/\beta$ with $x = 0$ (in this scenario is called exponential distribution). With $\alpha > 1$ the distribution begins at the source, $f(0) = 0$.

To model the radiation the analysis was carried out with the Normal and Gamma distribution, individually and in combination, that is, two Normal distributions and two

Gamma, respectively. The JMP software was used, filtering the information for each month, with a granularity of 5 min and limiting the records to the existence of radiation. In the first two analyzes the Kolmogorov - Smirnov - Lilliefors (KSL) and Cramer-Von Mises (CVM) goodness of fit tests are applied to determine whether or not the null hypothesis is rejected. In the case of Gamma behaviors, goodness of curve fit test was developed using the Pearson statistic with the simultaneous quantification of four parameters, obtaining the observed frequency directly from the measurements and testing the parameter values adjusting them to create minimization of the statistic of χ^2. The process of obtaining the parameters, for each month, was carried out in the Excel program so that said test maximized the probability of the right tail of the χ^2 itself. The hypothesis test applied in the adjustment of the goodness of fit is:

- Create classes in the histogram. There are as many classes as 5 min measurements exist in each month.
- Locate the original data in each class, i.e., the observed frequency (*ofr*) is found.
- Create the hypothesis test (HT). H0: Do the original data follow two Gamma distributions with their parameters α_a, β_a and α_b, β_b? H1: does not comply with the above.
- Prepare the expected frequency table (*efr*).
- Calculate the statistical χ_v^2: $\chi_0^2 = \sum_{i=1}^{k} \frac{(ofr_i - efr_i)^2}{efr_i}$. Where: v represents the degrees of freedom (DF). $v = k - P - 1$, with k the number of classes and P the parameters to be determined.
- The criterion for rejection of H0 is: $\chi_0^2 > \chi_{v,\alpha}^2$
- If it is not possible to reject, we can assume, with confidence of (1-α) % that the data set does meet the double Gamma distribution.

Approach Index to Measurements
In order to demonstrate the reliability of radiation simulation, an indicator was established to demonstrate proximity to measured data. The proximity index to measurements (Ipm) is defined with the help of the following expressions:

$$\phi = \frac{dr_{pS}}{dr_{pT}} \tag{2}$$

$$f_{dif} = (\phi - 1)\left[\frac{fda_T}{fda_S}\right](f) \tag{3}$$

$$I_{am} = (1 - f_{dif})(100) \tag{4}$$

Where ϕ is the ratio of the simulated reference splines (dr_{pS}) and the theoretical one obtained with the information (dr_{pT}) [17], f_{dif} is the fraction of difference and is a function of the fractions of days of good theoretical radiation (fda_T), of that provided by the simulation (fda_S) and of the random factor $f = \frac{1}{\sigma^2}$ where σ^2 is the variance of the combined simulation of the crossed gamma adjusted to the nearest integer.

Fraction of High Radiation Days
To determine the percentage of days with better radiation were found two monthly values,

these are: reference distance (rd) represented by the radiation peak measured from the spline reference frame and high distance (hd) estimated from the points observed with the highest magnitude. In this way the fraction of high radiation days was found: $F_{hr} = \frac{rd}{hd}$. When there are days of higher radiation the spline "rises", thus both distances are close, indicating the presence of a greater number of days where the radiation is considered high.

Radiation Conformation

The structure of the monthly radiation matrix (Rad), which represents the 12 months of the year, consists of 192 elements consisting of 12 rows and 16 columns. Its configuration is as follows: the elements located in the first six positions correspond to the β's of the polynomials of each month, obtained from the characterization of radiation [17]; the number of days (nd) is found in column seven, the following three parameters are the maximum reached value, that is, the peak radiation (pr), the magnitude of the reference spline (rd) and the minimum value (mv). The start (sr) and end (er) readings of the radiation measurement form columns eleven and twelve and the last four are the coefficients of α and β of the two Gammas distributions; in this way, α_a and β_a equal the simulation on sunny days and α_b and α_b represent the cloudy days.

2.3 Photovoltaic Systems

Standardization of PV Power

The analysis of the solar systems was carried out in two parts. In the first one the radiation was directly related, in the days with the best resource (the PV systems in their design are independent of environmental variations in their operation), and the production of the PVAs measured by the following equipment: AE1037, AE1038, AE1044, AE2000 AND AE2005. It is important to remember that the systems measured by AE1038 and AE1044 correspond to exactly the same facilities in their architecture and type of technology. However, power variations were found in four months, and consequently, the analysis of the park two only covers the months of July, August, September and October. The second section corresponded to the characterization of the power obtained by the meters AE2010 and AE4360; different polynomial adjustments without transformation were tested finding few correlations, so it was decided to analyze the transformation with logarithm base 2 in the response (power) to improve the experimental space of measurements and to clearly represent its behavior. The reason for using transformation with base logarithm 2 instead of the traditional natural logarithm was to observe improvement in correlation by reducing the base exponent e to 2, better adjusting both curves to the "m" type characteristic.

In the absence of congruence in the measured time interval, the equivalence of power was thus obtained every five minutes on the basis of the radiation collected. This results in their behavior over that period of time, homogenizing the information between generated power and measured radiation.

Association Functions (r's)

The monthly relationship between the measurements of energy produced and radiation received is found with polynomial functions in the form of reasons that allow it to be segmented to any granularity. This intrinsically characterization links other particularities such as type of technology, connections between cells, geometric construction, etc. In addition, since each PV system has its nominal power referenced at 1,000 W/m^2, the peak functions (rp) are obtained. Thus we have Eqs. 5 and 6:

$$r = \frac{E}{R} \tag{5}$$

$$r_p = \frac{E_p}{R_p} \tag{6}$$

Where E is the energy produced by each PVA, R represents the measured radiation, E_p and R_p describe the energy and radiation in maximum conditions, respectively. It is worth mentioning that in the PVAs of higher production the functions r and r_p were converted again with the help of the following property of the logarithms: $log_a N = \frac{InN}{In_a}$. Where a is the basis of logarithm and N is the number to be transformed.

From the above, it is possible to determine the simulated power (kW) of each of the PVA by means of Eq. 7.

$$P_{sim} = \left(\frac{P_n}{1000} \right) Rad_{sim} \left(\frac{r}{r_p} \right) \tag{7}$$

Where P_{sim} is the simulated power (kW), P_n is the rated power (kW) of each FV system, Rad_{sim} is the radiation (W/m^2) that the simulator generates, r and r_p are the associations between the energy produced and the radiation at a certain instant and in peak conditions, respectively. However, where radiation exceeds 1 kW/m^2 the PV production shall be higher than the nominal one.

3   Results

3.1   Radiation

Normal and Gamma Distributions
First of all, the adjustment with the normal distribution was developed, the KSL test was applied and the H0 was rejected, later, the Gamma distribution was tested, and this, without a doubt, is better approached to reality; however, the CVM goodness test also rejected H0. For simplicity, it has been decided to show only the radiation behavior of January through a histogram with their respective classes. Figure 3 shows the adjustment of the Normal distribution and Fig. 4 the corresponding analysis with the Gamma distribution, each with their respective tests of goodness of fit.

The reason for rejecting the adjustment of the normal distribution lies in the following fact: under this behavior, the average and the standard deviation of the data represent the possible best fit, clearly in the figure the null approach is observed.

When an asymmetric distribution, such as Gamma, is applied to the information, the methodology for achieving the best possible adjustment consists in optimizing the shape parameter (α) since it represents the region of greatest probability (area under the curve) and obtaining the average of the data to estimate the value of the scale parameter

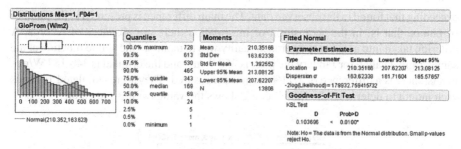

Fig. 3. Normal distribution for the month of January.

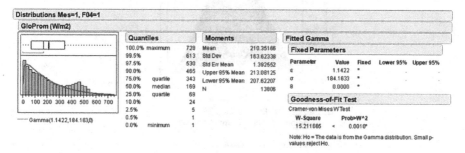

Fig. 4. Gamma distribution for the month of January.

(σ), due to the above, in the figure there is a better visual adjustment in the upper part and in the asymptotic low zone there is a mismatch. However, the proximity is greater compared to the normal distribution.

By reviewing the behaviors of the experimental points and histograms, it was detected that there is no single distribution; that is, there are two different probabilistic behaviors. Visually the first behavior, between 0 and 350 W/m^2, tends to be a gamma with $\alpha = 1$ (exponential) and the second to a normal one, its combined effect would generate the histogram of the data.

The previous combination was tested without the expected response. Due to this, two normal curves were associated, being equally rejected. When this possibility was ruled out, two crossed Gamma distributions were tested: the first represents the days of greatest radiation and the crossed one the low ones. When performing different tests, combining them and varying their characteristic parameters, the strong approximation with the radiations measured in each month is observed, generating them without spaces that serve as the input of the photovoltaic systems.

Radiation Simulation with Gamma Distributions

In order to find the parameters of the Gamma distributions that reflect an approach to radiation, four simulations were made, creating four years of radiation. Figure 4 warns the fourth simulation for the month of January.

In Fig. 5, 15,000 simulated points are observed every five minutes of the radiation, as well as the spline adjustment that reaches a correlation factor ($r = \sqrt{R^2}$) of 0.7141, exceeding that found in the observed data. The main difference is presented in the number of points, that is, in the acquisition of information there are absences of records. A criterion taken into account to approach reality was to maintain the spline function at the same original value, for January the peak is 350 W/m^2 and the original is 346.157 W/m^2, that is, there is a difference of 1.11% from the measured. They were simulated 10 times each month to determine the Ipm; Table 2 shows the values of this indicator.

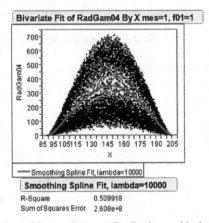

Fig. 5. Radiation simulation with two Gamma distributions with their corresponding spline fit for the month of January.

Table 2. Radiation measurement approach index.

Month	Ipm (%)	Month	Ipm (%)
January	98.9	July	94.9
February	98.6	August	95.4
March	98.1	September	98.7
April	93.4	October	97.6
May	97.3	November	98.1
June	97.6	December	96.9

As shown in the table, no Ipm exceeds the measured by 10%. April is the month where the difference is greater with 6.6%, due to intermittences of great duration, and in the months with low temperatures the simulator is closer to the measurements.

Matrix Rad
The matrix that was formed for the simulation of the particular radiation of each month is presented in Table 3.

Table 3. Matrix Rad

β_0	β_1	β_2	β_3	β_4	β_5	nd	hd	rd	mv	sr	er	α_a	β_a	α_b	β_b
$5.4e^3$	-184.1	2.2	$-1.06e^{-2}$	$1.79e^{-5}$	0	31	750	346.1	25	89	204	4.6	42	5.8	28
$4.0e^3$	-147.1	1.8	$-9.08e^{-3}$	$1.53e^{-5}$	0	28	975	445.2	60	84	210	5.6	48	5.7	45
$1.8e^3$	-83.1	1.2	$-6.17e^{-3}$	$1.06e^{-5}$	0	31	1000	537.3	30	79	216	6.2	48	7	45
$2.0e^3$	-89.0	1.3	$-6.63e^{-3}$	$1.14e^{-5}$	0	30	1280	654.4	30	69	226	5.7	47	7.5	45
$3.1e^3$	-143.0	2.3	$-1.52e^{-2}$	$4.51e^{-5}$	$-5.0e^{-8}$	31	1300	739.9	5	64	231	3.5	85	7.8	58
$4.8e^2$	-40.2	0.8	$-4.37e^{-3}$	$7.65e^{-6}$	0	30	1325	838.6	5	62	236	3	95	8.5	65
$2.6e^3$	-126.4	2.1	$1.37e^{-2}$	$3.93e^{-5}$	$-4.1e^{-8}$	31	1380	861.4	0	64	231	3.2	110	0	0
$3.7e^3$	-168.4	2.7	$-1.75e^{-2}$	$5.11e^{-5}$	$-5.6e^{-8}$	31	1350	834.2	0	69	226	3.3	100	0	0
$5.4e^3$	-232.7	3.5	$-2.32e^{-2}$	$6.99e^{-5}$	$-7.9e^{-8}$	30	1100	677.4	5	74	220	2.8	84	8.5	50
$6.2e^3$	-240.6	3.3	$-2.02e^{-2}$	$5.57e^{-5}$	$-5.6e^{-8}$	31	975	509.3	5	84	213	5	60	8.5	42
$5.2e^3$	-177.7	2.1	$-1.01e^{-2}$	$1.71e^{-5}$	0	30	800	339.5	5	89	204	5.1	62	8.2	30
$6.7e^3$	-224.1	2.6	$-1.26e^{-2}$	$2.14e^{-5}$	0	31	650	346.9	5	93	200	4.7	45	6.1	31

The simulator, automatically, decides the section of the matrix from which it will take the information when requesting the generation of a certain month. As a characteristic of the polynomials, a majority of negative odd coefficients are observed in contrast to the pairs, this means that, being the horizontal axis always positive, odd-order contributions compensate for ever increasing increases in even contributions. Since all functions are of 4th and 5th order, at least 3 curvature changes are possible, reflecting the radiation behavior. The parameters α and β of the Gamma distributions are highlighted in the matrix.

3.2 Photovoltaic Generation

r's Function

With the intention of exposing the three typical behaviors, it has been decided to present models of the functions found with their statistical analyzes. For this, Fig. 6, show the reasons of three AFVs measured by AE1037 (March), AE1044 (June) and AE2000 (March), respectively.

The characterization of the functions r's of the first PVA shows, on the one hand, the best adjustments in the months of March and December, with coefficients R^2 of 0.97 and 0.92 respectively; on the other hand, the approaches with less quality in the prediction are the months of May, July and September. Relations in parks 2 and 3 show better correlations between 0.91 and 0.99. In the three PVAs of lower power perfectly marked behaviors of "U" prevail in the "cold" and "M" in the "hot" months. The best correlations, in general, coincide in the fourth PVA and at the same time, their characterizations are more complex (4° and 5°), in the months where the temperature is low they are perceived behaviors in the form of "∩" and under this trend the reasons are better. The latter system has greater diversity in the behaviors found, however, it is still the high order functions that best fit.

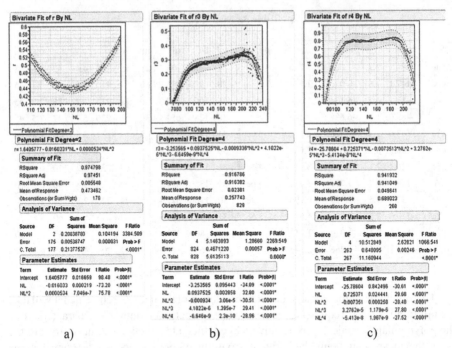

Fig. 6. r's function. (a) Park 1 for the month of March, (b) Park 3 for the month of June, (c) E01 Arfrisol for the month of March.

It is emphasized that in each of the analyzes meaningful relationships ($\alpha \leq 0.05$) are met and all the estimated parameters satisfy the tests of statistical behavior causing the regression.

Photovoltaic Power Simulation

Although the simulator has an interval where the user can request different powers of the PVA it was decided to use the CEDER nominals to compare the simulation with its consumption, the period requested was one year. Table 4 shows two of the most important characteristics: F_{hr} is the factor of days where the radiation is greater than the reference spline and P_{pmed} corresponds to the average peak photovoltaic power of all PVAs.

The table shows three months that would not cover, on average, the maximum power of the CEDER (40 kW). For its part, the summer months would supply this requirement without any difficulty, it would even be necessary to define which solar generators would interrupt its connection to the micro network. The above is clearly reflected in the F_{hr}, with an exceptional case being December, reaching 8.3% of days above the expected. During the months of June-August, P_{pmed} reached the nominal PV power installed. As the simulation reflects, lower production is frequently present in November.

Table 4 General monthly behavior of radiation and PV power.

Month	F_{hr}	P_{Pmed} (kW)
January	0.452	28.160
February	0.536	42.110
March	0.548	52.260
April	0.500	56.078
May	0.581	66.735
June	0.633	77.341
July	0.613	79.299
August	0.677	79.150
September	0.567	53.346
October	0.484	50.560
November	0.267	27.404
December	0.613	29.776

4 Conclusions

For the approach of the behavior of the monthly radiation is proposed a double distribution of probability Gamma, reaching a strong approximation to the reality shown by the Ipm, standing out as one of the few investigations that silver a double simulation. Moreover, achieving these results required only four simulations.

On the other hand, the PVAs have a similarity in the form of their regression curves according to the ambient temperature existing in each month, favoring the electric production cold climatic conditions. With the help of the relationships, under the best conditions between PV power and radiation, factors such as the geometry of PVAs, wiring losses, soil degradation and aging have been included in the characterization, which is not present in the measurements. Functions were also established at any granularity of time for future analysis. In all regression studies, the parameters meet the significance tests achieving a 95% confidence interval. In addition, the functions with the best correlations are independent of their degree.

All of the above has allowed us to establish, approximately, the capacity of the backup system needed in each month to meet the demand of the CEDER. Likewise, the results obtained will be raw material in the development of an energy management system of the same microgrid.

Acknowledgments. We would like to thank the CEDER by providing information for the development of this work.

References

1. Rudnick, H., Barroso, L., Skerk, C., Blanco, A.: South American reform lessons - twenty years of restructuring and reform in Argentina, Brazil, and Chile. Power Energy Mag. **3**, 49–59 (2005)
2. Mocarquer, S., Barroso, L., Rudnick, H., Bezerra, B., Pereira, M.: Balance of power. Power Energy Mag. **7**, 26–35 (2009)
3. Hernández, L., et al.: Artificial neural network for short-term load forecasting in distribution systems. Energies **7**, 1576–1598 (2014)
4. The Royal Academy of Engineering: The cost of generation electricity. Published by The Royal Academy of Engineering, London (2004)
5. Anderson, D.: Power system reserves and costs with intermittent generation. UK Energy Research Centre Working Paper (2006)
6. Lin, S., Chen, J.: Distributed optimal power flow for smart grid transmission system with renewable energy sources. Energy **56**, 184–192 (2013)
7. Skea, J., Anderson, D., Green, T., Gross, R., Heptonstall, P., Leach, M.: Intermittent renewable generation and maintaining power system reliability. IET Gener. Transm. Distrib. **2**, 82–89 (2008)
8. Chang, T.: Investigation on frequency distribution of global radiation using different probability density functions. Int. J. Appl. Sci. Eng. **8**(2), 99–107 (2010)
9. Sánchez, R., Aguirre, G., Sánchez, S., Alcalá, J.: Investigando variaciones aleatorias de radiación solar en Guadalajara, México. Revista Iberoamericana de Ciencias (2016)
10. Razika, I., Nabila, I.: Modeling of monthly global solar radiation in M'sila region (Algeria). IEEE (2016). 978-1-4673-9768-1/16
11. Assunção, H., Escobedo, J., Oliveira, A.: Modelling frequency distributions of 5 minute-averaged solar radiation indexes using Beta probability functions. Theor. Appl. Climatol. **75**, 213–224 (2003)
12. Soubdhan, T., Emilion, R., Calif, R.: Classication of daily solar radiation distributions using a mixture of Dirichlet distributions. Aricle soumis à Solar Energy (2008)
13. Jurado, M., Caridad, J., Ruiz, V.: Statistical distribution of the clearness index with radiation data integrated over five minute intervals. Sol. Energy **55**, 469–473 (1995)
14. Uribe-Pérez, N., Latorre, M., Angulo, I., De la Vega, D.: Aprovechamiento de los recursos renovables e integración de las TICs: ejemplo práctico de una Microred eléctrica. In: III Congreso Ibero-Americano de Empreendedorismo, Energía, Ambiente e Tecnología, pp. 161–166. Instituto Politécnico de Braganca, Portugal (2017)
15. Arroyo, I., Bravo, C., Llinás, H., Muñoz, F.: Distribuciones poisson y gamma: una discreta y continua relación. Prospect **12**(1), 99–107 (2014)
16. Bidegain, M., Diaz, A.: Análisis estadístico de datos climáticos, p. 15. Universidad de la República. Uruguay (2011)
17. López, R., Hernández, L., Jamed, L., Alonso, V.: Solar intermittency with Spline fit modeling. Microgrid case CEDER, Soria, Spain. In: I Ibero-American Congress of Smart Cities, pp. 592–601. Universidad Santiago de Cali, Colombia (2018)

Urban Data Analysis for the Public Transportation System of Montevideo, Uruguay

Renzo Massobrio[✉] and Sergio Nesmachnow

Universidad de la República, Montevideo, Uruguay
{renzom,sergion}@fing.edu.uy

Abstract. This article presents a study of the public transportation system in Montevideo, Uruguay, following a data science approach. More than 20 million records from the Intelligent Transportation System (ITS) are analyzed in order to characterize mobility in the city. Several useful pieces of information are obtained through data analysis, related to tickets sold, patterns of smart card utilization, most used bus lines and stops, and socioeconomic insights about passengers behavior. Practical case studies are also presented: anomaly detection in space and time, and a study of potential safety hazards due to reckless driving. The work reported in this article constitutes one of the first steps towards using data from the ITS in Montevideo to understand mobility in the city.

Keywords: Data science · Public transportation · Smart cities

1 Introduction

Public transportation plays a major role in urban mobility, as they are the most efficient, sustainable, and socially fair mode of transportation [9]. Understanding the interaction between citizens and public transportation systems is paramount in order to design and implement policies aimed at improving mobility.

Modern *smart cities* take advantage of technology to improve urban services [6]. Urban traffic and transportation systems are addressed under the paradigm of smart cities, in what is referred to as *smart mobility* [3]. Related to this concept are Intelligent Transportation Systems (ITS), which use technology to develop and enhance transportation. In addition to improving mobility, ITS allow collecting large volumes of urban data [7]. Large repositories of data offer a unique opportunity to gain valuable insights into the mobility of citizens [12]. In this context, urban data analysis arises as a tool to extract meaningful information from raw urban data to help decision-making processes in cities.

In 2010 an urban mobility plan was implemented in Montevideo, Uruguay, with the goal of restructuring and modernizing public transportation [1]. Under this plan, public transportation in the city was integrated into a unified system, which incorporates many of the characteristics common to ITS. Buses were equipped with on-board GPS units and ticket selling machines operated with smart cards. These devices represent new sources of urban data, which have a huge potential to help authorities understand mobility in Montevideo.

© Springer Nature Switzerland AG 2020
S. Nesmachnow and L. Hernández Callejo (Eds.): ICSC-CITIES 2019, CCIS 1152, pp. 199–214, 2020.
https://doi.org/10.1007/978-3-030-38889-8_16

This article presents a characterization of the use of the transportation system through urban data analysis, along with a series of case studies of potential use for these rich data sources. The article is organized as follows. Next section describes the data analysis process in smart cities. Section 3 describes the public transportation system in Montevideo, Uruguay. Specific case studies are described and analyzed in Sect. 4. Finally, Sect. 5 presents the conclusions and the main lines for future work.

2 Data Analysis in Smart Cities

This section introduces ITS in the context of smart cities, and urban data analysis as an efficient tool to extract meaningful information from urban data. Then, a brief review of related works in the literature is presented.

2.1 Smart Cities and ITS

The paradigm of smart cities proposes taking advantage of information and communication technologies to improve the quality and efficiency of urban services [6]. Smart devices embedded into traditional physical systems deployed on cities, generate vast volumes of data for the analysis. Extracting insights from the gathered data is crucial to improve decision-making in cities and to achieve quality improvements and increase the efficiency of public services.

Related to smart mobility, ITS integrate synergistic technologies, computational intelligence, and engineering concepts to develop and improve transportation. Automatic Vehicle Location (AVL) systems automatically determine and communicate the geographic location of a moving vehicle [17]. The transmitted locations of a fleet of vehicles can be collected at a central server to overview and control the group of vehicles. Due to its widespread availability, low cost, and precision, the most common technology to determine the location of vehicles in AVL is GPS. AVL technology is frequently incorporated in ITS and provides a rich source of data, as it can help to monitor and control the QoS provided by the transportation system to users.

Automatic Passenger Counters (APC) are electronic devices that can be incorporated to moving vehicles to record boarding and alighting data [5]. This technology is a major improvement over traditional manual passenger counts or surveys. Several implementations of this concept have been proposed including infrared lights in doorways of vehicles, scales to measure weight changes, and CCTV cameras coupled with computer vision software. The data generated by these systems allow identifying use patterns by linking boarding and alighting data with stop or station location [8].

Automatic Fare Collection (AFC) [4] automate the ticketing system on public transportation. AFC are comprised of fare media, devices to read/write onto these media, communication technologies, and back office systems. Contactless smart cards have become the de facto technology in AFC systems. AFC systems generate highly valuable data that can be processed to extract useful metrics for both day-to-day operation and long-term planning of transportation systems.

The development of smart tools that use data gathered by ITS has risen in the past years. These tools rely on efficient and accurate data processing (even in real-time), which poses an interesting challenge from the technological perspective. The methodology for analyzing sources of urban data to gain valuable insights to describe and improve the life of citizens is described next.

2.2 Urban Data Analysis

Data analysis is the process of collecting and processing raw data to extract meaningful information that provides supporting evidence for conclusions and helps decision-making processes. Multiple workflows have been proposed to describe the process of data analysis, and techniques under a variety of names have emerged in different fields of knowledge at both academia and industry.

The data analysis process starts and ends in the current reality. In urban contexts, the analysis starts with collecting raw data from a city and ends with communicating findings that can help stakeholders to shape the reality of that city to improve the quality of life of its citizens. In between, the data analysis process is comprised of several phases. Firstly, raw collected data must be processed. This phase include several tasks such as placing data into structures (e.g., tables), inspecting datasets, and cleansing data to detect missing or inaccurate records. After data processing, Exploratory Data Analysis (EDA) is performed [15]. This phase may lead to detecting further inaccuracies in the data and potentially requiring further cleansing. After EDA, statistical models and algorithms are applied to identify relationships between the studied data [11]. Finally, results are interpreted and communicated, mostly using visualization. When dealing with urban data, effectively communicating results is crucial, thus, the visualization phase is described in more depth in the following paragraphs.

2.3 Related Work

The advantages of using data analysis for social transportation have been studied in a thorough manner in the general review of the field developed by Zheng et al. [18]. The authors discussed the use of several sources of information, including vehicle mobility (e.g., GPS coordinates, speed data), pedestrian mobility (e.g., GPS and WiFi signals from mobile devices), incident reports, social networking (e.g., textual posts, user location), and web logs (e.g., user identification, comments). In the review, the advantages and limitations of using each source of data were discussed. Several other novel ideas to improve public transportation were also reviewed, including applying *crowdsourcing* techniques for collecting and analyzing real-time or near real-time traffic information, and using *data-based agents* for driver assistance and human behavior analysis. Finally, a data-driven social transportation system that integrates all the previous concepts and improves traffic safety and efficiency was proposed.

More related to the data analysis research included in this article, many works have studied urban mobility using smart card data from AFC in public transportation systems.

Bagchi and White [2] discussed the role of smart card data for travel behavior analysis. The transportation systems of Southport, Merseyside and Bradford in England were studied. The authors performed a simple study focused on the average number of trips and transfers made by passengers. The turnover rates were analyzed to identify the number of active users in the system. The research concluded that smart card data allow obtaining much larger samples than surveys to characterize transportation systems. However, certain information (e.g., purpose of traveling) cannot be inferred from these data. Thus, the authors conclude that smart card transactions are not an alternative to traditional data collection methods, but a useful complementary source of data.

Utsunomiya et al. [16] studied access and usage patterns of passengers in the transportation system of Chicago, US. The authors discussed the analysis using smart card sign-ups and transactions data, identifying the major issues encountered as well as general recommendations. The potential uses for smart card data were classified in categories: service planning, demand forecasting, pricing and fare policy definition, and market research. Seven days of recorded transactions were studied to analyze walking access distances, frequency of daily travel patterns, and passenger behavior by residential area. Frequent errors were due to missing transactions and incorrect bus route identification. In order to deal with these inconsistencies, the authors proposed combining smart card data with passenger counts and vehicle location from APC and AVL systems.

3   The Public Transportation System in Montevideo

This section presents the public transportation system in Montevideo, Uruguay, and the urban data analysis process to characterize its usage.

3.1   Overview of the City and Transportation System

Montevideo is the capital city of Uruguay, and extends to an area of only 530 km^2. Despite accounting for only 0.3% of the total surface of the country, nearly 40% of the total population lives in Montevideo.

The public transportation in Montevideo (Sistema de Transporte Metropolitano, STM), is comprised of 1528 buses operated by four private companies. The bus network consists of 145 main bus lines and 4718 bus stops, Bus lines have different variants, accounting for outward and return trips, as well as shorter versions of the same line. The total amount of bus lines when considering each variant individually is 1383. Figure 1 shows the bus lines that comprise STM according to data provided by [14].

Passengers of the public transportation system in Montevideo can use smart cards to pay for their tickets without physical money. STM smart cards are contact-less cards which are linked to the identity of the owner. Two different types of bus tickets are available which allow bus transfers: *one-hour* and *two-hours* tickets. One-hour tickets allow boarding up to two buses within an hour, while two-hours tickets grant unlimited bus transfers within a period of two hours. The fare scheme supports transfers between any bus line at any bus stop.

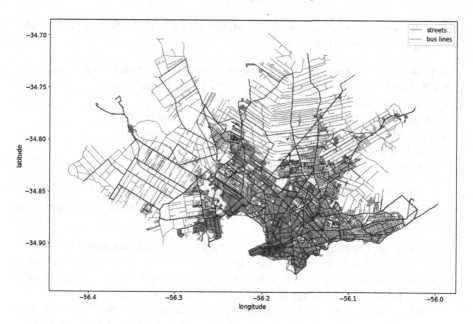

Fig. 1. Bus lines in STM

3.2   Data Collection and Cleansing

Data Collection. Many state agencies and local governments have web interfaces for publishing open data. In this context, the most useful web interface was the geographic information site at Intendencia de Montevideo (www.sig. montevideo.gub.uy), which holds geographic data of Montevideo including base maps, socioeconomic indicators, and transportation network data.

Besides using open data publicly available, the analysis included data regarding STM accessed through a collaboration between our research group and IM. The sources of these data are the AVL and AFC systems integrated in buses of the STM. The data corresponding to the full set of records of GPS bus location and bus ticket sales payed with STM cards during 2015 was released for research purposes. These large datasets comprise over 150 GB of raw data.

The bus location dataset contains information about the position of each bus in STM, sampled every 10 to 30 s. Each location record holds the following information:

- a unique bus line identifier.
- a unique trip identifier to differentiate trips of the same bus line.
- GPS coordinates.
- instant speed of the vehicle.
- time stamp when the GPS measure was taken.

Ticket sales data contain records related to each STM transaction made, including the following fields:

- trip identifier for the sale, which allows linking to the bus location dataset.
- GPS coordinates at the moment of the STM card validation.
- bus stop identifier.
- time stamp at the moment of the STM card validation.
- unique STM card identifier, hashed for privacy purposes.
- number of passengers traveling with the same STM card.
- leg number, for multi-leg trips that include transfers.

For the sake of clarity, the reported results correspond to tickets sold during May 2015. Pre-hoc analysis of the complete dataset showed that this month is representative of the full dataset.

Data Cleansing. Data cleansing is a mandatory step in data analysis that strives to detect and correct corrupt or inaccurate records [13]. Due to the lack of a backup source of information, records that appeared to be corrupted were simply filtered and deleted, according to the actions described next.

Vehicle location using GPS is prone to errors from a variety of sources. The most frequent error was records having a fixed value for both latitude and longitude, pinpointing to the middle of the Atlantic Ocean. Most likely, this was caused by an error message of the GPS unit being misinterpreted as a valid coordinate during data recording. 932.176 records suffered from this issue, accounting for nearly 4.6% of the total dataset. Additionally, 29.432 records corresponded to locations outside Montevideo. However, the dataset also holds the identifier of the boarding bus stop of each transaction, registered by the on-board GPS unit. Thus, even though the GPS measure at the moment of the transaction may fail, the boarding bus stop can be accurately determined from previous measures. Consequently, the bus stop identifier is more reliable than the raw GPS measure when defining the starting point of each trip.

Regarding time stamps of transactions, 74 sales corresponding to May 1st were filtered, since they correspond to Labour Day, a public holiday in which the transportation system is mostly inoperative. Those transactions represent a clear outlier from the remainder of the dataset. Similarly, only one transaction occurring on May 31st was present in the dataset. As a consequence, during the data analysis process, the month of May represents STM transactions occurring between May 2nd 00:00:00 to May 30th 25:59:59 of 2015.

Some transactions had trip identifiers which were not present in the GPS records. Since these records cannot be linked to their corresponding bus line, the 1634 records with this issue were discarded. Similarly, 22 transactions made with the same STM card during the same trip were detected in the original dataset. This might be explained by a synchronization problem between the bus and the centralized server where transactions are recorded.

Since the dataset corresponds to sales from 2015, some transactions refer to bus lines that were modified or no longer exist. These transactions (36.030 records) were also filtered from the dataset. Finally, 274.011 records were filtered, corresponding to transactions with identifiers of bus stops which were not part of the bus line route corresponding to the sale.

In summary, the complete data cleansing process consisted in filtering 311.772 out of a total of 20.359.835 records, accounting for 1.53% of the original dataset.

3.3 Characterizing Public Transport Utilization

This section presents the results from the data analysis process to describe the use of the transportation system in Montevideo from several perspectives.

Cardholders. The sales dataset holds transactions made with 654.228 STM cards. The public transportation system allows several passengers to travel together using the same STM card. Table 1 reports the number of passengers traveling with the same STM card. The vast majority of passengers use their personal STM card, with over 97% of transactions corresponding to individual ticket sales.

Table 1. Number of passengers traveling with the same STM card

# Passengers	Total	Percentage
1	19494451	97.24%
2	510043	2.54%
3	36454	0.18%
4	5468	0.03%
5+	1647	0.01%

Another interesting aspect that can be studied through data analysis is the frequency of use of the transportation system. Table 2 reports descriptive statistics of daily and monthly transactions per STM card. The *mean* number of transactions is reported, along with the standard deviation (*std*), the minimum (*min*) and the maximum (*max*) values, and the 25th (*Q1*), 50th (*Q2*), and 75th (*Q3*) percentiles. The 50th percentile corresponds to the median of the distribution of transactions per STM card. Monthly statistics consider all transactions done by each cardholder during May 2015. Daily transaction statistics only consider days for which at least one transaction was made.

When looking at monthly figures, cardholders perform over 30 transactions on average, nearly one transaction per day. However, the standard deviation is large, indicating a significant difference between regular and sporadic users of the public transportation system. The median of the monthly transactions is 22, nearly one transaction per working day in the month. Regarding daily use, the average cardholder performs 2.78 transactions each day that uses the transportation system. Figure 2 presents an histogram of daily transactions per STM card, considering only cards that made up to 10 transactions within the

Table 2. Descriptive statistics of daily and monthly use of STM cards

	STM transactions	
	Daily	Monthly
mean	2.78	30.65
std	1.53	28.14
min	1	1
Q1 (25%)	2	8
Q2 (50%)	2	22
Q3 (75%)	4	47
max	54	528

same day in order to remove outliers. Most cardholders perform two transactions per day, which probably correspond to direct trips used for commuting. It is interesting to observe that more cardholders perform four rather than three transactions. This might be explained by passengers commuting to work using a trip involving a transfer, thus, two transactions correspond to the outward trip and the remaining two transactions to the return trip.

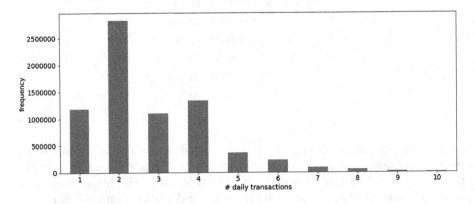

Fig. 2. Histogram of daily transactions per STM card during May 2015

A few interesting applications arise when looking at outliers within the STM use statistics. On the one hand, cardholders with very low activity can be identified by their card ID. For instance, in the studied dataset 15.440 cardholders performed only a single trip during the whole month of May 2015. Targeted marketing campaigns could be designed to encourage disengaged citizens to use the public transportation system more frequently. On the other hand, cardholders with large number of transactions can also be identified. In the studied dataset a single card was found to perform 54 transactions within the same day. Through data analysis, authorities may further investigate these situations in order to identify possible abuses to the rules of the transportation system.

Transactions per Bus Trip. Grouping STM transactions by their corresponding trip identifier provides a rough estimate for the number of boardings on each trip. Figure 3 presents a histogram of the number of transactions per trip. On average, 39.70 transactions are made in each bus trip (std: 28.16). The largest value encountered was a single trip with 249 transactions. It is worth noting that passengers might also board without using a STM card, so these figures represent a lower bound on the total number of boardings for each trip. Taking into account the capacity of the buses operating in Montevideo, the largest values may indicate overcrowding in some of the bus lines of the transportation system.

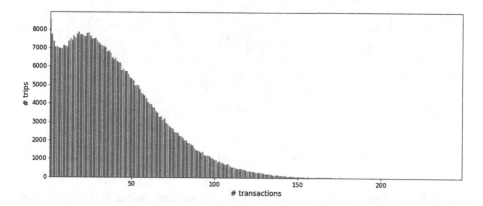

Fig. 3. Histogram of transactions per bus trip during May 2015

Most Used Bus Lines. Data analysis over the transaction data can be used to identify the most popular as well as the most underused bus lines. Figure 4 shows the ten most used bus lines. Some of the lines overlap since they correspond to different variants of the same line (e.g., outward and return lines). For each line the regular name (i.e., the name appearing in the front of the bus) is indicated in the map, along with its variant code indicated in parenthesis. The most used bus line is 183, closely followed by 181. Both lines connect the neighborhood of La Teja, located in the west side of Montevideo, with Pocitos, located in the south by the coastline. It is interesting to notice that none of the ten most used bus lines go into the city center.

Spatiotemporal Analysis of Transactions. The spatial and temporal dimensions of sales data can be combined, in order to gain insights that might not be evident when studying each dimension independently. Figure 5 shows an aggregated visualization of the spatiotemporal distribution of sales in Montevideo during May 2015. In this visualization the hours of the day are used as categories. Each transaction occurring at a given pixel in the image is categorized according to its time stamp. Then, the color of the pixel is set considering the amount of transactions on each category. The color mapping, which is detailed

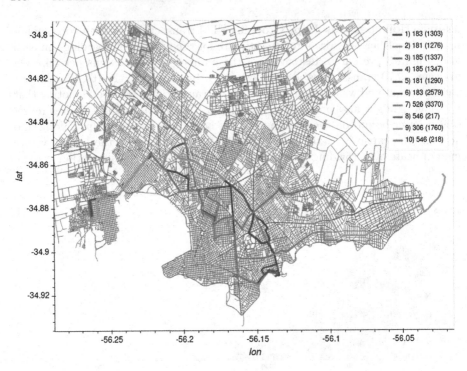

Fig. 4. Top 10 bus lines with most STM card transactions during May 2015 (Color figure online)

in the visualization, corresponds roughly to: red (12 a.m.), yellow (4 a.m.), green (8 a.m.), cyan (12 p.m.), blue (4 p.m.), purple (8 p.m.), and back to red, since hours and colors are both cyclic.

Firstly, it is observed that the city center has a prevalent blueish tone in the visualization. This corresponds to most transactions taking place between noon and the afternoon. This is consistent with the fact that many offices and public entities are located in this area of the city, thus, most transactions correspond to people commuting from the city center back to their homes by the end of the office-hours.

Another interesting fact arising from the spatiotemporal analysis of STM transactions is the clear difference between areas near the coast and areas farther away. It can be clearly observed that areas away from the coastline appear with more yellow and greener tones whereas areas closer to the coast have predominantly blue tones. This means that the majority of STM transactions in areas farther away from the coast occur earlier in the day than those near the coast. This can be explained by people commuting early in the day from these areas to workplaces located closer to the city center.

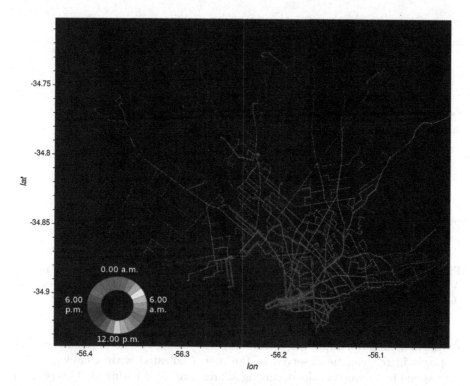

Fig. 5. Spatiotemporal distribution of trips in Montevideo during May 2015

4 Case Studies: Unexpected Events and Safety

This section outlines a series of case studies of uses of urban data analysis to detect special events and safety hazards within the public transportation system.

4.1 Anomaly Detection in the Spatial Dimension

Geolocation data of sales transactions can be used to detect abnormal situations in the transportation system. As an example, Fig. 6 shows a heatmap of transactions, along with the streets (in gray) and the bus lines (in blue). Two clusters of sales records (labeled A and B) appear in a street where no bus routes run. This represents a detour of one or more bus lines from their predefined routes. This may be due to an exceptional circumstance (e.g., road works) or due to a periodic event occurring certain days of the week (e.g., a flea market). Authorities can take advantage of this type of analysis to identify anomalies and make appropriate changes to bus routes and schedules.

4.2 Anomaly Detection in the Time Dimension

The time stamp of sales can be used to identify abnormal use patterns in the transportation system. Figure 7 shows an aggregated visualization of combined

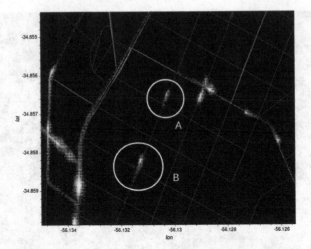

Fig. 6. Anomaly detection: example of detour. The blue lines represent bus routes. A and B are two clusters of transactions which occurred outside of the bus network. (Color figure online)

spatial and temporal information of smart card transactions data. A small cluster of pixels in red can be observed in the map (indicated with a circle), which correspond to a group of sales occurring approximately at midnight. This pattern significantly differs from the rest of the dataset. Given the location of these records, near an outdoor venue, the transactions probably correspond to a special event (e.g., a concert) taking place at night in this venue. In these occasions, bus companies usually assign buses to allow citizens to return to their homes

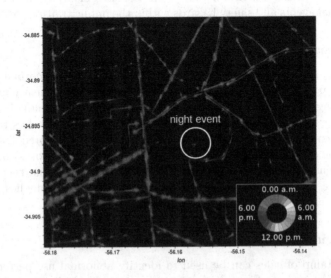

Fig. 7. Anomaly detection: example of event at midnight near an outdoor venue.

at the end of the event. Authorities can use urban data analysis to identify special events taking place in the city and implement strategies that improve the mobility of those attending these events.

4.3   Driving Behavior and Safety

Another interesting use for information is to analyze the spatial distribution of sales. Figure 8 shows a heatmap of transactions occurring in one-way streets. Arrows indicate the direction of each street and bus stops are represented using blue circles. The visualization shows that the spatial distribution of sales is skewed with respect to the location of the bus stops: more transactions occur after the location of the bus stop than before. This uneven distribution is probably caused by drivers moving the bus before all the boarding passengers validate their smart cards. This might represent a safety issue, since passengers are standing while validating their cards.

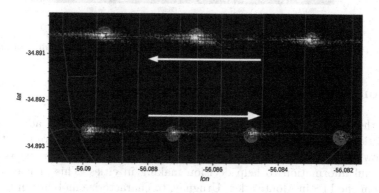

Fig. 8. Spatial distribution of transactions with regards to stop location: one-way streets

Figure 9 shows a heatmap of transactions near a roundabout, where a large number of transactions take place within the roundabout. Again, passengers are standing and validating their smart cards while the bus is moving. In fact, this might represent an even more serious issue, when drivers are also in charge of operating the smart card terminal. Driving and selling tickets at the same time is a risky behavior, frequently seen among bus drivers in Montevideo. The studied data provide evidences that support these observations. Authorities can use this type of data analysis to audit driving behavior, improving the safety of passengers and drivers of the transportation system.

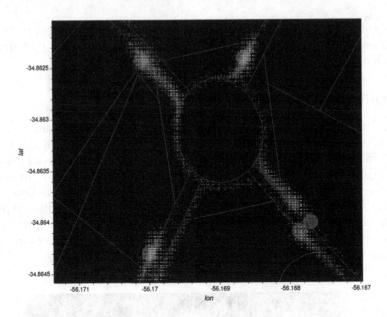

Fig. 9. Spatial distribution of transactions with regards to stop location: roundabout

5   Conclusions and Future Work

Under the paradigm of smart cities, ITS have emerged to take advantage of information and communication technologies to improve public transportation. ITS allow collecting massive amounts of urban data, which can be used to extract meaningful information to help decision making in cities. This article studied data from the ITS in Montevideo, Uruguay, to characterize mobility in the city.

The results reported in this article account for more than 20.4 million bus tickets sold using smart cards. During a data cleansing process, 1.53% of the records were filtered due to inconsistencies. Several insights were obtained through data analysis of the studied dataset, including: number of passengers traveling with the same smart card, frequency of use of the smart cards, number of bus transfers, number of transactions per bus trip, and most used bus lines and stops. A spatiotemporal analysis was also performed which revealed that citizens from areas farther away from the coastline start trips earlier than those near the coast.

Finally, some practical case studies on the use of data analysis on ITS data were presented, including: anomaly detection in space (to identify bus detours), anomaly detection in time (to identify events in the city), and a characterization of potential safety hazards due to reckless driving. Such analysis are useful for characterizing different aspects of mobility in smart cities [10,12].

The work reported in this article constitutes one of the first steps towards using data from the ITS in Montevideo to understand mobility in the city. As such, many lines of research remain to be explored in order to extract more and richer information that can be used to improve the public transportation system.

The data analysis reported in this article mainly focused in understanding the interaction between passengers and the transportation system. However, the available data sources offer the potential to study other very interesting aspects of mobility in the city. For instance, location data from AVL systems could be used to further study the QoS offered to citizens by the transportation system in terms of punctuality, frequency of lines, and load of passengers with regards to the bus capacity. Additionally, speed information of buses could be used to characterize the streets of the city and identify bottlenecks. This information could be used as input when designing new lines or re-designing existing ones.

Finally, it is worth noting that this work used ITS data from 2015. Since that year, the use of smart cards to pay for tickets has risen significantly. The proposed approach should be applied to recent ITS data when it becomes available publicly.

References

1. Abreu, P., Vespa, J.: Plan de Movilidad (2010). http://www.montevideo.gub.uy/sites/default/files/plan_de_movilidad.pdf. Accessed 30 Dec 2018
2. Bagchi, M., White, P.: The potential of public transport smart card data. Transp. Policy **12**(5), 464–474 (2005)
3. Benevolo, C., Dameri, R.P., D'Auria, B.: Smart mobility in smart city. In: Torre, T., Braccini, A.M., Spinelli, R. (eds.) Empowering Organizations. LNISO, vol. 11, pp. 13–28. Springer, Cham (2016). https://doi.org/10.1007/978-3-319-23784-8_2
4. Blythe, P.: Improving public transport ticketing through smart cards. Proc. Inst. Civil Eng.-Municipal Eng. **157**, 47–54 (2004)
5. Boyle, D.K.: Passenger counting systems. Transportation Research Board (2008)
6. Deakin, M., Waer, H.A.: From intelligent to smart cities. Intell. Buildings Int. **3**(3), 140–152 (2011)
7. Figueiredo, L., Jesus, I., Tenreiro, J., Ferreira, J., Martins, J.: Towards the development of intelligent transportation systems. In: IEEE Intelligent Transportation Systems, pp. 1206–1211 (2001)
8. Furth, P., Hemily, B., Muller, T., Strathman, J.: Using archived AVL-APC data to improve transit performance and management. Technical Report 113, Transit Cooperative Research program-Transportation Research Board (2006)
9. Grava, S.: Urban Transportation Systems. McGraw-Hill Professional Publishing, New York (2000)
10. Hipogrosso, S., Nesmachnow, S.: Sustainable mobility in the public transportation of Montevideo, Uruguay. In: II Iberoamerican Congress on Smart Cities (2019)
11. Judd, C., McClelland, G., Ryan, C.: Data Analysis: A Model Comparison Approach. Routledge, London (2011)
12. Nesmachnow, S., Bana, S., Massobrio, R.: A distributed platform for big data analysis in smart cities: combining intelligent transportation systems and socioeconomic data for Montevideo, Uruguay. EAI Endorsed Trans. Smart Cities **2**(5), 1–18 (2017)
13. Rahm, E., Do, H.H.: Data cleaning: problems and current approaches. IEEE Data Eng. Bullet. **23**, 3–13 (2000)
14. Servicio de Geomática - Intendencia de Montevideo: Líneas de Transporte (2012). http://geoweb.montevideo.gub.uy/geonetwork/srv/es/metadata.show?uuid=307ffef2-7ba3-4935-815b-caa7057226ce. Accessed 30 Dec 2018

15. Tukey, J.: Exploratory Data Analysis. Addison-Wesley Publishing Company, Boston (1977)
16. Utsunomiya, M., Attanucci, J., Wilson, N.: Potential uses of transit smart card registration and transaction data to improve transit planning. Transp. Res. Rec.: J. Transp. Res. Board **1971**, 119–126 (2006)
17. Zhao, Y.: Vehicle Location and Navigation Systems. Artech House Publishers, Norwood (1997)
18. Zheng, X., Chen, W., Wang, P., Shen, D., Chen, S., Wang, X., Zhang, Q., Yang, L.: Big data for social transportation. IEEE Trans. Intell. Transp. Syst. **17**(3), 620–630 (2016)

Bus Stops as a Tool for Increasing Social Inclusiveness in Smart Cities

Víctor Manuel Padrón Nápoles[1], Diego Gachet Páez[1](✉), José Luis Esteban Penelas[1], Germán García García[1], and María José García Santacruz[2]

[1] Escuela de Arquitectura, Ingeniería y Diseño, Universidad Europea de Madrid, c/Tajo s/n, Villaviciosa de Odón, Madrid, Spain
{victor.padron,diego.gachet, jluis.esteban}@universidadeuropea.es, gerggcl@gmail.com
[2] Facultad de Ciencias Sociales y de la Comunicación, Universidad Europea de Madrid, c/Tajo s/n Villaviciosa de Odón, Madrid, Spain
mariajo-se.garcia3@universidadeuropea.es

Abstract. In the last years, the concept of Smart City has moved from a predominantly technological perspective towards a more human based approach, where terms as sustainability and inclusiveness are presents and are part of a new concept referred as Human Smart Cities. In this context, the mobility of people and services represents one of the major challenges that cities must solve. Therefore, urban mobility policies must integrate new mobility needs as well as minimize the impact transportation has on the environment and the quality of life in our cities. Urban areas need to develop new sustainable urban mobility systems integrating traffic state, transport users demand, transport capacity providers, etc. These requirements involve the use of new techniques and methods as Big Data and IoT, but it is necessary to include a social component to ensure social inclusion and inclusiveness, sustainability and inclusiveness. In this paper, we describe some challenges regarding barriers to access new mobility systems and their relevant information. Therefore, we propose a smart bus stop taking into account cultural and socioeconomics characteristics of the transport users employing as a basis the access to information systems.

Keywords: Smart Cities · Inclusive transport · Smart bus stops · Mobility systems

1 Introduction

When designing Socially Sustainable Cities, we are doubtlessly faced with the opportunity to achieve social accessibility. Sustainability is related to two basic principles: a robust ecosystem and an equally strong social fabric [1]. The relationship between the social and ecological dimensions of unsustainability creates a vicious circle. In this context the transportation and mobility systems plays a major role in the context of sustainable and inclusive smart cities.

In April 2018, European Commission published the document "Transport in the European Union. Current Trends and Issues", which highlights the importance of social

S. Nesmachnow and L. Hernández Callejo (Eds.): ICSC-CITIES 2019, CCIS 1152, pp. 215–227, 2020.
https://doi.org/10.1007/978-3-030-38889-8_17

aspects in the development of an advanced European transport system: "From a social perspective, affordability, reliability and accessibility of transport are key. However, this has not been achieved across the board. Addressing these challenges will help pursue sustainable growth in the EU" [2].

The concepts of social inclusion and the digitalization of transport have to be harmonized in terms of accessibility, affordability, reliability and inclusiveness. Public transport plays a crucial role for mitigating the social exclusion of vulnerable and disadvantaged groups, affecting their access to basic services and their social and employment relationships. Accessibility should include all the stages of the journey, including the walking environment, so that people with mobility impairment can reach and use transport services; the design of transport facilities, addressing the specific needs of vulnerable groups; and safety and security in public transport, crucial issues which disproportionately affect women and the elderly.

It is clear the potential of new transport technologies and social innovation in mitigating social exclusion and providing flexible cost-effective transport services. Currently, there are identified specific policies, research priorities and recommendations for local transport, long-distance transport and tourism. They address problems such as: the need to combat low awareness of disabled passengers' rights; lack of information on accessibility of local transport; information presented not in accessible formats or not concise and reliable; low use of mobile apps and social media in the sector; low accessibility in suburban and rural areas; generally and major access barriers in interchanges and intermodal hubs.

2 Related Work and Background

In the context of smart cities there is an abundant literature related to transport and mobility as mentioned in [3]. As part of whole transportation in a smart cities several authors mention as an important component a smart traffic management system, including dynamic control of traffic signal lights based on traffic flow using technologies as wireless networks or powerful fiber-optic backbone [4], also there is an important volume of scientific literature describing the use of IoT (Internet of Things) technologies for quality of life improvement of citizens in smart cities through measures that leads to a healthy, green and sustainable environment. The potential benefits and challenges with the IoT service implementation for cities is visible for example in smart bus stops in Barcelona's (Spain) that are connected to the city's fiber-optic network offering services as online bus running schedule, information for foreign visitors, shows advertising, USB charging points for mobile gadgets and provide free Wi-Fi hotspots, giving waiting people access to the Internet using their mobile devices [5, 6].

As we aforementioned, the scientific literature in relation to the technological systems used in the transportation systems and their main elements is wide, however there is relatively little information available about social aspects of transportation and mobility and particularly referred to public transportation systems and their influence in the quality of life of groups of people at risk of social exclusion as for example immigrants, refugees, elders, people with disabilities etc.

2.1 Transportation and Social Inclusion

Social inclusion is a very complex concept. The EU defines social inclusion as a tendency to enable people at risk of poverty or social exclusion to have the opportunity to participate fully in social life, and thus enjoy an adequate standard of living considered normal in the society in which they live [7]. Social inclusion is especially concerned about people or groups of people who are in risk of deprivation, segregation or marginalization. Especially susceptible to exclusion are people or groups of people in situations of precariousness or belonging as a collective, stigmatized, either by their origin, gender (male or female), physical condition (disabilities), or sexual orientation, among other things.

In particular, groups of citizens who are especially vulnerable to exclusion, include persons with disabilities and older citizens (many of whom live alone), as well as persons on low incomes and the unemployed. As shown in Fig. 1, deserving special attention the situation of women, as some studies reveal that women have different travel patterns from men and that public transportation plays a crucial role in empowerment, access to opportunities and independence [8].

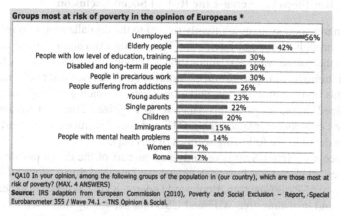

Fig. 1. Vulnerable and disadvantaged groups of citizens.

From the point of view of mobility and transportation the definition of social exclusion provided in [9] is particularly important due mobility in modern cities is an important factor in the people's life and that the reduced accessibility to opportunities, services or social networks are in partly due to insufficient mobility. The role of transport as a potential factor in creating social exclusion is well accepted and documented. Some identified barriers with which transport services can impact on social exclusion are for example, spatial, temporal, personal, psychological, cost and information access.

In order to successfully connect people to opportunities, public transport system should fulfil some criteria, as for example, it must be available, i.e. the public transport network should be easy reachable from people and offer good timetables and frequencies corresponding to patterns of social and working life, this is especially important for elder and handicapped persons. People also need to be kept informed of the services that are available both at smart stop and a whole transportation system. It must be accessible, i.e. vehicles, stops and the walking routes must be designed in such a way that everyone is able to use them without unreasonable difficulty and it must be affordable in the sense that people should not be paid a high fare for using public transport, at last public transport must be comfortable, safe and convenient.

It is clear that social inclusion and the digitalization of transport, have to be harmonized in terms of accessibility, affordability, reliability and inclusiveness. As mentioned in the study about "Social inclusion and EU public transport" [10] for the European Parliament's Committee on Transport and Tourism, public transport plays a crucial role for mitigating the social exclusion of vulnerable and disadvantaged groups, affecting their access to basic services and their social and employment relationships. Accessibility, for example, should include all the stages of the journey, including the walking environment, so that people with mobility impairment can reach and use transport services; the design of transport facilities, addressing the specific needs of vulnerable groups; and safety and security in public transport, crucial issues which disproportionately affect women and the elderly.

2.2   Smart Bus Stops to Decrease the Risk of Social Exclusion

Advances in transport systems are tightly related to the digitalization of physical transport assets, through the uses of Internet-of-Things, Big Data and Artificial Intelligence applications that joined with social innovation are producing new services such as shared mobility, multimodal transport planners, Mobility As A Service and public transport on demand. This combination of transportation assets, technological and social innovations is defined, in the scope of this paper, as a "Digitized Transport System" (DTS). An important component related with a DTS and social inclusion is a Smart Bus Stop described in detail in the following sections of this paper.

The concept of Smart Stop is recently new as part of the developments related to "Smart Cities" [11]. Several European cities have launched Smart Stops pilot projects. That is the case of Paris (one stop, Boulevard Diderot, 85 m2, accessible to persons with disabilities, and providing free WiFi and USB charge, among other services), London (100 ClearChannel bus shelters, using Google Outside service to provide information) and Barcelona (around 10 stops, with mobile based payment system). Other cities have incorporated some smart elements to traditional stops to supply more information to users, as arrival time of buses or other general information, without providing more interactivity.

Another example is the Smart Bus Stop (SBS) prototype of Hungarian company Aquis Innovo in Budapest. The design and development of the prototype (Fig. 2) was funded by EC (41000€). This prototype, which includes ticket vending, parcel delivery, passenger counting, passenger information, wireless, USB charging, bike rental, air condition, taxi order, tourist info, news, advertisement, weather forecast, reverse vending, surveillance and others services [12]. On the other hand, there are other smart furniture options, as outdoor bus ticket-kiosk (Portuguese OEMKIOSK) or information providing smart furniture (not a Smart Stop) adapted to people with disabilities as Portuguese TOMI as shown in Fig. 3.

Fig. 2. Aquis Innovo's Smart-Stop (Source: https://europa.eu/investeu/projects/smart-bus-stop_es.EUInvest).

Another example of advanced pilot project regarding Smart-Stop is the case of Aizuwakamatsu city, Japan. There, low consumption, bistable E-paper (only consumed power when the message changes) is solar powered and communicated with low power wide area (LPWA) wireless technology to provide information to users. This allows replacing paper timetables and improving user experience. Managed remotely through the Papercast data management platform, the multilingual displays will present live bus arrivals, timetables, route data, route transfers, service alterations (planned and unplanned) and a range of other travel advice [13]. Despite the huge potential of this technology, its penetration in many European cities is very limited and its adaptation to

Fig. 3. Outdoor TOMI accessible information kiosk (Courtesy TOMI World).

inclusiveness just is starting to be developed. One of the possible causes of this is the high mobile phone penetration.

The following sections describe in detail the architecture of a smart Bus Stop developed under the context of the MUSA (Advanced Sustainable Urban Furniture – Mobiliario Urbano Sostenible y Avanzado) project, a long-term project oriented to the development of smart bus stops based on the provision of information services with focus in inclusive, and social driven transport aspects.

3   MUSA Smart Stop Architecture

The MUSA project is being developed to start applying the aforementioned ideas in Madrid transport system, starting from a very popular point of interest: bus stops.

Our Smart Stop is a physical stop equipped with an interactive display and a computer system communicating with a set of cloud systems to provide different services to travelers publically available at the stop. The main of these services is a multimodal trip planner including options for walking, cycling, taxi, private and public transport. The interface to this urban equipment will be customized to increase the accessibility for those citizens that are at risk of exclusion. Smart stops will work as public access points and as travel assistants for low-income or disadvantaged groups of users; improving planning in real time and taking into account the unexpected events that can improves or disrupt transport operations. A Smart Stop, from inclusiveness point of view, is:

(a) An interactive bus stop available to the whole population. It is a public access point to a digitized transport system, which allow access to persons without apps or even without a smart phone
(b) It can work as a public access point and as a travel assistant for low-income or disadvantaged groups of users.
(c) It can improve the accessibility to DTS through customization of interfaces and reduction of cognitive demand.
(d) It can improve planning in real time taking into account unexpected events that can improves or disrupt transport operations.
(e) Through an attractive and customized interface it can foster the penetration of travel planning apps and its use by different users' segments.
(f)   These Smart-Stops can be implemented as "small" smart furniture providing a robust, essential electronic equipment that convert traditional stops into accessible Smart-Stops minimizing the modernization cost and having a wide use in the cities and rural areas.

The planning from users' point of view helps to characterize the demand on transport systems. This identified demand jointly with sensorization of transport means can be used by transport providers to customize and fine tuning their services in order to meet user requirement (Fig. 4) and increase satisfaction of their clients.

3.1   Sensorization of Buses

The efficiency of planning, from users' as well as from transport providers' point of view, is highly correlated to the level sensorization of transport means. For these reasons,

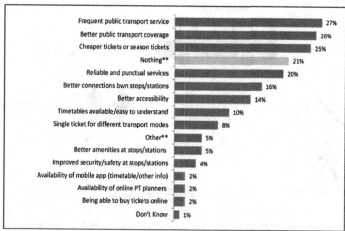

*Question: What would encourage you to use public transport more often?
**Spontaneous answer
Source: IRS adaption from EC (2014), *Quality of transport. Report*, Special Eurobarometer 422a / Wave EB82.2 – TNS Opinion & Social.

Fig. 4. Factors that can encourage the use of public transport.

two directions were taken. First, increasing sensorization of buses installing Automatic Passenger Counters (APC) to know the occupancy of the bus in real time, the availability of free places for wheelchairs and baby-strollers, as well as the flow of passengers in each bus stop [14]. Second, the design of a smart bus stop, which actually provides a public, accessible entry point to a digitized transport system.

The use of APC for transport providers is very important in order they can analyze the performance of buses in real time, the most demanded segment of routes or routes in highest demand and accordingly re-plan them, if deemed necessary, so as to increase efficiency of service and users' satisfaction. From users' point of view, the bus occupancy (or its probability) is crucial for an effective planning (it is useless, if the planed bus comes full and passengers cannot get on board).

Buses normally include ALV (Automatic Vehicle Location) using GPS and SC-AFC (Smart Card Automatic Fare). For a flat-fare service (where nowadays passengers do not check out when alighting the bus, as e.g. in Madrid), the next level of sensorization was the use of APC or Automatic Passenger Counters. There are different technologies for APC, infrared and vision systems (video cameras, stereo cameras and time-of-flight cameras).

The use of the latter can be adapted to detect free available places for wheel chairs and baby strollers, thereby supporting increased inclusiveness. Research about possible smart stop services are being performed. This can include not only public and private transport services, but also community communication services, publicity services, environment and health services, among others. Figure 5 shows the MUSA architecture.

Though for this project, infrared systems and stereo cameras were studied, we used simple video cameras from Retail Sensing, a Manchester company, to evaluate their performance in real-life conditions (Fig. 6). The cameras located on top of front and rear

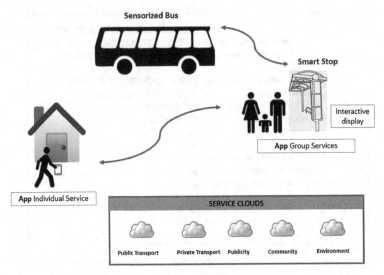

Fig. 5. Main components of MUSA architecture.

door use artificial vision algorithms to count in and out passengers. This information was sent through a 4G router to an MQTT server to make it globally available.

First, we tested them on Lab, then we installed then on buses and then we testing during daily operation of a bus in the center of Madrid (Figs. 7 and 8).

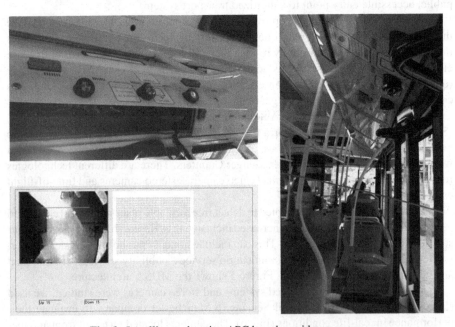

Fig. 6. Installing and testing APC based on video cameras.

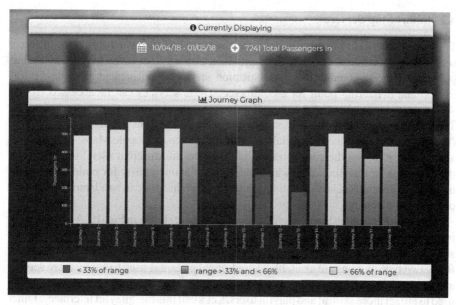

Fig. 7. Number of daily passengers entering in the bus (Courtesy Retail Sensing).

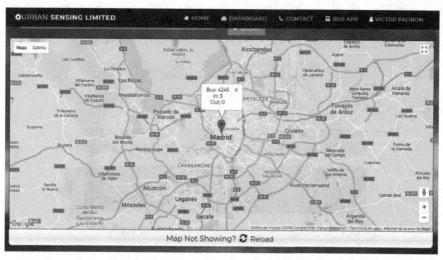

Fig. 8. Behavior of passengers' flow on one bus stop (Courtesy Retail Sensing).

Currently, a massive installation of APC systems using time-of-flight and Artificial Intelligence systems is taking place in Madrid buses. It is foreseeable that information about real-time occupancy of buses and availability of wheelchairs and baby stroller will be public available as Open Data.

3.2 Smart Stop Services

The smart bus stop is being designed as a smart furniture, which provides different services: information about public and private transport, reservation of trips, as well as publicity services, community communication services, environment awareness information and delivering point for e-commerce. These services can be accessed from a screen available in the stop which will connect passengers to a set of cloud services. The works on smart stop are currently in progress. Designed as a special software layer (Fig. 9), it can run on a commercial travel planner, such as Google Maps. This has two advantages; it allows the customization of interfaces for different users' segments and the collection of traveling data, which can be used anonymously for building mobility models and develop social innovation solutions. In addition, it can be adapted to different commercial planners.

The prototype of the Smart Stop and its interface are shown in Fig. 10. Advertisement is running on the background (in this case for musicals in the center of Madrid), different services are available in the lower carrousel. To intuitively attract user to different interfaces, two type of icons are available. A traditional picture is used to attract more serious and direct users. Let's call it the "conservative interface". And, a more playful icon is used to attract more skillful and playful users. Let's call this the "playful interface". Other future special services for assisting traveler with special needs (elder, reduced mobility, easier travel with kids or pregnant women) are also included in the interface. Other services as Community Services and Environment information are available following the already mentioned two icon policy.

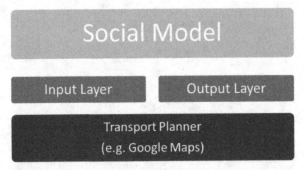

Fig. 9. Layering smart stop multimodal planning application.

The "conservative interface" of the public transport app is shown in Fig. 11. A box with the most frequently used destination from current stop is shown on top right corners, increasing the probabilities of reducing the interaction to minimum. Below, a box shows time and duration of the selected trip (cost will be available soon). Also, there is an option to select private or other type of alternative transport without leaving conservative mode of interaction.

Fig. 10. Main interface of the smart bus stop prototype.

A third box allows user to select any origin and destination, using a tactile keyboard on the screen. Finally, information about nearest bus stops can be searched. Typical interactive features of Google Maps are disabled, so conservative user cannot be distracted from their simple, direct interaction with the app.

Figure 12 shows the "conservative interface" fostering physical exercises by means of walking. In this case, time and duration of a trip walking and using public transport are similar, so the option of walking can be healthier for the user. This feature can be very interesting for elder people.

Fig. 11. Multimodal planner using public transport.

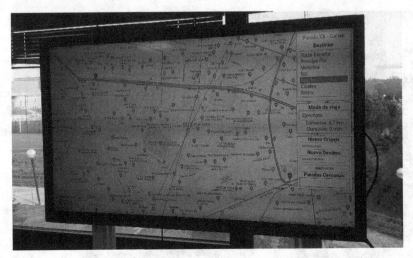

Fig. 12. Fostering physical exercise

4   Conclusions

This paper describes the first steps of development of a smart stop designed to increase social inclusiveness of modern, advanced, smart transport systems (digitized transport systems). Ensuring inclusiveness is crucial for ensuring that people not only can access and get full profit of advanced transport systems. It also helps characterize demand and allow transport providers a better planning and optimization of their resources increasing users' satisfaction.

Next step in the Smart Stop development is the study of more advanced interfaces, as those provided by the Voice Activated Personal Assistants or VAPA (e.g. Alexa) taking into account privacy concerns [15]. The design of this interface in the smart furniture creating a micro-space that isolates user and makes easier the interaction. This type of planning also can foster the use of VAPAs at home. Furthermore, VAPA systems have the potential to increase general accessibility of disabled people in general [16] and other target segments of users as well as decrease of the cognitive load and the effort of planning travels in the context of modern digitized transport systems. Taking into account privacy concerns and cybersecurity, it can be an effective double-approach to lack of digital competences and to reduce the impact of passivity of users.

Acknowledgments. This research was funded by Universidad Europea de Madrid grant number 2018/UEM06. We want to express our deep gratitude to all those persons and institutions that are helping and supporting us in the realization of this project. We want to thank the institutional support from the Municipal Transport Company (EMT) of Madrid, for the kindly support of its executives and technical staff; and at last, but not at least, to Asad Syed from Retail Sensing for his kindly support and sponsorship with the APC system. To all of you, thank you very much.

References

1. Verebes, T.: Master Planning The Adpative City. Routledge Taylor & Francis Group, London, New York (2014)
2. Transport in the European Union: Current Trends and Issues. https://ec.europa.eu/transport/sites/transport/files/2018-transport-in-the-eu-current-trends-and-issues.pdf. Accessed July 2019
3. Su, K., Li, J., Fu, H.: Smart city and the applications. In: 2011 International Conference on Electronics, Communications and Control (ICECC), pp. 1028–1031. IEEE (2011)
4. Wang, Z.: The application of wireless city technology in public administration. Journal of Chinese People's Armed Police Force, **24** (2008)
5. Cisco Espan~a. Internet of things world forum Barcelona 2013 (video), November 2013
6. Wallbank, P.: A geek's tour of Barcelona (2013)
7. Poverty and social exclusion. https://ec.europa.eu/social/main.jsp?catId=751&langId=en. Accessed July 2019
8. Samek, M., Pesce, F., Malgieri, P., Maffi, S., Rosa, C.: The Role of Women in the Green Economy. The Issue of Mobility. http://www.europarl.europa.eu/RegData/etudes/note/join/2012/462453/IPOL-FEMM_NT(2012)462453_EN.pdf. Accessed July 2019
9. Kenyon, K., Lyons, G., Rafferty, J.: Transport and social exclusion: investigating the possibility of promoting social exclusion through virtual mobility. J. Transp. Geogr. **10**, 207–219 (2003)
10. Social Inclusion in EU Public Transport. http://www.docutren.com/pdf/boletin/[IIIA% 201440].pdf. Accessed July 2019
11. Gretzel, U., Sigala, M., Xiang, Z., Koo, C.: Smart tourism: foundations and developments. Electron. Markets **25** (2015). http://doi.org/10.1007/s12525-015-0196-8
12. Aquis Innovo. https://europa.eu/investeu/projects/smart-bus-stop_es. Accessed July 2019
13. Papercast 2018. https://www.papercast.com/epaper_bus_stop_passenger_information_solu tions/products_e-paper_displays/. Accessed July 2019
14. Nápoles, V.M.P., Rodríguez, M.B., Páez, D.G., Penelas, J.L.E., García-Ochoa, A.G., Pérez, A.L.: MUSA–I. Towards new social tools for advanced multi-modal transportation in smart cities. In: Proceedings, vol. 2, p. 1215 (2018)
15. Moorthy, A.E., Vu, K.-P.L.: Privacy concerns for use of voice activated personal assistant in the public space. Int. J. Hum. Comput. Inter. **31**(4), 307–335 (2015). https://doi.org/10.1080/10447318.2014.986642
16. Pradhan, A., Mehta, K., Findlater, L.: Accessibility came by accident: use of voice-controlled intelligent personal assistants by people with disabilities. In: Proceedings of the 2018 CHI Conference on Human Factors in Computing Systems, Montreal, QC, Canada, 21–26 April 2018, pp. 1–13. https://doi.org/10.1145/3173574.3174033

Designing a Backbone Trunk
for the Public Transportation Network
in Montevideo, Uruguay

Claudio Risso[⊠] and Sergio Nesmachnow

Universidad de la República, Montevideo, Uruguay
{crisso,sergion}@fing.edu.uy

Abstract. Massive public infrastructure is usually structured into hierarchical levels, where different technologies handle different scales of requirements allowing most efficient and scalable implementations. In opposition to the aforementioned architecture, the public transport system in Montevideo (Uruguay) uses a single/flat level, with buses as the only means. This work explores the performance benefits and the cost feasibility of a new hierarchically segmented metropolitan trunk network for the public system in Montevideo, a problem that is tackled through combinatorial optimization approaches. The reference structure assumes light railway trams (LRTs) are used to massively transfer passengers between remote points of the city, while buses are reassigned as feeders of the new backbone in the network. The real-world example integrates demands information, realistic travel and waiting times as well as standard deployment costs. Results show that this new structure is economically competitive and significantly better in terms of quality of service.

Keywords: Smart cities · Public transportation · Network design

1 Introduction

Public transportation is a key element of nowadays societies, which directly impacts over several aspects of daily activities of citizens [16]. Moreover, it has a direct implication on sustainability, as the higher the rate of passengers using a public transportation system, the lesser the air pollution, the most efficient the use of energy, the most livable the city [13,15]. Public transportation is a very relevant problem in Latin American countries. Overall, public transportation serves a higher interest and delivers more benefits than private transportation. However, having a good public transportation system is not only a matter of good will. In order to succeed, public system travel times should plenty beat those of private vehicles, but the system also has to be economically competitive, reliable, and it has to provide seamless connectivity. There are many trade-offs to balance in such a design, which is not an easy task [2].

© Springer Nature Switzerland AG 2020
S. Nesmachnow and L. Hernández Callejo (Eds.): ICSC-CITIES 2019, CCIS 1152, pp. 228–243, 2020.
https://doi.org/10.1007/978-3-030-38889-8_18

Public transportation systems are studied within the concept of *smart mobility* [1] under the novel paradigm of smart cities [3]. In this context, Intelligent Transportation Systems (ITS) make use of technology to develop and enhance transportation [5], usually focusing on public media (e.g., bus, train, etc.)

In large cities, a successful public transportation system comprises different media, which compound a massive infrastructure. Paris Métro and London Underground move around 1.5 billion passengers per year; Moscow Metro is even larger with 2.5 billion. The problem of designing a public transportation system falls in the category of network design problems. As a general rule, large networks are structured into hierarchical levels that use different technologies to handle different scales of requirements. For example, consider access and backbone in telecommunications; high, medium and low voltage in electrical networks; or even subways, surface trains and buses in public transportation systems.

Regarding public transportation networks design, the related literature somehow integrates those technologies, aiming at having the higher *passenger per hour peak direction* media strategically connecting distant points within a city. Most reference works state the problem as a superposition of transportation technologies, where portions of the legacy infrastructure are considered definite. Most cities with massive transportation systems have designed their services correctively, adding elements to address specific situations, progressively improving the result without a coordinated design for the whole of the variables. The result of such a process is generally suboptimal.

This work explores the design of the trunk backbone network of a hierarchically integrated public transportation system. Design premisses are inspired in basic characteristics of resilient and scalable networks. The underlying model assumes a planning-from-scratch approach, where a few stations are set in accordance to demand data and other strategical concerns, while most of the trunk network topology is designed to minimize infrastructure costs and at the same time being competitive in terms of travel times. The design also assumes a two stages approach. First stage precisely comprises the backbone trunk or Rapid Transit System (RTS), which has the highest infrastructure investment. Buses are reassigned to the access function, i.e., they work as feeders for the previously planned backbone network. Thus, the layout of their lines is to be tackled in a second stage, which is out of the scope of this work. Variants of this model can integrate access times of users as a part of the problem.

The strict hierarchy of media intrinsic to the formulation of this problem, turns the new backbone network critical, since an interruption in a line operation could actually disconnect zones of the city. Thus, the design integrates topological constraints to minimize those risks, what constitutes an innovation of this work regarding existing literature. The work uses the city of Montevideo (Uruguay) as a real-world application case, a previously unexplored instance, which constitutes another contribution. The main results indicate that the proposed approach is economically able of being implemented in Montevideo.

This article is organized as follows. Section 2 presents the problem formulation, a description of the case study in Montevideo, and a review of related works. The proposed approach for the backbone transportation network design is also described in Sect. 2. Section 3 summarizes resolution details, while experimental analysis is reported in Sect. 4. Finally, Sect. 5 presents the conclusions and the main lines of future work.

2   Problem Formulation and Case Study in Montevideo

This section introduces the proposed approach to solve the problem of designing a backbone for a public transportation network, the mathematical formulation, and the case study of Montevideo, Uruguay.

2.1   General Considerations and Related Works

From an abstract point-of-view, the planning and location of new transport infrastructure must consider diverse urban or strategic affairs, such as: environmental issues, metropolitan land-use plans, integration of satellite cities into a larger metropolis, and even speculative real-estate concerns, because a better connectivity turns more desirable certain zones of a city. Many of these concerns are analyzed in the related literature [4, 9, 17]. The proposed approach integrates those high-level constraints in the analysis, but most of them are part of the design premisses rather than entities in the optimization model.

One of the advantages of having a transportation network hierarchically structured into two media (LRTs and buses) is that long-haul portions of most travels are carried out using trams/trains, which have the highest *passenger per hour peak direction*. Besides, for a given number of passengers to move, the road congestion and maintenance costs caused by a fleet of LRTs are much lower than buses, as buses are regarding private motor vehicles. Furthermore, electrical engines of LRTs feed directly from the electric grid. Having a mostly electrical public transportation system directly translates into environmental friendliness. Nowadays, electric buses are an available technology, but they use batteries, and the distance a bus can go with a full charge is incompatible with significant portion of current bus lines alignments. Reassigning buses to the access function minimizes distances and fosters the spreading of a fleet of electric buses. Finally, remote terminals serve as gateways to important urban centers nearby.

According to the literature [10], the design of a Rapid Transit System or RTS consists of two intertwined problems: a careful placement for stations and the crafting of the alignments for lines to connect them. Those entities are clearly interdependent, and optimally, the problem should be solved as a whole. However, a sequential approach helps to tackle the problem. A first step is *selecting key nodes* as main stations by their importance as origin or destination for trips. Designing an *optimized core network* is a second stage. This stage aims at connecting key-nodes with a good performance-to-cost ratio, which causes system effectiveness to be achieved while the overall efficiency is maximized. Finally, in order to optimally increase the total coverage of the lines, one might run a third step for *setting secondary stations* as a derived result from the previous alignments. A dual approach [9] analyses the problem as perceived from the user point-of-view. Hence, the attributes regard with *attraction accessibility*: the ease of reaching a station using any mode of transport; and *radiation accessibility*: the proficiency to reach a far-endpoint location.

This article combines both infrastructure and user perspectives of the problem. First of all, key-nodes are selected by the computation of the number of trips starting in each zone, referred to as *trip generation analysis* [10]. By considering those zones that add up to a significant percentage of the total trips, a good overall *attraction accessibility* is sustained. The number of lines to be deployed between those points is set from the number of trips starting and ending at each node/zone, what in turn is referred to as *trip distribution analysis*.

Potential edges for the alignments are selected by the broadness of streets and avenues. Such graph of potential corridors is planar and plenty connected, so secondary stations in this approach are defined as a collateral result of the backbone network, which is the main object of design in this work. Further details and considerations of literature [10], such as *Modal Choice Analysis*: allocation of trips among the currently available transportation systems; and *Trip Assignment Analysis*: assignment of trip flows for the specific routes on each transportation system that will be selected by the users, are appointed as future research. *Radiation accessibility* in this work relies upon the existence of a spread RTS connecting most important demand points in the city at very good end-to-end travel times.

In this work, two formulations of the problem are used to determine a reference topology for the backbone of a public transportation network in Montevideo. The case study and the two formulations are described next.

2.2   Case Study: Public Transportation Network in Montevideo

The case study solved in this article is the public transportation network of Montevideo, Uruguay. Public transportation in Montevideo is comprised of 1528 buses operated by four companies. The bus network consists of 145 bus lines with different variants, accounting for outward and return trips, as well as shorter versions of the same line. The total number of bus lines when considering each variant individually is 1383, a remarkably large number. The leftmost of Fig. 1 shows the bus lines of the system, on top of a road map (data from sig.montevideo.gub.uy). The city centre, marked as B in the rightmost of Fig. 1 is a hub in the bus network, with most lines converging to that area.

Bus lines are significantly large: the average bus line length is 16.7 km (standard deviation 7.1 km) and the median length is 16.4 km, with the longest line spreading over 39.6 km. Intuitively, these figures strike as remarkably large, considering that the total area of Montevideo is 530 km^2 and can be circumscribed to a rectangle of 26 × 37 km. This work follows literature recommendations: the design aims at integrating Montevideo with its metropolitan area [9] and key-nodes are mostly chosen according with their importance as traffic sources [10]. Table 1 shows the daily origin-destination trips matrix per-zone, considering not only Montevideo municipalities (A to G) but also demand from satellite cities, which are connected by national routes R1 to RInt. Table 1 accounts total trips

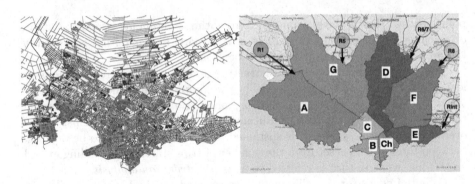

Fig. 1. Bus lines of the public transportation system of Montevideo, Uruguay

by any means. A recent survey [12] details how those trips are performed: *by-foot* 34%, *private vehicles* 32%, using *public buses* 25%, *motorcycles* 4%, *bicycles* 3%, *taxis, Uber and other apps* 1%, *other medias* 1%. These figures show how much space to grow public transport has.

Table 1. Origin-destination matrix for daily trips in Montevideo, Uruguay [12]

Destination Origin	A	B	C	Ch	D	E	F	G	R1	R5	R6/7	R8	Rint	Total
A	249,690	31,578	20,632	15,239	6,493	4,074	4,224	26,308	1,121	915	140	0	1,285	361,699
B	30,040	395,971	58,687	108,525	22,695	50,501	21,039	21,939	2,686	10,342	3,240	1,321	19,775	746,761
C	22,523	60,039	179,910	23,949	22,213	12,420	10,507	27,319	1,082	2,541	3,940	234	3,693	370,370
Ch	15,770	99,818	25,244	239,919	24,776	53,164	17,432	12,108	1,690	3,067	1,986	318	12,639	507,931
D	4,492	25,010	19,156	23,617	214,225	13,484	41,526	10,877	801	398	2,362	349	2,935	359,232
E	4,216	53,784	15,085	51,642	14,511	97,917	19,354	5,346	158	995	1,184	162	27,726	292,080
F	4,505	20,462	10,637	18,560	39,957	19,330	209,980	5,553	137	1,333	777	166	6,958	338,355
G	23,200	19,480	29,574	13,017	7,510	8,850	4,897	136,145	684	6,979	312	0	0	250,648
R1	966	3,803	1,172	639	727	78	137	684	67,299	405	90	0	285	76,285
R5	915	9,394	2,615	3,384	398	1,365	1,402	8,057	405	235,823	1,999	462	789	267,008
R6/7	152	3,326	3,723	2,142	2,275	1,114	561	381	90	2,369	70,024	3,129	3,352	92,638
R8	0	861	234	318	349	401	327	0	0	599	3,178	35,342	9,421	51,030
Rint	1,669	19,161	3,827	11,876	3,027	28,998	7,083	0	205	858	3,082	10,073	350,559	440,418
Total	358,138	742,687	370,496	512,827	359,156	291,696	338,469	254,717	76,358	266,624	92,314	51,556	439,417	4,154,455

Data in Table 1 are taken from a polling of the *Banco de Desarrollo de América Latina* [12]. As it counts in Table 1, the most important internal municipality is the city centre B, followed by Ch, which is geographically contiguous. Considering municipalities over the city border as connected with near cities, we conclude that areas in order of importance are the following: E+RInt, G+R5, D+R6/7 and A+R1. Thus, the case of study considered in this article for the LRT design defines five zones to be connected and seven key-nodes, which are definite for the optimization purposes. Design premises for the backbone of the public transportation network in Montevideo include:

– the backbone architecture is to be of *hub type*, with the city centre (zone B) as concentrator, since that zone is the main destination of trips in the city and its location as urban geographic centre makes it a natural candidate to articulate demands;

- three nodes are identified in the city centre: *Plaza Independencia* (PIN, node_1), *Tres Cruces* (XXX, node_id 2), and *Palacio Municipal* (PAM, node_id 3) for whom is supposed to exist a fast interconnection media, that allows to rapidly reach any of these nodes, whose far-end points are closer than 4 km;
- four *remote terminals* complete the set of key-nodes. They are *Carrasco* (CAR, node_id 4), *Cerro* (CRO, node_id 5), *Pocitos* (POC, node_id 6) and *Colón* (TCO, node_id 7). POC and CAR are introduced as new stations in the city, and they were included because of the number of trips of their zones, which respectively are Ch and E+RInt. CRO and TCO are actual bus stations by this date, and they are also among the most important origin-destination trips. They respectively correspond to A+R1 and G+R5.
- All lines connect the city centre (node_ids from 1 to 3) with some remote terminal (node_ids from 4 to 7). Trips between zones are assumed to relay in the centre. Besides, CAR, TCO and CER serve as gateway respectively terminals towards: East, North and West directions.

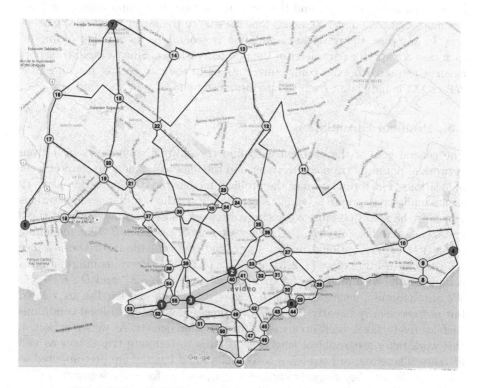

Fig. 2. Potential LRT network for the case study in Montevideo

Figure 2 shows the network of terminal and optional stations as well as potential connections between them. As we previously mentioned edges are select by the importance of streets and avenues. Optional stations are mostly defined by intersections of edges. In the chosen architecture, the remote terminals must be connected to the Centre by means of LRT lines to be displayed on the city. Remaining locations can be part of the solution (i.e., being a *station* of the proposed LRT) or not, depending on the convenience of their utilization. The *hub* architecture is that a passenger whose destination is not the Centre or any of the intermediate nodes of the line that he boarded, just makes a transfer in the Centre to the final destination.

Since buses are to be reassigned as feeders of the backbone, the last one becomes critical to keep trips running. That issue combined with the fact that LRTs operate at the surface (in opposition to a subway/underground service) and superficial vehicles are exposed to failures, induced to choose an organically robust design. Rather than using preset geometric pattern to assemble the network topology [11], the proposed approach relies upon typical criteria for network design: resiliency as a consequence of the degree of connectivity, i.e., of the number of physically independent paths connecting points. Thus, a specific condition of the design is that there is more than one physically independent line between each concentrator and the hub. In the case study, that number is 2 for terminals CAR, CRO and TCO, and 3 for POC, due to the larger number of passengers. In any case, the problem formulation is general, as the number of lines in each case is a specific parameter of the problem instance. Since a rapid transport mean is assumed to exist connecting stations in the city centre, reaching PIN, PAM or XXX is indifferent from the performance point-of-view.

2.3   Problem Formulation

The general goal of the problem is to find the optimal subnetwork of a given network of potential tram connections, and the lines assignment to connect a set of locations. The formulation of the problem models the transportation network as an undirected graph $G = (V, E)$, where V is the set of relevant stations and E is the set of possible connections between those stations. Some of these nodes compound the city centre $\mathcal{C}$, other are remote terminals $\mathcal{T}$. The remaining nodes $V \backslash \mathcal{C} \backslash \mathcal{T}$ are optional nodes, also called Steiner nodes. For the instance represented in Fig. 2, $\mathcal{C} = \{1, 2, 3\}$ and $\mathcal{T} = \{4, 5, 6, 7\}$. Previous information is complemented with functions for cost and delay: $C : E \rightarrow \mathbb{R}^+$ and $D : E \rightarrow \mathbb{R}^+$. We also assume a length function $L : E \rightarrow \mathbb{R}^+$. Costs and lengths are related but not necessarily linearly. They can be precisely adjusted to local conditions such as: rivers, lakes, built up areas, or urbanization density. As we see in Sect. 4, this work takes geographical lengths as a basis to compute trip delays as well as costs. Therefore, rail stretches costs, delays and lengths are precomputed as edges attributes; they respectively are: c_{ij}, d_{ij} and l_{ij} for every segment $ij \in E$.

Two versions of the problem are considered: *maximum resilience* and *maximum travel time limits* models. The main details and the formulation of each problem variant are presented next.

Maximum Resilience Problem. A simple version of the problem considers a given number of lines from every remote terminal towards the Centre, and it imposes that no line shares any edge with other. Consider the (realistic) case of requiring two lines from CAR (id 4), CRO (id 5) and TCO (node 7) to the Centre, and three from POC (node 6). Formally, given the non-directed graph $G = (V, E)$, a directed graph $\widetilde{G} = (V, \widetilde{E})$ is built by duplicating every edge in E considering both directions, except for those edges with nodes PIN (id 1), XXX (id 2) or PAM (id 3) as endpoints, for which only the incident edge is used. Let x_{ij} be a variable that accounts how much *flow* traverses the edge ij in $\widetilde{E}$.

$$
\begin{cases}
\min \sum_{ij \in \widetilde{E}} c_{ij} x_{ij} \\
\text{s.t.} \sum_{jk \in \widetilde{E}} x_{jk} - \sum_{ij \in \widetilde{E}} x_{ij} = 2, \; j = 4, 5, 7 \quad (i) \\
\quad\quad \sum_{6k \in \widetilde{E}} x_{6k} - \sum_{i6 \in \widetilde{E}} x_{i6} = 3, \quad\quad\quad\quad (ii) \\
\quad\quad \sum_{ij \in \widetilde{E}} x_{ij} - \sum_{jk \in \widetilde{E}} x_{jk} = 0, \; \forall j \geq 8 \quad (iii) \\
\quad\quad 0 \leq x_{ij} \leq 1, \quad\quad\quad\quad\quad\quad \forall ij \in \widetilde{E} \quad (iv)
\end{cases}
\tag{1}
$$

A formulation for this problem instance is that of Eq. 1. The idea is that a set of *flow paths* determine the sequence of edges used by each line. Equations group (i) in Eq. 1 force an outgoing net-flow of 2 units coming from nodes 4, 5 and 7. That number is 3 for node 6 because of equation (ii). Equations group (iii) imposes flow balance for every Steiner node, so traffic in this network can only drain out throughout nodes 1, 2 and 3. It is a well-known theoretical result that extreme points in the feasible region of network flow problems are integer, so we do not need to explicitly impose integrity to variables x_{ij}. Thus, equations group (iv) guarantees that any arc is either used ($x_{ij} = 1$) or not ($x_{ij} = 0$), and by at most one unit of flow (a line). The objective function aims at minimizing the total railway investments, which are the most significant in such a project.

Theorem 1. *The maximum resilience problem is within the polynomial time complexity class.*

Proof. Observe that formulation Eq. 1 is a pure linear programing problem, for whose kind there is at least one algorithm [8] *of polynomial-time complexity.* □

Maximum Travel Time Problem. Although simple to solve, the problem in Eq. 1 pushes physical independence beyond problem premises, since it does not allow any two lines to use a same edge. We only need such independence for lines coming from the same terminal, but lines from different terminals can share tram yards. Therefore, physical independence can be relaxed to allow lower costs without violating our design goals. Besides, we integrate some passengers Quality-of-Experience concerns to the formulation by setting maximum end-to-end travel times from terminals. The parameter TD_p specifies a threshold on the travel times between the terminal $p \in \mathcal{T}$ and the centre $\mathcal{C}$.

The problem formulation is presented in Eq. 2. The binary variable x_{ij} ($ij \in E$) indicates whether the edge connecting stations i and j is to be included in the solution ($x_{ij} = 1$) or not ($x_{ij} = 0$). Binary variable y_{ij}^{pr} only activates when the r-th line of terminal $p \in \mathcal{T}$ uses the segment $ij \in E$ on its way to-from the city centre. Variables θ_j^{pr} indicate whether or not the node (station) j is part of the route of the r-th line of the terminal station p.

$$
\begin{cases}
\min \sum_{ij \in E} c_{ij} x_{ij} \\
\text{s.t.} \sum_{pj \in E} y_{pj}^{pr} = 1, & 4 \leq p \leq 7, 1 \leq r \leq 2(3) \quad (i) \\
\sum_{ij \in E} y_{ij}^{pr} + \sum_{jk \in E} y_{jk}^{pr} = 2\theta_j^{pr}, & \begin{array}{l} j \geq 4, j \neq p, 4 \leq p \leq 7, \\ 1 \leq r \leq 2(3) \end{array}, \; (ii) \\
\sum_{r=1}^{2(3)} y_{ij}^{pr} \leq 1, & ij \in E, 4 \leq p \leq 7, \quad (iii) \quad (2) \\
\sum_{ij \in E} d_{ij} y_{ij}^{pr} \leq TD_p, & 4 \leq p \leq 7, 1 \leq r \leq 2(3), \; (iv) \\
4x_{ij} \geq \sum_{p=4}^{7} \sum_{r=1}^{2(3)} y_{ij}^{pr}, & ij \in E, \quad (v) \\
x_{ij}, y_{ij}^{pr}, \theta_j^{pr} \in \{0, 1\} & \begin{array}{l} \forall ij \in E, 4 \leq p \leq 7, \\ 1 \leq r \leq 2(3) \end{array} \; (vi)
\end{cases}
$$

Equations in group (i) in Eq. 2 set to exactly one the number of edges used by the r-th line of terminal p to come out from it. The index r can range from 1 to 2, or 3 when $p = 6$ (POC station). Equations in group (ii) force intermediate nodes to be used twice (inward and outward edges) or not at all. The combined effect of (i) and (ii) is to craft paths for each line of each terminal. Equations in group (iii) prevent from any two (or three) lines of the same terminal to use the same edge, which conveys physical independence. The left-hand side of equations in group (iv) accounts for the end-to-end traveling times for each line of each terminal p, which must be bounded by TD_p. The right-hand side of equations in group (v) counts how many times an edge is used by any line. Since lines from the same terminal cannot share an edge, and there are only four terminals, equations in group (v) are always satisfiable by setting x_{ij} to 1. That, however, increases the cost in the objective function to minimize. Suffices that a line is using edge ij to force the activation of the associated variable x_{ij}. For values of TD_p sufficiently large, travel times do not apply, and problem Eq. 2 becomes a relaxation of Eq. 1 that allows some additional degree of physical dependence. This fact can be used to estimate lower bound to the investments in tram yards.

Theorem 2. *The maximum travel time problem is within the NP-Hard time complexity class.*

Proof. Consider the Resource Constrained Shortest Path Problem (RCSP). Given graph $G = (V, E)$, a cost function $C{:}E \to \mathbb{R}^+$, a pair source "s" and target "t" nodes in V, resources usage functions $R_k{:}E \to \mathbb{R}^+$ for different kinds of resources $k \in \{1, \ldots, K\}$ and resource limits RL_k, the goal is on finding the minimum cost path from s to t in G that keeps the resources usage of each kind below RL_k. RCSP is proven NP-Hard in general [7], even for a unique resource.

Consider now a particular case of Eq. 2 where $C = \{s\}$, $T = \{t\}$ while set to 1 the number of lines connecting s and t (Eq. 2 allows in general to have more than one independently physical line from terminals, but it doesn't force it). This subproblem of the Maximum travel time problem is actually a RCSP variant where resources are link delays d_{ij} and the resource limit for that sole kind is TP_t, so single-resource RCSP is a polynomial reduction of Maximum travel time problem and the last one must be NP-Hard as well.   □

3   The Proposed Resolution Approach

This section describes the optimization methods applied for solving the two versions of the problem presented in the previous section.

Theorem 1 evidences the reduced intrinsic complexity of the maximum resilience problem version. State of the art linear programming solvers are able to tackle such problems for instances with hundreds of thousands of variables and constraints in very short times. The instantiation of the problem formulation in Eq. 1 for the problem instance described in Fig. 2 results in a linear programming problem with just 189 variables and 52 constraints. The problem instance was solved with the linprog solver of Matlab version 8.5.0 to find the optimum solution, using the interior point method. The problem was solved in 0.04 s executing in an Intel Core i5@1.8GHz processor with 8 GB RAM.

Due to the intrinsic complexity of the maximum travel time problem version (as proven by Theorem 2), it is not expected to find exact solution for large instances of the problem, regardless of particularities of the formulation. The instantiation of the problem formulation in Eq. 2 for the problem instance described in Fig. 2 results in an integer programming problem with 1515 variables and 987 constraints. The linprog solver of Matlab 8.5.0 was not able to find the optimum solution within a time limit of one hour. In order to tackle that much harder problem, our approach relied upon IBM ILOG CPLEX(R) Interactive Optimizer version 12.6.3 as the optimization software. A significantly more powerful hardware was also needed, in this case a HP ProLiant DL385 G7 server, with 24 AMD Opteron processor 6172@2.1 GHz and 64 GB of RAM. The overall execution time required for the resolution in that hardware was 30 s.

Empirical evidence demonstrated that for the real-world case study in Montevideo, even the harder version of the problem is possible of being solved with existing software and hardware. In consequence, we disregarded implementing ad-hoc heuristic algorithms to find good-quality solutions, being that the exact solution can be easily found in a matter of few seconds. However, we acknowledge that heuristic or metaheuristic approaches [14] must be needed in order to address more sophisticated problem variants and/or larger scenarios.

4 Experimental Analysis

This section presents the experimental analysis of the proposed approach for the transport system of Montevideo.

Table 2. Reference costs (c_{ij}) [million USD], lengths (l_{ij}) [meters] and delays (d_{ij}) [seconds] in the case study (public transportation system of Montevideo).

i	j	c_{ij}	l_{ij}	d_{ij}	i	j	c_{ij}	l_{ij}	d_{ij}	i	j	c_{ij}	l_{ij}	d_{ij}
1	52	24	263	84	12	13	34	3448	275	30	42	81	1478	157
1	53	65	1133	136	12	23	64	3218	262	31	32	36	509	99
1	54	45	690	110	12	25	82	4679	349	32	33	32	460	96
1	55	33	476	97	13	14	29	3283	265	32	41	38	772	115
2	25	116	2660	228	13	22	48	5500	398	34	35	12	410	93
2	33	49	821	118	14	22	30	3103	255	35	36	28	1231	142
2	34	135	2660	228	15	16	26	3037	251	35	39	126	2495	218
2	36	166	4203	321	15	20	27	2676	229	36	37	27	1182	139
2	39	97	2167	199	15	22	20	1888	182	36	39	107	2069	193
2	40	10	82	73	16	17	19	1822	178	37	38	118	2758	234
3	39	78	1642	167	17	19	29	2807	237	37	39	126	2463	216
3	40	100	1921	184	18	19	24	2282	205	38	39	37	542	101
3	49	103	1986	188	18	37	71	3727	292	38	54	31	410	93
3	51	54	1248	143	19	20	14	460	96	39	55	81	1543	161
3	55	31	410	93	19	21	23	1198	140	40	41	25	279	85
4	8	17	2380	211	20	21	26	1100	134	40	49	73	1297	146
4	9	14	1231	142	21	34	84	4728	352	41	42	72	1281	145
4	10	22	3267	265	21	37	31	1478	157	42	45	43	673	109
5	17	36	3776	295	22	23	78	3924	304	42	49	42	640	107
5	18	18	1707	171	22	36	74	4022	310	43	44	33	460	96
6	29	5	230	82	23	24	16	591	104	43	45	42	624	106
6	30	5	279	85	23	35	19	739	113	45	46	28	345	89
6	43	7	460	96	24	25	26	1116	135	46	47	31	410	93
6	44	4	230	82	24	34	10	279	85	46	48	71	1264	144
7	14	154	3185	260	25	26	10	279	85	47	49	55	1018	130
7	15	160	3201	261	26	27	59	1018	130	47	50	61	1379	151
7	16	186	3956	306	26	33	74	1445	155	48	49	99	1872	181
8	9	7	493	98	27	28	38	1806	177	48	50	74	1789	176
8	28	88	4712	351	27	31	52	1395	152	49	51	78	1740	173
9	10	12	1166	138	27	33	81	1527	160	50	51	49	1001	129
10	11	104	6600	464	28	29	21	1018	130	51	52	93	1806	177
10	27	98	5040	371	28	30	68	1395	152	52	53	62	1248	143
11	12	24	4285	326	29	44	29	361	90	53	54	99	2233	202
11	26	61	3300	266	30	31	37	542	101	54	55	38	542	101

4.1 Problem Instance

The problem instance models the public transportation network in Montevideo, according to the values reported in Table 2 for the topology presented in Fig. 2.
Values in Table 2 were defined according to the following procedures:

- Path lengths were taken from Google Maps service (maps.google.com).
- Travel times between stations (d_{ij} in Table 2) were computed applying the following start/stop model: (i) the LRT acceleration is $1.96\,\mathrm{m/s^2}$ (0.2 g), so standing passengers maintain equilibrium; (ii) deceleration is also of $1.96\,\mathrm{m/s^2}$ by the same comfort reason; (iii) the time required for passengers board/alight the train at each station is 60s, which is added as a fixed per-stop delay to every edge; (iv) cruise speed is 60 km/h, so it takes 8.5s to the LRT to get it.
- Regarding rail stretches costs, our approach relies on the study by Flyvbjerg et al. [6], adopting the worst per-kilometer value, since we are assuming elevated crossing point at some intersections.
- Constructions costs are based on lengths, but they are penalized by the urbanization density.

After computing the optimal solution for the *maximum resilience problem* variant for the case study (see Sect. 4.2), the resulting cost values were corrected by a coefficient so that the average per-kilometer cost to be 30 million USD, following the reference work by Flyvbjerg et al. [6]. Since the objective function in formulation Eq. 1 is linearly scalable, proportional modifications on the function change the objective value, but not the solution where it is attained.

4.2 Maximum Resilience Problem

The computed optimal solution for the maximum resilience problem variant has a cost of 2 744 million USD. Figure 3 sketches the solution for the maximum resilience variant of the problem, considering the reference values in Table 2.
Even though the solution for the maximum resilience problem finds rail stretches costs optimally, it allows more than one configuration for lines. For instance, swapping sub-tours between node 4 and 10 for lines CA1 and CA2 still gets a feasible solution with the same cost. Overall, the formulation in Eq. 1 does not determine configuration for lines. Nonetheless, it guarantees that at least a feasible configuration can always be crafted, and that whatever the features of the configuration, lines are independent and rails cost is optimal.
Figure 3 includes a proposal for the configuration of lines, chosen so that end-to-end travel times between lines of the same terminal are as balanced as possible. The attributes for each line are presented in Table 3

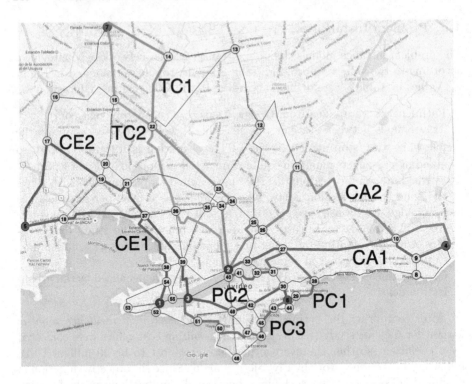

Fig. 3. Optimal solution for the maximum resilience problem

Table 3. Lines attributes for the reference alignment

Line ID	CA1	CA2	CE1	CE2	PC1	PC2	PC3	TC1	TC2
Cost (m.USD)	254	313	283	323	225	231	272	423	420
Length (m)	9785	16106	9292	13364	6091	4383	5467	13742	13314
Delay (s)	929	1308	900	1212	913	537	807	1236	1074

4.3   Maximum Travel Time Problem

Consider the problem formulation in Eq. 2 with end-to-end traveling times bounds TD_p of infinite value, i.e., without limits of time. This eliminates equations group (iv) in Eq. 2, so the result is a relaxation of the general formulation. The solution to that problem is a cycle spanning all terminals and node XXX (id 2), plus an additional path the for third line of Pocitos. That cycle borders the map in Fig. 2 and it is not suitable for passengers, since they would never use the secondary line because of its prohibitive traveling time. However, the cost of that solution is important, because it constitutes a lower bound for more realistic solutions. The solution of the relaxation of Eq. 2 has a cost of 1383 million USD.

Reference values of TD_p are based on Fig. 3, since travel times in Table 3 are much better than those of the actual public transportation system in Montevideo.

To allow a wide exploration of solutions, TD_p for a terminal p is defined as the end-to-end time of the worst lines configuration over railways associated to terminal p. For instance, for CAR that configuration is 4, 9, 10, 11, 26, 25 and 2, whose end-to-end travel time is 1323 s. By repeating that procedure upon remaining terminals, the other bounds result: 1266 s for CER, 913 s for POC and 1236 s for TCO. Using these TD_p values, line configurations in Fig. 3 are feasible in Eq. 2, so the solution cost computed for the maximum resilience problem is an upper bound for this problem variant. Thus, the optimal cost for this problem is between 1383 and 2744 million dollars. The exact solution for the maximum travel times problem is in fact below the average of those values, with a total cost of 1890 million USD. By prorating this amount among tickets annually sold (300 million) and considering a 30-year repayment period, a per-ticket cost of 0.21 USD over an actual average ticket cost of 1.12 USD (August 2019) is obtained.

Figure 4 sketches the optimal line configurations and Table 4 presents the main attributes for lines. In this case, the concept of *per-line cost* does not apply, because in this problem version lines share important portions of the tram rails.

Table 4. Lines attributes for the resilient and traveling time bounded problem

Line ID	CA1	CA2	CE1	CE2	PC1	PC2	PC3	TC1	TC2
Length (m)	12264	10951	12412	15169	2611	3399	7011	14513	14365
Delay (s)	1079	1273	1223	1252	499	614	832	1146	1204

End-to-end travel times in the solution of this problem version are better than in the previous one in three out of nine lines: CA2, PC1 and TC1. Per-terminal average traveling costs in the new solution are higher for Carrasco (5.1%), Colón (1.7%) and Cerro (17.2%), but they are lower for Pocitos (−13.8%), which moves much more passengers. In either case, differences are relatively low. A notorious difference is observed on the rail stretches cost, since the maximum time solution is 45.2% cheaper than the maximum resilience solution.

The average speed in both solutions are practically the same: 36.9 km/h vs. 36.6 km/h. Average travel times between remote terminals and the city Centre are significantly lower than in the current public bus system: 20 min vs. 55 min for Carrasco, 21 min vs. 61 min for Cerro, 11 min vs. 31 min for Pocitos, and 20 min vs. 65 min for Colón. Overall, the average speed-up provided by the new system is near to 3.

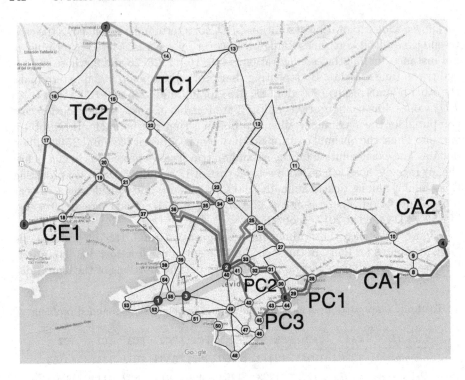

Fig. 4. Optimal solution for the maximum travel time problem

5 Conclusions and Future Work

This article presented a combinatorial optimization approach for the problem of designing a backbone trunk public transportation network for Montevideo.

Two variants of the problem were studied, accounting for maximum resilience and maximum travel time solutions. The best computed design balances investments costs with end-to-end travel times, getting to a reference solution with a cost of 1890 million USD, which can be assumed with a low increase of the ticket cost. The overall quality of service provided by the computed solution is significantly better than in the current bus system of Montevideo, with speedups of around three in the travel times between terminals and the city center.

The main lines for future work include integrating detailed distributions about inter-zone travel times and adding up the access portion of the network, not only to compute such additional travel times but also to estimate reduction in costs coming from reassigning busses to shorter trips.

References

1. Benevolo, C., Dameri, R.P., D'Auria, B.: Smart mobility in smart city. In: Torre, T., Braccini, A.M., Spinelli, R. (eds.) Empowering Organizations. LNISO, vol. 11, pp. 13–28. Springer, Cham (2016). https://doi.org/10.1007/978-3-319-23784-8_2
2. Ceder, A., Wilson, N.: Bus network design. Transp. Res. Part B: Methodol. **20**(4), 331–344 (1986)
3. Deakin, M., Waer, H.A.: From intelligent to smart cities. Intell. Build. Int. **3**(3), 140–152 (2011)
4. Dodson, J., Mees, P., Stone, J., Burke, M.: The principles of public transport network planning: a review of the emerging literature with select examples. Technical report 15, Griffith University (2011)
5. Figueiredo, L., Jesus, I., Tenreiro, J., Ferreira, J., Martins, J.: Towards the development of intelligent transportation systems. IEEE Intell. Transp. Syst. 1206–1211 (2001)
6. Flyvbjerg, B., Bruzelius, N., van Wee, B.: Comparison of capital costs per route-kilometre in urban rail. Eur. J. Transp. Infrastruct. Res. **8**(1), 17–30 (2008)
7. Handler, G.Y., Zang, I.: A dual algorithm for the constrained shortest path problem. Networks **10**(4), 293–309 (1980). https://onlinelibrary.wiley.com/doi/abs/10.1002/net.3230100403
8. Karmarkar, N.: A new polynomial-time algorithm for linear programming. Combinatorica **4**(4), 373–395 (1984)
9. Król, A., Król, M.: The design of a metro network using a genetic algorithm. Appl. Sci. **9**(3), 1–17 (2019)
10. Laporte, G., Marín, Á., Mesa, J.A., Ortega, F.A.: An integrated methodology for the rapid transit network design problem. In: Geraets, F., Kroon, L., Schoebel, A., Wagner, D., Zaroliagis, C.D. (eds.) Algorithmic Methods for Railway Optimization. LNCS, vol. 4359, pp. 187–199. Springer, Heidelberg (2007). https://doi.org/10.1007/978-3-540-74247-0_9
11. Laporte, G., Pascoal, M.: Path based algorithms for metro network design. Comput. Oper. Res. **62**, 78–94 (2015)
12. Mauttone, A., Hernández, D.: Encuesta de movilidad del área metropolitana de Montevideo. Principales resultados e indicadores (2017). http://scioteca.caf.com/handle/123456789/1078. Accessed 20 Aug 2019
13. Miller, P., de Barros, A., Kattan, L., Wirasinghe, S.: Public transportation and sustainability: a review. KSCE J. Civil Eng. **20**(3), 1076–1083 (2016)
14. Nesmachnow, S.: An overview of metaheuristics: accurate and efficient methods for optimisation. Int. J. Metaheuristics **3**(4), 320–347 (2014)
15. Rassafi, A., Vaziri, M.: Sustainable transport indicators: definition and integration. Int. J. Environ. Sci. Technol. **2**(1), 83–96 (2005)
16. Stjernborg, V., Mattisson, O.: The role of public transport in society—a case study of general policy documents in sweden. Sustainability **8**(11), 1120 (2016)
17. Škorupa, M., Kendra, M.: Proposal of backbone public transport lines in the upper Šariš region. Procedia Eng. **192**, 800–805 (2017)

Energy Storage Systems for Power Supply of Ultrahigh Speed Hyperloop Trains

Marcos Lafoz[✉] , Gustavo Navarro , Marcos Blanco , and Jorge Torres

Centro de Investigaciones Energéticas, Medioambientales y Tecnológicas (CIEMAT),
Av. Complutense, 40, 28040 Madrid, Spain
{marcos.lafoz,gustavo.navarro,marcos.blanco,
jorgejesus.torres}@ciemat.es

Abstract. The paper analyses the alternatives for the power supply of a Hyperloop type railway transport. The particular case of the technology of the Spanish company ZELEROS is studied. Specifications related to both a first prototype and a commercial system are presented and the power supply requirements analysed. After considering different alternatives, energy storage based on supercapacitors is obtained as a feasible and competitive solution for the power supply of this application due to the power/energy ratio and the cycles capability. A preliminary design methodology for the energy storage requirements is presented in the paper. Once selected the type of linear motor, the power supply scheme is presented, based on a motor-side power electronic converter and a DC/DC converter which connects to the energy storage devices. An additional low power grid-tie converter for the recharge of the energy storage system is also used. Different track sections are defined, connected to the power electronic converter through corresponding switches, being supplied sequentially when the capsule presence is detected along the track. The number of track sections depends on the limitations of voltage and current, defined by the power electronic converter selected and particular issues like current density selection and the evaluation of skin effect are very important for this application.

Keywords: Energy storage · Hyperloop · Power supply · Power electronics

1 Introduction, Historical Reference and Concept

According to the European Environmental Agency, in 2016, the transport sector contributed 27% of total EU-28 greenhouse gas emissions [1]. Emissions need to fall by around two thirds by 2050, compared with 1990 levels, in order to meet the long-term 60% greenhouse gas emission reduction target as set out in the 2011 Transport White Paper. Beyond the particular vehicles and the freight traffic, which means 72% of them, it is remarkable the pollution levels achieved by the air traffic, reaching even a higher level of pollution than the railway traffic in the range of distances of 500 km. On the other hand, railway traffic results not as competitive as air traffic for distances higher than 1,000 km.

© Springer Nature Switzerland AG 2020
S. Nesmachnow and L. Hernández Callejo (Eds.): ICSC-CITIES 2019, CCIS 1152, pp. 244–255, 2020.
https://doi.org/10.1007/978-3-030-38889-8_19

In this scenario, in 2013, the American entrepreneur Elon Musk, owner of Tesla and SpaceX [2] companies, launched the idea of a new ultrafast train, magnetically levitated and travelling along a low pressure tube. This mean of transport was named Hyperloop and it is considered as the 5th mean of transport, although is sustainability has been sometimes questioned.

Currently there are several projects to be mentioned [3], some other particular projects in America [4], some in Europe [5] and some in Asia [6] to develop this technology. In the case of Europe, a Commission has been created to define the operational specifications of this mean of transport, with the aim to ensure the interoperability between the different systems in operation across Europe.

The concept could be related to some very high speed trains developed in the 20th century, the magnetic levitation (maglev) trains [7–9]. In fact, the idea of the Hyperloop concept is not new, but it has some references from the 18th century, when the French inventor Denis Papin developed the idea of a tubular vehicle moving inside a tube as a result of the pressure difference between the front and rear parts of the vehicle. In the 19th century, this idea was materialized in England, in 1827, when the English inventor George Medhurst developed a vehicle moving along a rectangular pipe by the effect of a 1.07 atm pressure. It was named Atmospheric Railway. In 1867, in New York (USA), Alfred Ely Beach invented a similar device (see Fig. 1) which would become the first concept of suburban transport.

Fig. 1. Neumatic tube by Alfred Ely Beach, in New York (USA), 1867.

Back to the present time, the current operational requirements of the named system are related to the application both of freight railway traffic and of passenger traffic, connecting distances in the range of 1,000 km and maximum speed in the range of 700–1,000 km/h. At this range of speed the use of catenary and pantograph based systems is not possible since technology is does not support such conditions. Alternative systems need to be used for the traction of the moving part along the rails.

The technology is based on a railway line inside a pressurized tube, where several moving parts, hereafter capsules, are travelling between two points, with an utilization period estimated in the range of 1 and 5 min between capsules. The rail line can be divided in three areas: firstly, an acceleration area, between 5 and 10 km, where the capsule is accelerated with the help of a linear motor installed along the rail. Although different options are possible as traction motor, it is preferred the one with less weight in the moving part and more simplicity in the coils supplied along the track line. During this area, the capsule is accelerated to maximum speed. Secondly, the area where the capsule maintains the maximum speed. The losses are compensated by means of an on-board propulsion system that can be also based on different technological solutions. In the case of study, a compressor gets the air in front of the capsule, compresses it and subsequently it is expanded in a reaction turbine, in a similar way than in an aircraft. This air is not only used for the propulsion of the capsule but also for the levitation, in order to minimize the mechanical friction. The energy used for this process is covered by a set of batteries located on-board of the capsule. Finally, when the capsule arrives to the destination, it needs to be braked, using regenerative braking to recuperate part of the kinetic energy of the capsule. Additional braking systems are installed at the capsules in order to act in case of emergency.

Several studies have been accomplished in order to analyse the economic viability of this solution both in passengers and cargo [10].

Figure 2 shows the technology developed by the Spanish company ZELEROS [11], winner of the 2016 SpaceX competition in the category of best design and best propulsion system.

 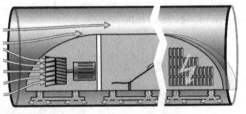

Fig. 2. Technology for Hyperloop form the Spanish company ZELEROS.

CIEMAT Institute is collaborating with the Spanish company ZELEROS in the development of the acceleration device and the power supply of the technological solution proposed. This paper will be focused in the study of the power supply for the acceleration of the capsules within the first area previously described.

2 Analysis of the Options for the Power Supply of the Capsules

The technical specifications for the acceleration device required by the system developed by ZELEROS are compiled in Table 1.

Table 1. Technical specifications for the acceleration area.

Maximum speed	Average acceleration	Acceleration time	Acceleration length	Maximum force	Mass
700 km/h (194 m/s)	2 m/s^2	97 s	10 km	100 kN	40,000 kg

First decision is the acceleration profile along the acceleration area. It is possible to choose a constant acceleration, applying a constant force, but it produces a maximum power level very high (around 15 MW in the study case) or, on the contrary, to select a more typical profile in industrial electric drives consisting of a first section of constant force and another section of constant power. In this case, the maximum power is lower (10 MW for the study case) and therefore more convenient for the design of electric equipment, although it requires a higher force value in the first section. The two options are presented in Fig. 2, but the second one is preferred since it gets a better dynamics for the moving capsule and allows to reduce the power, as well as the current intensity during the acceleration process.

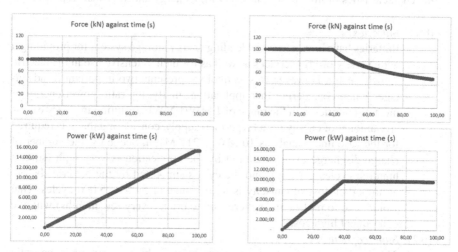

Fig. 3. Constant force profile (left) and constant power profile (right). (Color figure online)

According to the constant power profile from Fig. 3 (right), the theoretical amount of energy required for the acceleration of the moving capsule (not considering the efficiency of the system neither the additional power consumption of the auxiliary systems involved) with a maximum power of 10 MW can be estimated as the area under the red curve:

$$Energy = \tfrac{1}{2}(P_{max} \cdot T1) + P_{max} \cdot (T - T1) =$$
$$\tfrac{1}{2}(10\,MW \cdot 38\,s) + 10\,MW \cdot (97\,s - 38\,s) = 780\,MJ = 217\,kWh \qquad (1)$$

A value of 217 kWh has been obtained, used in the following calculations.

2.1 Power Supply Options for the Acceleration Linear Motor

Different options for the power supply of the linear motor installed in the acceleration area to achieve the maximum speed of the capsules are presented as following:

(a) *Direct connection to the electric grid*
    The first option is the direct connection to the electric grid. The advantages of this scheme are that: allows the use of a high voltage, very convenient for the supply of

the linear motor coils, since the voltage level can be transformed easily in the voltage level required; the connection is quite simple; the power supply is guaranteed. On the other hand, as inconvenient there is a higher cost of the infrastructure, the power consumption and the payment for the use of the grid, although the utilization time is quite low.

This is why it makes sense to consider the use of energy storage systems as an alternative.

(b) *Connection through an energy storage system*
Among the different energy storage technologies already existing in the market, nowadays three of them have been selected according to their maturity level and the characteristics of high power, not very high energy and very fast response.

(b.1) *Batteries*
Batteries have emerged as the leading energy storage system for providing a wide variety of grid services as well as for their extensive use in the electric vehicle sector. However, this technology presents two important disadvantages when considering this application: firstly, the ratio power/energy of most of batteries is in the range of 1 MW/1 MWh, resulting in a very excessive amount of energy for a Hyperloop supply, considering that it is required for the case under analysis 10 MW, 0.217 MWh. Secondly, the number of charge-discharge cycles required by the application is very high (several hundred cycles per day), and the cycles supported by the batteries before an important loss of capacity is in the range of 5,000–25,000 cycles. That would lead to replace the batteries quite often (every few months) with the consequent high cost.

(b.2) *Supercapacitors*
This technology results quite appropriate when considering the ratio power/energy offered by the commercial solutions, in the order of 1 MW/(5–10 kWh), very similar to the level required by this application.

On the other hand, the most important limitation is the isolation limit offered by the modules, allowing a voltage of 1,500 V. By using a topology with a middle point grounded it is possible to increase the voltage level to 3,000 V, still a quite low voltage level for the power level required.

A study based on three commercial solutions of supercapacitors have been accomplished and presented in Fig. 3. The three of them provide the same conclusion, which is that the most restrictive parameter for designing is the energy capacity, remaining some power capability underused, especially considering the low operation time, which does not increase the thermal necessities.

Nevertheless, the market trend for this technology goes towards getting supercapacitors cells with double the energy very soon (by 2020). In that case, the use of supercapacitors would be very suitable for this application, resulting economically competitive comparing with grid connection or batteries (Fig. 4).

Module type A: 80Wh, 64V	Module type B: 127Wh, 102V	Module type C: 158.4Wh, 144V
Number modules $= \dfrac{217\ kWh}{0.75 \cdot 80Wh}$ $\cong 3617$ modules	Number modules $= \dfrac{217\ kWh}{0.75 \cdot 127Wh}$ $\cong 2279$ modules	Number modules $= \dfrac{217\ kWh}{0.75 \cdot 158.4Wh}$ $\cong 1827$ modules
3000V / 64V_mod = 47 in series, 3617/47=77 groups in parallel	3000V / 102V_mod = 29 in series, 2279/29=79 groups in parallel	3000V / 144V_mod = 20 in series, 1827/20=92 groups in parallel
$I_{sc} = \dfrac{P_{max}}{U_{supercap\_min}} = \dfrac{10MW}{1500V} = 6.66\ kA$	$I_{sc} = \dfrac{P_{max}}{U_{supercap\_min}} = \dfrac{10MW}{1500V} = 6.66\ kA$	$I_{sc} = \dfrac{P_{max}}{U_{supercap\_min}} = \dfrac{10MW}{1500V} = 6.66\ kA$
• 6666/80=83 A per branch. • Supercapacitors underused.	• 6666/83=80 A per branch. • Supercapacitors underused.	• 6666/95=70.16 A per branch. • Supercapacitors underused.

Fig. 4. Dimensioning of energy storage systems required for the acceleration of a capsule, using three types of supercapacitor commercial solutions: A, B and C.

(b.3) *Flywheels*
　　　Other technologies as flywheels could be also used from the point of view of power/energy ratio and number of cycles capacity. However, the required high voltage level for the linear motor has a negative influence in the feasibility of using flywheels for this application since it would increase very much the cost.

3 Development of a 1/3 Reduced Scale Prototype of Linear Motor and Power Supply

First step before the opening of a commercial train line is the development of a test line for validation of the technology. A 1/3 reduced scale prototype of linear motor and power supply system is being currently accomplished. The technical specifications for this system are presented in Table 2. The power supply profile with the scheme of a constant power is shown in Fig. 5.

Table 2. Technical specifications for the acceleration area of the 1/3 scale prototype.

Maximum speed	Average acceleration	Acceleration time	Acceleration length	Maximum force	Mass
500 km/h (139 m/s)	20 m/s^2	7 s	0.5 km	80 kN	2,000 kg

3.1 Preliminary Design of an Energy Storage System for the Power Supply

Considering the previous specifications, a preliminary design of an energy storage system has been carried out. The methodology followed gets firstly a dimensioning based on the energy required, secondly on the voltage by associating the storage cells and finally validating the current required by the application.

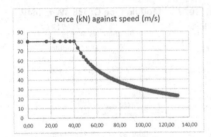
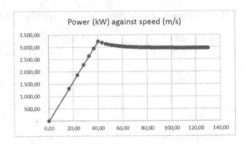

Fig. 5. Profile of force vs speed and power vs speed for the 1/3 reduced scale prototype.

(a) *Energy Dimensioning*

The energy required during the acceleration process can be calculated based on the kinetic energy associated to the maximum speed of the capsule. For this preliminary calculation, efficiency from electric to mechanic conversion has been considered 100% but it must be upgraded with the different efficiencies involved in the conversion process (mainly aerodynamic losses, magnetic levitation losses and Joule effect losses at the linear motor and the power distribution line along the acceleration area).

The energy value is given by (2).

$$E_{kinetic} = \frac{1}{2} \cdot mass \cdot v_{max}^2 = \frac{1}{2} \cdot 2{,}000 \cdot 139^2 = 19.32\,MJ \qquad (2)$$

Selecting one of the commercial modules with an energy of 80 Wh (64 V, 141F) and taking into account a deep of discharge of half of the total voltage, which means 75% of the total energy, the number of modules required to fulfill the energy is 90, as it is obtained from (3).

$$Number\,modules = \frac{Energy_{required}(J)}{deep_{ofdischarge(p.u)} \cdot Energy_{module(Wh)} \cdot \frac{3.6\,kJ}{Wh}}$$

$$Number\,modules = \frac{19.32\,MJ}{0.75 \cdot 80Wh \cdot 3.6\,J/Wh} \cong 90 \qquad (3)$$

(b) *Voltage Dimensioning*

The voltage selection depends on the maximum isolation voltage supported by the supercapacitor modules. Considering the same 64 V modules, and taking into account a middle point grounded topology (supports maximum of 3,000 V), splitting the previously calculated 90 modules in three branches of 30 series connected modules each, it is achieved a maximum voltage of 1,920 V. It remains the possibility to connect other 15 modules more in series per branch, increasing the energy of the complete system in 50% from the point of view of voltage limitation. The voltage of the storage system when reaching the discharge point is 690 V, voltage used to calculate the maximum current.

As a consequence, the already calculated 90 cells are distributed as explained above to fulfill the voltage requirements.

(c) *Current Dimensioning*

The most restrictive current occurs when the voltage is minimum in the energy storage system.

$$I_{supercaps\ P=cte} = \frac{P_{max}}{U_{supercap\_min}} = \frac{2.96\ MW}{690\ V} = 4,289\ A \tag{4}$$

That implies 1,429 A per each supercapacitor branch.

Considering that the maximum current of the module is 2,000 A and that the average current during the operation is in the range of 1,000 A, there is no limitation by current. However, it is very important to analyze the thermal effects of the current, since the temperature increase could lead to an important loss of capacitance in the supercapacitors. A thermal model is required to do an accurate study of the transient, not facing it at this point, but considering that the operating time is only 7 s, and although this is an important time from the point of view of the power electronics, it is not important for the supercapacitors due to their relatively high thermal inertia.

The already selected modules are therefore validated in terms of current.

3.2 Scheme of the Power Supply for the Reduced Scale System

As a result of Sect. 3.1, the prototype can be supplied by means of a set of series connected supercapacitors. The supercapacitors would be connected through a DC/DC converter to a DC-link and then, a power electronic converter supply the linear motor required for the acceleration. The recharge of the supercapacitors is done by means of a grid-tie converter (GTC), connected to the DC-link, but of much less power than the DC/DC converter. A 50 kW grid-tie converter is enough to replace the full energy of the system in less than 10 min. These elements are depicted in the scheme of Fig. 6.

As previously stated, the acceleration section needs a linear motor along 500 m in the reduced scale prototype. The design of this motor, although not accomplished in this paper, is based on the definition of a required maximum force, a velocity profile and some dimensional restrictions. Several solutions for the linear motor have been studied in the literature and most of them are based on permanent magnet machines [12]. However, a solution based on reluctance machine has been selected in this case because of the robustness, simplicity and reduced cost [13–15]. A decision of how to split the ampere·turns parameter into number of coil turns and the current has been considered, taking into account the voltage drop and the power electronics design.

On the other hand voltage requirements are also defined in order to compensate the electromagnetic force, the resistive voltage drop and the inductance transient, required to reach the current reference during the operation. As a result, the most suitable solution for the linear motor is to use different types of coils along the acceleration section. That is the best way to take advantage of the number of turns of the coil in order to adapt it to the electromagnetic force, according to the speed. The higher the speed, the lower the number of turns of the coil. Five different types of coils have been considered in this particular case of study, with a number of turns varying from 12 to 4 as increasing the speed or the distance along the track.

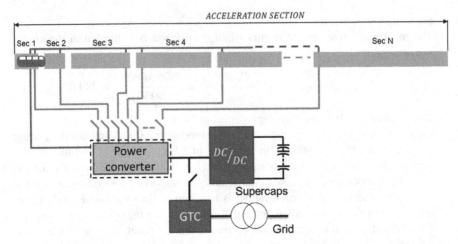

Fig. 6. Scheme of the power supply system proposed and the distribution in track sections.

A set of different track sections are calculated after considering the voltage and current limitations. For the prototype of study, a voltage of 4,000 V and current of 3,000 A have been selected due to the power electronic converter design. The methodology consists in adding a number of coils together, to be supplied at the same time by the power electronic converter, until a limit is reached in terms of voltage or current. Then, a new track section is defined. If a voltage limit is reached, a new track section with the same type of coil is considered. If the current limit is achieved, a new track section with a different type of coil is considered.

Other important issue related to the current is the selection of the current density at the linear motor coils (in order to determine the coils cable section), and the selection of the different track sections to be supplied at the same time by the power converter. Two current densities are being analysed for the calculation, 20 and 40 A/mm^2.

After running the procedure of track section calculation, the results are presented in Table 3, and the scheme of how the track sections are connected to the power electronic converter are described in Fig. 6.

Table 3. Number of track sections with different current density.

Current density	N = 12	N = 10	N = 8	N = 6	N = 4	Total number
20 A/mm^2	2	1	2	6	17	**28**
40 A/mm^2	2	1	2	6	19	**30**

Table 4 complements the information of Table 3 with the length of the different track sections along the acceleration area for one of the study cases, using 20 A/mm^2.

Skin effect needs to be also considered in this application since quite high frequencies are operating at the high speed area. Figure 7 presents how the ohmic resistance increases

Table 4. Length associated to the different track sections for the case of $J = 20$ A/mm^2.

Section	Coil type	Start (m)	End (m)	Section	Coil type	Start (m)	End (m)
1	$N = 12$	1	4	15	$N = 4$	192	216
2	$N = 12$	4	12	16	$N = 4$	216	238
3	$N = 10$	12	18	17	$N = 4$	238	261
4	$N = 8$	18	25	18	$N = 4$	261	284
5	$N = 8$	25	37	19	$N = 4$	284	306
6	$N = 6$	27	42	20	$N = 4$	306	329
7	$N = 6$	42	58	21	$N = 4$	329	350
8	$N = 6$	58	74	22	$N = 4$	350	372
9	$N = 6$	74	89	23	$N = 4$	372	393
10	$N = 6$	89	104	24	$N = 4$	393	414
11	$N = 6$	104	118	25	$N = 4$	414	436
12	$N = 6$	118	144	26	$N = 4$	436	457
13	$N = 4$	144	168	27	$N = 4$	457	478
14	$N = 4$	168	192	28	$N = 4$	478	500

with the speed. The effect is even more important when the current density is lower, since the cable section is bigger.

Position sensors will be deployed along the acceleration track in order to detect the presence of the capsule. That will provide the closing of switches, connecting each track section to the power electronics converter. Only one track section is supplied by the power converter at the same time being necessary only one power converter to supply the complete linear motor. That is an advantage compared to the power supply of previous

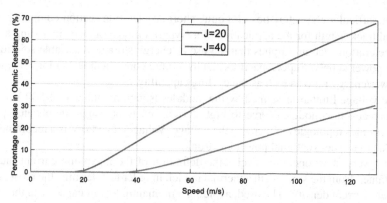

Fig. 7. Increase of the ohmic resistance due to skin effect for two values of current density (J).

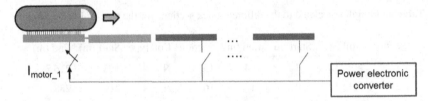

Fig. 8. Commutation of the different track sections switches from the power converter.

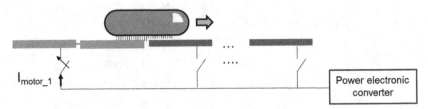

Fig. 9. Transition of the capsule from one track section to the next.

similar concepts as maglev [8, 16], where different power converters need to be installed along the track for the power supply, requiring high voltage equipment.

Figure 8 shows a scheme of how the different track sections are connected to the power electronic converter through the corresponding switches. During the transition of the capsule from one track section to the next (Fig. 9), only part of the coils are providing force, since only part of the supplied coils have their magnetic circuit closed [17]. The force will drop to ½ during a very short time each track section transition.

4   Conclusions and Next Steps

The conclusions of this study can be summarized in three points:

1. The particular characteristics of a quite short acceleration section compared to the total track length for the application of a Hyperloop type railway, including a close deceleration section, implies that the use of energy storage is a viable solution for the power supply. Supercapacitors results a quite convenient technology due to the power/energy ratio as well as the cycling capability.
2. The voltage limitation defined by the modules isolation voltage of 1,500 V for the supercapacitor modules force to high current levels or using complicated power electronics topologies to increase the voltage. Voltage of 4,000 V is a recommended value to use conventional power electronics.
3. For a very short operation cycles the definition of the maximum current must be obtained from the study with a thermal model, in order to determine the most appropriate current density to be used, avoiding a premature loss of capacity in the supercapacitors. A tradeoff between the material cost and the performance need to be found.

The next steps of the collaboration between CIEMAT and ZELEROS in the development of the 1/3 reduced scale prototype for technology validation are related to the manufacturing of the linear motor, power electronic converters and energy storage based on supercapacitors, as well as the deployment of the equipment in a 500 m testing track.

References

1. European Environment Agency: Greenhouse gas emissions from transport. https://www.eea.europa.eu/data-and-maps/indicators/transport-emissions-of-greenhouse-gases/transport-emissions-of-greenhouse-gases-11
2. Musk, E.: Hyperloop Alpha (2013). http://www.spacex.com/sites/spacex/files/hyperloopalpha-20130812.pdf
3. Chesteron, V., Kelvin, D.: Hyperloop-Opportunity For UK Supply Chain (2018). Final report. https://s3-eu-west-1.amazonaws.com/media.ts.catapult/wp-content/uploads/2018/10/08153525/00601_Hyperloop-Report.pdf
4. Hyperllop One. https://hyperloop-one.com/global-challenge
5. Hardt: European Hyperloop Program (2018). https://ec.europa.eu/eipp/desktop/en/projects/project-print-9401.html
6. Hyperloop Transportation Technologies. https://www.hyperloop.global/about
7. Ono, M., Koga, S., Ohtsuki, H.: Japan's superconducting Maglev train. IEEE Instrum. Meas. Mag. **5**, 9–15 (2002)
8. Ikeda, H., Kaga, S., Osada, Y., Ito, K., Mugiya, Y., Tutumi, K.: Development of power supply system for Yamanashi Maglev Test Line. In: Proceedings of Power Conversion Conference - PCC 1997, Nagaoka, Japan, vol. 1, pp. 37–41 (1997)
9. E.R.A. European Union Agency for Railways: Hyperloop – an Innovation for Global Transportation? https://www.era.europa.eu/sites/default/files/library/docs/hyperloop_innovation_for_global_transportation_en_1.pdf
10. ZELEROS Hyperloop Technology. https://hyperloopupv.com/projects/
11. Werner, M., Eissing, K., Langton, S.: Shared value potential of transporting cargo via hyperloop. Front. Built Environ. **2**, 17 (2016). https://doi.org/10.3389/fbuil.2016.00017
12. Chevailler, S.: Comparative study & selection criteria of linear motors. These no. 3569, Ecole Polytecnique Federal de Lausanne (2006)
13. Moreno Torres, P., Lafoz, M., Blanco, M., Navarro, G., Torres, J., García-Tabarés, L.: Switched reluctance drives with degraded mode for electric vehicles. In: Modeling & Simulation for Electric Vehicle Applications, Chap. 5. INTECH (2016)
14. Kolomeitsev, L., et al.: Linear switched reluctance motor as a high efficiency propulsion system for railway vehicles. In: Proceedings of International Symposium on Power Electronics, Electrical Drives, Automation and Motion (SPEEDAM), Ischia, Italy, pp. 155–160 (2008)
15. Kolomeitsev, L., et al.: Control of a linear switched reluctance motor as a propulsion system for autonomous railway vehicles. In: 2008 13th International Power Electronics and Motion Control Conference, Poznan, pp. 1598–1603 (2008)
16. Lee, K.: Advances in the application of power electronics to railway traction. In: 2015 6th International Conference on Power Electronics Systems and Applications (PESA), Hong Kong, pp. 1–4 (2015). https://doi.org/10.1109/pesa.2015.7398960
17. Kale, S.R., Laghane, Y.N., Kharade, A.K., Kadus, S.B.: Hyperloop: advance mode of transportation system and optimize solution on traffic congestion. Int. J. Res. Appl. Sci. Eng. Technol. (IJRASET) **7**(VII), (2019)

Noise and Ozone Continuous Monitoring in an Industrial Urban Area of Northeastern Portugal

Leonardo Campestrini Furst[1] , Manuel Feliciano[2(✉)] , Artur Gonçalves[2] ,
and Felipe Romero[3]

[1] Instituto Politécnico de Bragança, Campus de Santa Apolónia, 5300-253 Bragança, Portugal
[2] Centro de Investigação de Montanha (CIMO), Instituto Politécnico de Bragança,
Campus de Santa Apolónia, 5300-253 Bragança, Portugal
msabenca@ipb.pt
[3] Instituto de la Construcción de Castilla y León (ICCL), Valladolid, Spain

Abstract. The major environmental pressures associated with urban centers are noise and air pollution, making its monitoring of utmost importance to evaluate and reduce the exposure of the population to these environmental risk factors. In this study, continuous monitoring of sound pressure levels, ozone, nitric oxides, carbon monoxide concentrations, and local meteorological variables were performed during the winter and spring months of 2019 at the Mirandela industrial park. Ozone and nitric oxide levels followed a characteristic daily cycle, consistent with the diurnal evolution of radiation and the intensity of the main air pollution sources prevailing in the local. Hourly ozone levels were highest in July, reaching magnitudes of approximately 80 ppb. Ozone concentrations in the industrial park had a strong local influence, mainly related to the local nitric oxides emissions. The results also showed high influence of meteorological parameters on ozone production, especially during daytime. Regarding noise, typical daily and weekly patterns were observed, and sound pressure levels were compatible with those defined for mixed zones according to the Portuguese General Noise Regulation.

Keywords: Air quality · Noise · Monitoring · Industrial Parks

1 Introduction

The rapid urban expansion, associated with a high population growth rate over the last centuries, tends to influence and modify various environmental aspects, producing impacts on the air, water, soil, and biodiversity [1–4]. Under such circumstances, it is evident that the increase in urban traffic, expansion of industrial zones and suppression of vegetation are the main degradation factors of urban air quality and local meteorological changes [5]. In addition, a large part of the population is exposed to different levels of environmental noises, capable of producing diverse effects on human health and well-being [6]. Therefore, air pollution and environmental noise are the two major environmental pressures associated with decreased quality of life in cities [7].

© Springer Nature Switzerland AG 2020
S. Nesmachnow and L. Hernández Callejo (Eds.): ICSC-CITIES 2019, CCIS 1152, pp. 256–268, 2020.
https://doi.org/10.1007/978-3-030-38889-8_20

Air pollution is defined as a condition where one or more substances are present in the atmosphere at concentrations above normal ambient levels and particularly during a sufficiently long period to produce adverse effects on the health of humans, animals, and plants, or to cause material damage [8, 9]. According to the European Directive, noise corresponds to any unwanted sound or set of sounds that cause annoyance or may have an impact on human health, emitted by human activities, such as road traffic, rail traffic, air traffic and industrial sites [10].

Several studies emphasize the adverse effects of these components on human health [7, 11, 12], including respiratory and heart diseases [13, 14], causing annoyance and decreasing the cognitive ability [15, 16]. Thus, one of the great challenges of modern cities managers is providing quality of life to their inhabitants by improving the urban environment. To achieve this purpose, the monitoring of noise levels and air quality are extremely important to assess environmental risks, as well as to maintain or improve the environmental quality in urban centers [15, 17].

The main aim of this study was to study ozone, carbon monoxide, nitrogen oxides, and noise levels in the industrial park of Mirandela - Portugal. Since ozone is a very unstable secondary pollutant, its presence in the troposphere is partially related to the transport from the stratosphere, but the main contribution is its photochemical production, which occurs through the oxidation of hydrocarbons and carbon monoxide in the presence of nitric oxides and solar radiation [18]. For this reason, nitric oxides, carbon monoxide and, meteorological parameters were monitored in this research.

For the study, a monitoring system composed by one weather station, three gas analyzers and one noise sensor were installed in the Mirandela industrial park. The data collected during the winter and spring months of 2019 was used to correlate the different variables monitored with ozone production, and the system allowed further monitoring of the daily noise levels and the identification of the week noise profile. In the next sections of this paper a brief characterization of the industrial park, the methodological details of the study and the main air quality and noise results are presented and discussed.

2   Methodology

2.1   Industrial Park of Mirandela - Brief Description

This study was carried out in the urban industrial park of Mirandela (41°29′N/7°9′W), located in the northeastern region of Portugal, in the region known as Trás-os-Montes. The Industrial Park has an area of 33 hectares with 97 lots distributed to different industrial and commercial sectors. It comprises approximately 65 companies of different typologies such as sausage and granite factories, oil mills, carpentry, locksmiths and car repair shops. The Industrial Park is mostly surrounded by rural areas with olive trees plantations and open grassy spaces and is bounded by roadways to the west and south. The Mirandela downtown is southwest of the industrial Park.

2.2   Monitoring and Analyses

The air quality monitoring started in December 2018, with the collection of hourly data for carbon monoxide (CO), nitrogen oxides (NO, NO_2, NO_x) and ozone (O_3). All these gaseous pollutants were monitored according to the reference methods described by the Directive 2008/50/EC, using three gas analyzers: one ozone analyzer HORIBA APOA-370 (non-dispersive ultra-violet-absorption), one nitrogen oxides analyzer HORIBA APNA-370 (chemiluminescence) and one carbon monoxide analyzer HORIBA APMA-370 (non-dispersive infrared absorption). Noise monitoring started in February 2019 using the CESVA TA120 noise sensor, with measurements taken every minute. The noise sensor has class 1 accuracy according to IEC 61672-1 and was deployed outdoors due to the weather protection cover. In addition, a meteorological station was used to characterize the prevailing local weather conditions, measuring the direction and wind speed, solar radiation, temperature, relative humidity, and precipitation. The gas analyzers, weather station and, noise sensor showed in Fig. 1 have the capacity to send data remotely via GPRS system, enabling the data to be accessed through a remote server.

Fig. 1. Set of the monitoring equipment used in the study: (A) Weather station; (B) air intake; (C) smart noise sensor; (D) gas analyzers container.

Based on the solar radiation data, the days were divided into daytime (8:00–19:00) and nighttime (20:00–7:00) to determine the correlation coefficient between the variables and the local and regional contribution to the prevailing O_3 levels. These separate timeframes were chosen considering the ozone formation and depletion mechanisms that have a strong dependence on solar radiation. It should be mentioned that in this study it was adopted the Coordinated Universal Time (UTC).

Concerning noise, a daily and weekly profile were evaluated based on hourly average data observed during the spring months. Additionally, the noise assessment was based on the Portuguese General Noise Regulation (RGR) (Decree-Law No. 9/2007 of 17 January). The RGR does not set noise limits to industrial parks itself, but any activity located in an industrial park has to comply with criteria established in RGR for sensitive receivers (i.e., spaces where people live or stay) near industrial areas. The criteria set for those receivers depend on the classification established in the municipal master plan for the area where they are located. These areas can be classified into sensitive and mixed zones. The RGR defines sensitive zones as areas for residential use, schools, hospitals or similar, and recreational or leisure spaces, and may also contain small shops and services that do not operate at night, while mixed zones in addition to the uses for sensitive zones may contain shops, services, and industries working all day.

In the master plan of Mirandela the residential areas near the industrial park are classified as mixed zones. For these areas, the RGR specify the limit value of 55 dBA for the night noise indicator (Ln) and a 65 dBA for the day-evening-night noise indicator (Lden). Based on this, for research purpose, the monitoring point was evaluated as a mixed zone.

3   Results and Discussion

3.1   Daily Profile of Ozone Levels and Its Precursors

Figure 2 shows the variation of solar radiation, ozone and its precursors throughout the day.

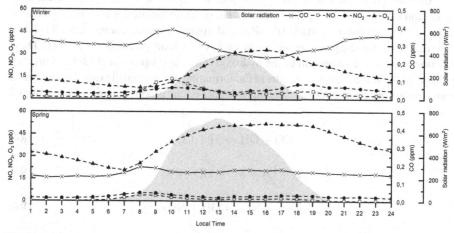

Fig. 2. Average hourly variation of NO_2, NO, CO, O_3 and solar radiation during winter (top) and spring (bottom).

The higher concentrations of the primary pollutants (CO and NOx) registered between 8:00 and 10:00 and between 17:00 and 18:00, coincides with the greatest intensity of traffic associated with the beginning and end of the daily activities inside and outside the industrial park. The higher levels of these primary pollutants in winter show clearly the influence of other combustion sources, such as domestic combustion for heating water and ambient air in dwellings.

In winter, ozone concentrations increase from 8:00 until they reach a peak of 33 ppb at 16:00. It is also noted that during rush hour (about 18:00), the increase in NO and NO_2 concentrations did not imply a significant increase in ozone concentration, partially explained by the prevailing low solar radiation. The ozone pattern in spring and winter was similar, however as the days are longer and the incidence of solar radiation is higher, there are some differences. At spring, ozone concentrations rise from 7:00 to reach its peak at 14:00, remaining stable until 19:00. Considering also that O_3 production depends on the concentration of NO, NO_2, CO, and volatile organic compounds, these gases are consumed as the O_3 concentration increases.

The reactions between O_3, NO, and NO_2 (R1–R3) are part of a well-established null-cycle [18]. Thus, during daylight hours (R1–R2), NO, NO_2 and O_3 are typically balanced on a condition referred to photostationary state [19]. For this reason, it is possible to observe in winter an ozone concentration near 30 ppb between 14:00 and 17:00 and in spring a concentration near 50 ppb between 13:00 and 19:00.

$$NO + O_3 \rightarrow NO_2 + O_2 \tag{R1}$$

$$NO_2 + hv \rightarrow NO + O \tag{R2}$$

$$O + O_2 + M \rightarrow O_3 + M \tag{R3}$$

An atmosphere only with nitrogen oxides do not favor the ozone production, as ozone can be recycled during the reactions. However, in the presence of other precursor gases such as carbon monoxide (R4–R6) and volatile organic compounds (R7–R11), new reactions are triggered, resulting in excess of ozone production [20, 21]. These reactions lead to the formation of the hydroxyl (OH), hydroperoxyl (HO_2) and organo-peroxyl (RO_2) radicals, which results in the formation of nitrogen dioxide without ozone consumption and, consequently, leading to higher ozone production rates by reactions 2 and 3.

$$CO + OH \rightarrow H + CO_2 \tag{R4}$$

$$H + O_2 + M \rightarrow HO_2 + M \tag{R5}$$

$$HO_2 + NO \rightarrow OH + NO_2 \tag{R6}$$

$$CH_4 + OH \rightarrow CH_3 + H_2O \tag{R7}$$

$$CH_4 + O_2 + M \rightarrow CH_3O_2 + M \tag{R8}$$

$$CH_3O_2 + NO \rightarrow CH_3O + NO_2 \tag{R9}$$

$$CH_3O + O_2 \rightarrow HCHO + HO_2 \tag{R10}$$

$$HO_2 + NO \rightarrow OH + NO_2 \tag{R11}$$

3.2 Relation Between Air Quality and Meteorological Variables

Tables 1 and 2 show the daytime and nighttime correlation coefficients between hourly means of individual pollutants (CO, NO, NO_2, NO_x and O_3) and the meteorological parameters for winter and spring. The values in bold were those that show a significant correlation at the 0.05 level (2-tailed). Similar to Agudelo–Castaneda et al. [22], a positive correlation was found between nitrogen oxides and carbon monoxide during daylight, indicating that both gases have the same source, mainly related to combustion processes (e.g. motor vehicles and industries).

Table 1. Spearman correlation coefficients between hourly mean CO, NO, NO_2, NO_x, O_3 and meteorological parameters for winter nighttime and daytime

Winter daytime								
	CO	NO	NO_2	O_3	T.	R.H.	W.S.	S.R.
CO	1	**0,780**	**0,693**	**−0,688**	**−0,685**	**0,629**	**−0,559**	**−0,246**
NO		1	**0,800**	**−0,622**	**−0,543**	**0,502**	**−0,410**	−0,154
NO_2			1	**−0,356**	**−0,281**	0,238	**−0,380**	**−0,251**
O_3				1	**0,852**	**−0,901**	**0,715**	**0,518**
T.					1	**−0,895**	**0,586**	**0,485**
R.H.						1	**−0,554**	**−0,543**
W.S.							1	**0,474**
S.R.								1
Winter nighttime								
	CO	NO	NO_2	O_3	T.	R.H.	W.S.	S.R.
CO	1	**0,771**	**0,840**	**−0,791**	**−0,568**	**0,608**	**−0,358**	**0,160**
NO		1	**0,802**	**−0,672**	**−0,391**	**0,443**	**−0,346**	**0,134**
NO_2			1	**−0,518**	**−0,283**	**0,304**	**−0,300**	0,076
O_3				1	**0,739**	**−0,860**	**0,458**	**−0,295**
T.					1	**−0,702**	**0,328**	**−0,177**
R.H.						1	**−0,288**	**0,392**
W.S.							1	0,088
S.R.								1

T. – Temperature R.H. - Relative Humidity W.V. - Wind Speed S.R. – Solar Radiation

Ozone showed a significant positive correlation with solar radiation and temperature during the daylight hours. This relation reverses during the night, due to the lack of solar radiation for ozone synthesis. This trend is observed in other studies [23, 24], showing that a favorable temperature and high solar radiation increase the photochemical reactions that generate ozone [25]. Moreover, based on reactions 1 to 3, an inverse relationship

Table 2. Spearman correlation coefficients between hourly mean CO, NO, NO$_2$, NO$_x$, O$_3$ and meteorological parameters for spring nighttime and daytime

Spring daytime

	CO	NO	NO$_2$	O$_3$	T.	R.H.	W.V.	S.R.
CO	1	0,675	0,781	−0,091	−0,375	0,330	−0,031	−0,223
NO		1	0,906	−0,402	−0,340	0,369	0,001	−0,211
NO$_2$			1	−0,211	−0,325	0,296	−0,096	−0,327
O$_3$				1	0,531	−0,706	0,313	0,328
T.					1	−0,825	0,159	0,498
R.H.						1	−0,175	−0,528
W.V.							1	0,160
S.R.								1

Spring nighttime

	CO	NO	NO$_2$	O$_3$	T.	R.H.	W.V.	S.R.
CO	1	0,142	0,458	−0,032	−0,302	0,164	−0,069	−0,009
NO		1	0,684	−0,369	0,071	0,178	−0,193	0,403
NO$_2$			1	−0,392	−0,033	0,113	−0,377	0,200
O$_3$				1	0,450	−0,715	0,702	−0,059
T.					1	−0,681	0,345	−0,013
R.H.						1	−0,482	0,057
W.V.							1	0,058
S.R.								1

T. – Temperature R.H. - Relative Humidity W.V. - Wind Speed S.R. – Solar Radiation

between ozone and nitrogen oxides is also observed, which can be confirmed by the negative correlation between these gases.

The results also showed a negative correlation between CO and O$_3$, since carbon monoxide reacts with hydroxyl radicals (R4) producing HO$_2$ radicals (R5) and, consequently, NO$_2$ (R6) which is photo-dissociated to produce O$_3$ through the reactions 2 and 3.

It is also observed in Tables 1 and 2 that the wind speed has a positive correlation with ozone concentration and a negative correlation with nitrogen oxides and carbon monoxide. Agudelo–Castaneda et al. [22] explain that this phenomenon may occur due to high wind speeds, which leads to the dispersion and mixing the gases from local sources, favoring ozone transport and formation reactions taking place in the atmosphere. Moreover, Markovic and Markovic [26] also justify the positive correlation between wind speed and ozone levels due to the transport of ozone produced on the main roads to the measurement point. There is also an expected negative correlation between ozone and relative humidity, since as relative humidity increases the major photochemical paths of

O_3 removal will be lowered [27]. High humidity levels are associated with cloudy days and less sunshine, thus reducing photochemical processes [27].

3.3 Local and Regional Contributions to Ozone Formation

To determine the local and regional contribution to ozone formation, potential ozone levels ($O_3 + NO_2$), also called total oxidant levels (OX), were related to NOx, following the same analysis used in other studies [19, 28, 29]. For this purpose, daily average values (day and night) of OX were evaluated against the values of NO_X. For each data distribution, a linear regression was applied, thus providing an equation, in which the slope represents the local contribution (NO_x-dependent), while the intersection represents the regional contribution (NO_x-independent). Figure 3 presents the linear regressions lines obtained for each of the studied months. The regional contribution represents the background OX concentration, while the local contribution is related to the local production/destruction [28].

When OX levels increase as a function of NO_X, the NO_X contributes mainly to ozone production; when the OX levels decrease, means that NO_X influences the processes of ozone depletion; and when OX levels remain relatively constant as a function of NO_X, indicate that NO_X contributes in equal parts to the production and depletion of ozone.

Based on the regression analysis from December 2018 to June 2019, it was possible to obtain the slope and intersection for each period. These results are presented in Fig. 4 showing the monthly local and regional dependence of OX. It is noticeable that values of the local contribution are higher than the values of the regional contribution, thus indicating that for the industrial park of Mirandela OX production occurs mainly locally due to primary pollutants emissions.

For the regional component, there is a tendency to an increase in the concentration of OX, because the intensification of solar radiation helps photochemical processes. This same tendency was observed in the study of Notario et al. [29]. Regarding the local component, for daytime, an increase in OX concentration is observed from January to May, indicating that during this period NO_X favors ozone production. For the nighttime the relationship is inverse, suggesting that that NO_X is mainly related to ozone depletion mechanisms.

3.4 Noise Monitoring

Figure 5 shows the hourly averages values during the spring months. Between Monday and Friday, the noise profile throughout the day is very similar, with the lowest averages observed between 1:00 and 3:00 at night. Subsequently, noise rises until 8:00, when activities start in the industrial zone, remaining relatively stable until 12:00. At his time, there is a decrease in noise levels due to lunchtime, where most activities stop in the industrial zone. After 18h00 the noise level decreases due to the finish of the work hours. During the weekend, noise levels are lower than during working days, although Saturday levels are higher than those registered on Sundays because some activities operate on Saturday.

Figure 6 presents the daily average night noise levels (Ln) and the day-evening-night-noise (Lden) levels during the spring days. The Portuguese Decree-Law No. 9/2007 of

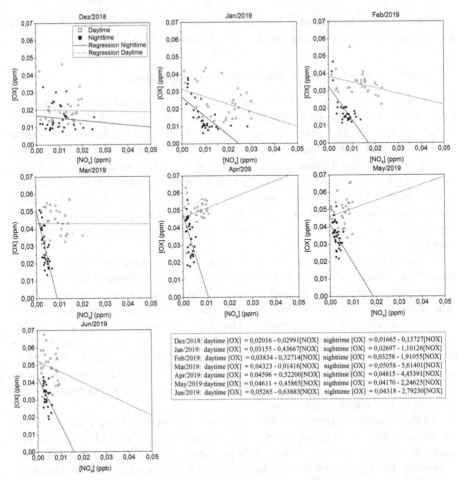

Fig. 3. Daily variation means of regional [OX] with NOx during the months of winter and spring for daytime and nighttime.

17 January establishes for Lden a limit of 65 dBA and for Ln a limit of 55 dBA for mixed zones. During the evaluation time the night indicator was exceeded on April 4th, 15th, and 24th, and May 8th and 24th, reaching the values of 57.0, 56.7, 56.4. 56.0 and 55.6 dBA respectively. As the values of Ln are very close to the established limit and observing that only occurred five days in three months, it can be inferred that a singular event resulted in this phenomenon, so they are values not very relevant for the acoustic characterization of the industrial zone.

It should also be noted that although there are no legal limits for industrial parks, the observed values are within the legal limits for mixed zones, meaning that noise generated by activities developed in industrial park of Mirandela, including traffic road have little impact on the acoustic environment of the sensitive receivers located in its vicinity.

During working days, noise remains relatively stable, close to 60 dBA, thus indicating that the noise sources in the industrial park have a typical behavior over the week.

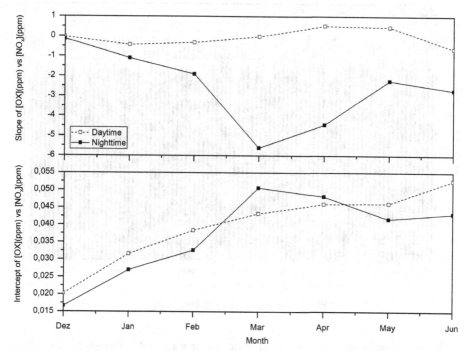

Fig. 4. Monthly variation of regional (intercept) and local (slope) OX in the Industrial Park of Mirandela.

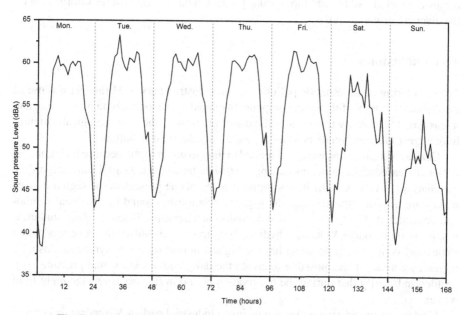

Fig. 5. Average hourly variation of sound pressure levels for spring weeks.

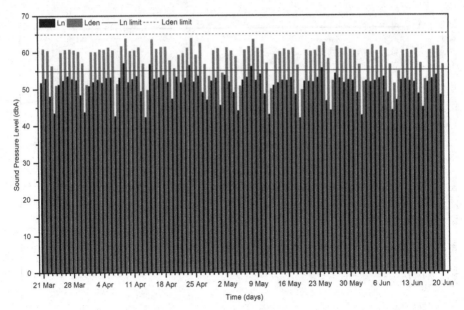

Fig. 6. Ln and Lden levels for Spring

It is noteworthy that only one fixed noise sensor was used in this study, and, for a better acoustic characterization of the industrial zone, it would be necessary to install more noise sensors, considering that the sound is attenuated due to the obstacles and the distance traveled. Additional monitoring points would also add useful information on the diversity of noise sources.

4 Conclusions

The monitoring of atmospheric pollution in the industrial park of Mirandela was useful for the identification of the main components related to the local ozone production, and it was possible to verify that besides the ozone precursors, the meteorological variables have a great influence on its production, especially the solar radiation.

CO and NO emissions were also related mainly to urban traffic because their concentration increased at the same time during the rush hours in the industrial zone. Regarding the analysis of OX vs NO_x, it was found that the ozone present in the region derives mainly from local influence, and the negative relationship found for the local component indicates that NO_x favors ozone depletion mechanisms. Thus, in future studies, it is suggested to monitor VOCs and hydrocarbons to know the different ozone production routes and verify which pollutant has the highest impact on ozone synthesis. Also, by monitoring noise, it was possible to create the daily and weekly sound pressure level profiles and, verify that during the observation period in five occasions the night limit was exceeded.

Continuous monitoring will continue in the industrial park of Mirandela, in order to obtain the ozone and noise profile for all seasons of the year.

Acknowledgments. This study was part of the Trans-National Project Rehabind. The authors would like to thank the Spain-Portugal Transnational Program (POCTEP), with the Financial Support from the European Union under Program FEDER (European Regional Development Fund). The authors acknowledge all the support provided by the Mirandela City Council for the execution of this work.

References

1. Molina, M.J., Molina, L.T.: Megacities and atmospheric pollution. J. Air Waste Manag. Assoc. **54**, 644–680 (2004). https://doi.org/10.1080/10473289.2004.10470936
2. Ren, W., et al.: Urbanization, land use, and water quality in Shanghai: 1947–1996. Environ. Int. **29**, 649–659 (2003). https://doi.org/10.1016/S0160-4120(03)00051-5
3. Imperato, M., Adamo, P., Naimo, D., Arienzo, M., Stanzione, D., Violante, P.: Spatial distribution of heavy metals in urban soils of Naples city (Italy). Environ. Pollut. **124**, 247–256 (2003). https://doi.org/10.1016/S0269-7491(02)00478-5
4. Seto, K.C., Güneralp, B., Hutyra, L.R.: Global forecasts of urban expansion to 2030 and direct impacts on biodiversity and carbon pools. Proc. Natl. Acad. Sci. U.S.A. **109**, 16083–16088 (2012). https://doi.org/10.1073/pnas.1211658109
5. Romero, H., Ihl, M., Rivera, A., Zalazar, P., Azocar, P.: Rapid urban growth, land-use changes and air pollution in Santiago, Chile. Atmos. Environ. **33**, 4039–4047 (1999). https://doi.org/10.1016/S1352-2310(99)00145-4
6. Morel, J., Marquis-Favre, C., Viollon, S., Alayrac, M.: A laboratory study on total noise annoyance due to combined industrial noises. Acta Acustica United Acustica **98**, 286–300 (2012)
7. Hänninen, O., et al.: Environmental burden of disease in Europe: assessing nine risk factors in six countries. Environ. Health Perspect. **122**, 439–446 (2014). https://doi.org/10.1289/ehp. 1206154
8. Seinfeld, J.H., Pandis, S.N.: Atmospheric Chemistry and Physics: From Air Pollution to Climate Change. Wiley, Hoboken (2016)
9. Jacobson, M.Z.: Atmospheric Pollution. Cambridge University Press, Cambridge (2016)
10. European Parliament and of the Council: Directive 2002/49/EC of the European Parliament and of the Council of 25 June 2002 relating to the assessment and management of environmental noise (2002)
11. Linares, C., Díaz, J., Tobías, A., Miguel, J.M.D., Otero, A.: Impact of urban air pollutants and noise levels over daily hospital admissions in children in Madrid: a time series analysis. Int. Arch. Occup. Environ. Health **79**, 143–152 (2006). https://doi.org/10.1007/s00420-005-0032-0
12. Muzet, A.: Environmental noise, sleep and health. Sleep Med. Rev. **11**, 135–142 (2007). https://doi.org/10.1016/J.SMRV.2006.09.001
13. Ji, M., Cohan, D.S., Bell, M.L.: Meta-analysis of the association between short-term exposure to ambient ozone and respiratory hospital admissions. Environ. Res. Lett. **6**, 024006 (2011). https://doi.org/10.1088/1748-9326/6/2/024006
14. Gan, W.Q., Davies, H.W., Koehoorn, M., Brauer, M.: Association of long-term exposure to community noise and traffic-related air pollution with coronary heart disease mortality. Am. J. Epidemiol. **175**, 898–906 (2012). https://doi.org/10.1093/aje/kwr424
15. Jacquemin, B., et al.: Annoyance due to air pollution in Europe. In. J. Epidemiol. **36**, 809–820 (2007). https://doi.org/10.1093/ije/dym042
16. Basner, M., et al.: Auditory and non-auditory effects of noise on health. Lancet **383**, 1325–1332 (2014). https://doi.org/10.1016/S0140-6736(13)61613-X

17. Eldien, H.H.: Noise mapping in urban environments: application at Suez city center. In: 2009 International Conference on Computers & Industrial Engineering, pp. 1722–1727. IEEE (2009)
18. Jacob, D.J.: Heterogeneous chemistry and tropospheric ozone. Atmos. Environ. **34**, 2131–2159 (2000). https://doi.org/10.1016/S1352-2310(99)00462-8
19. Clapp, L.J., Jenkin, M.E.: Analysis of the relationship between ambient levels of O_3, NO_2 and NO as a function of NO_x in the UK. Atmos. Environ. **35**, 6391–6405 (2001). https://doi.org/10.1016/S1352-2310(01)00378-8
20. Hewitt, C.N., Jackson, A.V.: Atmospheric Science for Environmental Scientists. Wiley-Blackwell, Hoboken (2009)
21. Wallace, J.M., Hobbs, P.V.: Atmospheric Science: An Introductory Survey. Elsevier Academic Press, Cambridge (2006)
22. Agudelo-Castaneda, D.M., Calesso Teixeira, E., Norte Pereira, F.: Time–series analysis of surface ozone and nitrogen oxides concentrations in an urban area at Brazil. Atmos. Pollut. Res. **5**, 411–420 (2014). https://doi.org/10.5094/APR.2014.048
23. De la Guardia, M., Armenta, S.: Quality of Air. Elsevier, Amsterdam (2016)
24. Teixeira, E.C., de Santana, E.R., Wiegand, F., Fachel, J.: Measurement of surface ozone and its precursors in an urban area in South Brazil. Atmos. Environ. **43**, 2213–2220 (2009). https://doi.org/10.1016/J.ATMOSENV.2008.12.051
25. Pudasainee, D., Sapkota, B., Shrestha, M.L., Kaga, A., Kondo, A., Inoue, Y.: Ground level ozone concentrations and its association with NO_x and meteorological parameters in Kathmandu valley, Nepal. Atmos. Environ. **40**, 8081–8087 (2006). https://doi.org/10.1016/J.ATMOSENV.2006.07.011
26. Markovic, D., Markovic, D.: The relationship between some meteorological parameters and the tropospheric concentrations of ozone in the urban area of Belgrade. J. Serb. Chem. Soc. **70**, 1487–1495 (2005). https://doi.org/10.2298/JSC0512487M
27. Nishanth, T., Satheesh Kumar, M.K., Valsaraj, K.T.: Variations in surface ozone and NOx at Kannur: a tropical, coastal site in India. J. Atmos. Chem. **69**, 101–126 (2012). https://doi.org/10.1007/s10874-012-9234-5
28. Jenkin, M.E.: Analysis of sources and partitioning of oxidant in the UK—part 2: contributions of nitrogen dioxide emissions and background ozone at a kerbside location in London. Atmos. Environ. **38**, 5131–5138 (2004). https://doi.org/10.1016/J.ATMOSENV.2004.05.055
29. Notario, A., et al.: Analysis of NO, NO_2, NO_x, O3 and oxidant ($OX = O_3 + NO_2$) levels measured in a metropolitan area in the southwest of Iberian Peninsula. Atmos. Res. **104–105**, 217–226 (2012). https://doi.org/10.1016/J.ATMOSRES.2011.10.008

Multiobjective Household Energy Planning Using Evolutionary Algorithms

Giovanni Colacurcio[1], Sergio Nesmachnow[1(✉)], Jamal Toutouh[2],
Francisco Luna[3], and Diego Rossit[4]

[1] Universidad de la República, Montevideo, Uruguay
{giovanni.colacurcio,sergion}@fing.edu.uy
[2] Massachusetts Institute of Technology, Cambridge, USA
toutouh@mit.edu
[3] Universidad de Málaga, Málaga, Spain
flv@lcc.uma.es
[4] Universidad Nacional del Sur, Bahía Blanca, Argentina
diego.rossit@uns.edu.ar

Abstract. This article presents the advances in the design and implementation of a recommendation system for planning the use of household appliances, focused on improving energy efficiency from the point of view of both energy companies and end-users. The system proposes using historical information and data from sensors to define instances of the planning problem considering user preferences, which in turn are proposed to be solved using a multiobjective evolutionary approach, in order to minimize energy consumption and maximize quality of service offered to users. Promising results are reported on realistic instances of the problem, compared with situations where no intelligent energy planning are used (i.e., 'Bussiness as Usual' model) and also with a greedy algorithm developed in the framework of the reference project. The proposed evolutionary approach was able to improve up to 29.0% in energy utilization and up to 65.3% in user preferences over the reference methods.

1 Introduction

Energy management is a crucial issue in nowadays societies. Many strategies have been proposed to guarantee an increased access to the energy resources at affordable costs for citizens, while ensuring the preservation of natural resources and the protection of the environment [15].

For implementing effective energy management policies, innovative technologies must be integrated in easy-to-use and efficient systems, which must include specific features to be useful for both energy companies and citizens. In order to be applied by energy companies, management systems must include capabilities for performing realistic simulations, controlling, and planning the electricity market. From the point of view of citizens, system must provide easy-to-use applications to monitor and manage the energy consumption at household level.

© Springer Nature Switzerland AG 2020
S. Nesmachnow and L. Hernández Callejo (Eds.): ICSC-CITIES 2019, CCIS 1152, pp. 269–284, 2020.
https://doi.org/10.1007/978-3-030-38889-8_21

The capabilities of monitoring, controlling, and managing the energy consumption and generation are very important to provide good quality of service (QoS) and user experience, especially when considering the emphasis on citizen engagement, environment protection, and economic considerations, under the novel paradigm of smart cities [4].

Residential buildings significantly contribute to the total energy used in the world. According to statistics from the USA Energy Information Administration, the average household in the USA and Canada uses about 12,000 kWh of electricity. In Europe the figure is less than 10,000 KWh, but also significant. Some household appliances make the biggest contributions to consumption, including heaters and air conditioning (40–45%), electronic and kitchen appliances (~30%), water heaters (15%–20%), and cooling (5%–10%) [16]. Energy utilization patterns are not too different in developing countries, where the impact of energy consumption is also very important.

The related literature indicates that systems based on planning the use of *deferrable appliances* allow improving energy efficiency at domestic level [12,14]. Deferrable appliances are those whose demand for energy can be postponed or interrupted (such as dishwashers, washing machines, etc.), causing a negligible impact on the QoS provided to users. This is an important approach that takes into account the different prices of electricity and the availability of (non-storable) energy from renewable sources.

In this line of work, this work presents the application of evolutionary algorithms (EAs) to solve the problem of planning the use of household appliances considering user preferences. A multiobjective approach is considered, aiming at simultaneously maximizing user satisfaction (evaluated in terms of the QoS offered according to the specified preferences) and minimizing the total energy consumed, which is directly related to the total cost of the electricity bill for the user. The main results indicate that the proposed approach is able to find appropriate plannings that improve over situations where no intelligent energy planning are used (i.e., '*Bussiness as Usual*' model) and also with a greedy algorithm previously proposed in the framework of the reference project.

The main contributions of this research are: *(i)* formulating a novel multiobjective household energy planning problem accounting for user satisfaction and energy consumption; *(ii)* devising a specific EA to address the problem, using a linear aggregation approach for the objectives; and *(iii)* evaluating the proposed evolutionary approach over realistic scenarios, built by using real data of household energy consumption from well-known repositories.

The research reported in this article is developed in the context of the Cloud Computing for Smart Energy Management (CC-SEM) project [6,7], which proposes building an integrated platform for smart monitoring, controlling, and planning energy consumption and generation in urban scenarios. The project integrates cutting-edge technologies (Big Data analysis, computational intelligence, Internet of Things, High Performance Computing and Cloud Computing) and specific hardware for energy monitoring/controlling built within the project.

The article is organized as follows. Section 2 presents the formulation of the multiobjective household energy consumption planning and a review of related works. The proposed evolutionary approach for household energy planning is described in Sect. 3. The experimental analysis is reported in Sect. 4. Finally, Sect. 5 presents the conclusions and the main lines of future work.

2   The Household Energy Planning Problem

This section introduces the household energy planning problem, the multiobjective formulation addressed in this article, and a review of related works.

2.1   General Considerations

The goal of the study is to develop a system to help end-users to take appropriate decisions concerning the use of household appliances in a given planning period (e.g., daily, weekly, etc.). The problem consists in scheduling the use of different household appliances to minimize the electric bill, taking into account the end-user preferences, electricity prices, and the available contracted power.

The planning period is divided in slots considering the user preferences. For every slot, each user can indicate a value that represents the priority of using a certain appliance in that time. Higher values of priority represent a higher desire of using the appliance. In case that users do not indicate their preferences, machine learning is applied to infer preferences from the analysis of historical utilization data. Classification methods can also be applied to characterize the household power consumption, regarding neighboring houses and socio-economical data, such as for other public services [10].

The problem formulation assumes that the energy cost is known for each time interval. These values are publicly available from the energy companies, for example from the National Electricity Company (UTE) in Uruguay. Also, the maximum contracted power for each user is known, from the contract details provided by the energy company. The contracted maximum power can only be surpassed by a small amount (up to 30%) in a short period of time, without causing a short circuit. Schedules that includes such a surplus are penalized.

2.2   Problem Formulation

The multiobjective version of the household energy planning problem addressed in this article considers the following elements:

- a set of users $U = (u_1 \ldots u_N)$, each user represents a house in a city;
- a set of time slots $T = (t_1 \ldots t_M)$ in the planning period;
- a set of domestic appliances $L = (l_1 \ldots l_K)$ for each user;
- a function $E : U \to \mathbb{N}$, where $E(u_i)$ indicates the maximum electric power contracted by user u_i;
- a penalty term ρ applied to those users that surpass the maximum electric power contracted;

- a function $D : L \times U \rightarrow \mathbb{N}$, where $D(l_k, u_i)$ indicates the average time of utilization of appliance l_k for user u_i;
- a function $C : T \rightarrow \mathbb{N}$, where $C(t_j)$ indicates the utilization cost (per kW) of the energy in time t_j;
- a function $P : L \rightarrow \mathbb{N}$, where $P(l_k)$ indicates the power (in kWh) consumed by appliance l_k;
- and a function $UP : U \times L \times T \rightarrow \mathbb{N}$, where $UP(u_i, l_k, t_j)$ indicates the preference of user u_i to use the appliance l_k at time t_j;

Lets consider the binary variable x_{kj}^i, that indicates if appliance l_k of user u_i is turn on at time t_j; and function $y(x_{kj}^i)$ that indicate the time period in which appliance l_k of user u_i is turned on continuously (without intermediate turn off) from time t_j: $y(x_{kj}^i) = m - j$ with $m = \max r / \forall h \in (j, r) \ x_{kh}^i = 1$.

The problem proposes finding a planning function $X = \{x_{kj}^i\}$ for the use of each household appliance that simultaneously maximizes the user satisfaction defined in Eq. 1 (given the users' preference functions) and minimize the total energy consumed (see Eq. 2).

$$f(X) = \sum_{i=1}^{N} \sum_{j=M}^{T} \sum_{k=1}^{K} UP(u_i, l_k, t_j) \times \delta_{kj}^i \tag{1}$$

$$\text{with} \quad \delta_{kj}^i = \begin{cases} 1 & \text{if } y(x_{kj}^i) \geq D(l_k, u_i) \\ 0 & \text{otherwise} \end{cases}$$

$$g(X) = \sum_{i=1}^{N} \sum_{j=M}^{T} \sum_{k=1}^{K} x_{kj}^i \times C(t_j) \times P(l_k) + \rho \times \psi_{kj}^i \tag{2}$$

$$\text{with} \quad \psi_{kj}^i = \begin{cases} P(l_k) - E(u_i) & \text{if } P(l_k) - E(u_i) \geq 0 \\ 0 & \text{otherwise} \end{cases}$$

Two scenarios are defined for defining the penalty model used for those situations in which the household consumption exceeds the maximum power contracted. The first scenario (*soft penalty*) is when the user exceeds the maximum power contracted for less than 30% of it. This is the maximum value of energy consumption that can exist without a short circuit occurring. In that case, the solution is penalized by a 30% of ρ. The second scenario (*hard penalty*) is when the user exceeds the maximum power contracted in a value greater than or equal to 30%. Therefore, that plannings are penalized entirely by the penalty term ρ.

Function UP considers the energy consumption measurements of electrical devices reported by Kolter and Johnson [5]. For each minute of the day, in the period of a month, the user preference is defined considering how many times each appliance was turned on for each appliance at that minute.

Function D uses consumption values of user appliances from a representative day. The duration of using for the appliance was studied, defined as the number of consecutive minutes in which it remained powered on [2].

2.3   Related Works

The analysis of the related literature allows identifying several hardware- and software-based methods for household energy consumption characterization and planning. The main related works are reviewed next.

The main line of work related to the proposed research has been developed by Soares et al., who studied the household electricity demands and categorized a set of appliances, according to their use and management strategies that can be applied to them [13]. An initial work [14] introduced a model based on integer non-linear programming for energy utilization planning, with the aim of reducing cost. The authors applied an EA to minimize the cost of invoice and violations to the maximum contracted power. The EA allowed to reduce up to 40% the energy cost for the users with respect to a reference scenario without demand management. Later, the authors proposed minimizing cost and maximizing user satisfaction [12], which is the main motivation for the work proposed in our research. Results showed that the cost reduction was 22–24%. However, no trade-off solutions were computed, so different users with equal contracted power and equal preferences should adapt to the same planning. Additionally, no studies were carried out in different urban levels (buildings, neighborhoods, etc.) or used real data.

Our previous work [11] presented a hardware and software platform for intelligent monitoring and planning of energy consumption in homes. The proposed system integrates a hardware controller for energy efficiency, a communication protocol to improve data transmission, and a software module for planning and managing household devices. The proposed solution was implemented applying the Internet of Things (IoT) paradigm, allowing the integration of computational intelligence techniques. A greedy algorithm was proposed for planning, considering user preferences and a maximum allowed power consumption. Results showed that it is possible to reduce the energy consumption of a water heater to 38.9% and that two water heaters and an air conditioner can be optimized simultaneously without reducing QoS. These results suggest that the proposed approach is useful for energy consumption planning in homes.

Bilil et al. proposed a characterization of household appliances and a dynamic planning method for collaborative microgrids [1]. Two multiobjective optimization problems were studied, accounting for the activation and power profiles of appliances. A simulation procedure was applied to generate the instances of these problems and NSGA-II was used to solve them. The instances consisting in 40 microgrids that inclulde a flexible deferrable appliance, such as a water heater, and a non-flexible one (i.e., dishwasher). For the experiments, a residential load curve based on U.S. user profiles was used. The results showed that the load curve can indeed become very flat by applying the proposed bi-level multiobjective optimization scheduling approach.

The analysis of the related works indicates that there is room to contribute with solutions focused on the development of systems to implement the management of domestic demand through the integration of IoT technologies and computational intelligence algorithms.

3   The Proposed EA for Household Energy Planning

This section describes the proposed EA to solve the household energy planning problem.

3.1   Evolutionary Algorithms

EAs are stochastic techniques that emulate natural evolution to solve optimization, search, and learning problems. They are useful for solving complex real-world problems in multiple application areas [9].

An EA is an iterative technique (each iteration is called *generation*). In each generation, probabilistic operators are applied on a set of individuals (the *population*). The initial population is generated by applying a random procedure or using a specific heuristic for the problem to be solved. Each individual encodes a tentative solution to the problem and has a *fitness* value that determines its suitability to solve the problem. The goal of the EA is to improve the fitness of individuals in the population. In order to achieve this objective, *evolutionary operators* are applied iteratively, such as the *recombination* of parts of two individuals and the random *mutation* of an individual's coding. These operators are applied to individuals selected according to their fitness, thus guiding the EA toward tentative solutions of higher quality that replace old individuals. The stop criterion usually involves a fixed number of generations, a quality level on the fitness of the best individual, or detecting convergence. The EA returns the best solution found in the iterative process, taking into account the fitness function considered for the problem. Algorithm 1 presents the generic schema of an EA with a population P.

Algorithm 1 Schema of an evolutionary algorithm.

1: **initialize**($P(0)$)
2: $t \leftarrow 0$ ▷ generation counter
3: **while** not stop criterion **do**
4:      **evaluate**($P(t)$)   ▷ evolutionary cycle
5:      parents←**selection**($P(t)$)
6:      children←**variation operators**(parents)
7:      newpop←**replacement**(children,$P(t)$)
8:      t++
9:      $P(t)$←newpop
10: **end while**
11: **return** best individual found   ▷ best fitness value

In this article, a traditional EA using a linear aggregation approach is used to solve household energy planning problem. Although the aggregation approach is often outperformed by Pareto-based methods for multiobjective optimization, it is a common approach in the literature, because of two main advantages: (i) it is suitable for multiobjective optimization problems with a convex Pareto front, and (ii) it is computationally efficient, so it is recommended when the times available to perform the planning is short [3].

3.2   The Proposed EA for Household Appliances Planning

The main features of the proposed EA for household appliances planning are described next.

Solution Encoding. A problem-specific encoding is used to represent solutions. The proposed encoding considers for each user a vector $X = (x_0, x_1, \ldots, x_T)$, where T is the total number of timesteps (i.e., minutes) in the planning period. Each element x_j in the encoding is a vector of binary values $x_j = (b_1, b_2, \ldots, b_L)$, where L is the number of appliances considered in the planning and each value b_i indicates if the appliance is on on timestep j.

Figure 1 presents an example of solution encoding for an instance of the problem considering five appliances. In the example, at timestep (minute) i, appliances #1, #2, and #5 are ON, while appliances #3 and #4 are OFF.

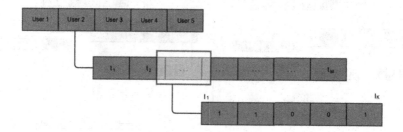

Fig. 1. An example of the proposed solution encoding.

Fitness Assignment. The fitness function of the proposed EA corresponds to an linear aggregation of the power consumption and user satisfaction functions: $F = \alpha \times f(X) - \beta \times g(X)$. Several combinations of weights (α, β) were studied in order to properly weight each objective function and provide a useful search pattern. The main results of the analysis are reported in Sect. 4.3. The combination that allowed computing the best results was $(\alpha = 0.65, \beta = 1)$.

Initialization. The population of tentative solutions is initialized by applying a randomized method that assigns to each appliance a probability $\gamma = 0.6$ (value tuned in preliminary experiments) to be ON at each time step, following a discrete non-uniform distribution. Assigning a slightly larger probability to each appliance to be ON than to be OFF allows starting the evolutionary search for a more diverse set of solutions. The value of γ was set to provide an equal pressure to both objectives, considering the weights defined in the previous paragraph.

Selection. The standard tournament selection was applied in the proposed EA. Preliminary experiments demonstrated that tournament selection provides an appropriate selection presure to guide the search. After a preliminary configuration analysis, the size of the tournament was set to two individuals, and the best of them is selected.

Evolutionary Operators. Ad-hoc evolutionary operators were conceived to provide efficacy and diversity to the search, working with the proposed solution encoding. The proposed evolutionary operators are:

- *Recombination.* An ad-hoc version of the Single Point Crossover operator was conceived to recombine solutions. A cutting point is selected for each user and a new planning is created for each user, using information from the first parent (before the cutting point) and from the second parent (after the cutting point). Figure 2 presents an example of the application of the proposed recombination operator between two solution for a problem instance with three users and six appliances for each user.

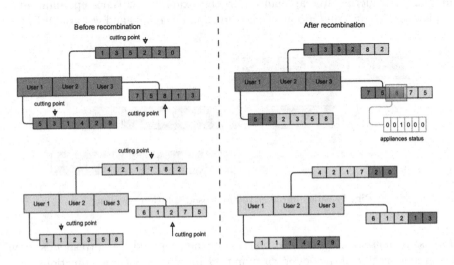

Fig. 2. An example of the proposed recombination operator.

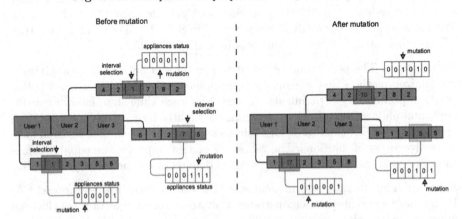

Fig. 3. An example of the proposed mutation operator.

Mutation. The mutation operator modifies the current state of an appliance. First, a specific time interval is randomly selected for every user, according to a uniform distribution. An appliance is then randomly selected (applying a uniform distribution) from all belonging to that user, and its state is changed (on/off or viceversa). Figure 3 presents an example of the mutation operator.

3.3 Development and Execution Platform

The evolutionary approach was implemented using the ECJ library, a Java-based evolutionary computation system developed at George Mason University (cs.gmu.edu/~eclab/projects/ecj). ECJ includes easily modifiable classes for solving optimization problems. The experimental evaluation was performed on a Dell Power Edge server, Quad-core Xeon E5430 processor at 2.66 GHz, 8 GB RAM, from Cluster FING, Universidad de la República, Uruguay [8].

4 Experimental Analysis

This section presents the experimental analysis of the proposed EA for household energy consumption planning.

4.1 Problem Instances

A set of problem instances was build using real data.

Raw energy consumption data for appliances were obtained from the REDD dataset [5], sampled every three seconds for a period of one month. Appliances included in the problem instances were selected considering: (i) the categorization of household appliances according to their operating profiles and purposes [14]; (ii) the average and maximum time of use of each appliance; and (iii) several other parameters, including the number of activations and energy consumption measurements, the number of houses where each appliance is present, the frequency of activation, etc. Six appliances were selected: dishwasher, microwave, dryer, air conditioning, oven, and refrigerator. The planning period is one day.

Energy consumption data in the REDD dataset was averaged over intervals of 15 min, and the resulting values were analyzed to define the preferences of using each appliance for each user. The overall energy consumption data were studied for each day. One representative weekday and one representative weekend day was determined for each appliance, in order to define the daily power consumption in each case. Real energy prices from the National Electricity Company (UTE) in Uruguay (https://portal.ute.com.uy), considering an average residential plan (contracted power of 3.7 kWh) were used.

Six problem instances were generated (Table 1) accounting for different number of users, appliances, and consumption patterns (weekday/weekend).

Table 1. Proposed problem instances

#	name	users	appliances in the instance	consumption pattern
1	small.1 (s1)	2	(2,3)	weekday
2	small.2 (s2)	2	(2,3)	weekend
3	medium.1 (m1)	4	(4,4,3,2)	weekday
4	medium.2 (m2)	4	(4,4,3,2)	weekend
5	large.1 (l1)	6	(5,5,4,4,3,2)	weekday
6	large.2 (l2)	6	(5,5,4,4,3,2)	weekend

4.2   Baseline Algorithms for Results Comparison

Two baseline strategies were implemented for evaluating the results of the proposed EA for household appliances planning: a greedy algorithm and a Business-as-Usual (BaU) planning strategy, which are described next.

Greedy planning strategy. Greedy algorithms iteratively build solutions based on a taking optimal local decisions in each step. A greedy algorithm from the literature [11] was adapted for baseline comparison. The proposed strategy searches the best time intervals to switch on each appliance d_k, according to the user satisfaction and cost, considering the linear aggregation fitness function using $\alpha = 0.65$, $\beta = 1$ (Algorithm 2).

BaU planning strategy. The BaU strategy proposes assigning ON times to each appliance without planning. These plannings have good user preference values, but suboptimal cost values.

4.3   Linear Aggregation Fitness Function

The analysis considered the candidate values $\alpha \in \{0.3, 0.65, 0.75, 1.0\}$ and $\beta \in \{0.3, 0.5, 1.0\}$. The EA was executed over three medium-size instances of the problem (two, four, and six devices). Table 2 reports the mean and interquartile range (IQR) of the best fitness value computed in 30 independent executions of the proposed EA for the three instances solved, using the studied configurations.

Figure 4 presents a trade-off analysis of solutions computed using different values of (α, β) for instance #3 (results are representative of those obtained for other instances). The combination (0.65,1.0) allows computing the best trade-off solutions regarding user satisfaction and total energy/price.

Algorithm 2 Greedy algorithm for household appliances planning

---

procedure INTERVALMAXPREFCOST(initMin,u_i,d,X)
   prefCost ← 0; duration ← 0
   for (m=initMin; m< t_M; m++) **do**
     if duration < $D(d, u_i)$ **then**
       if $\sum_{k=1}^{K} x_{km}^{i} \times P(d_k) + P(d) < E(u_i)$ **then**
         prefCost ← prefCost + $\alpha \times UP(u, d, m) - \beta \times C(m)$
         duration ← duration + $(t_{m+1} - t_m)$
       else
         prefCost ← 0
         duration ← 0
       end if
     else
       return [m, prefCost]   ▷ interval found
     end if
   end for
   return [m, prefCost]   ▷ no interval found
end procedure

$X \leftarrow \vec{0}$
for ($i = 1$; $i \leq N$; i++) **do**   ▷ for each user
   for (k=1;i≤K;k++) **do**   ▷ for each appliance
     prefCost ← 0; bestPrefCost ← -1; bestmin ← 0   ▷ search best interval
     for (m=t_1; m< $t_M - D(d_k, u_i)$; m++) **do**
       [min, prefCost] = IntervalMaxPrefCost(m, d_k, u_i, X)
       if prefCost > bestPrefCost **then**
         bestPrefCost ← prefCost
         bestmin ← min
       end if
     end for
     for (m=bestmin $-D(d_k, u_i)$; m ≤ bestmin; m++) **do**
       $x_{km}^{i} \leftarrow 1$ ▷ set appliance ON
     end for
   end for
end for

4.4 Parametric Configuration Analysis

EA parameters must be adjusted to determine the configuration that allows computing the best results. The analysis was performed over three problem instances, different from those used in the evaluation to avoid bias. After an initial evaluation, the population size was fixed at 150 individuals.

Three relevant parameters of the proposed EA were studied: number of generations used as stopping criterion (G), recombination probability p_C and mutation probability p_M. Candidate values for each parameter were: $p_C \in \{0.1, 0.25, 0.5\}$; $p_M \in \{0.1, 0.05, 0.01\}$; and $G \in \{2500, 5000, 10000\}$. All combinations of parameter values were studied by performing 50 independent executions of the proposed EA for the three problem instances considered in the analysis. The metric considered in the analysis was the linear aggregation fitness function defined in the previous subsection.

Table 2. Best fitness values computed using different values of (α, β)

α	β	instance #1		instance #2		instance #3	
		median	IQR	median	IQR	median	IQR
0.3	0.3	15.81	1.09	179.83	0.55	132.35	6.68
0.3	0.5	11.02	1.54	167.94	2.03	110.10	4.54
0.3	1.0	4.27	6.39	128.55	28.66	54.82	13.56
0.5	0.3	34.06	0.81	311.32	28.66	253.95	5.11
0.5	0.5	26.75	1.06	298.80	23.71	224.47	12.21
0.5	1.0	13.53	10.28	269.83	26.03	175.11	40.39
0.65	0.3	47.28	2.08	409.91	1.76	342.66	6.57
0.65	0.5	39.87	0.83	398.45	1.34	316.32	8.40
0.65	1.0	25.48	6.12	369.21	3.91	257.55	39.03
0.75	0.3	54.85	2.79	475.64	0.39	405.86	10.03
0.75	0.5	48.52	3.20	462.74	35.73	373.95	4.11
0.75	1.0	30.18	3.43	433.82	3.23	304.31	21.64
1.0	0.3	81.21	4.41	640.62	0.59	548.20	5.64
1.0	0.5	71.46	4.55	628.42	2.76	524.55	9.10
1.0	1.0	52.05	2.89	597.33	0.24	454.48	20.50

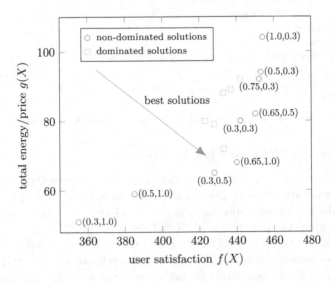

Fig. 4. Trade-off analysis of solutions computed using different values of (α, β)

The methodology for selecting the best configuration included: (i) the Shapiro-Wilk statistical test was applied to check normality, taken as a null hypothesis that the results followed a normal distribution; as p-values less than 0.05 were obtained, the null hypothesis was discarded and it was assumed that the fitness results follow a non-normal distribution; (ii) the Friedman's rank test was applied, taken as a null hypothesis that the fitness distributions for the different configurations were not different, as p-values less than 0.05 were obtained, the null hypothesis was discarded and the results significantly differ from each other.

Table 3 reports the fitness values computed in the parameter setting experiments for a representative problem instance. Overall, the best results (i.e., largest fitness median and also lower IQR) were obtained using configuration #11 (values $G = 10000$, $p_C = 0.1$, and $p_M = 0.1$). Henceforth, these values were used in the validation experiments of the proposed EA.

Table 3. Parameter setting results for the proposed EA

configuration	fitness		configuration	fitness	
(G, p_C, p_M)	median	IQR	(G, p_C, p_M)	median	IQR
(2500, 0.1, 0.01)	7.88	10.45	(10000, 0.5, 0.1)	40.27	7.61
(5000, 0.1, 0.01)	38.74	11.71	(2500, 0.25, 0.1)	40.73	7.01
(10000, 0.1, 0.01)	40.04	6.98	(5000, 0.25, 0.1)	41.64	6.76
(2500, 0.5, 0.01)	9.26	11.17	(10000, 0.25, 0.1)	40.72	8.67
(5000, 0.5, 0.01)	39.22	9.37	(2500, 0.1, 0.05)	39.60	6.97
(10000, 0.5, 0.01)	39.28	9.88	(5000, 0.1, 0.05)	40.22	9.23
(2500, 0.25,0.01)	9.06	9.22	(10000, 0.1, 0.05)	40.58	7.95
(5000, 0.25,0.01)	39.39	10.18	(2500, 0.5, 0.05)	38.66	7.39
(10000, 0.25,0.01)	38.69	11.76	(5000, 0.5, 0.05)	39.59	10.07
(2500, 0.1, 0.1)	41.77	8.88	(10000, 0.5, 0.05)	40.79	11.62
(5000, 0.1, 0.1)	41.30	8.46	(2500, 0.25, 0.05)	38.17	10.32
(10000, 0.1, 0.1)	**42.57**	**6.46**	(5000, 0.25, 0.05)	41.67	8.38
(2500, 0.5, 0.1)	40.62	7.22	(10000, 0.25, 0.05)	41.00	8.44
(5000, 0.5, 0.1)	41.28	8.65			

4.5 Experimental Results

Table 4 reports the median of the best fitness computed by the EA and the comparison with the reference algorithms (greedy and BaU). The relative improvement on fitness values (Δ_f) and on each objective function (Δ_{cost}, Δ_{pref}) over each reference algorithm refA is computed as $\Delta = (f(\text{EA}) - f(\text{refA}))/f(\text{refA})$.

Results in Table 4 indicate that the proposed EA is able to improve significantly over the greedy algorithm regarding the fitness values.

Table 4. Experimental results: fitness values and improvements of the proposed EA over the baseline greedy algorithm and the BaU strategy.

Instance	f(EA)	Greedy				BaU			
		f	Δ_f	Δ_{cost}	Δ_{pref}	f	Δ_f	Δ_{cost}	Δ_{pref}
Weekday									
Small.1	14.1	11.0	28.3%	22.6%	56.2%	−7.6	284.6%	81.1%	16.0%
Medium.1	340.0	239.4	42.0%	27.2%	65.3%	69.5	388.9%	77.9%	19.4%
Large.1	407.8	347.9	17.2%	20.8%	47.3%	−187.1	317.0%	70.6%	22.0%
Weekend									
Small.2	323.7	252.1	28.4%	25.1%	44.9%	67.4	383.1%	76.6%	25.8%
Medium.2	253.4	197.2	28.5%	29.0%	48.1%	153.8	64.7%	60.6%	20.8%
Large.2	369.8	351.9	5.1%	19.7%	37.4%	−299.9	224.2%	72.2%	31.6%

Considering the baseline results computed by the proposed greedy algorithm, improvements of up to 42.0% were obtained in instance medium.1. Results also suggest that consumption patterns during the weekend are harder to plan for the EA, as the improvements over the greedy algorithm reduced to 5.1% in instance large.2. This can be explained due to the interactive utilization of household appliances in weekends, when people are at home a significantly larger periods than in weekdays. Regarding the improvements on user satisfaction and cost, the plannings computed by the proposed EA allow reducing more than 20% the electric bill, and preferences improve more than 40% in all the studied scenarios.

The EA computed significantly cheaper plannings than those of BaU, which systematically failed to provide good cost values, indicating that users do not take the correct decisions to turn on home appliances in this regard, and they can benefit of having an automated planning offered by a recommendation system. In addition, preferences on the solutions computed by the EA were 16–31% better than BaU. The obtained improvements over a BaU strategy are consistent with results reported in previous works for a reduced subset of home appliances (air conditioner and water heater) [11].

The obtained results suggest that the proposed evolutionary approach is accurate for computing household energy consumption plannings accounting for both energy costs and user satisfaction at the same time. The proposed approach is a first step towards designing an intelligent recommendation system for end-users.

5   Conclusions and Future Work

This article presented an evolutionary approach to address the problem of household energy planning, as a first approach to develop an automated recommendation system for end-users. This is a relevant problem for both energy companies and citizens under the novel smart city paradigm.

A mathematical formulation for the problem was proposed, considering the optimization of user preferences and energy consumed/cost. A specific EA was proposed to solve the problem, simultaneously optimizing both criteria using a linear aggregation multiobjective function and ad-hoc evolutionary operators.

A set of six realistic problem instances built using real data were considered in the experimental evaluation of the proposed EA. The analysis compared the EA results with two baseline planning methods (greedy and business-as-usual).

The experimental results showed that the proposed EA is able to compute accurate plannings, accounting for significant improvements on the problem objectives. Regarding the baseline greedy algorithm, improvements of up to 42.0% were obtained in the proposed multiobjective function, accounting for an average reduction of more than 20% in the energy consumption (and thus, on the electric bill) and preferences improved more than 40% in all the studied scenarios. Regarding the BaU strategy, the EA computed significantly cheaper plannings and user preferences improved up to 31%, in line with previous results from our research group.

The obtained results suggest that the proposed evolutionary approach is accurate for computing household energy consumption plannings accounting for both energy costs and user satisfaction at the same time. Overall, the proposed algorithm showed to be effective for addressing the considered optimization problem. The analysis demonstrated that users can significantly benefit of having an automated planning offered by a recommendation system.

The main lines for future work are related to study explicit multiobjective algorithms to solve the problem, in order to compute several trade-off solutions at the same time. The problem formulation can be extended to include the noisy nature of user preferences in order to define an uncertainty optimization problem. In this regard, robust evolutionary approaches should be studied to solve this problem variant. Finally, new real problem instances can be generated, especially using data from the National Electricity Administration (UTE), in Uruguay.

References

1. Bilil, H., Aniba, G., Gharavi, H.: Dynamic appliances scheduling in collaborative microgrids system. IEEE Transactions on Power Systems **32**(3), 2276–2287 (2016)
2. Chavat, J., Graneri, J., Nesmachnow, S.: Energy disaggregation of household appliances based on pattern consumption similarities. In: Iberoamerican Congress on Smart Cities (2019)
3. Coello, C., Van Veldhuizen, D., Lamont, G.: Evolutionary algorithms for solving multi-objective problems. Kluwer Academic, New York (2002)
4. Deakin, M., Al Waer, H.: From intelligent to smart cities. Intelligent Buildings International **3**(3), 140–152 (2011)
5. Kolter, J., Johnson, M.: Redd: A public data set for energy disaggregation research. Workshop on Data Mining Applications in Sustainability. **25**, 59–62 (2011)
6. Nesmachnow, Sergio, Hernández Callejo, Luis (eds.): ICSC-CITIES 2018. CCIS, vol. 978. Springer, Cham. https://doi.org/10.1007/978-3-030-12804-3

7. Luján, E., Otero, A., Valenzuela, S., Mocskos, E., Steffenel, L., Nesmachnow, S.: An integrated platform for smart energy management: the CC-SEM project. Revista Facultad de Ingeniería (2019)
8. Nesmachnow, S.: Computación científica de alto desempeño en la Facultad de Ingeniería, Universidad de la República. Revista de la Asociación de Ingenieros del Uruguay 61(1), 12–15 (2010)
9. Nesmachnow, S.: An overview of metaheuristics: accurate and efficient methods for optimisation. International Journal of Metaheuristics 3(4), 320–347 (2014)
10. Nesmachnow, S., Baña, S., Massobrio, R.: A distributed platform for big data analysis in smart cities: combining intelligent transportation systems and socioeconomic data for montevideo, uruguay. EAI Endorsed Transactions on Smart Cities 2(5), 153478 (2017)
11. Orsi, E., Nesmachnow, S.: Smart home energy planning using IoT and the cloud. In: IEEE URUCON (2017)
12. Soares, A., Antunes, C., Oliveira, C., Gomes, A.: A multi-objective genetic approach to domestic load scheduling in an energy management system. Energy 77(1), 144–152 (2014)
13. Soares, A., Gomes, A., Antunes, C.: Categorization of residential electricity consumption as a basis for the assessment of the impacts of demand response actions. Renewable and Sustainable Energy Reviews 30, 490–503 (2014)
14. Soares, A., Gomes, A., Antunes, C., Cardoso, H.: Domestic load scheduling using genetic algorithms. In: European Conference on the Applications of Evolutionary Computation. pp. 142–151 (2013)
15. Turner, W., Doty, S.: Energy management handbook. The Fairmont Press (2007)
16. U.S. Energy Information Administration (EIA): Energy use in homes, https://www.eia.gov/, June 2018

Control of a Bidirectional Single-Phase Grid Interface for Electric Vehicles

Matheus Montanini Breve[1,2] and Vicente Leite[2(✉)]

[1] Universidade Tecnológica Federal do Paraná, Cornélio Procópio, Brazil
matheus.m.breve@gmail.com
[2] Research Centre in Digitalization and Intelligent Robotics (CeDRI),
Instituto Politécnico de Bragança, Bragança, Portugal
avtl@ipb.pt

Abstract. The number of electric vehicles is expected to increase exponentially in the next decade. This represents a huge potential for grid support, such as energy storage in their batteries, with advantages for grid operators and for customers. For this purpose, flexible power interfaces are required. This paper presents a simulation of a bidirectional single-phase power interface between an electric vehicle battery and the grid. The proposed system is fully simulated and counts with features such as vehicle-to-grid, vehicle-to-home and grid-to-vehicle. All power flow and the controllers for these modes of operation are described in detail. The simulation was developed in a Software-in-the-Loop scheme to facilitate a future physical implementation with a Hardware-in-the-Loop platform. The proposed system was extensively tested via simulation, the results proving the system is stable, able to change operation modes smoothly and definition of the exchanged active and reactive powers.

Keywords: Bidirectional interface · Electric vehicle · V2G · V2H

1 Introduction

According to estimations from the International Energy Agency (IEA) around 120 million electric vehicles (EV) will be on the road globally by 2030 [1]. Thus, EVs might serve as a distributed energy storage system that can be integrated with the electric grid [2–4].

This integration was first devised in 1997 [2] and has since been frequently referred as vehicle-to-grid (V2G) technology [3], with its various aspects being analyzed in depth by many authors [5–8]. If V2G technology is adopted by the majority of EV owners, it has the potential to be not only useful to grid operators, but to customers as well. Enabling information and power exchange between grid operators and electric vehicles owners would allow customers to optimize charging based on electricity prices, for example. Grid operators, on the other hand, could benefit from an additional grid stabilization source, which could prove useful in a scenario where the usage of photovoltaic energy and wind energy is also growing.

S. Nesmachnow and L. Hernández Callejo (Eds.): ICSC-CITIES 2019, CCIS 1152, pp. 285–299, 2020.
https://doi.org/10.1007/978-3-030-38889-8_22

The possibility of a bidirectional power flow could also be used to power homes during short electricity shortages and electric grid instabilities, technology called Vehicle-to-Home (V2H). Vehicle-to-Home is one of the features built in the latest model of the aforementioned Nissan Leaf [9]. V2H could help reduce consumption of grid power in periods of the day when demand is highest and thus costlier, or simply as a backup power supply in case of emergencies. This technology, explored for example in [10,11], could become important taking into account the expanding connectivity between home appliances in a Smart Home scenario and the growing number of households with renewable energy sources, like photovoltaics (PV).

In this context, this paper presents the simulation of a bidirectional single-phase power interface between an electric vehicle and the grid with MATLAB® and Simulink. The presented system counts with features such as grid-to-vehicle (G2V) for battery charging, vehicle-to-grid (V2G) for grid support and vehicle-to-home (V2H), as well as allowing seamless transitions between these operation modes. The simulation is assembled in a Software-in-the-Loop (SiL) scheme with the power and control structures simulated in the discrete domain and with different simulation rates. This allows for future testing in a Hardware-in-the-Loop (HiL) platform, for which only small parameter adjustments are needed.

The paper is divided in five sections, the first being a brief introduction about concepts such as V2G and V2H and their relevance. The second section contains details on the implemented system structure, such as the control algorithms employed and power topology used. The third section explains the computational model created in Simulink and the simulation results are listed in the fourth section. The fifth and last section contains the conclusions.

2   System Structure

The power structure chosen to accomplish the integration of an electrical vehicle with the electric grid is arranged in a dual-stage configuration and composed of five parts. This structure is the most commonly employed [12] and counts with two dedicated power processors, similar to the structure employed in [10,13,14]. The parts are:

- Vehicle, represented as a battery;
- Bidirectional DC/DC converter (BDC);
- Bidirectional single-phase voltage-source inverter (BADC or VSI);
- Output filter to reduce current harmonic distortion;
- Grid and common-coupling point (CPP).

A simplified block diagram of the proposed system structure can be seen in Fig. 1. The connection lines between the blocks represent the bidirectional nature of the power flow in the system.

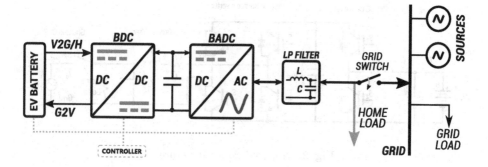

Fig. 1. Proposed system structure

2.1 Power Topology

Figure 2 shows the power topology of the bidirectional interface in greater detail. The bidirectional DC/DC converter (BDC) is a power converter that alternates between two modes of operation, step-down (buck) and step-up (boost) modes, respectively charging (G2V) and discharging the battery (V2G and V2H).

The bidirectional single-phase voltage-source inverter (BADC) is a full-bridge inverter with two IGBT inverter legs and free-wheel diodes. The output filter is a low-pass LC filter to lower the harmonic distortion in the inverter current output waveform. The grid is represented by an AC source with capability of exchanging any given amount of active and reactive power, thus acting as an infinite bus. The common-coupling point represents where home loads can be connected to and the point which, after a grid fault condition is detected, remains energized in case the V2H feature is enabled.

The power structure is controlled by two control algorithms, the BDC and BADC control algorithms. Table 1 contains a summary of the system operation modes and the control targets of the BDC and BADC control algorithms.

Table 1. Summary of system operation modes and the respective control targets of the DC/DC and DC/AC converters

Operation modes			Control target	
Mode	Grid tied	Battery	BDC	BADC
G2V	Yes	Charging	CV and CC charging	DC bus voltage
V2G	Yes	Discharging	DC bus voltage	P and Q
V2H	No	Discharging	DC bus voltage	AC voltage

2.2 BDC Control Structure

The BDC control strategy can be divided in three subsystems, as shown in Fig. 3.

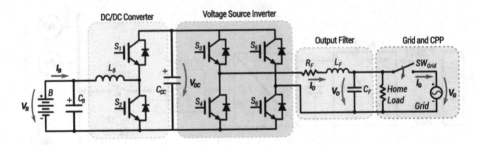

Fig. 2. Proposed power structure

The *"Charging Current Reference Generator (G2V)"* subsystem generates a battery current reference, I_B^*, to control the charging current in G2V mode. The battery charging current is determined by two charging modes, constant current (CC) and constant voltage (CV). In CC charging mode the current reference $I_{B_{CC}}^*$ can be set to equal the maximum or a given percentage of the battery nominal charge current. In CV charging mode a PI controller generates a battery current reference, $I_{B_{CV}}^*$, to maintain the battery voltage constant.

The *"Discharging Current Reference Generator (V2G/H)"* subsystem contains a PI controller that will determine the battery current needed to maintain the DC link voltage constant at a set voltage. This V_{DC} control method is used both in V2G (grid-connected) and V2H (grid-isolated) modes.

The *"Battery Current Controller"* subsystem controls the BDC PWM duty cycle to maintain the battery current at the setpoint, in turn given by the two aforementioned subsystems. It contains a PI controller comparing the battery current reference I_B^*, given by the two aforementioned subsystems, and the measured battery current value I_B, generating a BDC control signal. This signal is converted to a PWM signal generator to drive the IGBT gates in the BDC converter to achieve the desired battery current.

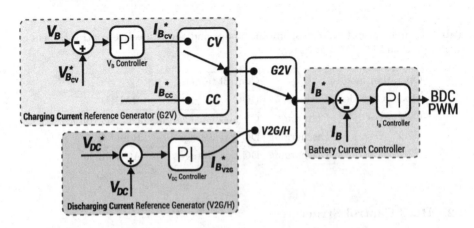

Fig. 3. Proposed BDC control structure

2.3 BADC Control Structure

The BADC control algorithm can be subdivided in two different modes: the grid-connected and grid-isolated modes.

Grid connected modes include the G2V and V2G operation modes. An overview of the grid-connected control algorithm is shown in greater detail in Fig. 4. The system operating in G2V mode is responsible for controlling the battery charging current and voltage. In V2G mode it controls the active and reactive power exchange with the grid. The control algorithm of the two grid-connected operation modes are explained as it follows:

- **V2G mode**: in V2G mode, the active and reactive power are set externally by P_{REF} and Q_{REF}. Since the active power delivered to the grid is proportional to the output current d-component, i_d, and the reactive power proportional to the output current q-component, i_q, converting these power quantities into the desired dq-components of the output current requires power calculations in dq-theory. These calculations result in dq-current references, i^*_{Od} and i^*_{Oq}, which are fed into classical PI controllers, that in turn give out V'_d and V'_q, called voltage demand values [15].
- **G2V mode**: in G2V mode the VSI is responsible for maintaining the DC link voltage constant, acting similar to the BDC in V2G mode. In this mode a PI controller compares the DC link voltage, V_{DC}, with the reference value, V^*_{DC}, and generates the needed current to be extracted from the grid and injected into the DC link I^*_{DC} to maintain the DC bus voltage constant. An unitary power factor is also maintained, since the q-component of the grid current is kept null, unless reactive power compensation while charging the battery is needed. Thus, in this mode there is a 180° phase difference between the VSI voltage and current output.

As displayed in Fig. 4 the dq-current controllers only calculate the demand values V'_d and V'_q. In order to obtain the true V_d and V_q values, a process called decoupling is necessary. Decoupling takes into account the dynamics of the inverter AC-side, including output filter. Signals such as θ_{PLL} and $||V_G||_{PLL}$ represent respectively the grid voltage phase and amplitude, needed for grid synchronization. These signals are calculated via a Phase-Locked Loop (PLL) based on the structure devised in [16].

2.4 Grid-Isolated Mode (V2H)

The transition from grid-connected to grid-isolated mode is activated following the detection of a grid fault by the grid fault detection module. This module detects large frequency or amplitude variations in the grid voltage and, if the manually-defined thresholds are surpassed, it sends a signal ordering the disconnection from the grid, opening the grid switch as shown in Fig. 1. If the grid-isolated mode is allowed, the system control algorithm changes following the fault detection and it starts operating in grid-forming mode, also called grid-isolated mode, disconnecting itself from the grid.

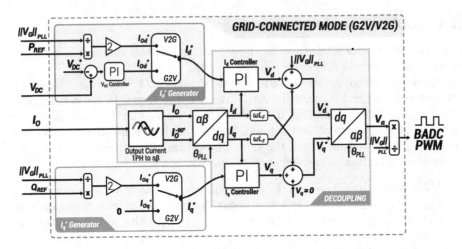

Fig. 4. Proposed BADC current control structure in grid-connected modes

In grid-isolated mode (V2H) the VSI must be controlled with a fixed sinusoidal voltage reference, since grid synchronization is not possible, being the system responsible for generating a grid. This voltage reference in V2H mode is obtained via the system represented in Fig. 5.

This system uses a fixed frequency reference, 50 Hz, to generate a signal ωt via a discrete integrator. The maximum value of ωt is limited 2π, that is, $360°$, given that the integrator is reset when ωt reaches this value. An initial phase, θ_0, given by a PI controller for re-synchronization with the grid, is added to the resulting signal and the sum $\omega t + \theta_0$ is converted into a sinusoidal reference with a 230 V RMS value. The peak voltage is divided by the DC link voltage to obtain the PWM reference signal corresponding to a 230 V RMS output.

The voltage output requires a closed-loop control as shown to ensure a steady V_{RMS}^* voltage regardless of the load, up to the specified inverter power limits. The controller output is limited to a $\pm 5\%$ variation to prevent over-voltage conditions.

2.5   Grid Re-synchronization

In the event of grid reconnection in stand-alone (V2H) mode, the VSI output might be at a different frequency or out-of-phase in relation to the grid voltage and thus a grid re-synchronization strategy is required. For that, an initial phase, θ_0, is given by a PI controller. The controller compares and reduces the difference between the grid and output phase by altering the initial phase value, which is added to the resulting signal generator. The phase difference is calculated by converting the grid and output phase signals into sinusoidal signals and then the difference between them. This results in another sinusoidal signal, whose amplitude relates to the phase difference. This way it is possible to define a threshold value and, if the calculated RMS value, that is, the difference, is lower

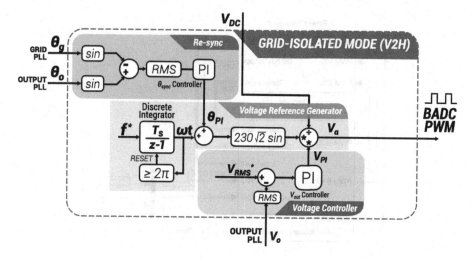

Fig. 5. Voltage reference generator in grid-isolated (V2H) mode

than the threshold the system reconnects itself with the grid, thus enabling seamless transition between grid-isolated and grid-connected operation modes.

3 Computational System Model

This section concerns the methods and materials used to create a computational model (Fig. 6) of the power structure as shown by Fig. 7 and the respective control algorithms as displayed in Fig. 8.

Figure 6 shows that the main parameters are set externally, that is, an external user or higher-hierarchy controller can determine the operation mode while grid-connected (G2V/V2G), the power to be exchanged with the grid (power references), if the grid-isolated mode (V2H) is allowed and if the system is enabled. This reflects a the context in which higher-hierarchy controllers determine the needed V2G services, that is, what each vehicle with this system will provide.

The simulation of the system was carried out with the software MATLAB® and Simulink by MathWorks, as well as the *Specialized Power Systems* library under Simscape.

The power structure was developed and simulated in the discrete domain with a simulation step time of 2 μs (500 kHz). The power structure is shown in Fig. 7.

The control algorithms are simulated with a longer simulation step time of 100 μs (10 kHz) and are displayed in Fig. 8. Thus, the simulation was developed in a Software-in-the-Loop (SiL) scheme to facilitate a future physical implementation with a Hardware-in-the-Loop (HiL) platform.

The computational model reflects the experimental platform found in the Polytechnic Institute of Bragança (IPB), that counts with a real-time control interface based on the dSPACE DS1103 Controller Board and IGBTs switches

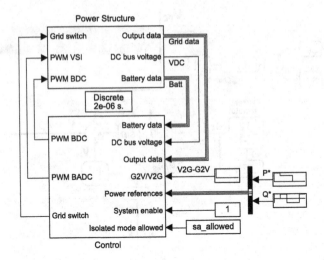

Fig. 6. SiL system representation modelled in Simulink

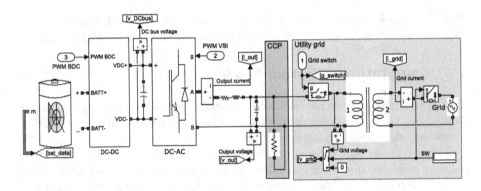

Fig. 7. Power structure modelled in Simulink

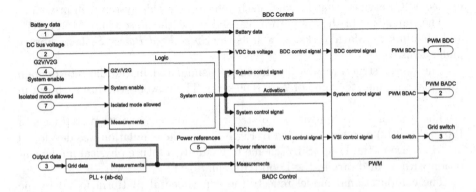

Fig. 8. Control structure modelled in Simulink

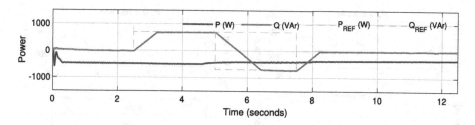

Fig. 9. Power references and measured power in G2V mode

in the PM75RLA120 power module with a maximum switching frequency of 10 kHz, the frequency used to simulate the power system representation.

4   Computational Results

The following results demonstrate the different system modes of operation, including operation while connected to an electric grid, thus including V2G and G2V operation modes with varying power references, as well as the V2H operation mode and the transitions between the main modes of operation.

4.1   Operation in Grid-to-Vehicle (G2V) Mode

During continuous G2V operation the grid current phase is opposed to that of the voltage, that is, a 180° phase difference. In this simulation the active and reactive power references were also varied during the simulation to show operation in 4 different power combinations:

- CC charging mode and null reactive power;
- CC charging mode and 700 VAr;
- CV charging mode and −700 VAr;
- CV charging with null reactive power.

Since the active power withdrawn from the grid is defined by the battery charging algorithm - approximately 490 W in constant-current mode, the active power reference is given either by the CC or CV charging schemes.

The active power in G2V mode is not set externally, but rather internally by the battery charging controller. This can clearly be seen in Fig. 9 where the power reference line does not have any influence on the power being withdrawn from the grid to charge the battery. A change between different charging modes can also be seen at the 5 s mark, showing the change from a CC to a CV charging scheme. The reactive power can be set externally and, thus, the system can simultaneously charge the battery and act as an active power factor corrector if needed.

Figure 10 shows the current and voltage outputs in 3 power combinations while operating in G2V mode.

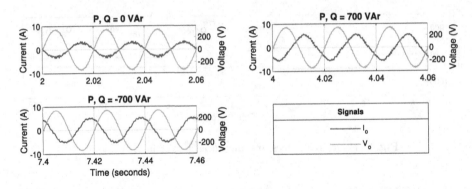

Fig. 10. VSI output current waveform in G2V mode

4.2 Operation in Vehicle-to-Grid (V2G) Mode

In this simulation the active and reactive power references were varied during the simulation. The simulation lasts 12.5 s and shows the system operating in 5 different power combinations, reflecting the existence of an external controller to determine the needed power in a micro-grid, for example. The tested power combinations are listed as it follows:

- 1000 W and null reactive power;
- 700 W and 700 VAr;
- 700 W and −700 VAr;
- 0 W and −700 VAr;
- 0 W and 700 VAr.

Figure 12 shows the results obtained in this mode of operation. It shows the power references set externally, that is, the active and reactive powers desired, and the measured power exchanged with the grid, which follow these external parameters. The results prove that the system is able to operate in two power quadrants, that is, with positive active power - delivered to the grid - and either consuming or injecting reactive power (Fig. 11).

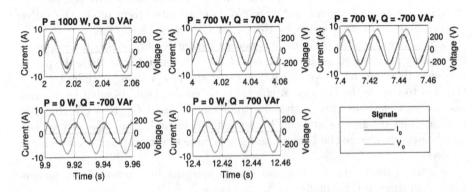

Fig. 11. VSI output current waveform in V2G mode

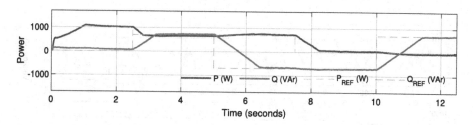

Fig. 12. Active and reactive power at VSI output and their reference values in V2G operation mode

4.3 Grid-Tied Operation Mode Transitions

The following results, visible in Figs. 13 and 14, prove the system capability of switching between V2G and G2V operation modes maintaining system stability. All the switching operations are only performed when the output current crosses zero in order to reduce transients.

Figure 13 exhibits the VSI output current waveform, output power, DC link voltage and the battery voltage and current during the transition from G2V to V2G. The transition is requested at the 2 s mark, but executed at the next current zero crossing. Figure 13 shows the transition of the current phase in relation to the grid voltage, from being in-phase before the 2 s mark and becoming in opposite phase after the 2 s mark.

Figure 14 exhibits the VSI output current waveform, output power, DC link voltage and the battery voltage and current during the transition from V2G to G2V. The transition is requested at the 2 s mark, but executed at the next current zero crossing. Figure 14 shows the transition of the current phase in relation to the grid voltage, from being in opposite phase before the 3 s mark and becoming in-phase after the 3 s mark.

4.4 Seamless Transition - From Stand-Alone to Grid-Connected

This subsection contains the results obtained by simulating the system grid-isolated feature (V2H), including the seamless transition and smooth grid re-synchronization strategy after a grid reconnection is detected. For this test the grid voltage was set to be leading 45 degrees compared to the V2H voltage reference.

Figure 15 shows more details of the re-synchronization and transition processes from V2H to V2G and Fig. 16 from V2H to G2V. Both figures display the output and grid phases, the error between them, the grid status, the current and voltage waveforms and the power output during these test conditions.

The transition from V2H to grid-tied operation modes is always executed when a voltage zero-crossing is detected to ensure a smooth transition. Complete re-synchronization takes approximately 3.2 s starting after detecting the grid presence for G2V and 1 s for V2G.

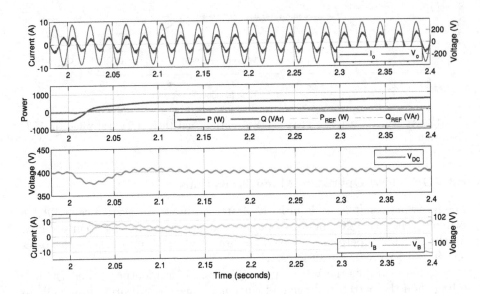

Fig. 13. VSI output current waveform, output power, DC link voltage and battery voltage and current during transition from G2V to V2G.

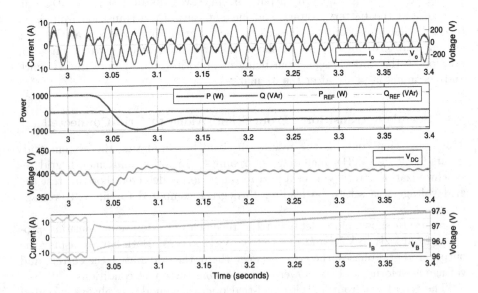

Fig. 14. VSI output current waveform, output power, DC link voltage and battery voltage and current during transition from V2G to G2V.

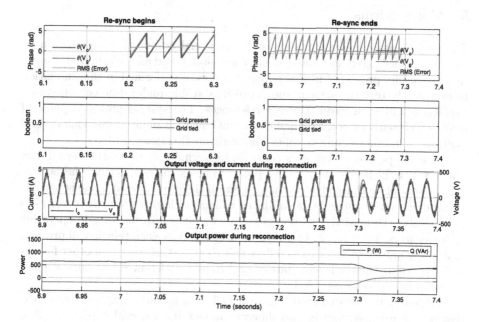

Fig. 15. Re-synchronization and transition from grid-isolated (V2H) to grid-tied V2G mode.

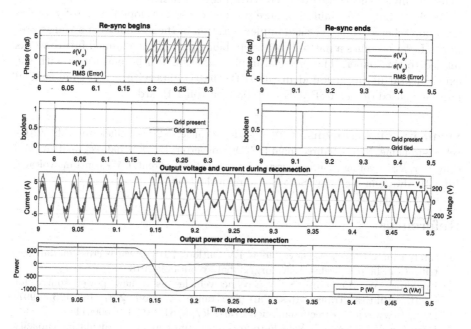

Fig. 16. Re-synchronization and transition from grid-isolated (V2H) to grid-tied G2V mode.

5   Conclusions

The implementation of a single-phase bidirectional power interface between an electric vehicle battery and the grid was successful, based on the achieved computational results presented in this paper. Tests were performed in the simulation to extensively test the system and prove it is stable under different operation conditions and with varying power references. The system proved capable of dealing well with external requests or events such as mode transitions or grid faults as well, maintaining stability and with small transients.

Since the proposed system is controlled externally, that is, an external user is able to set the active and reactive power to be exchanged, decide whether the battery should be charged or discharged and if the grid-isolated mode is permitted, the proposed system is useful in the context of higher-hierarchy controllers to determine the needed V2G services. This way it is possible for grid operators or aggregators, for example, to determine which service each vehicle will provide, controlling numerous vehicles as a fleet and coordinating, based on other factors such as current battery levels, state of health, user preferences, the duration and type of services to be provided.

A simulation-validated system in which all these features are packed together, that is, battery charging in two different modes (G2V), grid support (V2G), grid-isolated (V2H), reactive power compensation, as well as allowing manual selection of the operation mode and switching between them smoothly, is not found in any of the literature cited within this document.

Besides that, the simulation here presented was developed in a Software-in-the-Loop scheme, thus, physical implementation of the system with a Hardware-in-the-Loop becomes a natural next step, being part of the planned future works related to this paper. The physical implementation will be performed with the experimental platform found in the IPB, that counts with a real-time control interface based on the dSPACE DS1103 Controller Board.

Summary of Acronyms. G2V - grid-to-vehicle; V2G - vehicle-to-grid; V2H - vehicle-to-home; BDC - bidirectional DC/DC converter; BADC - bidirectional DC/AC converter; VSI - voltage-source inverter; CC - constant current; CV - constant voltage; HiL - Hardware-in-the-Loop; SiL - Software-in-the-Loop.

References

1. International Energy Agency: Global EV Outlook 2018: towards cross-modal electrification. https://webstore.iea.org/global-ev-outlook-2018
2. Kempton, W., Letendre, S.E.: Electric vehicles as a new power source for electric utilities. Transp. Res. Part D: Transp. Environ. **2**(3), 157–175 (1997) http://www.sciencedirect.com/science/article/pii/S1361920997000011
3. Kempton, W., Tomić, J.: Vehicle-to-grid power fundamentals: calculating capacity and net revenue. J. Power Sources **144**(1), 268–279 (2005)

4. Kempton, W., Tomić, J.: Vehicle-to-grid power implementation: From stabilizing the grid to supporting large-scale renewable energy. J. Power Sources **144**(1), 280–294 (2005)
5. Sovacool, B.K., Axsen, J., Kempton, W.: The future promise of vehicle-to-grid (V2G) integration: a sociotechnical review and research agenda. Annu. Rev. Environ. Resour. **42**(1), 377–406 (2017)
6. Tan, K.M., Ramachandaramurthy, V.K., Yong, J.Y.: Integration of electric vehicles in smart grid: a review on vehicle to grid technologies and optimization techniques. Renew. Sustain. Energy Rev. **53**, 720–732 (2016)
7. Mwasilu, F., Justo, J.J., Kim, E.K., Do, T.D., Jung, J.W.: Electric vehicles and smart grid interaction: a review on vehicle to grid and renewable energy sources integration. Renew. Sustain. Energy Rev. **34**, 501–516 (2014)
8. Ferdowsi, M.: Plug-in hybrid vehicles - a vision for the future. In: 2007 IEEE Vehicle Power and Propulsion Conference, pp. 457–462, September 2007
9. Nissan: Vehicle to Home Electricity Supply System. https://www.nissan-global. com/EN/TECHNOLOGY/OVERVIEW/vehicle_to_home.html
10. Pinto, J.G., et al.: Bidirectional battery charger with grid-to-vehicle, vehicle-to-grid and vehicle-to-home technologies. In: IECON 2013–39th Annual Conference of the IEEE Industrial Electronics Society, pp. 5934–5939, November 2013
11. Vittorias, I., Metzger, M., Kunz, D., Gerlich, M., Bachmaier, G.: A bidirectional battery charger for electric vehicles with V2G and V2H capability and active and reactive power control. In: 2014 IEEE Transportation Electrification Conference and Expo (ITEC), pp. 1–6, June 2014
12. Sharma, A., Sharma, S.: Review of power electronics in vehicle-to-grid systems. J. Energy Storage **21**, 337–361 (2019)
13. Leite, V., Ferreira, A., Batista, J.: Bidirectional vehicle-to-grid interface under a microgrid project. In: 2014 IEEE 15th Workshop on Control and Modeling for Power Electronics (COMPEL), pp. 1–7, June 2014
14. Zgheib, R., Al-Haddad, K., Kamwa, I.: V2G, G2V and active filter operation of a bidirectional battery charger for electric vehicles. In: 2016 IEEE International Conference on Industrial Technology (ICIT), pp. 1260–1265, March 2016
15. Samerchur, S., Premrudeepreechacharn, S., Kumsuwun, Y., Higuchi, K.: Power control of single-phase voltage source inverter for grid-connected photovoltaic systems. In: 2011 IEEE/PES Power Systems Conference and Exposition, pp. 1–6, March 2011
16. Ciobotaru, M., Teodorescu, R., Blaabjerg, F.: A new single-phase PLL structure based on second order generalized integrator. In: 2006 37th IEEE Power Electronics Specialists Conference, pp. 1–6, June 2006

Author Index

Aguilar-Jiménez, Jesús Armando 162
Alfaro-Mejía, Estefanía 1
Alonso-Gómez, Víctor 38, 135, 185
Aragüés-Peñalba, Mònica 70

Beltrán, Ricardo 162
Blanco, Marcos 244
Breve, Matheus Montanini 285

Chavat, Juan 54
Chillón-Antón, Cristian 70
Colacurcio, Giovanni 269

Dávila-Sacoto, Miguel 38
Díaz-González, Francisco 70

Escamilla-Ambrosio, P. J. 109
Espinosa-Sosa, O. 109

Feliciano, Manuel 256
Figueiredo, Luís Guilherme Aguiar 121
Franco-Mejía, Edinson 1
Fuentes, Andres Felipe 80
Furst, Leonardo Campestrini 256

Gallardo-Saavedra, Sara 38, 135
Gallegos-García, G. 109
García, Germán García 215
Girbau-Llistuella, Francesc 70
Gonçalves, Artur 256
González, Luis G. 38
González-San Pedro, Edgar 162
Graneri, Jorge 54

Hernández-Callejo, Luis 1, 38, 109, 135, 146, 162, 176, 185
Hernández-Martínez, Bhishma 135
Hipogrosso, Silvina 93

Jamed-Boza, Luis Omar 185

Lafoz, Marcos 244
Lebrusán, Irene 9
Leite, Vicente 25, 121, 285
Llonch-Masachs, Marc 70
Loaiza-Correa, Humberto 1
López-Meraz, Raúl A. 185
López-Zavala, Ricardo 162
Luna, Francisco 269

Maidana, Wellington 25, 121
Massobrio, Renzo 199
Monge, Oscar Izquierdo 176
Morales-Aragonés, José Ignacio 135
Morales-Olea, M. 109

Nápoles, Víctor Manuel Padrón 215
Navarro, Gustavo 244
Nesmachnow, Sergio 54, 93, 146, 199, 228, 269

Obregón, Lilian J. 176

Páez, Diego Gachet 215
Penelas, José Luis Esteban 215
Porteiro, Rodrigo 146

Ramírez-Salinas, M. A. 109
Ribeiro, Gabriela Moreira 25
Risso, Claudio 228
Romero, Felipe 256
Rossit, Diego 269

Santacruz, María José García 215
Scotta, Isabella Cristina 25

Tamura, Eugenio 80
Torres, Jorge 244
Toutouh, Jamal 9, 269

Velázquez, Nicolás 162

Printed in the United States
By Bookmasters